PEDAGOGIES OF CROSSING

Pedagogies

Perverse Modernities

A SERIES EDITED

BY JUDITH HALBERSTAM

AND LISA LOWE

M. Jacqui Alexander

MEDITATIONS ON FEMINISM,

SEXUAL POLITICS, MEMORY,

AND THE SACRED

# of Crossing

DUKE UNIVERSITY PRESS   DURHAM & LONDON   2005

*The distribution of this book is supported
by a generous grant from the Gill Foundation.*

FOR YEMAYÁ

CONTENTS

ACKNOWLEDGMENTS

This book has been a long journey without distance, and the travelers have been varied and many. I am indebted to the regional feminist movement in the Caribbean, members of the Caribbean Association for Feminist Research and Action, the SISTREN theatre collective of Jamaica, Development Alternatives for Women (DAWN) of the Bahamas, and the Audre Lorde Project of Brooklyn, New York, the only national organization committed to lesbian, gay, bisexual, transgender and two-spirit people of color communities, for the consistency with which you bring a deep vision for social justice into the nitty-gritty work of political organizing. You bring a politics of hope to these perilous times of empire-building and you consistently sustain those of us who temporarily sojourn in the academy. I am also indebted to those who are fearless in providing models of activist scholarship, including among others, Jennifer Abod, Angela Davis, Brenda Joyner, Margo Okazawa-Rey and Julia Sudbury; to writers Chrystos, Dionne Brand, Kamau Brathwaite, Audre Lorde, Cherríe Moraga and Toni Morrison, whose work brings us always to the edge of uncompromising consistency; to Angela Bowen (also grammarian extraordinaire), Linda Carty, Gloria Joseph (patient revolutionary and outrageous critic), Barbara Herbert, Jerma Jackson, Gary Lemons, Gail Lewis, Chandra Talpade Mohanty, Papusa Molina, Amit Rai and Gloria Wekker for your love, abiding friendship, astute eyes and staunch intellectual companionship; to fellow travelers Marion Bethel, Carole Boyce Davies, Tristan Borer, Drucilla Cornel, Cynthia Enloe, Janet Gezari, Monisha dasGupta, Ana-Louise Keating, Andrée Nicola McLaughlin, Gita Patel, Chandan Reddy, Tracy Robinson and Alissa Trotz; to Jinny Chalmers, who first suggested this collection, and Lynn Comella, who began its painstaking assembly; to Jessica Badonsky, Sangeeta Budiraja, Nova Vaughn-Burnet, Ana Christie, Claudia Veronica Brignolo-Giménez, Annalis Herman, Tamara Irons, Paul Lai, Silvia Panzironi, Ursula Wolfe-Roca, David Sartorious, Giovanna Torcio, and Heather Sibley for exceptional research assistance; to Payal Banerjee, Nova Gutierrez, and Constanza Morales-Mair for your commitment to excellence and generous support at crucial junctures; to Susannah Driver-Barstow and Jody Shapiro for keen readings of chapters 3 and 4 and chapter 5 respectively; to AnaLouise Keating for your generosity and the keen editorial sense you brought to chapter 6; to Beverly Hutchinson and Urayoana Trinidad, your healing touch worked as restorative on many an occasion; and to Maggy Carrot and Sylvia Villaroel for unconditional friendship and a quiet passion that teaches how not to take the world for granted.

I dedicate chapter 4 to The Mobilization for Real Diversity, Democracy and Economic Justice, which directed its labor toward overturning instrumental diversity at the New School University between 1996 to 1998, and to all undergraduate and graduate students as you learn that the journey with the life of the mind and the journey with life are twin streams in the same dreaming. I circulated early drafts of the chapter to thirty-five members of The Mobilization and I am especially grateful to Saradhamanidevi Boopathi, Scott Carter, Jan Clausen, Mustafa Emirbayer, Leslie Hill, Gary Lemons, Kerry MacNeil, Laura Poitras, Amit Rai, Gregory Tewksbury and Michelle Zamora for your willingness to revisit the political struggle, wade into your memories and transform my recollections. Mirangela Buggs, Mustafa Emirbayer, and Janet Gezari, your generosity, exceptional thoroughness, and political adeptness made the final draft suited for the public eye. I thank among others Brenda Joyner, Sy Khan and Colia Clarke for pivotal conversations and support when the going was rough and I thank all of our supporters, academics and activists, poets and public intellectuals who wrote letters of solidarity that simply put, kept us going.

To the organizers of Theorizing Transnationality, Gender and Citizenship of the Women and Gender Studies Institute at the University of Toronto, public lecture series 2002–2003 and the Thinking Sex Transnationally series at the University of Seattle at Washington where preliminary sketches of chapter 5 were first presented, I am grateful for your commitment to create and maintain intellectual neighborhoods that cross the boundaries of the academy.

Chapter 6 honors Cherríe Moraga and Gloria Anzaldúa who gave birth to the original vision of *This Bridge Called My Back*. To Vincent Woodard and the Black Cultural Studies Seminar at Tufts, I am thankful for the provocatively fruitful discussions that enlivened chapter seven. And I am enormously grateful to Payal Banerjee, Honor Ford Smith, Tamara Irons, Cassandra Lord, Susan Mintz, Rubie Nottage, Robin Riley, Tracy Robinson, Cara Schlesinger, Rhoma Spencer and Xochipala Maes Valdez for your generosity during the apparently unending last-minute crunch in the assembly of notes and fragments of data and the attention you brought to formatting and style; to Pat Murphy, you bring to proofreading an unusual combination of craft and wit; to Carolyn Watson for your diligent reading of the entire manuscript, and to Laurie Prendergast for your astute indexing.

My sincerest appreciation to Judith Halberstam and Lisa Lowe, series editors of Perverse Modernities, for your staunch commitment to this project; the copyeditor and anonymous readers for your attunement to the intellectual vagaries of *Pedagogies;* Raphael Allen, former acquisitions editor at Duke who first demonstrated interest in this book; Ken Wissoker, editor-in-chief for your dedication, guidance and acuity; Justin Faerber for your meticulous attention; Katie Courtland and Michael McCollough for your efficiency and warm professionalism; and Courtney Berger for your sensitive attention to administrative matters.

I am humbled by the process of making spiritual community—the ongoing work of pursuing different Sacred paths to knowing and of the ongoing challenge involved in internalizing, that is living, the belief that all things are interconnected. I am indebted to my teachers: Danny Dawson who introduced me to my Bakôngo teacher Bunseki Kimbwandende Kia Fu-kiau, whose steady guidance led me straight to Mayombe in the Kôngo to his teacher/father/uncle Papa Vweba, who has since transitioned;

Paulo Bispo, Suzette James, Patricia James, Florence Jean-Joseph, Joan Noray, Verna St. Rose Greaves, Baba Henry White and my youngest brother Ngozi Obasi Umoja for that rare combination of unconditional love and spiritual likemindedness; the ceremonial fire-keepers and water carriers determined to honor Spirit: Cherríe Moraga, Celia Herrera-Rodriguez, Carmencita Vicente of the Saraguro Medicine Lodge, Ecuador, and Xochipala Maes Valdez; those committed to the search for cosmic truth without borders, Minister Marie Knight and members of Gates of Prayer, Harlem, New York; Mama Lola; Madrina Teresa Ramirez; Ojugbona Juanita Rodriguez; Norm Rosenberg and Ticia Roth of Pangea Farm; Luisa Teish; Mother Veronica; and Marta Morena Vega.

And finally my deepest gratitude to my ancestors on whose shoulders I stand; to Maya, my daughter, you teach me always about grace and courage; and to Xochipala Maes Valdes, my partner, for the honesty of your love and for your commitment to show up for this appointment with life.

On Living the Privileges of Empire

I did not awake this morning to the deafening noise of sirens or the rocketing sound of nonstop bombs. I did not awake to the missiles that fall like rain from the sky, exploding on contact with land, staking out huge craters within the earth, collapsing people into buildings, trees into rubble, men into women, hands into feet, children into dust.[1] Two thousand tons of ammunition in three hours. Forty-two air raids in one day. Twenty-seven thousand air raids in a decade.[2] I did not awake this morning to the taste of desolation, nor to the crusts of anger piled high from decades of neglect. I did not awake to the familiar smell of charred flesh, which sand storms use to announce the morning raid. I did not awaken in Basra to the familiar smell of hunger, or of grief for that matter, residual grief from the last twelve years that now has settled as a thick band of air everywhere. Breathing grief for a lifetime can be toxic. Breathing only grief simply kills. I did not awake in Falluja, symbol of the post-election settlement wager: votes in exchange for bombs. I awoke this morning from a comfortable bed, avoiding the interminable queues for rations of fuel or food, because I have the privilege to choose to live, unlike many who have lost their lives in the insatiable service of imperialism.

What do lives of privilege look like in the midst of war and the inevita-

ble violence that accompanies the building of empire? We live the privilege of believing the official story that the state owns and can therefore
dispense security, that war is over, that silence is a legitimate trade for
consent in the dangerous rhetoric of wartime economy; the mistaken
belief that we can be against the war yet continue to brand this earth with
a set of ecological footprints so large and out of proportion with the rest
of life on the planet that war is needed to underwrite our distorted
needs;[3] to consume an education that sanctions the academy's complicity
in the exercise and normativization of state terror; to continue to believe
in American democracy in the midst of an entanglement of state and
corporate power that more resembles the practices of fascism than the
practices of democracy; to believe that no matter how bad things are here
they are worse elsewhere, so much so that undermining the promises of
American democracy is an eminently more noble and therefore legitimate undertaking, more so than the undermining of democracy in any
other place in the world; to assume that the machineries of enemy production pertain to an elsewhere, not operating within the geographic
borders of the United States of North America. One of the habits of
privilege is that it spawns superiority, beckoning its owners to don a veil
of false protection so that they never see themselves, the devastation they
wreak or their accountability to it. Privilege and superiority blunt the loss
that issues from enforced alienation and segregations of different kinds.

Pedagogies' central metaphor is drawn from the enforced Atlantic
Crossing of the millions of Africans that serviced from the fifteenth
century through the twentieth the consolidation of British, French, Spanish, and Dutch empires. At the time I conceived of the book in 2000, the
world had not yet witnessed the seismic imperial shifts that characterize
this moment. In one sense, then, *Pedagogies* functions as an archive of
empire's twenty-first-century counterpart, of oppositions to it, of the
knowledges and ideologies it summons, and of the ghosts that haunt it.
The book has assumed such a consciousness, and necessarily so since we
are living witnesses or casualties of empire's egregious practices. None of
us now alive lived that first round, at least not in a direct way, but we can fill
in the outlines provided by these contemporary excesses: in the return to a
Republican-led militarized Reconstruction that polices the national body
as it amplifies its global reach;[4] by the U.S. state's cynical deployment of

tradition in a way that upholds the heterosexualization of family and of morality so as to eclipse any apprehension of the immorality of empire; in the recirculation and rearticulation of myths of (American) origin and destined might through an ideological force-field that manufactures and feeds an enemy made increasingly by the day more grotesque, while purveying a faith-based politics tied to the oxymoronic "armies of compassion";[5] in the disappearance of immigrants and the increased incarceration of women and people of color, drawing sharp fault lines that continue to make of citizenship a more fragile, highly contingent enterprise—the requirements of citizenship for empire are disturbingly antithetical to those requirements of citizenship for collective self-determination;[6] by the way this moment presses up against what democracy has been made to mean, since empire requires sacrifice—the sacrifice of consent— unable to function, as William Pitt suggests, within the slow, cumbersome machine of constitutional democracy on its back;[7] by the fact that this moment not only challenges but also undermines epistemic frameworks that are simply inadequate to the task of delineating these itineraries of violence that are given other names such as democracy and civilization; by probing our function and location as radical intellectuals (and I intend the term intellectual in the broadest sense of a commitment to a life of the mind whether or not one is linked to the academy) along the lines that Stuart Hall suggests—that is, our ethical commitments, the contours and character of our class affiliations and loyalties, and the interpretive frameworks we bring to bear on the histories to which we choose to be aligned; and, importantly, how we assess the size and scope of the wager involved in displacing collective self-determination with corporate institutional allegiances. We can fill in the outlines of empire since its multiple contradictions are everywhere seen in the hydra-headed quality of violence that constitutes modernity's political itinerary as its ideological cognates, militarization and heterosexualization, are exposed. We can fill in the outlines of empire since we have seen the ways in which freedom has been turned into an evil experiment—that is, in George Lammings's words, "the freedom to betray freedom through gratuitous exploitation."[8] We can fill in the outlines when we see how empire's ruthless triumph demystifies the corruptibility of the self, without respect for those who believed themselves incorruptible. Perhaps empire never ended, that psychic and material will to conquer and appropriate, twentieth-century movements for decolonization notwithstanding. What we can say for sure is that empire makes all innocence impossible.[9]

Why Pedagogies, and Why Pedagogies of Crossing?

This book spans what feels like a lifetime compressed into a decade. It is an inventory of sorts of my multifaceted journey with(in) feminism, an inventory that is necessarily pluralized by virtue of my own migrations and the confluence of different geographies of feminism. In this volume I am concerned with the multiple operations of power, of gendered and sexualized power that is simultaneously raced and classed yet not practiced within hermetically sealed or epistemically partial borders of the nation-state. I am also concerned with the unequal diffusion of globalized power variously called postmodernism or late capitalism, yet understood in these pages as the practice of imperialism and its multiple effects. Put differently, one of my major preoccupations is the production and maintenance of (sexualized) hegemony understood, in the Gramscian sense, as a map of the various ways that practices of dominance are simultaneously knitted into the interstices of multiple institutions as well as into everyday life. To understand the operation of these practices I traveled to various sites of crisis and instability, focusing to a large extent on the state, whose institutions, knowledges, and practices stand at the intersection of global capital flows, militarization, nationalisms, and oppositional mobilization. While differently located, both neo-imperial state formations (those advanced capitalist states that are the dominant partners in the global "order") and neo-colonial state formations (those that emerged from the colonial "order" as the forfeiters to nationalist claims to sovereignty and autonomy) are central to our understandings of the production of hegemony.[10] The nodes of instability include heterosexuality's multiple anxieties manifested in the heterosexualization of welfare and the defense of marriage in the United States and the criminalization of lesbian and gay sex in Trinidad and Tobago and in the Bahamas; the consolidation of the military-industrial-prison complex that both promotes the militarization of daily life and the most contemporaneous round of military aggression and war; the ideological production of various hegemonic identities: the soldier, the citizen patriot, the tourist, and the enemy on the part of state institutions and corporate capital; the integration of the corporate academy into the practices and institutions of the state at this moment of empire and therefore made integral to the machineries of war; knowledge frameworks, particularly those that bolster and scaffold modernity's practices of violence that signify as democracy, such as cultural relativism; the global factory and its naturalization of immigrant women's labor; and the moments and places where apparently oppositional social locations and practices become rearticulated and appropriated in the interests of global capital, as is the case of white gay tourism. These nodes of instability form, as well, the base for the thematic organization of the seven chapters in this volume.

In this book I am disturbed by these products of domination and hierarchy, particularly the psychic products that fossilize deep in the interior, forcing us to genuflect at the altar of alterity and separation, the altar of the secular gods of postmodernity, experienced as hypernationalism and empire. Physical geographic segregation is a potent metaphor for the multiple sites of separation and oppositions generated by the state, but which are also sustained in the very knowledge frameworks we deploy and in the contradictory practices of living the oppositions we enforce: the morally consuming citizen versus the morally bankrupt welfare recipient; the patriot versus the enemy; the loyal citizen versus the disloyal immigrant; "us" versus "them"; the global versus the local; theory versus practice; tradition versus modernity; the secular versus the sacred; the embodied versus the disembodied. And disturbance works as a provocation to move past the boundaries of alienation, which explains why *Pedagogies* is centrally concerned with the promise that oppositional knowledges and political mobilizations hold and with the crafting of moral agency.

If hegemony works as spectacle, but more importantly as a set of practices that come to assume meaning in people's everyday lives (that is, the ways in which ordinary people do the work of the state and the work of war), then all spaces carry the potential for corruptibility. Lesbian, gay, bisexual, transgendered and two spirit-communities, transnational feminist constituencies, women of color political mobilizations, and subordinated knowledges within the academy that have traded radicalism for institutionalization all carry these reciprocal antagonisms and contradictions. Thus, for this reason, but not for this reason alone, the stakes are quite high. Building oppositional practices within and across multiple simultaneous sites is imperative in political struggle as is the cultivation of the discipline of freedom and collective self-determination in terms that supercede those of free-market democracy. Yet, oppositional consciousness is a process rather than a given before the fact of political practice. And further, we cannot afford to be continually, one-sidedly oppositional.

Pedagogies is intended to intervene in the multiple spaces where knowledge is produced. I have deliberately chosen to interrupt inherited boundaries of geography, nation, episteme, and identity that distort vision so that they can be replaced with frameworks and modes of being that enable an understanding of the dialectics of history, enough to assist in navigating the terms of learning and the fundamentally pedagogic imperative at its heart: the imperative of making the world in which we live intelligible to ourselves and to each other—in other words, teaching ourselves. Because within the archaeologies of dominance resides the will to divide and separate, *Pedagogies* points to the reciprocal investments we must make to cross over into a metaphysics of interdependence. In the same way in which Paulo Freire narrated our ontological vocation to become more fully human, these pedagogies assemble a similar ontological imperative, which pertains to learning and teaching.[11] And since there is no crossing that is ever undertaken once and for all, this ontological imperative of making the world intelligible to ourselves is, of necessity, an enterprise that is ongoing.

Since the central metaphor of this book rests in the tidal currents of the Middle Passage, we should want to know why and how this passage— The Crossing—emerged as signifier. If here I am concerned with embodied power, with the power derived from the will to domination, I am simultaneously concerned with the power of the disembodied and the stories that those who forcibly undertook the Middle Passage are still yearning to tell, five centuries later. One such story is that of Kitsimba, who numbered among those who through the door of no return were shuttled from the old Kôngo kingdom to the Caribbean, circa 1780. Kitsimba unexpectedly showed up in this collection, so unabashedly bound up with materialism, that my aim is not so much to tell the story of her capture but to convey a particular meaning of pedagogy. Indeed, her emergence is pedagogy in its own right: to instruct us on the perilous boundary-keeping between the Sacred and secular, between dispossession and possession, between materialism and materiality—the former having to do with the logics of accumulation, the latter with the energy and the composition of matter. She has traveled to the heart of feminism's orthodoxies to illustrate that the personal is not only political but spiritual, to borrow Lata Mani's felicitous formulation.[12] She is here to meditate on the limits of secular power and the fact that power is not owned by corporate time keepers or by the logics of hegemonic materialism. As I show in chapter 7, within Kitsimba's universe reside the very categories that constitute the social, the most crucial of which is Time. Yet in the world she inhabits, dominant corporate, linear time becomes existentially irrelevant. Indeed it ceases to have any currency at all.

Put differently, pedagogies that are derived from the Crossing fit neither easily nor neatly into those domains that have been imprisoned within modernity's secularized episteme. Thus, they disturb and reassemble the inherited divides of Sacred and secular, the embodied and disembodied, for instance, pushing us to take seriously the dimensions of spiritual labor that make the sacred and the disembodied palpably tangible and, therefore, constitutive of the lived experience of millions of women and men in different parts of the world. Once Kitsimba appeared to claim the book's closing chapter, the title of this entire collection surfaced. Thus, I came to understand pedagogies in multiple ways: as something given, as in handed, revealed; as in breaking through, transgressing, disrupting, displacing, inverting inherited concepts and practices, those psychic, analytic and organizational methodologies we deploy to know what we believe we know so as to make different conversations and solidarities possible; as both epistemic and ontological project bound to our beingness and, therefore, akin to Freire's formulation of pedagogy as indispensable methodology. In this respect, *Pedagogies* summons subordinated knowledges that are produced in the context of the practices of marginalization in order that we might destabilize existing practices of knowing and thus cross the fictive boundaries of exclusion and marginalization. This, then, is the existential message[13] of the Crossing—to apprehend how it might instruct us in the urgent task of configuring new ways of being and knowing and to plot the different metaphysics that are needed to move away from living alterity premised in difference to living intersubjectivity premised in relationality and solidarity.

Pedagogies cannot be adequately assembled, however, without attention to the social relations of teaching in the multiple makeshift classrooms we inhabit, and so it is no accident that the gestation period for this collection coincides with much of my life as a teacher. *Pedagogies* thus pertains to what we are prepared to teach, the methodologies of our instruction and the particular challenges that arise in the task of demystifying domination. Still, the classroom is Sacred space. In any given semester a number of Souls are entrusted into our care, and they come as openly and as transparently as they can for this appointment.[14] To be sure, resistances develop as serious engagement morphs into confrontation with inherited nationalisms and their conceptual and identity structures. But outside of courses for which there is mandatory matriculation, the desire to show up stems from our curriculum that brings a promise to satisfy some yearning, as faint or as well-formed as it might be, to imagine collectivities that can thrive outside of hegemony's death-grip. I have not always been successful in simply teaching in order to teach, to teach that which I most needed to learn. More often I intended my teaching to serve as a conduit to radicalization, which I now understand to mean a certain imprisonment that conflates the terms of domination with the essence of life. Similar to the ways in which domination always already confounds our sex with all of who we are, the focus on radicalization always already turns our attention to domination. The point is not to supplant a radical curriculum. The question is whether we can simply teach in order to teach.

The Crossing is also meant to evoke/invoke the crossroads, the space of convergence and endless possibility; the place where we put down and discard the unnecessary in order to pick up that which is necessary. It is that imaginary from which we dream the craft of a new compass. A set of conflictual convergences of my own migrancy, rendered more fragile under empire, and the genealogies of feminist, neocolonial, and "queer" politics that are simultaneously transnational, all reside here. It is a place from which I navigate life, using the foot I keep in the Caribbean, the one I have had in the United States since 1971, the arithmetic of which continually escapes me, and yet a third foot, desirous of rooting itself deep in the forest of Mayombe in the Kôngo. Living and thinking this dialectic means refusing to insist on two feet, which would be the recipe for sheer imbalance. It means turning my three legs into the legs of the deep, round cooking pot used to prepare medicine on the open fire. Three feet make the stretch more necessary, more livable, more viable. Yet none of the preoccupations of these pedagogies could have surfaced in the absence of these very genealogies: a regional feminist movement in the Caribbean, which by the mid 1980s had begun to chart the failures of anticolonial nationalism, implicating capitalism and colonialism in the unequal organization of gender, and by definition, charting the terms of how feminism would be understood and practiced; a movement of black women in Britain whose political consciousness as excolonial subjects produced a series of political campaigns that implicated the British state in colonialism at home (practices around immigration and racism in housing and hiring) and colonialism abroad ("we are here because you were there"); and the political movement and theory of collections such as *This Bridge Called My Back, Home Girls,* and *Sister Outsider,* which squarely brought dominant U.S.-based feminism to its own crossroads, challenging it to a personal and epistemic self-reflection out of which feminism has never been the same.[15] These same texts provided some of the context in which I came to lesbian feminist consciousness as a woman of color in the mid-1980s. As Chandra Talpade Mohanty and I wrote in *Feminist Genealogies,* we were not born women of color but rather *became* women of color in the context of grappling with indigenous racisms within the United States and the insidious patterns of being differently positioned as black and brown women.[16] Thus, the analytical elements that comprise this volume intimate my own intellectual and political history, marking its convergence with cross-currents of different feminisms and belatedly with "queer" theorizing both inside and outside the academy, both elsewhere and here.

If I Could Write with Fire: A Word on How to Read

Heuristically speaking, each chapter in this book possesses its own analytic integrity and as such could be made to function and be read on its own. Intersecting thematics are restated under apparently different frameworks in the hopes of sharpening the analytic agility we bring to understanding a world, an event, a life that is infinitely encrusted and layered and that ultimately demands different modes of intelligibility. For instance, all of the chapters that critique capitalist and state practices foreground the ideological imperatives that are deployed to function as truth or otherwise naturalize violence. Yet in chapter 4, there is a particular insight I gleaned from using apparently normative categories, such as speech and rights, to trace the ways in which the putative race-neutral market of diversity discourses of the corporate academy masked coercions of different kinds and how speech became acts that carried the capacity "to rank, legitimate, discriminate and deprive."[17] It was instructive to put this formulation to work, so to speak, so that it could attend to the interstices of power and show that the vocabularies of rights and truth could be made to disrupt dominant regimes, particularly when the claimants are not the ones imagined to formulate the operating discourses of power.

With essays written at different times, spanning the ten years from 1994 to 2004, the organization of this book is not necessarily linear. For instance, a version of chapter 3, "Whose New World Order? Teaching for Justice" was first delivered as an address to the Great Lakes Women's Studies Association in 1994. Its discursive sensibilities, however, bring it into closer ideological proximity to the contemporary imperatives of empire-building that have been engineered by the ideologies of the U.S. national security state apparatus. The Gulf War of 1991, one of the immediate precursors of "the new world order," staged a cynical dress rehearsal for the invasion of Iraq in 2003, and even that starting place is contingently arbitrary. Furthermore, the methodological template for the book as a whole unfolds not in chapter 1 but in chapter 5. Yet the preoccupation in chapter 5 with modernity's traditions and violences would have been nearly impossible had I not waded through the points of confluence between the neocolonial and the neo-imperial, the hegemonic and the oppositional, and the reciprocal traffic among them, or had I not understood cultural relativism's analytic and political intransigence—the thematics of earlier chapters. Thus, the placement of chapter 5 is intended to bring methodological rather than chronological coherence to the book's framing. In what follows I touch briefly on the content of each chapter, after which I discuss what is at stake in assembling these particular pedagogies.

Three interlocking themes frame this collection. In part 1, "Transnational Erotics: State, Capital, and the Decolonization of Desire," I include two chapters to serve as a foreground to the sexualization of subjectivity on the part of the heterosexual neocolonial state and white gay capital, both of which mobilize lesbian and gay bodies for their sex: one in the service of the heterosexualizing imperatives of nation-building and imperial tourist consumption, the other in the service of a sexual economy of gay desire where "native" bodies are made to assume, as in satisfy, the anxieties of colonial scripts and gay capital accumulation simultaneously. The meeting ground occupied here by the hegemonic and the oppositional is a troublesome one. Chapter 1, "Erotic Autonomy as a Politics of Decolonization," which was first published in 1997, focuses on the ideological rescue of heterosexuality through the passage of the 1991 Sexual Offences and Domestic Violence Act in the Bahamas. This legislation criminalized lesbian and gay sex, while ostensibly protecting some women against domestic violence, rape in marriage, and different forms of sexual harassment. I examine in this chapter how citizenship is premised in heterosexual terms and how lesbian and gay bodies are made to bear the brunt of the charge of undermining national sovereignty, while the neocolonial state masks its own role in forfeiting sovereignty as it recolonizes and renativizes a citizenry for service in imperial tourism. In the process of this examination I map the profound crisis of legitimation, which the feminist movement provoked for the state, and I chart what was at stake in the heterosexualization of the nation and the lengths to which the state was willing to go to protect itself and heteropatriarchy at the same time.

In chapter 2, "Imperial Desire/Sexual Utopias," first published in 2000, I shift the site of analysis from the neocolonial state to the practices of white gay corporate tourism, while I attend to the conditions of miscegenation between heterosexual and gay capital. Here neocolonialism is made to assume a form different than that premised in chapter 1. Its agents are not the indigenous, anticolonial, nationalist class but the heirs of imperialism residing in imperialism's centers, who are involved in rewriting the colonial script that sexualizes and fetishizes the "native" back into tradition. I provide a sobering note on the dangers of offering up sexual freedom alone on the broken platter of U.S. democracy in order to secure or ostensibly guard the boundaries of modernity, and ultimately I urge queer studies and queer movements to take up questions of colonialism, racial formation, and political economy simultaneously.

In part 2, "Maps of Empire, Old and New," I illustrate how the itineraries of empire are organically linked by virtue of the substantial amount of ideological trafficking that occurs among them. The political economies of corporate capital within the global factory and those of the state in which the academy figures centrally draw a great deal of sustenance from each other. The ideological fodder for both is provided by analytic traditions developed within the academy itself. In chapter 3, "Whose New World Order? Teaching for Justice," I interpret the manufacture of the "new world order" as a mechanism on the part of neo-imperial states to manage the global crisis of the 1980s and 1990s. If neocolonial states managed internal rupture by using heterosexuality in defense of nation, as I show in chapter 1, neo-imperial states covered their own internal ruptures by managing what they produced as the new world order, deploying it as an ideological and material anchor to secure a range of corporate and state interests, particularly interests in militarization. In this chapter I point to corporate restructuring in the shift to a service economy and to the processes through which the academy becomes one such industry by participating in its own kind of downsizing and in the rewriting of knowledges that comport with the imperatives of empire. What is the academy's role in an era of globalization? The genealogies of consciousness and political organizing among women workers in global factories in places ranging from Mexico and the Caribbean to India and Canada, who foreground the fact of their hunger for justice ("tenemos hambre de justicia"), are juxtaposed with the urgency of teaching for justice in the academic factory, thus challenging us to develop radical pedagogies that do not erase the knowledges of these very women who redefine "survival" to mean collective self-consciousness.

In chapter 4, "Anatomy of a Mobilization," I build on chapter 3 as an archaeology of just what transpires in the academy when downsizing and fiscal conservatism morph into curricular conservatism. The site of this examination is the New School for Social Research (now the New School University), which is renowned for its traditions of progressivism. The moment is 1997, when a political mobilization that involved a coalition of faculty, staff, and security guards challenged the hiring and epistemic practices of the School that produced a climate of exile—the very circumstance that prompted scholars to flee European fascism and American anti-Semitism and establish the School in the first place. Because my own temporary position there sharpened the contradiction between hypervisibility and a rotating-door policy that erased the knowledges of women of color, this chapter charts the failures of normative multiculturalism, liberal pluralism, and the eclipse of the white liberal Left in the context of the schism that emerged between the School's liberal public identity and its regressive internal practices. In light of this, I track the sizable stakes that are attached to the diffusion of radical transnational feminist frameworks in a corporate context that requires an instrumental diversity so as to better position white bodies only as knowledge producers.[18]

In chapter 5, "Transnationalism, Sexuality, and the State," I provide the analytic grounding for the first four chapters. To do so I exhume the ghost of cultural relativism and the traditions that mark the itineraries of modernity by offering a way to theorize violence that does not fix violence in tradition alone. By taking the regulatory practices of heterosexualization within three social formations—the colonial, the neocolonial, and the neo-imperial—I push up against the limits of linearity by arguing instead for the ideological traffic (in the words of Payal Banerjee) that occurs within and among them. In conjoining discourses that have been internally segregated and temporalities that have been simultaneously distanced—the colonial is oftentimes never imagined to traffic within the neo-imperial, for instance—I make it possible to see that there can be no good heterosexual democratic tradition over and against a bad heterosexual primitive tradition. There also can be no false deduction that democratic heterosexualization is simply more benign in its alignment with modernity than traditional heterosexualization, which in its alignment with backwardness is simply more pernicious. Within this frame it is analytically impossible to position heterosexualization and the attendant discourses and violences of homophobia as imbricated within tradition only—in the presumably cordoned-off geographies of sexuality in the Caribbean. This chapter shows how they are simultaneously constitutive of the practices of modernity as well.

The third and final theme is charted in part 3, "Dangerous Memory: Secular Acts, Sacred Possession," where I position memory as antidote to alienation, separation, and the amnesia that domination produces. Chapter 6, "Remembering *This Bridge*, Remembering Ourselves," which was first published in 2002 in *This Bridge We Call Home: Radical Visions for Transformation,* is an excavation of the costs of a collective forgetting so deep that we have even forgotten that we have forgotten. Twenty years after the initial publication of *This Bridge Called My Back,* this chapter returns to the moment of my first encounter with that book in order to weave a discontinuous thread to the present through the examination of several questions: Who are we now as women of color twenty years later? Have we lived differently? Loved differently? Where do we come to consciousness as women of color and live it, at this moment? Have we crossed into a new metaphysics of political struggle? Did *This Bridge* get us there? Did it coax us into the habit of listening to each other and learning each other's ways of seeing and being? Who are we now, twenty years later? Why do we need to remember?

In this chapter I focus on certain contentious relationships between African American and Caribbean women who share a similarly fractious history of racism, but whose differential forgetting of colonization and slavery has occasioned a contemporary politics of blame. I deal explicitly with heterogeneity within the seemingly homogeneous category of woman of color by seeking to determine what residency in adopted homes might teach us about the continuities between home and exile. In doing so I confront the challenge of using rememory to take account of the effects of suspicion and betrayal. There is a great deal of urgency in reimagining wholeness as a necessary part of a pedagogy of crossing, the very point of the book's final chapter.

Chapter 7, "Pedagogies of the Sacred," gets squarely at the question of transgenerational memory. There I engage memory not as a secular but rather as a Sacred dimension of self. I examine how sacred knowledge comes to be inscribed in the daily lives of women through an examination of work—spiritual work—which like crossing is never undertaken once and for all. Spiritual work is different from the category of domestic labor or of cheapened migratory labor in the exploitative capitalist sense, although the spiritual workplace is usually constituted as home. Drawing on my own position of priest in two African-based spiritual communities of Vodou and Santería, of mixed gender and sexualities, I trace the ways in which knowledge comes to be embodied and made manifest through flesh, an embodiment of Spirit.

All of the elements with which feminism has been preoccupied—including transnationalism, gender and sexuality, experience, history, memory, subjectivity, and justice—are contained within this metaphysic that uses Spirit knowing as the mechanism of making the world intelligible. But primarily because experience has been understood in purely secular terms, and because the secular has been divested of the Sacred and the spiritual divested of the political, this way of knowing is not generally believed to have the capacity to instruct feminism in the United States in any meaningful way, in spite of the work of feminist theologians and ethicists. It is a paradox that a feminism that has insisted on a politics of a historicized self has rendered that self so secularized, that it has paid very little attention to the ways in which spiritual labor and spiritual knowing is primarily a project of self-knowing and transformation that constantly invokes community simply because it requires it. In spite of the work of Gloria Anzaldúa, Cornel West, bell hooks, and the more recent work of Lata Mani, Leela Fernandes, and others, there is a tacit understanding that no self-respecting postmodernist would want to align herself (at least in public) with a category such as the spiritual, which appears so fixed, so unchanging, so redolent of tradition. Many, I suspect, have been forced into a spiritual closet. Ultimately, then, I argue that a transnational feminism needs these pedagogies of the Sacred not only because of the dangerous diffusion of religious fundamentalisms, and not only because structural transformations have thrown up religion as one of the primary sites of contestation, but more importantly because it remains the case that the majority of people in the world—that is, the majority of women in the world—cannot make sense of themselves without it. We would all need to engage the Sacred as an ever-changing yet permanent condition of the universe, and not as an embarrassingly unfortunate by-product of tradition in which women are disproportionately caught. Moreover, many individuals would not have survived the crossing without it; many have been persecuted because of it. Pedagogies in this universe of the Sacred are ongoing.

On Writing, Memory, and the Discipline of Freedom

Different voices inhabit this text. The ideological "I" (to use a term by Sandra Paquet)[19] that wrote "Erotic Autonomy" in 1997 is not the same "I" writing here in this introduction, nor the "I" that wrote "Pedagogies of the Sacred." Rather, that "I" has shifted and transformed, so much so that different voices emerge. Audre Lorde would have us believe that this shift in voice is that of the poet bringing faint yet decipherable whispers of freedom, a conjunction of the aesthetic of creation, the beauty of the Sacred and the flight of imagination. Modulations in voice, therefore, are not solely speech—perhaps not about speech at all—but instead are about an opening that permits us to hear the muse, an indication of how memory works, how it comes to be animated. But whose memory, whose voice, and whose history?

In a fundamental sense *Pedagogies of Crossing* moves from the betrayal of secular citizenship and dispossession to sacred citizenship and possession, from alienation to belonging, from dismemberment to rememory. And it does so not in any discrete, noncontradictory, linear way, not in any way that suggests that there is no traffic between and among them, but rather as a way to indicate that possession can be a guided, conscious choice. Perhaps that muse emerges at the cusp of the vise between dispossession and possession, but she would have been refused entry had surrender and stripping not occurred. Had I not been stripped to the elementals and made to see that the experience of wartime, for instance, at the seat of empire (whose effects are starkly divergent even as immigrant from the external casualties of war), made its own cumbersome demands including provoking the fear of deportation from a site of neglect; had I not been thrown up against the underbelly of capitalism's insecurity in the absence of full-time employment; had I not been forced to enroll in the never-ending school where Spirit as teacher is determined to use a curriculum in which the syllabus is given at the end of each lesson and then, only partially so; and had I not been forced to enter fire to tap the roots of its capacity to change the shape of things the muse would have been denied entry, turned back at the border of self-pity, cowardice, and the knowledge of corruptibility—the borders of the self—to inhabit another, more receptive land. I was neither author nor mediator of that stripping even as I was being required to own it, to possess it and be possessed by it, to wear it as an indispensable something that belonged to me, yet not only to me. Stripping is a methodology in the most literal, perhaps mundane, sense of constituting the practices through which we come to know what we believe we know. At stake is not only whether emotion is made to count in the knowledge process, but *how* it is made to count. I leave it to Kitsimba's narration in chapter 7 to fill in the details of that telling.

So what does possession mean after all at this time of empire in the United States? How would it be possible to annul the psychic legacy of an earlier contract that premised U.S. freedom and democracy in manifest destiny? To oppose freedom to violence is to sharpen the fault line where democracy butts up against empire. It begs also for new definitions of both freedom and democracy. What is democracy to mean when its association with the perils of empire has rendered it so thoroughly corrupt that it seems disingenuous and perilous even to deploy the term. Freedom is a similar hegemonic term, especially when associated with the imperial freedom to abrogate the self-determination of a people. How do we move from the boundaries of war to "the edge of each other's battles"?[20] How many enemies can we internalize and still expect to remain whole? And while dispossession and betrayal provide powerful grounds from which to stage political mobilizations, they are not sufficiently expansive to the task of becoming more fully human. I do not mean here the sort of partial, contingent humanism on which Enlightenment rationality rested, but rather one that dares to cultivate a moral imagination that encompasses the full, unromanticized dimensions of human experience. Some of us undertook that perilous journey of the Atlantic Crossing only to jump overboard to escape the intolerable. Others of us arrived at Ibo Landing in the Carolinas and intuited the conditions of our would-be capture, turned around and walked right back on the water. Still others of us have forgotten the call, choosing instead to be accountable to the imperatives of affirmative action, torn between the desire to build fleeting careers and the practice of freedom. And still pedagogies that are derived from the Crossing are not chattel or moveable property to be selectively owned by Africa's descendants alone. Such ownership can only rely on use value to determine the structure of relationships to self and collectivity. We would have to practice how to disappear the will to segregation. The terms of this new contract will have to be divined through appropriate ceremonies of reconciliation that are premised within a solidarity that is fundamentally intersubjective: any dis-ease of one is a dis-ease of the collectivity; any alienation from self is alienation from the collectivity. It would need to be a solidarity that plots a course toward collective self-determination. Among its markers will be the knowledge that "all things move within our being in constant half embrace: the desired and the dreaded; the repugnant and the cherished; the pursued and that which [we] would escape."[21] It will entail the courage to reimagine the patriot along the lines that Adrienne Rich suggests in *An Atlas of the Difficult World*, where a patriot is one who wrestles for the Soul of her country, for her own being; where a patriot is a citizen trying to wake from the burned-out dream of innocence to remember her true country.[22] It will entail a freedom whose texture consists of honesty and discipline, the kind of which Howard Thurman speaks when he defines freedom as moral choice pertaining both to the character of one's actions and the emotional and spiritual quality of one's reactions.[23] Accountability is indispensable to both. It will entail the desire to forge structures of engagement, which embrace that fragile, delicate undertaking of revealing the beloved to herself and to one another, which James Baldwin sees as the work of the artist. "The artist does at [her] best what lovers do, which is to reveal the beloved to [herself] and with that revelation to make freedom real."[24] It will entail gentle determination and Pablo Neruda's idea of a burning patience to choose freedom so as to better build archaeologies of freedom, which, in the first and final instance, can only be lived.[25] This is the Spirit in which I offer this book.

I

TRANSNATIONAL EROTICS

State, Capital, and the Decolonization of Desire

1

Erotic Autonomy as a Politics of Decolonization: Feminism, Tourism, and the State in the Bahamas

In 1994 Marion Bethel wrote the following tribute to the members of Developing Alternatives for Women Now (DAWN)[1] and in memory of the women of the suffrage movement who severed the colonial connection between property ownership, respectability, and citizenship.

> *And the Trees Still Stand*
> We are here
> because you beat back the bush
> because you raked rocks and stones
> because you pitched scalding tar
> to make that road
> You uprooted lignum vitae trees
> to turn that uncharted road
> into a journey with landmarks
> And because you replanted
> those trees of life
> we are here[2]

In this poem Bethel establishes a deliberate link with a particular history of women's political struggle in the Bahamas. Foregrounded in her incantation is a conscious political move on the part of women in the contemporary women's movement in the Bahamas to choose from particular feminist genealogies and from particular histories of struggle, especially at a moment when the legacy of British gentility and respectability threatens to mold Bahamian identity. According to Bethel, the choice of a legacy is an uncharted road strewn with entangled brush; it is a tumultuous journey out of which a path must be cleared. But Bethel also suggests that the political and strategic work of movement-building involves danger, pitching scalding tar, simultaneously deploying tools that might entrap, ensnare, or liberate. These symbols of contradiction and liberation deliberately evoke the ideological dialectic in which the women's movement is now positioned.

The history to which the contemporary women's movement lays claim is one that contradicts the imperial legacy of nineteenth-century and early-twentieth-century organizations, such as the Queen Mary Needlework Guild, the Women's Corona Society, and the Imperial Order of Daughters of Empire, all of which drew their ideological strength from the British imperial state whose fledgling infrastructure was established in 1718. These were organizations whose ideologies of "gentility" and femininity gave primacy to service—service to the queen and to the British nation, which in practice meant servicing white militarized masculinity as "daughters" during the Second World War. In essence, then, femininity was deployed in the service of, and out of allegiance to, British colonial norms.[3] Women in the suffrage movement and in the National Council of Women, however, sought to contradict this imperial legacy of Britain as patriarch by attempting to reconcile the imposed epistemic opposition between woman and citizen that was characteristic of colonial relations of rule.[4] This evolution—from daughter, to lady, to citizen—epitomized political contestation among women's organizations in the Bahamas, and ultimately emerged as a major point of contestation with the state. Should woman be perennial daughter raised as lady, always already defined by her relationship to men? Or, should woman and citizenship signify a certain autonomy—what we might regard as erotic autonomy—and sexual agency?

Women's sexual agency and erotic autonomy have always been troublesome for the state. They pose a challenge to the ideology of an originary nuclear heterosexual family that perpetuates the fiction that the family is the cornerstone of society. Erotic autonomy signals danger to the heterosexual family and to the nation. And because loyalty to the nation as citizen is perennially colonized within reproduction and heterosexuality, erotic autonomy brings with it the potential of undoing the nation entirely, a possible charge of irresponsible citizenship, or no responsibility at all. Given the putative impulse of this eroticism to corrupt, it signals danger to respectability—not only to respectable black middle-class families, but most significantly to black middle-class womanhood. In this matrix, then, particular figures have come to embody this eroticism, functioning historically as the major symbols of threat. At this moment in the neocolonial state's diffusion of sexualized definitions of morality, sexual and erotic autonomy have been most frequently cathected on the body of the prostitute and the lesbian. Formerly conflated in the imaginary of the (white) imperial heteropatriarch, the categories "lesbian" and "prostitute" are now positioned together within black heteropatriarchy as outlaw, operating outside the boundaries of law and, therefore, poised to be disciplined and punished within it.[5]

A great deal of analytic work has been done by feminists in different parts of the world on demystifying the state's will to represent itself as disinterested, neutered, or otherwise benign.[6] We now understand how systems of sex and gender operate at the juncture of the disciplining of the body and the control of the population.[7] Feminists have clarified the patriarchal imperatives at work within the state apparatus, making it possible to examine the ways in which masculinized gestures of normalization exert and deploy force, generate new sexual meanings, displace and reinscribe old meanings, and discipline and punish women in disproportionate ways for a range of imputed infractions, not the least of which has to do with being woman. Much less work has been done, however, on understanding how heterosexualization works within the state apparatus, how it is constitutively paradoxical, that is, how heterosexuality is at once necessary to the state's ability to constitute and imagine itself and becomes, at the same time, a site of its own instability.[8]

In this chapter, I want to extend an earlier analysis I made of the operation of these processes of heterosexualization within the state.[9] Specifically, I want to combine the twin processes of heterosexualization and patriarchy—what Lynda Hart calls "heteropatriarchy"—in order to analyze the significance of a moment of crisis when state-sponsored violence moved to foreclose desire between women. The passage of the 1991 Sexual Offences and Domestic Violence Act, which criminalized lesbian sex and moved to reestablish primogeniture under the guise of protecting women against domestic violence, signals for me the mobilization of an unstable heteropatriarchy, reelaborating and reinventing itself at a moment of crisis. But why was it necessary for the state to shore up its inherited power? Why this reinvention of heteropatriarchy? What, to use Lynda Hart's terms, are the productive breaks in this symbolic order that require the state to clothe itself, as it were?[10] I want to argue here that heteropatriarchy functions in ways that supercede the sexual. At this historical moment, for instance, heteropatriarchy is useful in continuing to perpetuate a colonial inheritance (which is why I use the term neocolonial) and in enabling the political and economic processes of recolonization.

Before proceeding further, let me provide a brief synopsis of the relevant legislation in order to mark the terrain on which I interrogate the questions of recolonization, heteropatriarchy, and their contradictions in the face of feminist popular mobilization. The most crucial elements of the Sexual Offences and Domestic Violence Act include the following provisions: (1) Sexual assault, sexual abuse, sexual harassment, and domestic violence are considered criminal offenses. A system of mandated reporting is to be used in the case of incest and sexual abuse of minors. Parents or guardians, teachers, employers, and medical practitioners are required to report suspected sexual abuse to the police, with a fine of $5,000 for failure to report; (2) Adult male sexual intercourse with another male, and adult female sexual intercourse with another female, are both criminal offenses, with a maximum penalty of twenty years imprisonment; (3) Prostitution is a criminal offense (before the passage of the act it was not); and (4) Anyone with HIV infection who has sex without disclosing their HIV status faces a penalty of five years imprisonment, if convicted.

In examining the state's gesture of simultaneously "protecting" some women while criminalizing others, I offer a theorization of the shape and contours of sexual politics within the neocolonial state through the lens of heteropatriarchy. While the black nationalist party (the People's Liberal Party) wrested power from an elite group of white owners in 1972, it seized ownership of some of the more popular symbols of the black working-class political struggle, such as the Burma Road rebellion and the right of women to vote, as its own benevolent achievement. This was one of its earliest attempts to erase the memory of popular struggle. It narrowed its own vision of popular nationalism, turning the mobilization of women, youth, trade unions, and churches, on which it relied for support, into a constitutional convention organized in Britain. There, the queen was retained as head of state. The imperial government retained control over foreign affairs and defense, while the Bahamas lost sovereignty over those portions of Bahamian territory that were negotiated away under the earlier leadership of the United Bahamian Party (UBP).[11] Thus, part of what I narrate here is the extent to which these early politics of compromise and erasure, the state's desire to neutralize political struggle through its control over the instruments of co-optation and coercion, foreshadow the more contemporary politics of recolonization.

My use of the term recolonization refers to the ways in which political and economic strategies are made to usurp the self-determination of the Bahamian people. In this regard, heteropatriarchal recolonization operates on at least three levels simultaneously. At the discursive level it operates through law, which is indispensable in the symbolic and material reproduction and consolidation of heteropatriarchy, and in the elaboration of a cathectic structure based primarily in sexual difference. In light of this, I will demonstrate the ways in which the law forges continuity between white imperial heteropatriarchy—the white European heterosexual inheritance—and black heteropatriarchy. This unity is crucial to the creation of a marginal underground of noncitizens, historically figured around the "common" prostitute and the "sodomite" (killed by Balboa to mark the advent of imperialism), now extended by the neocolonial state to include lesbians and people who are HIV infected.[12] To the extent that citizenship is contained within heterosexuality, the state can produce a group of nonprocreative noncitizens who are objects of its surveillance and control—subjected to its processes of normalization and naturalization that serve to veil the ruses of power.[13]

Also at the discursive-juridical level, I establish continuity with white European inheritance by analyzing accounts of domestic violence. State managers recodified the text of this new law in terms of class-based symbols of the matrimonial home, in a way that continued the somewhat orderly patrilineal transfer of private property under the most disorderly and injurious circumstances of wife beating, rape, sexual abuse, and incest. This literal resituation of the law of the father and the privileges of primogeniture through state domestication of violence not only distanced parliamentary patriarchy from domestic patriarchy, but also narrowed the definitions of violence that feminists had linked to the organizing episteme of heteropatriarchy itself.[14] From the official story, we know almost nothing about women's experiences of violence in the home, which were ideologically fragmented in the legal text. Women were made culpable for not reporting these acts (perpetrated against themselves and their daughters) and the burden of criminality shifted onto them, thus drawing them more tightly into the state mechanisms of surveillance—positioning them simultaneously as victim and manager—all under the ideological gaze of the heteropatriarchal state as "protector." Finally, discursive recolonization occurs, as well, in the legal reinvention of normative, dyadic heterosexuality and in the mythic reelaboration of sexual decadence as the basis for the destruction of the nation of Sodom and Gomorrah, and now, by extension, the Bahamas.

Heteropatriarchal recolonization operates through the consolidation of certain psychic economies and racialized hierarchies as well as within various material and ideological processes initiated by the state, both inside and beyond the law. These actions can be understood as border policing; in this instance, the unequal incorporation of the Bahamas into an international political economy on the basis of serviceability—that is, tourism. Attempts to guard against the contamination of the body politic by legislating heterosexuality are contradictorily bolstered by state gestures that make borders permeable for the entry of multinational capital. Making the nation-state safe for multinational corporations is commensurate with making it safe for heterosexuality, for both can be recodified as natural, even supernatural. Thus, tourism and imperialism become as integral to the natural order as heterosexuality, and are indispensable in state strategies of recolonization.

Methodologically, I focus here on tourism because it has been the major economic strategy of modernization for the Bahamian state. It has now been transformed from its tentative beginnings as a leisure activity of an imperial elite, the domain of a primarily British foreign mercantile class, to a mass-based tourism dominated by North Americans and Canadians. Currently, approximately two-thirds of the gross national product of the Bahamas is derived from tourism.[15] For our purposes, the significance of tourism lies in its ability to draw together powerful processes of sexual commodification and sexual citizenship. The state institutionalization of economic viability through heterosexual sex for pleasure links important economic and psychic elements for both the imperial tourist (the invisible subject of colonial law) and for a presumably "servile" population (which the state is bent on renativizing). It would seem that at this unstable moment of heteropatriarchy, socializing citizens into heterosexuality through legal mandate and through service in tourism is more urgent for the state than socializing them into self-determination, one of the major promises of anticolonial nationalism.

Psychic recolonization occurs, then, not only through the attempts to produce a servile population in tourism, but also through the state's attempts to repress, or at least to co-opt, a mass-based movement led by feminists. Put differently, it seems that law—positioned as order—functions both to veil ruptures within heteropatriarchy and to co-opt mobilization of another kind, that is, the sort of popular feminist political mobilization that made the break visible in the first place. It would be necessary for the state to work, and work hard, to recast the official story, to displace popular memory of the people's struggle with its own achievements (in this instance, the Sexual Offences and Domestic Violence Act of 1991). But the fact is that Bahamian feminism, however ambiguously or contradictorily positioned, helped to provoke the political rupture by refusing the state conflation of heterosexuality and citizenship, and by implicating the state itself in a range of violences. In this regard, then, and as a prelude, I would like to locate myself within this narrative.

I write as an outsider, neither Bahamian national nor citizen and thus outside the repressive reach of the Bahamian state, recognizing that the consequences of being disloyal to heterosexuality fall differently on my body than on the bodies of those criminalized lesbians in the Bahamas for whom the state has foreclosed any public expression of community. Against the state's recent moves to reconsolidate heterosexuality, I write as an outlaw in my own country of birth. Both in Trinidad and Tobago and in the Bahamas, state laws confound lesbian identity with criminality. I write, then, against the "myth of lesbian impunity."[16] However, I am not an outsider to the region, for feminist solidarity crosses state-imposed boundaries. And unlike the Bahamian state, which almost entirely aligns itself with the United States and foreign multinational capitalist interests, a regional feminist movement, of which Bahamian women are a part, consciously chooses links with the wider Caribbean region and with diasporic women living elsewhere.

I live in the United States of North America at a time when the U.S. state is still engaged in reinventing and redrawing its own borders, engaged in the constant creation of categories of "noncitizen," "alien," "immigrant," and "foreigner."[17] Although I am a "legal" alien, I am also subject to being convicted of crimes variously defined as "lewd, unnatural, lascivious conduct; deviant sexual intercourse; gross indecency; buggery, or crimes against nature."[18] I am simultaneously writing against hegemonic discourses produced within metropolitan countries, and even within oppositional lesbian, gay, and bisexual communities that position the so-called Third World as barbaric—in contrast to American civilized democracy—even in the midst of the daily escalation of racist and homophobic violence that the state itself legitimates, the sexualization of citizenship from both secular and religious fundamentalisms, and the consolidation of heterosexism and white supremacy through population control policies that link the terms of foreign aid (read imperialism) to the presence of nuclear families.[19] I write also out of the desire to challenge prevalent metropolitan impulses that explain the absence of visible lesbian and gay movements as a defect in political consciousness and maturity, using evidence of publicly organized movements in the United States as evidence of their originary status in the West and their superior political maturity. These imperial tendencies within oppositional movements have occasioned a marked undertheorization of the imbrication of the imperial and the national, of the colonial within the postmodern.[20] Such theorization might enable a more relational and nuanced reading of the operation of state processes between neocolonial and advanced capitalist states around their systematic practices of heterosexualization, for clearly both states, although differently positioned, are constantly involved in the reconsolidation of borders and the repressive deployment of heteropatriarchy in domains other than the sexual.[21]

In what follows, I analyze the ways in which the state reinvented heteropatriarchy within the Sexual Offences and Domestic Violence Act by way of two examples: first, by analyzing the literal resituation of the law of the father and of primogeniture that preserves intact the transfer of property within disrupted heterosexual marriage; and second, by looking at the minute ways in which the state works to reinvent heterosexuality by, on the one hand, creating a class of loyal heterosexual citizens and, on the other hand, by designating a class of subordinated noncitizens including lesbians, gay men, prostitutes, and people who are HIV infected, thereby reviving the myth of the apocalyptic destruction of Sodom (and now by extension the Bahamas) by an oversexed band of nonprocreative noncitizens. I will show how the state actively socializes loyal heterosexual citizens into tourism, its primary strategy of economic modernization, by sexualizing them and by positioning them as commodities. I end by foregrounding the contradictory location of Bahamian feminism, since it has been forced to rely on a corrupt nationalist state that continues to draw on imperial constructions of sexuality as it reinvents itself as the savior of the people.

Domesticating Violence:
Feminists Publicize the "Private"

For many women in the Bahamas, the popular feminist mobilization of the mid-1980s recalled the time three decades earlier when the women's suffrage movement agitated for—and won—the right for all women to vote. Then, the colonial state had made ownership of property, wealth, whiteness, and masculinity the primary conditions of citizenship. In fact, owners of real property could vote more than once if they owned land in several places.[22] Universal adult suffrage, however, severed the colonial links among ownership of property, colonial respectability, manliness, and rights of political representation. It conceded the right to vote to the majority of black Bahamians (both men and women), the bulk of whom were working class. Not only did the contemporary feminist movement reach back and draw on earlier strategies of political education and mobilization such as public meetings, marches, rallies, petitions, and demands for legal protection, but like its progenitor it also refused the narrow designation of "the woman question," choosing instead to formulate its political vision in terms of a mass-based struggle for popular justice. In general, both the movement for universal suffrage of the 1950s and the political platform of violence against women of the 1980s and 1990s were formulated in terms that implicated sexual politics in the very organization of social relations, rather than seeing it as a peripheral category of significance only to women.

The recent mobilization based on violence against women functioned as a point of convergence for many different women's organizations. Among them were the Women's Desk, contradictorily positioned between the state machinery and the women's movement; lodges with an active membership anchored within an African-based spiritual cosmology; the Women's Crisis Center; professional women's organizations such as Zonta; church-affiliated women's groups; and autonomous feminist groups. All of these groupings had different, often conflicting theories about the origins of violence and the most effective strategies to combat it.[23] Nonetheless, for the majority of them violence was both defined in terms of its social history and as "offenses," such as rape, incest, battering, and sexual harassment perpetrated by men against women. The combined work of these organizations—particularly the Women's Desk, which used workshops and seminars to help identify "violent crimes against women"—gave collective force to a political agenda that shaped a public conscience for more than a decade.[24]

Prior to 1981 when the Women's Desk was created, the Women's Crisis Center had begun to document an increased incidence of rape and incest. After a major mobilization against rape, it turned its attention to the violence of incestuous familial relations. Most acts of incest were committed against girls under ten years old.[25] Female victims of incest outnumbered male victims by a ratio of almost ten to one. Girls as young as five and even three were being brought to hospitals where they were diagnosed with spontaneous orgasms and sexually transmitted diseases.[26] Combined cases of physical and sexual abuse were being reported to social services at a rate of three to five cases daily. Together, these data shattered the myth of the sanctity, safety, and comfort of the matrimonial home. Two marches to "take back the night" had underscored violence on the streets, where "strangers" committed at least 25 percent of all physical and sexual abuse. In addition, a series of radio and television broadcasts sponsored by the Women's Crisis Center challenged the media's partial silence on the issue of physical and sexual violence perpetrated against women. When the media did report these incidents, they gave the impression that the abuses were idiosyncratically imagined and enforced or simply irrational and, therefore, extreme.[27]

But it was the widespread occurrence of incest that prompted the Women's Crisis Center to turn it into a major organizational focus. In addition to insisting that it be removed from the colonial penal code and treated instead as a separate crime, the first petition, which the center drafted in March 1988, demanded that the proceedings against such crimes occur in chambers; that the names of survivors not be published; that some safe refuge be provided for girls taken out of homes; that the professional reporting of sexual abuse to the police be mandatory; and that court-mandated psychological evaluation and treatment be provided for the offenders. Besides organizational endorsement from the church (which sidestepped the question of violence against women to define incest as an infraction against the Divine) and some members of the medical profession (who worried that if incest continued, family groups would be extinct by the year 2000), civic groups, lawyers, and on the order of ten thousand other Bahamians who were not organizationally affiliated but who signed petitions agreed that evidence needed to be presented to the state about pervasive sexualized violence and that the state ought to do something that neither private organizations nor individual citizens felt empowered or had the capacity to do. Indeed, the mobilization pointed to something far deeper and far more profoundly disturbing than individual criminality or individual concupiscence suggested—that is, it gave official recognition to what many Bahamians knew, or suspected to be true: that the normalization of violent sex inside and outside of the family had produced a profound existential dilemma. Something had gone terribly amiss in the human organization of things. And in "a small place" like the Bahamas such a public, mass-based move to denaturalize violence could not help but infuse the fabric of daily life with a new, albeit contentious, vocabulary on sexual politics. It challenged inherited definitions of manliness, which had historically been based on ownership—sometimes as owner of property—but more often as owner and guardian of womanhood.[28]

Not all segments of the movement understood violence in terms of physical and sexual abuse. Once violence was denaturalized, however, it could be linked to the imperatives of the political economy whose logic was underwritten by heteropatriarchy itself. This is precisely what DAWN aimed to do by its act of refusing the inherited legal conflation of wife and mother and arguing instead that the existing legal mandate that required wives to cohabit with their husbands and, implicitly, to bear offspring did not necessarily require motherhood,[29] and thus that women, those with "husbands" and those without, were free to engage in heterosexual sex for pleasure alone, without having to satisfy the patriarchal state's desire for biological paternity or for reproduction.[30]

Within the broad framework of reproductive freedom, DAWN politicized the state's recirculation of the modernization discourses of the 1950s, which had marked women's bodies with a recalcitrant, unruly sexuality: a sexuality that reproduced so much that it posed a threat to the "body politic," threatening ultimately "development" and "progress." In its public mobilizations against the introduction of Norplant and other pharmaceuticals into the Bahamas, DAWN implicated the state, organized medicine, and Planned Parenthood in the imperial forfeiture of women's agency. The state had acquiesced to the unexamined introduction and diffusion of Norplant, an invasive birth control procedure, without women's knowledge or consent. Thus, it helped to reinforce a metropolitan pharmaceutical ideology of the Third World as a silent, willing receptacle for the technologies of development and modernity.[31] Generally, then, DAWN challenged state enforcement of compulsory motherhood and, with it, the overall colonization of citizenship and subjectivity within normative heterosexuality. The organization expanded the definition of violence against women to include ongoing state economic violence and the "silent" destruction of "citizens" and "noncitizens" alike. In this regard, DAWN aligned itself with the regional feminist movement of the Caribbean in that it understood violence against women as part of a continuum of patriarchal violences expressed in different sites. Violence within the domestic sphere, then, did not originate there but drew strength from, and at times was legitimated by, organized state economic violence, which was itself responsible for the increase in sexual violence in the home.[32]

It was this larger feminist vision of the historicized violences of heteropatriarchy, only partially understood as "sexual offenses," that the state co-opted, narrowed, and brought within its juridical confines as the Sexual Offences and Domestic Violence Act. The passage of this legislation became a major symbol of victory for women and for feminists. Incest, sexual harassment, and sexual assault of a spouse (*almost* defined as rape) were introduced as new crimes. An act of incest by an adult on a minor or dependent carried, on conviction, the possibility of life imprisonment or a minimum sentence of seven years. But there were significant changes that the movement had not intended. Only the attorney general, not the women who were the victims of incest, sexual harassment, or assault, could be relied on to present true testimony to the court. And in the text of the legislation, sexual offenses were spatially separated from domestic violence, thereby contradicting what women had demonstrated: that almost all instances of violent sex were accompanied by violent physical coercion. In addition, the urgent popular demand for professionals to report on incest and sexual abuse of minors and dependents became legally diffuse. The legislation stated the following:

> Any person who a) is the parent or guardian of a minor; b) has the actual custody, charge or control of a minor; c) has the temporary custody, care, charge or control of a minor for a special purpose, as his attendant, employer or teacher, or in any other capacity; or d) is a medical practitioner, or a person registered under the Nurses and Midwives Act, and has performed a medical examination in respect of a minor, and who has reasonable grounds for believing that a sexual offence has been committed in respect of that minor, shall report the grounds for *his* belief to a police officer as soon as *reasonably practicable*.[33]

The penalty for the failure to report was a fine of $5,000 or imprisonment for two years, which was the same penalty for an employer who sexually harassed an employee.

But precisely because there are significant disjunctures between what women demanded and what was conceded, and precisely because women (and not just *any* person) are drawn into the state's mechanisms of surveillance in ways they had not anticipated, we can argue that the state folded its own interests into a disciplining narrative that it could later claim as evidence of its benevolent paternalism. History was being constantly retold in the media in these terms: "Women's crisis week proclaimed by Prime Minister Linden Pindling . . . [is] aimed at increasing public awareness of family violence"; "Bahamians in forefront of sexual harassment legislation"; "MPs pass sexual offences bill to provide greater protection for women on the job. . . . [This is] an important piece of social legislation, particularly [those] sections outlawing sexual harassment on the job and domestic violence."[34] Parliamentarians thus invoked a Bahamas residing at the pinnacle of constitutional evolution: "We happen to have, unlike the British, a written constitution which has embodied in it . . . certain principles with regard to freedom of conscience and rights of privacy."[35] These statements illustrate the state's desire to own the popular narrative of struggle, to convert it into a hegemonic narrative of deliverance, to be seen as initiated *only* by itself as benign patriarch. It is crucial, therefore, that we understand the uses to which "sexual offenses" and "domestic violence" were put. How were these social and material practices converted into categories that were deployed by the state to do its own work, the work of the state?

Ensuring the Law of the Father:
Domestic Violence as Proxy

The law's new provision relating to domestic violence made it possible for *any* party in the marriage to apply to the supreme court for an injunction that would restrain the other party from molestation or from using violence. Nowhere in the text of the law are there definitions of domestic violence, except in a single vague reference stating that the supreme court might consider attaching a power of arrest to the injunction, in cases where the court is satisfied that "the other party has caused actual bodily harm to the applicant"; instead, there are definitions of the following: "apartment," "child of the family," "dwelling," "matrimonial home," "mortgage," and "mortgager." But why is property foregrounded along with its simultaneous conflation with marriage? How is it that domestic violence came to be narrowly codified as "actual bodily harm" in contrast, presumably, to imagined or psychic harm or fear of threat? Why is there a spatial distancing in the legal narrative between "actual bodily harm" as an element of domestic violence on the one hand and incest and rape in marriage on the other? Are these not enacted within the same sphere that has been ideologically coded as the "domestic"? Are they not undertaken by the same patriarch?

The conflation of property with marriage is not coincidental. The Bahamian legislation borrowed directly from the British Domestic Violence and Matrimonial Proceedings Act of 1976 and 1983, and in this way it inherited the underlying epistemological frame that immediately codified matrimony and coverture in terms of the obligations of the "wife" and the economic and fiduciary responsibilities of the husband.[36] In almost all instances, the discussion of marriage was accompanied by a discourse on the disposition of proprietary interests, in the event of marital rupture.[37] In fact, this is precisely what the law intervened to adjudicate. The legislation states:

> On an application for a [restraining] order under this section, the court may make such order as it thinks just and reasonable having regard to the conduct of the parties to the marriage in relation to each other and otherwise, to their respective needs and financial resources. . . . [It] may not order a party occupying the matrimonial home or any part thereof . . . to make periodical payments to the other in respect of the occupation . . . [or] impose on either party obligations as to the repair and maintenance of the matrimonial home, or the discharge of any liabilities in respect of the matrimonial home.[38]

Given the disproportionate gendered ownership of property in favor of men and the frequency with which financial paternity is adjudicated through the courts, the legislation guarantees only a *promise* of financial restitution for women during moments of rupture; clearly, here, this is not about *any* party in a marriage.

This framework of coverture, which has an explicit operating assumption that the "wife is her husband's charge,"[39] together with the historic link that has been drawn between property ownership and maleness, work to fix the notion of the propertyless housewife, of woman as non-owner, as a wage earner, perhaps, but not the owner of wealth.[40] It is difficult to obtain statistics on the accumulation of wealth in the Bahamas, but an analysis of household income gives at least a partial sense of where wealth might reside, as well as some sense of whether the legal injunction to the "discharge of liabilities" and the promise of financial restitution might be fulfilled. As an individual moves up the income ladder in the Bahamas, the gap demarcating gendered earning capacity becomes significantly greater.[41] At the highest earning capacity, women's earnings become almost insignificant: 4 percent of men earn upwards of $60,000, as opposed to just over 0.5 percent of women. In contrast, approximately 58 percent of the population earned less than $20,000 in 1988, and 30 percent of those households earned less than $10,000 annually. Women's changing relationship to marriage is indicated by the fact that about 40 percent of all households in the Bahamas are headed by women, the mean household income of which is $12,000.[42] And thus being female is made into an index of poverty. The earning capacity of state managers, on the other hand, places them among the highest recorded earners, in class proximity, if not in class affiliation, with the white indigenous owning class, from whom they presumably distanced themselves in the anticolonial struggle.[43] Indeed, this was the very class that disenfranchised the black Bahamian working-class majority by using property ownership and wealth as rights to political representation.

If we were to invest these statistics with some degree of authority, we would have to conclude that households are not the primary sites for the generation of wealth, and that the more likely site is in the profit generated by multinational capital. Eighty-five cents on every tourist dollar is returned to corporations that are based abroad. Thus, we can conclude that the state's gesture of domesticating violence speaks to its ideological support for primogeniture—a system of property inheritance and transfer that rests solidly upon, and ultimately remains with, wealthy men.[44] Not only does the neocolonial state protect the economic interests of its own state managers, but it also protects those of the small indigenous owning class, whose interests are often eclipsed by multinational interests. If, as the state purports, the law intervenes on behalf of women, it also intervenes on its own behalf to ensure that heterosexual disruption does not shift the fiscal responsibility of the matrimonial patriarch onto that of the public patriarch. And while in the contemporary Bahamas this may be somewhat of a misplaced worry—since the state is constantly eroding its share of the social wage to favor privatized multinational economic strategies—the state continues to draw on notions of women as nonessential wage earners in order to preserve this ideological disjuncture between the public and the private, and it does so at the same time that it relies on women to compensate for severe state retrenchments. In practice, many women do not earn wages at all.[45] Of those who are unemployed, more than 61 percent are women.[46] Economic violence is thus enacted both publicly and privately. And domestic violence legislation, ostensibly framed to protect women's interests, now works to continue primogeniture and to ensure property transfer within a small white upper-class stratum and the more recently constituted black upper-middle class.

The ideological production of primogeniture is even more starkly exposed in examining women's relationship to these legal "protections." For working-class and poor women, the dissolution of property (which emerges as the major trope in the legal discussion) is of no consequence in the face of violent masculinity, for these women own neither "dwelling" nor "apartment" and they are neither "mortgager" nor mortgagee. On "domestic" day (Friday), which is the day that many working-class women appear in the magistrate's court seeking maintenance for their "natural and legitimate" children, or injunctions against their battering partners, it is not the ownership of property that has brought them there but, at least in part, the lack of it. Indeed, their lack of property ensures that at the day's end their cases would not have been heard, nor would the summonses they had demanded been served.[47] For middle-class and upper-middle-class women who may own property, one of the primary questions they confront is how to disentangle themselves from the web of well-established social relationships that protect *their* middle-class and upper-middle-class "husbands" from being defined, or accorded the same treatment, as criminals—a category that the law has apparently reserved only for working-class women, lesbians, gay men, prostitutes, and Haitians.[48] The proximity of these middle-class men to the central domains of power that cross party affiliation ensures legal, cultural, and gender immunity from demotion in status, from the immediate popular scourge of working-class resentment over the disjuncture between what upper-middle-class "husbands" profess to do and what they actually do— that is, the semblance of respectability and the disproportionate rewards they inherit and/or mobilize through it. Ultimately, they are protected from shame.[49] For most women who stand outside the legal definitions of "party to a marriage," no such claims can be made for relief from the court. Domestic violence as a legal construct—or, more accurately, women's experience of physical, sexual, and psychic violence together in a space that has been designated as private—operates as a proxy to ensure the allocation of private property within a disruptive heterosexual marriage. However, the shift in women's relationship to, and dependence on, marriage (for the last three decades the percentage of children in the Bahamas born outside of heterosexual marriage has averaged 58 percentage of all live births) might well increase the state's anxiety around questions of heterosexual middle-class respectability.[50] Moreover, the relative inability of indigenous classes to accrue wealth would not interrupt the continued gendered accumulation of private property. Thus, state support of primogeniture, of itself as benign patriarch, and of its interest in the property relations of heterosexual marriage all become much more urgent and significantly more fragile in the face of such threats.

By offering only minor allusions to the widespread occurrence of "domestic" violence in a legislative narrative that is ostensibly dedicated to eradicating it, and by making it possible for "*any* party" in the marriage to be perpetrator and "victim" of that violence, the legal text authorizes and flattens the asymmetrical exercise of power within domestic relations. This apparent gender neutrality or sexual democratization by fiat conveyed in the term "*any* party" is only possible, of course, because the state has detached sexual assault from physical violence, the very mechanisms through which male power operates, the very ones that feminists politicized.[51] Indeed, the text arbitrarily recodes women's experiences of violence in the domestic sphere, within the confines of a class-specific and race-specific matrimonial home, recast with fictions of harmony, order, and shades of the sacred. In so doing, it works to mask the political terrain of the immediate feminist struggle against violence, attempting now to contain a broad, popular movement within the courts in terms that are largely antithetical to that popular memory. Now, women who are beaten or raped are rendered triply suspect: as woman, as "victim," and as possible impostor (even extortionist), positioned to retrieve their legitimacy by relying on the authority of the attorney general, who alone must determine the veracity of their complaints. Women seem to carry no legitimacy of their own. The legal mandate for women to report crimes of incest and the sexual abuse of themselves and their daughters reinforces the popular-cultural sentiment that women are culpable for the sexual "lapses" in heteromasculinity. This does not take into consideration the context in which women's lives are situated, especially when telling demands the confessional mode that law itself appropriates.[52]

To the extent that the state as ideal typical patriarch chides women for wanting more (in light of the entanglements around implementing the law), or dismisses their demands for the transformation of the mechanisms of punishment (even as women's demands are being misnamed in the service of disciplining and criminalizing womanhood, while authorizing patriarchal violence), women are forced publicly to remain focused on the court system and its skewed, narrow definitions of violence in order to legitimize their broader claims.[53] The gesture works to place women in the role of perennial supplicant, as permanently grateful, and as guardian of the minimal.

"Domestic" violence as a legal construct, in its capacity to be placed within the boundaries of law (albeit nominally, and simultaneously recodified as the disposition of property within the matrimonial home) and to be outside of the law (in the sense of the patriarchal refusal to legislate seriously against it), aims to discipline and even to foreclose an emancipatory praxis that might demystify patriarchal power within the home. Such a praxis might imagine the domestic sphere as a space where one form of patriarchal power coagulates yet disperses to produce different kinds of violence that include wife-beating, incest, rape, and the sexual abuse of girl children and young women, because both girls and women are figured as sexual property. Thus, the spatial separation of physical abuse from sexual abuse on which the legal text insists dissolves almost instantaneously in the face of pervasive practice, for it is the *same* patriarch within the boundaries of the *same* home who disciplines and terrorizes through physical *and* sexual force, turning daughters into women, women into wives, and both into mothers. It seems a travesty, then, that a set of complicated psychosexual practices, so poorly under-stood and undertheorized, so urgently awaiting historical and cultural specification, conspires in the instance of the legislation to further crimi-nalize women for not reporting. It seems a travesty to position women as *the* cultural reproducers of heteropatriarchy, as complicit in its reproduc-tion, so much so that the state appears to be more progressive than vio-lent domestic patriarchy, and more progressive than women whose mo-bilizations instigated state action.

Configuring the Nation as Heterosexual: The Time When There Were No Lesbians and Gay Men in the Bahamas

Here I want first to read the injunctions and stipulations within the Sexual Offences and Domestic Violence Act as a strained self-reflection on forms of heterosexualized violence, which include incest, rape, sexual assault, and sexual harassment. I described earlier the ideological frag-mentation within the legal text that made these forms of violence appear as if they were either idiosyncratic or individually imagined. But given their pervasiveness and their widespread occurrence, the politicization of which originated within the feminist movement, we might question whether these forms of violence were not a permanent or at least a long-standing element of heteromasculinity. As expurgated, these forms of violence must have had an original placement within heterosexual desire. If that violence were to interrogate itself thoroughly, it would be com-pelled to move outside the boundaries and limits inscribed by law. Within the legal narrative, however, only displacement can occur, for the legal discourse is conducted narrowly, as if incest and rape were only to be understood as sins against God or crimes against man, or as if they primarily took place on the outside, as if there were no ideological and material links between state/parliamentary patriarchy and domestic pa-triarchy, for instance, and as if homosexuality could only be imagined as residing at the pinnacle of perverted heterosexualized violence. Ulti-mately, this narrow content resides within the rhetorical form prescribed within law, and this is why, methodologically, it is crucial to take them apart.

The conflations within the legal narrative are by now familiar: the systematic conflation of perverted heterosexual violence, such as rape or incest, with same-sex desire, which establishes a continuum of criminality in which same-sex desire is the apotheosis of a range of offenses including murder, robbery, dishonesty, lying, rape, domestic violence, adultery, fornication, and incest. Thus constructed, the psyche of criminality *is* the psyche of homosexuality. Moral weight—or, more accurately, "the logic of the narrative's discrimination"—is established through the designation of penalties that are attached to these crimes.[54] Both "unnatural crimes" of "adult male sexual intercourse with another male," and "adult female sexual intercourse with another female" are second only to possible life imprisonment for rape. In fact, if minimum sentencing penalties were to be enforced (seven and fourteen years on first and second convictions, respectively), these "unnatural crimes," with sentences of twenty years upon conviction (if committed in a public place), carry the most severe penalty of all possible sexual sins and crimes. Unlike other crimes, there are no mitigating circumstances to which one could appeal for mercy from the court, or presumably from God.

During the course of parliamentary debates, state managers drew from a motley assortment of symbols to displace the reflection on heterosexuality. There were brief moments when they directed the gaze at each other, but the confrontation foreclosed debate altogether. Instead, they pondered the weightiness of their task and whether their own moral caliber permitted them to attend to this most crucial of national tasks:

> The real answer [to crime] does not lie with this parliament, except in so far as the example that we as parliamentarians give by the manner in which we live our lives . . . and because the lives we live shout so loudly that nobody listens to what we say . . . it becomes imperative that once we take on the mantle of responsibility and become public servants, we recognize that every aspect of our lives is a daily mirror.[55]

The daily lives told another story, however. Corruption was widespread: "Officials [were] taking money left and right every day from people they [were] having dealings with," and "since most of the complaints about sexual harassment were about ministers," state managers were not quite sure whether a certain criminal element, most often associated with the streets, or the home, had crept into parliament's own august halls. They wondered what to do with their own "sodomites" within parliament:

> Buggery as it is called in this law is an absolute offence . . . But I can't accuse honorable members of parliament of committing criminal offences . . . the rules prevent me from doing so, even if I wanted to . . . It is reasonable to assume that this place has its share of gays, even parliament is not excluded.

And what of the police force, one might ask, whose historic mission it was to fulfill the state mandate of surveillance? Who was going to arrest the police who are that way inclined? Did the homosexual "proclivity" of not telling on each other privilege sexual loyalty above loyalty to state and nation?

> You will not have any homosexual who will consent to have, or carry on homosexual activities or sodomy with another homosexual making complaints against the other one. The only way you will be able to catch a homosexual and prosecute him is if you have informants . . . Separate from that you will never get them . . .

Were criminal penalties sufficient to reverse such unnatural proclivity?

> When they go to jail, do they stop being lesbians, stop being homosexuals? Does the urge disappear?

Surely a distinction ought to be made between force and consent:

> Shouldn't the lesbian who has committed this crime by forcing herself upon somebody else be treated more severely than two lesbians, who are consenting adults? There should be a distinction between fondling, for instance, and the actual act itself. The actual abominable act!

State managers pondered aloud the implicit contradiction of criminalization for homosexual parliamentarians when adulterous heterosexual ones, while immoral, had not yet been treated as criminal. They wondered whether "normal" husbands and wives performed sex acts that resembled buggery. The answer was not clear-cut, however. Did God intend heterosexual buggery?

These acts which are made offences are not exclusive. Let's check it out and see if it is what God intended for that offence to be between husband and wife.

In the end, the parliamentarians conceded their authority to medicine and science:

The doctors and the scientists will be able to tell us whether that causes any physical problems; obviously if it did cause much physical harm it wouldn't be carried on.

Understanding for a brief moment the extent of the power of fiat that resided in the office of the attorney general regarding questions of sexual harassment, and assuming that the attorney general would always be male, they puzzled over the conflictual operation of fiat in *his* hands in cases when *he* was the sexual harasser. As state managers noted:

Many an attorney general has committed the offence of sexual harassment.

In the end, however, these confrontations were reduced to party disagreements and, as reported in the media, rested on the (then) opposition's objection to the state's desire to legislate the private lives of citizens. And because these disagreements were merely cosmetic, they were not sufficient to undo the underlying conflations on which the heterosexual imaginary insists. Thus, it seems that the law continued to provide a "civilized," presumably neutral, objective mode of escape from a major ontological conundrum: how to accord lesbians and gay men the respect of fully embodied human beings, not reduced to a perfunctory mind/body dichotomy, in which the dismembered body could be imagined only as a dangerous sexual organ. As one state manager put it:

Just because he is a sissy does not mean he might not go to heaven . . . I don't believe his soul is a sissy . . . It's only the body, his sissy body.

What about protecting the constitutional rights of bodies detached from their souls, which were not human beings after all? Once homophobia began to govern the disciplinary mechanisms, it seemed to matter little to state managers whether homosexual "sin" and "crime" could be constitutionally sanctioned, or whether homosexuality was simply anathema to it.

Overall, no other kind of critique or interrogation was necessary because the law had presumably emptied the society, emptied heterosexuality of the chaotic, the disorderly, the criminal. Both the law and heterosexuality had been sanitized to function as the repository of order, returning each to an originary moral position. Thus articulated, the law presumably satisfied its civilizing mission, functioning silently, as early British mandates had commissioned it to do, while constructing and defending its own hierarchies.[56] The parliamentarians put it well: "The laws we pass are intended to keep us civilized." The law can dispense only what it has been destined to do and, simultaneously, it can provide a rationale for state intervention to ensure order, in this instance, for the viability of the nation. It could provide the "moral" ground to expunge anything that threatens that viability.

The state's self-reflection on heterosexuality, although strained, is important at another level. It is enacted from a dual gaze: from a recognition of seeing itself, coupled with the pervasive worry about how it is seen—by Bahamians and by church pundits, but more notably by those who bestowed independence. The worry is buried in the discussion of constitutionality and the prerequisites of mature, civilized governance. This is how the question was posed as the government presented its case for the passage of the Sexual Offences and Domestic Violence Act:

> Does the state have the right to define dimensions of sexual conduct between its citizens? Does the government have the right to enter the bedrooms of the citizens of this country?

It then provided its own (un)ambivalent response:

> The government has decided that it thinks, in its wisdom, that the state has the right to define the dimensions of social and moral relationships between men and women, and to define the dimensions which are lawful and thereby . . . the dimensions which are unlawful.

But the moral difficulty resided in the historical dilemma in which both the state and the church found themselves—in the very question that the Wolfenden Commission of England had debated three decades earlier:

the relationship between the sinner and sin, between illegality and immorality, the distinction between sin and crime. As state managers urged rhetorically:

> Let us preach against homosexuality and preach against lesbianism as a sin, but should we put someone into jail for what we believe is an unnatural sex act?

Conducted in parliament under the symbolically watchful eyes of the British royal pedigree, this debate on sin and crime adhered to the very discursive parameters outlined by them—the same governors who had disciplined the oversexualized, infantilized "native." Remember that the racialized psychic impasse of colonization reflected Britain's own fictive construction: "They cannot govern themselves." Nationalism may have contradicted the imperial discourse that used the fictions of science to explain "native" *incapacity* to govern in terms of biology, but the psychic residue of colonization continued to operate to convert double consciousness into a double bind.[57] Acting through this psychic residue, neocolonial state managers continued the policing of sexualized bodies, drawing out the colonial fiction of locating subjectivity in the body (as a way of denying it), as if the colonial masters were still looking on, as if to convey legitimate claims to being civilized. As the parliamentarians reflected:

> We have to be careful that we do not give the public, who still have to understand the functioning of this independent state of ours, the wrong impression, when we know the situation is entirely otherwise. That is one thing I respect the British for . . . although I didn't want them to dominate my country. The true fact of the matter is that the Englishman would tell you what the facts of the situation are on one side and interpret the facts as his opinion somewhere else . . . I accept that that is the constitutional position.

Not having dismantled the underlying presuppositions of British law, however, black nationalist men, now with some modicum of control over the state apparatus, continue to administer and preside over these same fictions.

Moreover, no nationalism could survive without heterosexuality—

nationalism needs it no matter how criminal, incestuous, or abusive it might be. Heterosexuality still appears more conducive to nation-building than does same-sex desire, which appears hostile to it—for women presumably cannot love themselves, love other women, and love the nation simultaneously. As one state manager, in his haste to honor divine will, explained: "One thing God did was to give man an undying urge to ensure the survival of the human race." But what is attributed to God is also avidly embraced by the state. We still need to understand the processes through which heterosexuality is reified, as well as the kinds of mythologies that the state recirculates to ensure its ideological longevity and to ensure that the moral boundaries that mark the closet will not in any way be contravened. It is to these questions that I now turn.

The State of the Closet, or the State and the Closet

The state has always conceived of the nation as heterosexual in that it places reproduction at the heart of its impulse. The citizenship machinery is also located here, for the prerequisites of good citizenship and loyalty to the nation are simultaneously housed within the state apparatus. They are sexualized and ranked into a class of good, loyal, reproducing, heterosexual citizens, and a subordinated, marginalized class of noncitizens who, by virtue of choice and perversion, choose not to do so. But there are additional ways in which the state works through law to position the nation as heterosexual. There are three primary gestures. The first, which I discussed earlier, is the normalization of violent heterosexuality and same-sex desire. The second gesture is the organization of an internal homophobic discourse on homosexual ontology, on the nature and origins of homoeroticism and its passion and desire, which operated through a contradictory, quasi-scientific discourse to present itself as truth about character. As noted by one state manager:

> You see the lesbian, the natural lesbian and the natural homosexual, God created them the way they are . . . The good doctor from Garden Hills has said that homosexual tendencies are not inherited ones.

While intimately aware of its own ignorance ("I don't have any scientific basis for what I am saying . . . but I think I am free to project my own views . . . I checked with the speaker of the house and he thought so too"), this homophobia utilizes systems of classification that are replete with minute details of physiognomy and anatomy, which, much like colonial discourse, function to interpret important dimensions of self. The legislative hearings overflow with convoluted pronouncements such as these:

> Buggery is completed on penetration and we are being very candid so that we can understand. Penetration of the anus by any member I suppose. But if you are talking about the offence of buggery, then penis. That's it . . . And in the case of lesbianism, then it is two women who have sexual intercourse. You see what I mean . . . What I am getting at here is that in the case of buggery, what we call homosexuality, the whole sexual act itself is penetration of the anus with the penis . . . In the case of lesbianism there is no penetration necessary. Stimulation of the vulva for anything would amount to sexual intercourse . . . They are not the same thing . . .
>
> If you have a man who stimulates the anus of another man by any means, but does not penetrate, he is not guilty of buggery. Do you see what I mean? . . . The nature of the lesbian act is different from the male homosexual act. There is no anatomical comparison possible, so [with] the whole question of the homosexual, there is no anatomical comparison.

And it is in these spaces of open meaning—open, as well, to confusion and wide interpretation and arrived at without consensus, and where strands of "evidence" are culled idiosyncratically from science, medicine, and common sense—that homophobia comes to reside.

The third strategy involved in the legal resituation of the heterosexual is a gesture that invoked nostalgia for an idyllic Bahamas, free from Western decadent incursions—a Bahamas not peopled by lesbians and gay men. The ideological scaffolding for these three moves was assembled through the twin paradoxical strategies of spectacularization and the erasure of lesbians and gay men, which served in the end to reposition and naturalize hegemonic heterosexuality.

Erasure is most immediately visible in the nostalgic invocation of sexual "purity," imagined within a geography and a home that only heterosexuals inhabit:

It is true, as the honorable member of St. Michael has said, that as we grew up, as we developed, we knew nothing, or very little of these learned responses, or these alternative lifestyles . . . Homosexuality was something that [in the past] was extremely rare . . . In our communities, when I was younger, we probably knew, and could count on one hand, those people who engaged openly in homosexuality.

But what does it mean to invoke such nostalgia and to suggest that some originary, unambivalent moment for the heterosexual founding of a Bahamian nation could be immediately recuperated and collectively made intelligible? What is the historical time frame within which this contradictory memory is summoned?

Presumably the time in which there were no lesbians and gay men in the Bahamas coincided with the era of the consolidation of colonization, the period that provided the ideological moorings for anticolonial nationalism. Here it is important to counter the mythology of sexual purity. The nineteenth century witnessed an ongoing struggle for power among different kinds of white masculinities: the wrecker, the rogue, the pirate, and the white gentleman.[58] The white masculine rogue and wrecker actually laid the groundwork for Ernest Hemingway's twentieth-century discovery of Bimini, which signaled the symbolic and material transfer of imperialism from British to American hands. With this transfer came the installation of tourism, the major site for the commodification of black women's bodies for sexual pleasure. It was in this period of the consolidation of the colonial nation that sodomy laws were introduced as one of the potential offenses against the white, male British person. The legal elimination of the sodomite, who at the onset of colonization was the indigenous Indian, helped to anchor the belief that white European heterosexual interests were best matched with those of the colonized, and that European civilization was necessary to conquer the savage sodomite, a point to which I return in chapter 5. Whether the contemporary Bahamian state can apprehend the continuities between its own gestures of violence and erasure and those of the colonial state is as significant as the fact that both are engaged in promoting and extending the heterosexual inheritance. "I am just a normal Bahamian male," said one state manager, "and a normal Bahamian male is *not* homosexual."

The belief in the perils of American imperialism and homosexuality—
that "the whole concept of the acceptability of homosexual behavior
between consenting adults is essentially an American phenomenon" that
Bahamians have adopted—means, at least in the state's view, that there is
no space for indigenous agency for lesbians and gay men, who presumably
become homosexual by virtue of Western influence. There is no consensus
among state managers about origins. Thus, the summoning of memories
around heterosexual inheritance marks an attempt to foreclose any coun-
terhegemonic memory of an insurgent sexuality that would have to be
housed outside of state structures on account of the excessive sexualization, codification, regulation, and discipline exerted upon those very
bodies. Communities of lesbians in the Bahamas, who claim neither
Western decadence nor the protection of the white European father, in
tandem with the work of many Caribbean feminists in Suriname, Curaçao, Jamaica, Grenada, and Carriacou, elaborate such a counterhege-
monic memory and subsequently form the bases of community around
mati work, kachapera, manroyals, and zami, which interrupt the state's
continued adjudication of heterosexual inheritance.[59] The point here is
one of the paradoxes of negation: "That which a culture negates is necessarily included within it."[60] State managers are caught in a contradictory
homage to the West as the harbinger of civilization and progress, on the
one hand, and as the harbinger of sexual destruction on the other. Clearly,
for feminists, a continued challenge lies in constructing a contemporary
vocabulary for same-sex desire beyond the point where the hegemonic
and oppositional meet.

The violent erasure of insurgent sexualities in the period of "flag
independence" can be linked more directly to the state's activity in re-
establishing the nation as heterosexual, in ideological and material terms,
imagined and practiced through patriarchy and masculinity. It has meant
redrawing a fictive nation as masculine and patriarchal at this historical
moment when popular masculinity has generated the belief that men
would have to leave the Bahamas to keep their masculinity intact. In the
wake of the passage of the Sexual Offences and Domestic Violence Act,
popular fears surfaced of a nation of women (read lesbians), who had
rendered men homeless and nationless by exercising their newly bestowed power to report coercive sex as marital rape, to report the pimps

who sexually exploit them, to report the fathers, cousins, and uncles who incest them, and to report their bosses who sexually harass or exploit them. These fears dovetail with an overall state impulse to control and criminalize women.[61]

The legislative fiction of the nation as masculine means reasserting the foundation of masculinity in procreation so that same-sex masculinity is positioned as femininity engaged in sex purely for satisfying desire (sissies), presumably not in the interest of the nation. And same-sex femininity is really femininity in drag—that is, woman as man-hater who defies biology, medicine, and psychiatry, who anatomically, according to state managers, cannot be compared to homosexual man, heterosexual man, or heterosexual woman. She is a species unto herself, who engages in something approximating normal sex. In the absence of a penis, she can only "stimulate the anus or the vagina or vulva of another," purely for satiating pleasure, presumably not in the interest of the nation.

In addition, the fiction of the nation as masculine masks the mass mobilization of women for the nationalist movement. Without women, state-generated popular nationalism could not have consolidated itself. The popular, mass-based suffrage movement of the 1950s, which was the vehicle for universal suffrage, provided visibility for an emerging black nationalist state, anxious to signal to Britain its newly acquired knowledge about citizenship, rights, and loyalties, and, therefore, its capacity for self-rule.[62] In a real sense, this mass movement of the 1950s was disciplined through the accession of the vote, which state managers usurped and claimed as their own accomplishment. The official narrative would record the Voting Rights Act of 1962 as among the earliest and most significant of its achievements, erasing the memory of that popular struggle and the significance of the women involved: Mother Butler, Mother Donaldson, Doris Johnson, Eugenia Luckhart, Mary Ingraham, Mable Walker, U. J. Mortimer, Gladys Bailey, Georgina Symonette, and Marge Brown—the very women for whom Marion Bethel dedicated the poem cited at the beginning of this chapter.[63] Ultimately, the fiction of the nation as masculine attempts to cancel out the economic when the state relies on tourism as its primary economic strategy and when it, in turn, rests on women's bodies, women's sexual labor, and the economic productivity of women's service work in this sector to underwrite the economic viability of the nation.

The paradoxical counterpart of erasure in the consolidation of hegemonic heterosexuality is spectacularization. State managers relied heavily on biblical testimony in order to fix this specter, using reiteration and almost incessant invocation to God and to Sodom:

> As the legend goes, God destroyed a whole city because of corruption. In the nineteenth chapter of Genesis, it tells how the cities of Sodom and Gomorrah were destroyed because of homosexuality. This is a very important defense to me. And I am now living in the Bahamas and I would not want the country destroyed because of homosexuality.

But how did same-sex love come to find itself in Sodom and in the Bahamas? How do sexuality and geography collide? Unfortunately, neither the biblical discourse nor the state-generated discourse on the origin of homosexuality are settled on these questions. State managers were not quite clear whether "homosexual tendencies [were] inherited ones," whether "*they* were born like that," or whether "the vast majority of *them* were induced or enticed into *that* condition by succumbing to the temptation of those homosexuals who [held] high office in the country." But they did not require answers to those questions, for the power of Sodom rested in its capacity to provide "the most important defense" for state managers, to operate as truth, despite contentious ecclesiastical debate about the impetus for destruction. Sodom requires no point of reference other than itself; it can assert authority without comparison, evidence, or parallel.[64] Its power lies in its ability to distort, usurp, or foreclose other interpretative frameworks, other plausible explanations for its destruction, or other experiential dimensions of homosexuality that oppose and refuse state constructions of the criminal, presumably reinforced by biblical authority. Such formulations would take the place of an over-determined state preoccupation with what lesbians and gay men do in bed and the ostensible power of our sex in destroying the nation. The myth of Sodom sexualizes and eroticizes and, in so doing, reduces ontology to the body, a contradictory move for black state managers, a "race" people for whom the justification for slavery presumably carried biblical weight, to premise citizenship in physiognomy, the very basis of the colonial refusal to admit agency and self-determination.

The conflation of lesbian and gay sexuality with mass destruction and with ominous, apocalyptic visions of genocide spill beyond biblical legend into other domains. For state managers, no place was safe:

> I thought the number of them was growing, and I thought they were engaged in various forms of activity . . . The atmosphere at Her Majesty's prison is conducive to homosexual activity . . . This is where you take it when you can't have it . . . Most of them are in influential positions; they use these positions to intimidate and corrupt young boys and young girls . . . Some of them have such influential positions that they control hundreds of people, sometimes thousands.

Sexualization and destruction are complete with the prostitute's body and the "AIDS infested body," spreading contagion and destruction:

> They have one single commodity with which they deal, that is their body . . . with that AIDS-infested body, they seek to ply their trade to get the cocaine to feed their habit.

The significance of these parliamentary discussions on sexual practices is that they invest homosexuality with the power to corrupt otherwise loyal citizens of the nation, even those who are temporarily outlaws. Criminality does not forfeit heterosexuality or heterosexual citizenship. However, criminalized homosexuality forfeits citizenship, because within homosexuality inheres the power to dissolve the family, the foundation of the nation and the nation itself. Homosexuals occupy relative rather than absolute citizenship, or rather none at all, and would now have to earn rights in order to move outside the closet and regain entry into the moral heterosexual community they have presumably contravened.[65] Because the requirement of citizenship is the requirement to be heterosexual, the state can now create a context for establishing its own secular narrative of salvation and deliverance. According to its understanding, only an act of God—not even that of state managers who can only legislate the unenforceable ("homosexuals will never tell on each other")—might extend a gesture of mercy toward the Bahamas to save it from sexual destruction.

In the interim, however, the state can act as savior and deliverer. It can simultaneously claim a biblical pedigree and appropriate the powerful, foundational biblical narrative of deliverance in which Moses, God's chosen deliverer, brings the Hebrews out of bondage. The Progressive Liberal Party appropriated a version of the theme from Exodus—"This land is mine, God gave this land to me"—as a mobilizing symbol.[66] How this symbol was put to use in the service of the economic, to position the state as heterosexual patriarch and economic savior, is the subject I explore in the discussion that follows.

"This Land Is Mine":
Tourism as Savior and Other Fictions

Earlier, we saw how the state eroticized the dissolution of the nation and produced apocalyptic (mythic) visions of disease and mass destruction premised in prostitution and in the practice of lesbian and gay sex. Several different bodies were called on for this task: the prostitute body (with potential disease, imagined as working class, and thus a perennial threat to middle-class respectability and femininity); the sodomite body (often imagined as white European, or white Bahamian, and financially well-off, objectified, and hypersexualized); and the immoral lesbian body (simultaneously spectacularized and hidden, lying somewhere outside of the heterosexual imagination, yet a perennial threat to domestic space). All of these bodies were conjoined in the state-constructed imperative to circumscribe boundaries around the body politic (making it safe for imperialism), or establishing quarantine within it (making it safe for loyal heterosexual citizens).

The eroticization of the dissolution of the nation is made visible by the state while it masks its own role in the eroticized production of citizenship and in the commodification of the nation as broker for multinational capital interests, so much so that even the notion of the nation-state is made unstable. Whose hands hold the power of national extinction when eighty-five cents of every tourist dollar made by state-supported multinational capital reverts to those corporations in their countries of origin? Moreover, sexual "symbolic" consumption practices provide a real base for the social processes of capital accumulation from which the state disproportionately benefits.[67] For whom, one might ask, is it "better in the Bahamas?"

In the discussion that follows, I examine tourism against the state narrative of its economic importance to citizens in order to foreground the processes of the commodification of sexual pleasure, the production of loyal sexualized citizens who service heterosexuality, tourism, and the nation simultaneously. There are profound, contradictory implications of socializing a population as "natives" five hundred years after colonial conquest, instead of socializing them for self-determination, the promise of anticolonial nationalism.

At the outset, we need to understand the state-managed semiotic system and its generative role in the excessive production of a tourist culture through which the Bahamas is inscribed and managed. Admittedly, the system functions differently for (imperial) tourists and has different implications for Bahamians, according to their racial or gender status; different implications for prostitutes whose sexual labor marks them as potential vectors of disease; different implications for women who do "legitimate" grossly underpaid work as chambermaids and cooks, or who otherwise service white femininity through more personalized services such as hair braiding and the like. For the tourist, the state-managed system adheres to the feminization of nature through symbols of unspoiled virgin territory, waiting to be transformed and possessed by imperial heterosexual design; the evocation of a land steeped in pathos and, by extension, mystery; a rewriting of history and the renovation of the narrative of colonization as a celebratory one of mutual consent, reminiscent only of imperial travel writing and rescue narratives.[68] For Bahamians, it involves the excessive production of a tourist culture and the almost painstaking building of an ideology that premises loyal Bahamian citizenship upon loyalty to tourism.

While state managers in the Ministry of Tourism presented Bahamians to the outside as perennially willing, hardworking people, underneath they worried about how to turn a recalcitrant population into a band of "warm and genial Bahamians," who were indeed ready and willing to serve. Every major throne speech delivered in parliament devoted substantial time and space to the benefits and rewards of tourism. Tourism promised civilization, modernity, and progress. According to the prime minister, "tourism and resort development [would] provide the main thrust for the vast program of economic expansion that [would] take the Bahamas to First-World status . . . it [would] make the Bahamas one of the finest, world-class tourist and resort destinations." Further, tourism promised increased spending, "Some $400m . . . between 1988 and 1992 to provide new tourist facilities and upgrade existing ones." Tourism also promised jobs, "at least 3,000 permanent jobs in the tourist industry alone," and it extended a special invitation to Bahamians to join the international community in the rehearsing of history: "By 1992, the 500-year anniversary of Columbus' landing in the Bahamas, the infrastructure and accommodations [would] be in place in San Salvador, thereby enabling us to host the international community at that historic island."[69]

Was this ideology generated in order to veil the economic difficulties in tourism? At the time, there were several media reports of a "big slump in tourism," "sluggishness," "layoffs in the hotel industry," and a "general decline in the volume of tourist days." Besides, what did First World status mean in the midst of unemployment? The state responded by accelerating its appeals to tourists: "Let a Bahamian introduce you to the Bahamas." Tourists were promised "warm and genial Bahamians," personalized services with a host family whose "leisure, occupational or religious interests [were] similar" to theirs. Advertising brochures displayed photographs of colorfully garbed black women with flowers in their hair. In practice, however, it proved difficult for the state to mobilize the "hundreds of volunteers" promised to tourists.

State managers faced additional problems. There were rumors of "poor attitudes," "bad service," and downright "rudeness" on the part of Bahamians. In response to this, the ministry initiated a major smile campaign in which Bahamians were urged to remind themselves to be courteous to tourists by wearing smile buttons. But Bahamians refused to smile. So each year thereafter, the ministry was forced to devise new strategies. The state could not quite accomplish such a formidable task on its own—this promised conversion of former sullen "slaves" into a contemporary band of smiling obsequious "natives"—so the Rotary Club, linked to the local Chamber of Commerce, which blamed the government for its own economic plight, took matters into its own hands. The

Rotarians wanted Bahamians to see that "tourism affect[ed] them too." It produced a set of bumper stickers rhetorically asking ordinary Bahamians (including the 58 percent working in the tourist industry) "What have you done for tourism today?"[70] The expectation was that Bahamians would come to see that their interests were inextricably linked to the tourist presence and that their daily duty as Bahamians rested in an ongoing consciousness of the tourist. That consciousness had material implications as well, for in any given month the number of tourists was likely to exceed the number in the total population.

In 1990, for instance, there were 3.6 million visitors, a monthly average of 302,000 in a population of 259,000.[71] In public television broadcasts, the Rotarians maintained that "in almost all instances the dollar start[ed] with the tourist." They hoped that Bahamians would adopt the Rotary's own motto of "service above self"; that they would learn to adapt "even if the tourists annoyed" them; or, at the very least, that they would stop to help tourists instead of rudely "speeding past" in their cars. Unlike the Rotarians, the prime minister assured Bahamians that they were not to blame for their own poor attitudes and the bad service they gave to tourists. The blame rested, instead, at the door of "hard-nosed, high pressure, North American management techniques," that were introduced insensitively into an island culture.[72]

But what were the symbols on which the state relied? A major symbol in the state-organized system for the tourist depended on the organization and creation of paradise, with all of its comforts and contents. Paradise actually exists, of course, in the form of Paradise Island, the name given to what was previously, and most unattractively, called Hog Island.[73] Paradise exists, as well, in an obsessive preoccupation with cleanliness and order. A case in point is the set of instructions developed by the Ministry of Tourism for use by those in the Straw Market, where women are the major owners and sellers. The instructions state: "The stall and its immediate surroundings *must* be kept clean and tidy at *all* times"; "Goods *must* be displayed on or around the said stall only and in *no other unauthorized location*. They may not be hung from ceilings, on louvers, or anywhere else except with the expressed permission of the Ministry of Tourism." "Only the stall owners and two other helpers will be allowed at the stalls." "*Loud* and *boisterous* behavior, as well as the use of *obscene language* will not be tolerated." As Mr. Pindling, former prime minister and minister of tourism, admonished the nation: "People visit the Bahamas to relax and have a good time and they want to do so in a peaceful and *clean* environment." The labor involved in creating such peace and cleanliness thus rested squarely upon Bahamians. There should be no beggars or homeless people in and around Nassau, for they might contaminate paradise. There should be no evidence of the sordid effects of economic decay that would suggest that paradise was not paradise after all.

From the advertisements, it seems that there is something for everyone in paradise. In the words of the Ministry of Tourism: "The law now says you can cruise the Bahamas duty-free; some people have been doing it for years": cruising grounds, care-free, tax-free, sex and capital combined. "For those who believe wild life should be preserved": nature and sex combined. "Come to Bimini . . . only 50 miles away from Hemingway's hideaway—home of the Hemingway championship tournament": the provision of "world-class" facilities, by which is meant European facilities, for after all, underdeveloped paradise peopled by natives is quite different from imperial paradise inhabited by the civilized.[74]

Columbus may have first landed in San Salvador, but it is Hemingway who owns the discovery of Bimini way after nineteenth-century tourism took hold and, as the irony of imperial history would have it, twenty miles from San Salvador, the site of the origin of "New World" colonization. Hemingway occupies an important psychic space in the American literary imagination, and in the imagination of Bahamian state managers as well—for they continue to market its attractiveness on the basis of its proximity to North America (particularly the U.S. South) and to the legend of Hemingway's discovery of Bimini. It was there that Hemingway fashioned the narratives in which he commanded the presence of black people and erased them.[75] It was there that he perfected the practice of having black people anticipate the desires of white people, even before whites gave voice to them. It was in Bimini, then, that he developed the trope of serviceability of black people, the serviceability on which tourism is anchored. In addition, it was in Bimini that Hemingway developed his prowess for shooting sharks and fish (the basis of current championships) recirculating the traditions of white, predatory, roguish (hetero)-

masculinity, daring and powerful enough to dominate nature.[76] And in spite of claims that Hemingway was gay, his refusal to disaffiliate from whiteness bears all the markings of imperialism, linking him to what Toni Morrison identifies as "American Africanism."[77] I am not making an argument here for marrying Hemingway's presumed homosexuality with the contemporary homosexual, even if I were able to identify such a figure. I am interested, however, in foregrounding the imperial, for in the contemporary period the erotic consumptive patterns of white gay tourism follow the same trajectory as those of white heterosexual tourism (the subject of the chapter that follows). In his faithfulness to white masculinity as rogue and pirate, in his construction of the availability of Bimini as "a blank, empty space" and his view of the "serviceability of black people," Hemingway continued the imperial narrative that preceded him. Accordingly, nature figures as raw material for American (European) creative expansiveness, positioned to collude in phantasmic representations of black people. These rhetorical strategies are the very ones that state and private corporations utilized to market Bahamians and the Bahamas to the rest of the world.

Of course, Hemingway's "discovery" of Bimini also becomes a powerful signifier that later inaugurates the escalated transfer of political, economic, and cultural hegemony in the region from British to U.S. hands.[78] Researchers at the North American Commission on Latin America have found that the Caribbean is perhaps more thoroughly dominated by transnational capital than any other region of the Third World. The Caribbean hosts the branches, subsidiaries, and affiliates of more than 1,740 U.S. corporations and an additional 560 companies affiliated with other foreign firms. The Resource Center in the United States reports that more than three quarters of all hotel rooms in the Bahamas are owned directly or indirectly by North American interests, including Playboy, Resort International Britannia Beach Hotel, Sheraton, and ITT. Approximately 13 percent of all U.S. finance-related investment abroad is located in the Bahamas. In addition, there are U.S. military installations, missile-tracking stations, the U.S. Navy and Coast Guard, and an underwater testing and evaluation center there.[79] Given what we know about the link between militarized masculinity and the growth of heterosexual prostitution elsewhere, it would be most plausible to assume that such prostitution exists in the Bahamas as well. Yet in the legislation it is the prostitute who bears the brunt of criminalization.

The organization of this psychic syntax of availability and serviceability is disturbing, both in the production of the tourist and in the (re)production of the "native."[80] The mass production of the imperial tourist psyche rests in the power of an ideology that summons an entire population (particularly women) into service; for the tourist it rests in the belief that the foreign currency spent is indispensable to the operation of the economy and vital for the local population. This, of course, results in another kind of psychic occlusion, the most significant being that the organization of tourism is presented so as to erase the role of the tourist in the production of tourism itself. What is kept invisible is the penalty for violating the rules of the Straw Market as well as the extent to which the state disciplines the population to ensure that it works to make things "better in the Bahamas" for tourists and not for itself. "Tourists are almost never aware of the perceptions 'natives' hold about them," Jamaica Kincaid suggests. "It never occurs to the tourist that the people who inhabit the place cannot stand you . . . that behind the closed doors they laugh at your strangeness."[81] Nor are tourists aware that the well-practiced rituals of dissemblance that characterize friendliness have more to do with the rituals of asymmetry and survival, or the desire to keep a job when few are available, than with fictions of "native" character.

The state's reliance on silence and invisibility tends to erase the work that women do to make it better for tourists and worse for themselves. I am referring here to the level of superexploitation in the workforce, the reductions in household income, and the increase of women-headed households in poverty at a time of excessive tourist production of the economy. Someone has to work to make it better in the Bahamas; 58 percent of the workforce *works* to do so, the largest percentage of whom are women. Simply put, Bahamian women are not the beneficiaries of tourism, and the erasure of this fact makes it possible for the state to impute a willingness on the part of women in the Bahamas to be complicit in the terms of their own exploitation and erasure in the same way that it made women complicit in and responsible for (hetero)sexualized violence within the home. Still, there is a contradictorily ironic state reliance on women who do sex work. Everyone knows about the links between prostitution and the hotel and soldiering business; there is no mistake that sex is what is being sold. What inheres within this mask of "respectability" is that all self-respecting black gentlemen know the rules of the game, how to buy and sell sex and how to maintain a guarded reticence about it; yet no respectable woman can sell sex to tourists and retain respectability. It is ostensibly the "common" whore who prostitutes her labor (in the service of the nation) to make Bahamas better for the tourist. State managers rely on the dubious boundaries the sex worker is made to inhabit, the boundaries of (im)morality and (il)legality, to maintain and consolidate the silence.[82]

Sexual commodification and consumption are evident not only in the earlier trope of the imperial rescue of virgin land but also in other ways that women's bodies are commodified. White-owned private capital need not be as discrete as black masculinity, which must carry the burden of respectability for the world. A set of postcards designed by Charm Kraft Inc. (printed in Ireland and distributed by Island Merchants Ltd., which owns sole rights of distributorship) markets white femininity and the availability of their sex as part of tourism. An invitation to "Come to the Bahamas where summer never ends" is accompanied by photos of semi-nude white women with the caption, "Feeling Hot, Hot, Hot . . . in the Bahamas." In another, "Ooh, Bahamas: want to do something besides stroll along white sand beaches, swimming in aquamarine waters? Well there's always biking." All of these advertisements are accompanied by white seminudity. The cards project such a surreal quality that it is difficult to ascertain whom they represent. Do they ultimately erase the women who trade in sex? Are they so homogenized, so hypercommercialized, and so generic (they could be on beaches anywhere) that their objectification becomes cliché? It would be important to determine the extent to which this sexual commodification pertains, as well, to the homosexual male body, and whether it enters another underworld, as it were, when the gay body, tourist or indigenous, turns prostitute, either as an extension of gay culture or exploited as another exotic part of the transnational trade in sex.[83]

Black women are also sexualized and exoticized in this tourist drama. In fact, white imperial tourism would not be complete without eroticized blackness. The script finds expression in commercial advertising and in the production of certain fetishes that are signified as "culture." Bahama Mama (Bahama Papa has been recently added to complete the heterosexual ideology of family nuclearity) is a buxom, caricatured, hypersensualized figure that can be bought in the market in the Bahamas. She can also be consumed as "hot and spicy sausage" at any "Nice and Easy" convenience store in the United States. Upon their return home, tourists can continue to be intoxicated by the Bahamas by ordering a bloody Mary with Bahama Mama—alterity as instruments of pleasure. European fantasies of colonial conquest—the exotic, the erotic, the dark, primitive dimensions of danger, dread, and desire—converge here on virgin beaches and aquamarine waters, enabled by black state managers and their white multinational counterparts. Black masculinity is deeply complicit in managing phantasmic constructions of black femininity, satisfying white European desire for restless adventure and for what is "rare and intangible."[84]

Ultimately, tourism as a metasystem makes it possible for the state to circumscribe boundaries around the nation while servicing imperialism. The evidence for this is that the state simultaneously reenacts the dissolution of the nation through these political economic gestures, which it ideologically recodes as natural, as (super)natural, or as savior of the people. It presented itself as economic savior of the people through tourism, legislating against "disease-infested AIDS bodies," at a time when tourism was experiencing one of its worst slumps. The Sexual Offences and Domestic Violence Act has made it possible to have imprisoned (for five years) anyone with an HIV infection who has consensual sex without disclosing their HIV status. Thus, tourism is not only an economic activity but also an important ideological site for the dissolution of the nation and for the construction of a national identity fashioned from the proclivities and desires of the imperial masculine subject, the invisible subject of the legal text. It has assisted in the production of a specific cultural form dutifully chiseled from a mold produced *elsewhere*. Five hundred years after the Conquest, girls as young as seven work in the Straw Market, offering songs to tourists in exchange for twenty-five cents. For whom is it "better in the Bahamas?" What does it mean to resocialize a generation into the benefits of rediscovery, to rewrite the history of Bahamians as one of "pirates and princes," and to prepare one's country, one's identity, in the service of service, to argue that "as Bahamians we have many, many personalities . . . we can be whatever *you* want your vacation to be"? How precisely are citizens to be socialized for self-determination and autonomy through the tropes of rediscovery? How is it tenable for black state managers to insist on independence and yet adopt strategies that are diametrically opposed to it: to socialize citizens into heterosexuality and not into self-determination?

In whose interest is heteropatriarchy reinvented? Our discussion suggests that black heteropatriarchy takes the bequeathal of white colonial masculinity very seriously, in its allegiance to the Westminster model of government, in its belief in an originary nuclear family (which is not the dominant family form in the Bahamas), and in its conscientious management of law and the reproduction of its false ontologies.[85] The legal subject of colonial law, which black heteropatriarchy now continues to adjudicate, was neither slave nor woman. Heteropatriarchal nationalist law has neither sufficiently dislodged the major epistemic fictions constructed during colonial rule, nor has it dismantled its underlying presuppositions. Nor has the (in)visible subject of imperial law been entirely replaced, not in nationalist law, not in any of the neocolonial state's contemporary gestures to adjudicate the imperial through law, not within the political economy. The ideal typical citizen is still premised within heterosexuality and maleness. When citizenship is premised in these terms, all of those who occupy a marginalized status—working-class and poor women, sex workers, lesbians and gay men, and those who are HIV-infected—continue to be positioned as noncitizens. Yet, a retreat from demands for state accountability will make it more possible for the state to continue to premise citizenship in masculine and heterosexual terms, and to continue to make women irrelevant to the project of nation-building.

Central also to the reinvention of heterosexuality is the state's attempt to foreclose lesbian desire, however voyeuristically imagined by state managers, in a manner reminiscent of the detailed surreptitious sexual narratives of Britain's nineteenth-century Purity Society. There was never an organized demand to criminalize lesbianism during the political mobilization for the passage of the Sexual Offences and Domestic Violence

Act. The organized feminist demand coalesced around restraining violent domestic patriarchy. Behind closed doors, however, state managers
sought to keep the erotic within the boundaries of the domestic heterosexual home, disrupted as it was by wife beating, rape, and incest. If
husbands now had to rely on the consent of their wives for sex, if they
could no longer resort to physical and psychic violence or coercion in the
matrimonial home, if, in other words, domestic patriarchy were in perennial need of restraint, then heterosexuality itself was at risk and, therefore, needed to be defended. On no account could it be relinquished. Put
differently, from the state's vantage point erotic autonomy for women
could only be negotiated within the narrow confines of a disrupted heterosexual. Autonomous eroticism could only go so far: it could not leave
the confines of the matrimonial bed to inhabit a space that could be
entirely oppositional to it, entirely unaccountable to it, or even partially
imagined outside of it. Much like the colonial master narratives in which
masters could not imagine or anticipate their absence (for power cannot
predict its own destruction) so, too, does heterosexuality remain unable
to imagine *its* own absence. The state as surrogate patriarch can distance
itself from violent domestic patriarchy only temporarily, however, in
order to appear more progressive than it. But ultimately the state comes
to the defense of the domestic patriarch in legally recouping the matrimonial bed. While women and feminist groups may make demands on
the state, undoing this historical, homosocial, and ultimately homophobic bonding is a formidable task indeed.

Despite differences in their ideological and material class base, women
and women's groups appear to have derivative access, if not direct access,
to state power. Small size, in this instance, facilitates fluidity and, one
might argue, a certain proximity to the halls of power. But at times,
fluidity entangles women in the presumably open but largely coercive
web of patronage from which the state draws loyalty, especially in a
context where the state is the major employer. But there is a certain
duplicity attendant with coercive power: there are risks and costs embedded in women's decisions to engage, in their decisions to craft the very
terms of engagement, or in their refusals to engage at all. Shifting political
alignments among women's groups and differences among working-class
women's organizations reflect shifts in situational power, although the

power of discursive definition is not insignificant. But this power is of a different valence than state-coagulated power, sometimes permeable, at times coercive, at times securing its own interests on behalf of patriarchal nation. Given the fact that the state is able to contravene almost entirely women's own definitions of domestic violence and of sexual and physical abuse, and that it can construct its own narrative of heterosexual deliverance, it has at least partially created a defined space where women struggle over situational power, while the state continues to exert its inherited power. In this sense, then, the political-economic serviceability of working-class women in tourism is matched by women's serviceability in another domain: the state can now draw on women's political mobilizations as evidence of its own legitimate, advanced form of political governance, as evidence of its mature evolution, and as evidence that democracy is working. The establishment of the Woman's Desk provides international legitimacy for the state, which is now seen as adhering to international conventions of progress. The links that these groups have established make it possible for the state to permit entry only to certain women as symbolic representatives of women's struggles while simultaneously continuing to diffuse narrow definitions of femininity. Can feminists rely on a patriarchal state that draws epistemic fodder from sexualized, imperial, regressive symbols, while making emancipatory demands on it? Can feminists continue to lay claims on a corrupt state? What are the responsibilities of feminists within the state apparatus to those on the outside? Needless to say, major challenges remain for feminist organizations, for while they have provoked significant ruptures in heteropatriarchy that have propelled the state into working harder to reconstitute itself, those gains have not interrupted the dominant sexualized practices within tourism in the Bahamas.

As feminists, we have understood the meaning and limits of state repression. Yet we need a deeper appreciation of the nuanced ways in which heteropatriarchy is indispensable to it. As the organizing episteme within the state, heteropatriarchy is avidly mobilized to serve many fictions. Most significantly, it enables a homosocial, homophobic, and, in a real sense, bankrupt state to position itself as patriarchal savior to women, to citizens, to the economy, and to the nation.

At this moment in the evolution of the Bahamian state, emancipatory feminist projects are hard pressed to continue to draw legitimacy from the state. It seems crucial for the feminist movement to reformulate a new vocabulary for an understanding of domestic violence, for instance, in terms that are not located within the state's mechanisms of surveillance. Instead of being premised within the state's misrepresentation of domestic violence and its deployment of the law of the father, feminists would need an emancipatory praxis to dissolve the carefully programmed dimensions of the survivors' internal psychic landscape that has taught "if mih man don't beat me, he don't love me"; "is so man stop"; or that a daughter is "too womanish for she own good and it can't have two women living in one house"; or that more generalized, internalized shame that begets the silent conviction that women are women's worst enemies and only men are women's best friends. There is an urgent need for an emancipatory praxis that deconstructs the power of heterosexual lore that positions women as their own worst erotic enemies and rivals, that might explode mothers' inherited discomfort with the emerging, restless sexuality of their own daughters, a sexuality that is often viewed as threatening or anxious to usurp. We might have to speak the unspeakable and name the competitive heterosexuality, an unnamed homosexual desire between mother and daughter, its complicated, as yet unspecified, origins, and its contradictory societal sanctions. It would be an emancipatory praxis anchored within a desire for decolonization, simultaneously imagined as political, economic, psychic, discursive, *and* sexual.

Thus a major challenge lies in crafting interstitial spaces beyond the hegemonic where feminism and popular mobilization can reside. It would mean developing a feminist emancipatory project in which women can love themselves, love women, and transform the nation simultaneously. This would mean building within these interstices new landmarks for the transformative power of the erotic, a meeting place where our deepest yearnings for different kinds of freedom can take shape and find rest.

2

Imperial Desire/Sexual Utopias:
White Gay Capital and Transnational Tourism

Sexualized, gendered, cross-cultural bodies . . . have histories of
production in the United States at the nexus of academic and non-
academic discourses. These histories are histories of tourism and
exploitation. They are histories that simultaneously seek and produce
commodities as queered fetishes, feminized fetishes and nativized
fetishes.—GITA PATEL, "Sleight(s) of Hand in Mirror Houses"

During much of my work on the Bahamas I only narrowly engaged the
question of the organization and production of gay tourism, assuming
largely that the processes of ideological and material exploitation, of
which Gita Patel speaks in the epigraph above, followed a trajectory that
was intrinsic to heterosexualized tourism and the operation of neocolonial states alone. I had neither imagined a systemic, interdependent
relationship between heterosexual capital and gay capital, nor had I considered that capitalist competition might push these two systems to draw
from the same epistemic frameworks, to consume from the same site, as
it were, in much the same way that black capitalism had been called on to
do a similar kind of work for white capital.[1] All of these ways of thinking
changed, however, after a trip I took to Jamaica.

In the process of traveling to Negril Beach in Jamaica, after driving
past Hedonism II on Norman Manley Boulevard, I witnessed the area's

covert racial trade in illicit sex—an issue of which everyone was aware (including the police) but reluctant to discuss.[2] This trade pertained as much to heterosexual practice as it did to same-sex desire among men. The transactions seemed to carry that same covert valence of unnamed knowing that Shyam Selvadurai described on a beach in Sri Lanka, in his coming-of-age novel *Funny Boy*:

> The sun was setting, and the beach was quite crowded with foreigners and local villagers. We sat in silence, watching the sky change color at the horizon. Then, Jegan leaned forward in his chair and looked keenly at something on the beach. My father regarded him, curious. Jegan turned to him and said, "Is what is happening what I think is happening?"
>
> I turned to look down the beach now, wondering what Jegan had seen. There was nothing out of the ordinary. As was usual at this time, there were many foreign men around. A lot of them were talking to young boys from the village.
>
> "Yes," my father said.
>
> "And they come back to the hotel?"
>
> My father shrugged. "Sometimes."
>
> "You don't mind?"
>
> "What am I to do? They have paid for the rooms. Besides, if I tried to stop it, they'd simply go to another hotel on the front."
>
> "But isn't it illegal?"
>
> My father chuckled. "I don't see any police out there, do you?" He poured himself another drink. "It's not just our luscious beaches that keep the tourist industry going, you know. We have other natural resources as well."[3]

Of course, natural resources are the backdrop for nativizing sensibilities, and for Patel's notion of the nativization of fetishes. In one sense this scene in Sri Lanka bears close resemblance to the sexual contours of Bahamian tourism that I described in chapter 1. And it raises an important question regarding whether the erotic consumptive patterns of white gay tourism followed the trajectory that had been mapped by white heterosexual capital. In thinking through the legend of Ernest Hemingway's "discovery" of Bimini and the state's use of it to market

Bahamian attractiveness primarily to American tourists, I wondered whether Hemingway's (presumed) homosexuality might have made a difference to the kind of narratives he crafted about the Caribbean. It could have been the case that Bahamian state managers deployed the discourse of imperial discovery to enhance and advance their own first claim to inheritance, which might not have been at all what Hemingway had intended.[4]

White gay tourism need not, of course, be built upon Hemingway's discursive inventions. First, his own gayness can be disputed. Second, he writes well before the widespread formation of gay identity communities in the United States. Yet I believe he illustrates the manner in which discursive, which is to say ideological, production can and does serve as the basis for certain consumptive practices, in this case, accumulation within tourism. And if we were to conclude that Hemingway was gay, and believe that the social facts of identity shaped knowledge, we would have to ask how and why his narratives of travel so closely resemble heterosexual travel narratives. But it is not only the possible case of a single resemblance that is crucial here, even for a figure who occupies as important a place in the American imaginary as Hemingway. When the generative scripts of heterosexual tourism and those of gay tourism are examined, we see that they traverse a similar imperial geography; that they draw on similar epistemic frames to service an imagined Western tourist. It is this similarity that requires our analytic and political attention, for it suggests that the material and ideological gestures of recolonization and renativization may not be the province of heterosexual capital or neocolonial state managers alone. Rather, both segments of capital appear to depend on one another, and to compete with one another through that (inter)dependence. In this regard, the contiguity between heterosexual and homosexual male desire under the seal of a shared colonialist appropriative approach vetted through race and ultranationalist representations of the West demands close scrutiny.

What is disturbing about this development is that if we invoke a common experience of (sexual) queerness as the ground on which to establish *global* solidarity communities, where is this queer "native" to fit? Who is this "native" within the discourses of anthropology, fetishized as sexual other at the inauguration of imperialism, now recolonized by white gay capital through tourism? Admittedly, these economies of the erotic had been forced underground by heterosexual capital, but they now function above ground, borrowing from the heterosexual tropes of sexual serviceability to invent and imagine themselves. What can we make of the similarity between regressive homophobic state gestures and the practices of gay capital? Does capitalism inevitably commodify and fetishize, despite whose face it wears? What is to be the relationship between gay capitalism and gay political praxis? What is the content of "gay"? What kinds of solidarity communities do we wish to construct, and what kinds of geographies of desire and pleasure are possible, and necessary, in light of the conflation of the erotic and the exotic? What are to be the politics of the erotic under the increasingly fragmented and alienating conditions created by the operations of capitalism itself? What critical political stances are required when the oppositional begins to assume the shape of the hegemonic, when the hegemonic simultaneously continues to insinuate itself into the oppositional in aggressive and destructive ways?[5]

These are not easy questions to undertake at this moment, particularly because attempts at deep self-reflexivity within marginalized communities run the risk of perverse appropriation and distortion by right-wing movements, whose secular and religious arms are unrelenting in their desire to mobilize homoerotics as a pretext to refuse citizenship. The idea of the gay consumer as a prosperous, perhaps undeserving, elite is now so prevalent that it has become politically dangerous. As Amy Gluckman and Betsy Reed have argued, in order "to bolster antigay campaigns in Colorado, Oregon, and Maine, right-wing groups seized on the legal advances that lesbian and gay men won to position homosexuals as a privileged minority, as a group requiring unnecessary 'special rights.' "[6] While some of these campaigns have been waged with the full support of conservative segments within the black church, opposition does not only originate from the outside. Deep fissures and contradictions around continued male privilege, class hierarchy, and nationalism also exist within a fractured gay community in which there is little consensus about the terms on which a mass movement could be constructed. Indeed, it seems that when "the lesbian and gay movement goes to market," as Alexandra Chasin argues, radical political praxis is forfeited.[7] Many predominantly white gay organizations in the United States refuse to confront racism or the unequal effects of the very processes of globalization in which we are imbricated and, therefore, continue to reproduce. Tourism itself results from globalization, even while it simultaneously relies on it. Further, an early epistemic marriage between queer theorizing and the dominant methodologies of poststructuralism in the U.S. academy has had the effect of constructing queer theory in a way that eviscerates histories of colonialism and racial formation, frameworks that could themselves point the way to a radical activist scholarship in which race, sexual politics, and globalization would be understood together rather than being positioned as theoretical or political strangers.

The more specific purpose of this chapter is to delineate how globalization matters in the production of gay consumer identities. In presenting the outlines of a genealogy of interdependence and competition between heterosexual capital and gay capital, my aim is to elaborate how gay imperial production of sexual utopias is undertaken in the West, and I will do so by examining the International Gay Travel Association, the largest membership organization for gay travel, and by analyzing the travel/vacation guides of the *Spartacus International Gay Guide*, which owns the largest share of this market. These guides have become formative ideological tools in a transnational tourist trade at a moment when tourism itself is the largest growth area of gay capital. Again, I foreground the imperial, not only because the unequal dichotomies between consumer/producer and producer/audience adhere to a First World/Third World hierarchy, but also because implied within this nexus of sexual transaction is the production of a "queer fetishized native" who is made to remain silent within his local economy in order to be appropriately consumed. By nativization, I am referring to an ongoing process through which an essential character is attributed to the indigenous—the "native"—which derives largely from relationships to geography or to a particular territory, which in turn structures the context within which this "native" is to be imagined and understood. The effects of nativization are several. It seems that in order to satisfy the terms of an earlier imperial contract, this fetish cannot live and breathe, ideologically that is, for purposes other than the foreign or the sexual, nor is he permitted to travel. Nativism operates best in its own place. Nor can the "native" be his own sexual agent, for that would contravene one of the basic tenets of the imperial script. Here I use "he" because the subject/agent/producer/citizen within this gay tourist economy is almost always imagined as a white, able-bodied, and upwardly mobile man who lives in the West. There are presumably no cultures of whiteness in the Third World. This traveling agent assumes his rightful place in the competition between two segments of capital. He is the same agent/citizen that white heterosexual capital has produced as the quintessential gay consumer, possessing a perennially changing set of needs and desires that only capitalism can satisfy. While citizenship based in political rights can be forfeited, these rights do not disappear entirely. Instead, they get reconfigured and restored under the rubric of gay consumer at this moment in late capitalism. Heterosexual capital makes it appear that the only gay people are consuming people, and that the only gay consuming people are white and male. In this universe, whiteness and masculinity operate together through a process of normalization that simultaneously overshadows lesbians, working-class gay men, and lesbians and gay men of color of any class. This erasure is necessary to produce this above-average homosexual consuming citizen.

In what follows, I begin an examination of these issues by first outlining what is at stake for heterosexual capital in creating what has come to be known as "the gay marketing moment." Despite claims to the contrary, heterosexual capital's gesture of rolling out the "welcome mat" has less to do with hospitality than with the creation of a new consumer and a new market, both of which must be contained.[8] But what does gay capitalism do with the gay consumer who is the construct of the heterosexual imaginary? In the second section of this chapter, I use the specific example of gay tourism and its ideological production of gay travel guides to demonstrate that gay capital mobilizes the same identity and operates through a similar set of assumptions as does heterosexual capital. These systems not only mutually construct each other but also compete for a market that each is anxious to usurp. Both are engaged in nativizing and colonizing moves, which I had assumed earlier were generated by processes of heterosexualization alone. Finally, I end by suggesting that if we are to build effective solidarity movements that embody pleasure while not simply reifying it, we need to understand and confront these orientalizing discourses and practices of travel, the fantasy of the "silent native," and their possible effects on urban metropolitan racisms.

Manufacturing the Contemporary Gay Consumer: U.S. Heterosexual Capital Rolls out the "Welcome Mat"

Despite the widespread deployment of "woman" and the marketing of white middle-class femininity as central ideological tropes of white heterosexual capitalism, the quintessential homosexual consumer within the contemporary racialized, gendered political economy of the United States is invented and imagined as male and white. This often masculine man (akin to, although somewhat different from, the ["real"] Marlboro man), is well educated and, on that basis, correspondingly well paid. The one "glitch" in this profile is that he "happens" to be homosexual.[9] This corporate construction of his homosexuality as coincidence—perhaps incidental to the buying point—paradoxically helps to instill the idea that gay identity has the potential to disrupt the "mainstream" heterosexual market. Through advertising he is summoned to consume, yet he is made to be hidden so that his sexuality need not become the subject of his consumption. For instance, in 1992 a *New York Times* article titled "Tapping the Homosexual Market" announced that "for the first time advertisers [were] vying for homosexuals' buying power, though they [worried] about offending mainstream consumers."[10] The significance of this buying power lay in the apparent statistical fact that it outstripped that of the very "mainstream" consumer who presumably took offense at homosexuality. The statistical weight for such a conclusion came from a survey conducted in that same year by the Chicago company Overlooked Opinions, which found that the average household income for lesbians was $45,827 in 1992, while for gay men it was $51,325, which, the survey states, was "well above the average annual household income in the United States, which stood at $36,520."[11] In 1999, Community Marketing confirmed that the trend of above-average income had continued. Some 75 percent of lesbians and gays who travel had incomes of more than $40,000 per year, and 23 percent had incomes of over $100,000, compared to 9 percent of the population of the mainstream (heterosexual) American travelers.[12]

Those who customarily alert capitalists to the consumptive proclivities of the affluent announced that gay men spent two out of every three "queer" dollars; 80 percent dined out more than five times in any month; 48 percent were homeowners; and, together, 43 percent of lesbians and gay men took more than 162 million trips in 1991 alone.[13] Overall, by 1999, 85 percent of those surveyed reported taking vacations in the previous year (compared to 64 percent of the national average), 36 percent took three or more vacations, and 45 percent traveled overseas, compared to just 9 percent of the national average.[14] These statistics appear with vigorous frequency, particularly in the gay press where they operate with the power of myth in the sense that they no longer require either explanation or context from which to derive legitimacy. Indeed, they suggest that no matter how tainted gay dollars appear, no potential market can escape capital's logic to transform them into an arena of competition or a site for potential profits.

Over the last decade and a half there has been an acceleration in the commercial interests that investigate "gay and lesbian niche marketing," some of which was spurred by white gay men themselves who work in the corporate sector. As early as 1996 an amorphous "Wall Street" became poised to recruit lesbians and gay men to help roll out not the proverbial red carpet but rather the "welcome mat" for gay investors, believing that gay corporate executives are best suited to engage "gay" clients. One mutual fund in California, Sheppard and Meyers, specifically guides gay investors toward "gay friendly" companies, of which it believes there are 375 in the United States.[15] But perhaps the most frequently referenced guide was one that promised to point the way toward "untold millions," advising businesses about how they might position themselves for the impending "gay and lesbian consumer revolution." This text was written by Grant Lukenbill, who describes himself as "America's leading authority on marketing to gay and lesbian consumers." Lukenbill argues that as companies across America battled for an increased share in the market, many of them ignored the vast untapped market segments of consumers ready and waiting to throw their economic weight behind those companies that acknowledged "who they [were] and what they want[ed]." Lesbians and gay men were a new "defined consumer segment," an attractive "niche" with the ability to "bolster corporate image, its market savvy and its competitive advantage."[16] "Twenty million new customers!"[17] All areas of consumption were targeted as arenas where the struggle for this newly defined population would take place: alcohol, drugs (complicated in the age of worsening HIV infection), clothing, film, cigarettes, and travel. So lucrative was the market that in the same year of the publication of *Untold Millions,* Lukenbill shifted his attention from heterosexual market interests, turned his subjects into his audience, and provided advice in the form of a "guide" on astute, socially responsible spending.[18]

Finance capital, which includes investment and mutual funds, retirement estates, credit and insurance companies, and the viatical services they provide, has also discovered the well-off gay consumer, yet it differs significantly from its counterparts in the economy of travel. While investment and mutual funds rely on well-off, able bodies capable of travel, these segments of finance capital are organized to underscore the specter of vulnerability and of death.[19]

Of course, death is rarely directly invoked. The euphemism of "viatic," which means "of or pertaining to supplies for a journey," as in traveling provisions, masks the anxiety about death at the same time that it underscores it. The provisions or supplies necessary for the journey of people living with AIDS are advertised on the same pages as those presumed to be able-bodied travelers. In mainstream gay magazines such as *Out* and the *Advocate,* as well as in regional newspaper/publications such as *New York, Homo-Xtra, Metro-Source,* and *Gay and Lesbian New York,* advertisements for gay travel options seem to live comfortably with agencies offering cash in exchange for life insurance policies. Such hyperawareness of the "needs" of the dying at once script people with AIDS as dying rather than living with disease, or as people who are expected to die soon. While this narrative clearly contradicts the model of the ideal traveler—dead bodies do not travel—it stands uncontested and not even discussed.

Despite the manufacture of this particular gay consumer and the faith in his potential to generate "untold millions," the gay market is constantly mediated by heterosexual capital's anxiety about how the gay consumer is to be (re)presented. In its pursuit of "gay" dollars, heterosexual capital has worried aloud about how it might pursue those (tainted) dollars without "offending mainstream consumers." Homophobia, then, is temporarily positioned as a threat to profits. Yet, in this instance, concern is focused not so much on corporate homophobia, but on the homophobia of the "mainstream consumer." Capitalism is able to position itself as being more progressive than the "mainstream," progressive enough to "sell" to homosexuals and, even in some instances, to hold out the promise of befriending them, as depicted, for example, in an advertisement by General Motors in Chicago, "where customers become friends."[20] Not surprisingly, certain fractions of capital have moved to utilize heterosexism as a competitive wedge in this contest for the gay consumer. In its financial advice, American Express found it necessary to remind well-to-do "unwed" gay men and lesbians of their vulnerability, of the fact that they cannot "count on the protections that married couples [take] for granted; unlike married couples, [they cannot] pass to each other assets of more than $10,000 a year, without exhausting the $600,000 gift and estate tax exclusion [they] might want at death."[21] *They*, therefore, require protection. The struggle for this consumer, alive or dead, is thus so fierce that heterosexual capital feels entirely compelled to use the perversity of heterosexism to mold lesbian and gay men into well-behaved consumers.

This is not the only instance in which capitalism has been caught between its own market imperatives and the ideological casing around the identities of its potential buyers, caught in the contradiction, to use Bessie Smith's words, of wooing an audience of which it is contemptuous.[22] In this instance, contempt can be read through the violence of erasure that comes from a dual marketing strategy that hides "gayness" in the heterosexual market while accentuating it in the gay market. With this strategy, capital creates images that presumably elude the heterosexual consumer but also are suggestive enough that the homosexual consumer —who consumes more avidly than his heterosexual counterpart—gets the point that he, too, is the intended subject of consumption. Ultimately, within a sexualized market, advertisements in the gay media are most often refracted through the sexual—the very trope through which all homosexuals are imagined.

The same strategy manifests itself in the singular line of advertising directed toward the lesbian and gay community, seemingly constructed to reassure lesbians and gay men that while gay erasure is necessary for the functioning of heterosexual capitalism, there is an appropriate place for visibility—the lesbian and gay press.[23] Within these pages, American Airlines announced a "new partnership" in "gay travel value." "Seaspirit, the only ship designed specifically for gay travelers," offers the promise of "a positive gay experience you will never forget." It is in the gay press we learn that Detours Travel Guides ("for those who don't necessarily travel the straight and narrow") has teamed up with U.S. Air to save money for traveling "companions." Subaru, advertising in the *Windy City Times: The Chicago Gay and Lesbian Weekly* secures its legitimacy by making itself "the proud founding sponsor of the Rainbow Endowment." Similarly, the Private Water Corporation announces itself in the same publication as the proud sponsor of the Gay Games in 1995. These ads are never to be found in the mainstream press such as the *New York Times*, nor in advertisements for AT&T, Time Warner, or the Disney Corporation, the very companies that provide medical benefits to domestic partners, or have been named as gay-friendly firms and, therefore, safe for gay investments. It is indeed a paradox that more than three decades after the gay movement deployed pride in identity to destabilize the internalized shame of heterosexism, heterosexual capital now moves to redeploy gay identity in the service of legitimizing its own heterosexual pride.

Transnational corporations that have successfully established themselves as gay friendly in the United States have not, however, been similarly successful in establishing corporate policies that uphold the dignity of those who labor in the Third World. The Haiti Justice Campaign has shown, for instance, that the Disney Corporation exploits its workers in Haiti by paying them the abysmally low wage of twenty-eight cents an hour.[24] No doubt, winning access to health and other benefits as domestic partners is a considerable victory, given the intent of the membership of the Baptist Convention, the largest Protestant denomination in the United States, to undermine it. If solidarity politics were not so narrowly grounded in the sexual, however, one could conceive of an alliance between U.S.-based employees, who have fought for domestic partner benefits, and those who mobilize with the Haiti Justice campaign against the Disney Corporation and its subcontractors, who have been instrumental in the creation of an exploited, predominantly female labor force in export processing/producing zones. But if prominent gay capitalists continue to believe that "American businesses do not have to become the forum where lesbian and gay political battles are fought," and perhaps, by extension, political battles of any kind, then such alliances are indeed hard to imagine.[25] Thus we need to ask ourselves: What is the structure of privilege that determines who rolls out this welcome mat and who is allowed to walk on it? What is the intended destination of privilege?

In the face of a normalizing process that links earning power to consumption and agency, we know very little about the earning or owning power of different racialized groups in our communities. These ads have effectively sealed a relationship between white gay citizenship and white gay consumption, only after two decades. While the obligatory lesbian gets appended to "gay" as the descriptor to consumer, lesbians, as Danae Clarke has argued, "have never been targeted as a separate consumer group within the dominant configuration of capitalism, either directly through the mechanism of advertising, or indirectly through media representation."[26] Overall, their messages codify an image of gay *as* white, able-bodied, and perennially upwardly-mobile, thereby making these characteristics a proxy for both production and consumption. White gay men are either positioned as trendsetters in a leisure economy, or as followers of style, not agents in politics. And with the ostensible capacity to consume more than "ordinary" citizens consume, gay people can be pressed into spending the income that stands higher than these ordinary consumers. But perhaps there is a certain history at work here, for it is not the case that capitalism permanently shies away from creating markets where none existed before, or from boosting existing ones; from finding, in other words, new areas to colonize. There was indeed a time when heterosexual capital wanted nothing to do with the gay consumer. Now it seems that the very crises that have come about as a result of aggressive globalized expansion have forced heterosexual capital to consume on the same site, as it were, with homosexual capital—a fraught arrangement indeed. The ideological scaffolding of that arrangement is the topic to which I turn in the section that follows.

White Gay Tourism and the
Construction of Sexual Utopias

More than two decades ago, John D'Emilio argued that capitalism was indispensable in the creation of gay identity. It freed the individual from kinship and family-based economies, thus enabling women and men to enter a paid labor force in which production was socialized: "Only when individuals began to make their living through wage labor, instead of as parts of an independent family unit, was it possible for homosexual desire to coalesce into a personal identity—an identity based on the ability to remain outside the heterosexual family, to construct a personal life based on attraction to one's own sex."[27] But if, as D'Emilio maintains, capitalism created the conditions for the emergence of a gay identity, it has also been able to appropriate that identity, in the sense that both production and consumption, the twin anchors of commerce, are made to construct it. Given how consumer appropriation functions, however, this consuming gay individual is free only virtually, for at times heterosexual capital wants access to gay dollars while at other times it wants those dollars to remain hidden.[28] I am not arguing that this colonization has been enabled by a quiescent community, for as Danae Clark has shown, lesbian communities in particular have used "selected strategies of (re)appropriation, resistance and subversion," as a way of diffusing stereotypical images that have been generated.[29] But the deployment of strategies of appropriation suggests that processes of reification draw little from the real lives of pulsing, contradictory, provisionally organized communities. For gay capital, on the other hand, queer dollars need not be hidden. They need not be bleached of anything before they are spent. But they *do* need to be spent. And it is this imperative that provides the uneasy meeting ground for both gay and heterosexual capitalists, who have reified the same consuming subject in their struggle for profits.

Stonewall marked a watershed in the emergence of gay commercial enterprises, replacing the quasi-visible underground sexual economy of bathhouses and mail-order businesses with a range of enterprises that straddled a thin line between the political and the commercial. By 1995, the same year that lesbian and gay consumers were believed to be the source of "untold millions," and three years after the *New York Times* had announced that advertisers were vying for homosexual buying power, *Out* announced that business had come out of the closet. Gay liberation had spurred a new development of commercial enterprises: bookstores, counseling services, porn shops, newspapers and magazines, and clothing boutiques. While the surge of lesbian and gay businesses in the late 1980s and in the 1990s meant that more queer dollars were being spent within the lesbian and gay communities than before, the *Out* article asserted that the bulk of queer dollars still ended up in the coffers of straight businesses. This is the conjuncture at which gay capital began its more visible emergence, working from the assumption that gay providers know best how and what to provide as gay services to gay consumers. More important, gay providers assume that they are best able to organize a sexual economy of desire for gay people. Gay tourism has been premised and perfected on these same assumptions, so much so that it is now the greatest commercial area of gay growth. The gay and lesbian travel sector now positioned as the "cream puff" market for the travel industry is worth approximately $54.1 billion, roughly 10 percent of the U.S. travel market, and since tourism and being gay are believed by entrepreneurs to be inextricably linked, along with the notion that travel constitutes "an important part of gay identity," it becomes as well a crucial site for the interpolation of consumer citizenship.[30]

Sexual consumption within gay tourism, as within heterosexual tourism, is a transnational phenomenon, traversing different national borders that often are the same geographies that were established during the earlier phases of imperialism. Travel guides comprise one of gay tourism's primary ideological anchors, and their discursive expression elaborates a certain intransigent colonial relationship in which a previously scripted colonial cartography of ownership, production, consumption, and distribution all conform to a First World/Third World division in which Third World gay men get positioned as the objects of sexual consumption rather than as agents in a sexual exchange. If, as Gita Patel's quote in the epigraph suggests, colonialism has assisted in the production of commodities as nativized fetishes, and if gay tourism conforms to this same colonial hierarchy, then it would seem that white gay capital becomes an active participant in the same processes of nativization and recolonization that heterosexual tourism helped to inaugurate. This form of tourism, then, might also assist in recirculating an earlier colonial myth that attempted to replace subjectivity with the sexualized "native" body, the same myth that neocolonial state managers in the Bahamas circulated as a way of denying citizenship to lesbians and gay men.

White gay tourism's transnational structure is perhaps best embodied in the International Gay Travel Association (or the IGTA, which in 1998 appended the word lesbian to its title), which represents itself as a travel resource and a clearinghouse for gay travel information. Based in the United States with a corporate companion in Germany, the association has grown from a charter group of five members in 1983 to over nine hundred enterprises of lesbian and gay-owned and "gay-supportive" businesses within the travel industry in different parts of the world. It behaves as an umbrella organization by assembling a growing network of hotel and resort owners, travel agents, tour operators, and airline and cruise line representatives as well as "ancillary" businesses such as advertising agencies, car rental firms, video producers and distributors, travel clubs and associations, and travel accommodation guide publishers. Still, the primary flow of IGLTA's resources is directed toward travelers in the United States and Europe, where the bulk of its membership is based. Different segments of the industry—highly integrated in terms of finance, management, research and development, and marketing and advertising —are also located in the West, which functions usually as a tourist generator, while the Third World functions as receiver. The getaway place is located elsewhere, outside the West, and is envisioned as having something that can be used, however temporarily. This elsewhere can be coveted, then, for its use value or its serviceability—a strip of beach, a hotel, a club, or a much-needed place for cruising.

It is difficult to ascertain precisely how this market operates, primarily because paid membership and informal networks of "who is who" seem to be the sole paths to belonging and to gaining access to information. I can only speculate, for instance, that tour operators play an important role in designing all-inclusive packages, organized by gay-friendly travel agents on gay-friendly airlines with gay-friendly people. A class-based computer technology fuels transnationalization, providing quick and easy access to the "Rainbow Mall" on the Internet, where one can obtain a "personal invitation" for membership in "the largest growing and dynamic organization: the International Gay and Lesbian Travel Association."[31] While the IGLTA designates travel and travel guides as "ancillary" services, however, I want to suggest that they are highly formative in fashioning desires, tastes, and satisfaction among both producers and consumers. Primarily because of the quasi-underground character of the transnational sale of gay sex, its location somewhere between the illegal and the immoral and, because in most instances the threat of homophobic violence can express itself swiftly and with grave consequences, the guides function as a travel curriculum on which gay tourists seriously rely. Information on the kind of pleasure that is sold; who sells and consumes it; the conditions under which it is sold: the ambiance, the mystery, and the "friendliness" of the people (which needs to be more intimate and personable than the friendliness of even the most gay-friendly corporations in the United States) are all contained within this curriculum. Yet they are both elusive and real enough that they require codification: they need to conform to certain standards to which potential tourists in the "West" are accustomed. It may actually be the case that homophobia operates in a way that lesbian and gay travelers, to a much more significant degree than heterosexual folk, need to have the "unknown" made intelligible. Thus, traveling gay tourists rely heavily on these national and international gay guides to provide the signs, symbols, and terms through which leisure is understood, experienced, and interpreted. Rather than being "ancillary," then, these enterprises are crucial in the ideological arsenal upon which gay tourists rely. They are also crucial in the creation of the identities of those who produce and those who consume gay tourist services.

Overall, the market in gay travel guides has experienced a major shift from the earlier homespun, underground economy of the 1950s to a well-established enterprise for which heterosexual capital feels compelled to compete. Reputable publishing houses such as Ferrari International Publishers contend with *Bob Damron's Address Book* and the *Spartacus International Gay Guide* to establish the signs and symbols by which gay people travel. The market caters to local (San Francisco, Amsterdam), national (*Thai Scene Gay Guide*, the *Philippine Diary, Canada's Gay Guide*), and international economies, aiming to satisfy a range of pleasures and circumstance: rough guides for bargain hunters (*Rough Guides of London*);

nudity and seclusion for those with special tastes (Baxandall's *World Guide to Nude Beaches and Resorts*); cozy home experiences for those wanting a home away from home (*Mi Casa Su Casa: International Home Exchange and Hospitality Network*); and affinities of identity (*Gaia's Guide for Lesbians*). In most instances, these publishing houses are located in metropolitan centers in Amsterdam, Frankfurt, or San Francisco, from which distribution logically occurs. The acceleration of global flows of information reflects in the proliferation of Web-based sites such as sistertrip.com, Qguys.com, and internationalgaytravel.com, amounting to one and a half million resource guides in 2005 for lesbian, gay, and bisexual travelers. No other guide, however, has achieved the status, scope, or overall market edge as that held by the *Spartacus International Gay Guide*. I will now use it to anchor our discussion of the importance of curriculum in the culture of travel and the extent to which it, too, travels within the confines of an earlier colonial geography.

The *Spartacus International Gay Guide*, published by the Spartacus organization located in Germany, is a hefty, thousand-page compendium encompassing close to nine hundred countries. It maps a wide geography, from Albania to Zimbabwe, in a fairly standardized way: demographics and climate; the legal status of homosexuality; the location of bars, clubs, cruising areas, and religious, health service, and AIDS organizations. It describes itself as "the world's best and most famous gay guide . . . by gay men for gay men." Its popularity is confirmed by its numerous appearances on best-seller lists; the number of letters it receives from "friends" annually (some 12,000) from all around the world; its status as "the gay bible," which is suggestive of the authority it holds among readers preparing for gay travel; its robust sales (it has been reprinted five times, in 1988, 1990, 1995, 1996–1997, and 1997–2004); and its language accessibility (it is published simultaneously in English, German, Spanish, and French).[32]

Within its pages, the colonial is produced and maintained through four simultaneous discursive moves. The first, which I mentioned earlier, occurs through the reproduction of the boundaries of colonial geography. For instance, countries colonized by France, such as Martinique and Guadeloupe, are listed as pertaining to or belonging to France, while the colonial relations of seizure and possession go unmarked. France itself is similarly racially unmarked; it is made to function as white. Lest the white gay tourist be confused about the racial configuration of Guadeloupe and conflate "pertaining to France" with whiteness, the guide is quick to clarify that the majority of inhabitants in this country are of African descent; or, as in the case with Martinique, where the use of the phrase "exotic tropical beauty" becomes the trope for blackness.[33] Even where colonial rule has been nominally suspended, as in the case with Aruba, it is still presented "as an autonomous territory of the Netherlands."[34] The implicit representational impulse that anchors Europe and the West as the purveyors of progress and modernity becomes contradictory when neocolonialism enters the picture. For instance, the guide's entry on Indonesia states, "homosexuality has traditionally been an integral part of Indonesian culture . . . Only in the country's new Western style middle class has homophobia taken root."[35] How can the West be progressive in its own territory yet paradoxically instigate homophobia in the West? Or is it that Indonesia's middle class is deployed to deflect scrutiny from some of the most egregious practices of homophobia that occur in Europe and the United States so as to mask the racialized erotic anxieties that patrol the text?[36]

Second, the writer, the imagined reader, and the reader as a potential tourist consumer are all positioned as white and Western, and thus familiar to one another and within each other's cultural proximity and milieu. It is elsewhere—the unfamiliar Third World—that needs to be made intelligible. This intelligibility is achieved by deploying a language in which the presumed audience is already white. "Be among the first to experience the South Pacific's most exclusive all-gay resort!" Or, as the guide wrote about Burundi in 1988: "*We* know little about this little Central African agricultural country between Lake Tanganyika and Lake Victoria" (emphasis added).[37]

Third, the guide resorts to a nativist discourse that attempts to construct the "character" of Third World people. "Friendly" is the most frequently invoked descriptor here, a trait that is indispensable to the comfort of the foreigner and is the pivotal nub on which tourism can successfully operate. This "character" cannot, of course, be guaranteed to the tourist, as we saw in the case of the Bahamas, but at least it needs to be invoked, for without it the ambiance on which tourism is based will flounder. It is applied almost singularly to construct a Thai friendly character, creating a certain uniqueness that makes Thailand "nirvana" and "a single slice of paradise."

Finally, the guide reproduces and maintains the colonial through a mode of elaborating and narrating geography that places it within the genre of colonial travel literature. The entire marketing strategy is premised in terms of a paradisiacal neutral/natural frame in which the consumption of tourist services takes place. Indeed, it is premised as a specific kind of experience that least resembles daily life and in an artificial context in which almost everything is sanitized, paradise itself is sold as quintessentially natural.[38] Nature itself is wild, untamed, sometimes disappointing, but always alluring. Cruising in Barbados, for instance, can occur in "lots of bushes," and in Cuba one can go into "the small forest," whereas in France one goes into the "garden" or "behind the castle"—that well-known symbol of European royal pedigree. It can also conspire to provide the erotic frame for the meeting of white and nativized bodies. "The junction of the Amazon with the Rio Negro," we are told, "provides a spectacular natural wonder where one side of the river carries the typical orange hue while the other half retains the black color of the Rio Negro."[39] Thus, nature is made to complete the gesture of nativization, to provide the "exoticizing frame" for sexual consumption. This description is evocative of a more vivid moment in the *Men of South Africa II*, a South African gay porn video in which images of black people are intermixed with wild animals, providing what Ian Bernard has called an "exoticizing frame for white sex performers."[40]

When the colonial narrative is combined with the reification of the sexual, some particularly bizarre elaborations of "primitivism" can be produced. The Divine can be invoked to conspire in sexual consumption: Brazil offers "masses of gorgeous gods of all races."[41] The reader is told that Burundi, the same little country "of which we know little," is a place where "African Nature Religions" are practiced. This obscure detail cannot in fact be explained, since there is no such thing as "African Nature Religions." But it does not require an explanation; its obscurity can be made palatable for white gay Westerners only within the context of homosexuality: "*We* know little . . . but what *we* have heard sounds interesting: The country is governed by the Tutsi tribe for whom bisexuality is the norm."[42] Bisexuality and primitivism thus bind the exotic. But the bond can be temporary. By the time reports of civil war in Burundi began to receive global attention in 1996, when more than eight hundred thousand Rwandans, mainly Tutsi, were massacred by Hutu death squads, Burundi had disappeared from the exotic geography of white gay desire without a trace of explanation of the kind accorded the global shifts in right-wing homophobia, or the experience and politics of HIV infection—accounts that are widely known to distinguish *Spartacus* from other gay guides, such as *Damron's Address Book,* for instance.[43]

The disproportionate attention in the guide given to Germany and the United States, partly the result of corporate centralization, implies that gay bodies also use the metropolis as a place for pleasure. Yet, somehow, those who provide sexual service in the Third World are not presumed to be the travelers. Fetishes are not assumed to circulate in the reverse. That constructed Third World fetish is somehow not expected to journey from home simply in search of sexual pleasure in the First World; he is to be encountered in the authentic local geography, imagined back into the "native" context in order to conform to, and complete, the terms of a colonialist fantasy. Indeed, geographies become alive—that is, poised to be consumed as a feminized body. Geographies can, in Joseph Boone's words, be apprehended only sensually, and that mode of apprehension leaves no room for speech, no room for intellect.[44] The constructed Third World fetish can perhaps journey from countries "with poor literacy rates and living standards" for reasons of labor and economic gain; and he journeys to enjoy democratic freedoms in such places as the "interesting, modern and enlightened" metropolis of Canada, thereby fleeing his own country, which is inherently repressive, tradition-bound, and poor. The nativized fetish, as constructed, must not only remain at home, in "spectacular natural wonder," he must also remain silent, the same ideological requirement imposed on lesbians and gay men for whom heterosexual capital had rolled out the welcome mat. Unlike *Gaia's Guide* for lesbian travel, in which one finds lesbians characterizing the nature of their own lives in different countries, the *Spartacus Guide* grants the authority to speak to the editor/writer who journeys for first-hand knowledge. Authority is even granted to the German Embassy in different Third World countries, but never to the "native" who is made not to speak even the terms of his own sex. Ultimately this authority to compose and to speak as a way of coalescing male power (that is at once textual, sexual, and economic) is characteristic of phallocentric discourse, although in this instance it is reified in the name of homosexual rather than heterosexual pleasure.[45]

Pleasure and racial anxiety (ultimately, masculine) pervade these multiple texts. The West and non-West are brought into signification through male desire, but these are not relations of equivalence, for they do so within the boundaries of a geographical body that is feminized, entered and vitalized from that which resides outside of it. In this sense, signification is evocative of an orientalist homoerotic that is at once patriarchal and misogynist.[46] If travel consolidates consumer identity for well-to-do gay tourists from the West, then it is not only spending to satisfy material needs that is at stake but also the very construction of an erotic subjectivity that seeks and produces itself through fetishization at the same time that it produces commodities as queer feminized and nativized fetishes. And if subjectivity continues to be premised in the right to consume (witness the response of the executive director of IGLTA to the refusal of the Cayman Islands and Jamaican governments to dock gay cruise ships: "If Jamaica is unwilling or unprepared to welcome gay and lesbian tourists to [its] shores, then IGLTA is prepared to warn all of our member companies and associations that our tourist dollars are no longer welcome in that country"),[47] there is no need to shed the European self in order to become the other—rather it is the rabid inhabiting of that self in order to better consume the other.

But speech is costly. What "queer natives" have to say about the curriculum of travel, about globalization as a late-imperial travel culture, and about the possible links between nineteenth-century imperial travel narratives that evoke nostalgia for empire and these contemporary gay guides might well be dangerous. When "nativized" fetishes traverse the bounded sexual geographies assigned to them and move to the metropoles that constitute the home of the returned tourist, they are not only not in their assigned place—they do not live the lives invented by scripts of travel—but also they live in the contentious geographies of the metropolis, which at this moment in history are marked by profound dislocations in labor—known as immigration—which is itself one of the results of globalization. Immigrant geographies, like tourism, constitute global-ization. Within them, contestations around citizenship and belonging, around displacement and exile, constantly jostle for a local space that is already transnational. But nativist discourses produced about the else-where simply do not disappear, particularly because they circulate at home as well, weaving themselves into the existing practices of urban racisms, complicating a merely dichotomous relation between indige-nous black and white. Traveling white bodies return home and they return with the colonialist travel narratives that prepared them for travel into the racialized queer spaces of rice bars for Asian men, cha-cha bars for Latinos, and ding bars for black gay men. Orientalism operates at home. This is what Martin Manalansan's *Global Divas* cogently illus-trates. Gay travelogues such as *Philippine Diary* catalogue cruising places for men (read white) who like Asian men and are replete with an inven-tory of habits such as "unstable personalities, a penchant for gossip and a childish fascination with telephones" that are ostensibly characteristic of Filipino gay men everywhere, including those in the United States.[48] As Manalansan states, the ideological formulations in this text "are the same ones that confront Filipino gay men when they enter the shores of the American gay community." Thus, the very culture of "rice queens" shapes the designation of racialized bars that ultimately reify and fetishize cor-poreality.[49]

Of course, Filipino gay men constantly negotiate this spectacle of orientalism, subverting it and redeploying it at the same time that they disentangle its discursive practices in ways that reveal their instability, necessarily so since as Filipino immigrant men they simultaneously live between the cultural spaces of *bakla* that denote a mix of homosexuality, cross-dressing, hermaphroditism, and effeminacy. Put differently, Fil-ipino gay men author themselves. The point here is not to position some fixed authenticity against a monolithic orientalism but rather to take up the challenge as Manalansan illustrates, to position queer spaces from a particular marginalized gaze in ways that can provide "a complicated yet positioned view of a gay urban landscape in the late twentieth century."[50] It speaks to an urgent need for the reconfiguration of racial relationships in the home of the tourist, which the former "native" also now claims as home through projects that imbricate shifting political economies, the politics of immigration, and racial formation in these varied urban landscapes.

The reason that we must be deeply suspicious of reification and unrelenting in our desire to root it out is that it produces ontological distortions and paradoxes that have nothing to do with personhood. In the same way that individuals can never be chattel, so too they can never be only sex; it simply cannot be made to stand in for who they are—the very replication of dominant scripts. But here is where choices need to be made. We would need to locate these very contradictions as a way of opening up both analytic and political possibilities. One possibility would be to engage the kind of unconscious nationalism that enables one to "consume" the transnational abroad, with the assumption that it remains elsewhere. Another possibility is to attend to the effects of reification. Sexual consumption confuses personhood with bodies only, but bodies only do not provide fertile ground for constructing what Ella Shohat calls "critical communities of affinity."[51] Building such critical communities requires work, the most immediate of which is the recognition that racialization and immigration do matter for an alternative politics of sexual identity, just as globalization matters in structuring the kinds of economic and cultural choices we make. As the Audre Lorde Project has consistently shown, geographies of belonging and displacement need not be positioned as narrowly nationalist or bounded; rather, they can be mobilized within local spaces that attend to the racism and orientalism of (sexual) consumption by engaging practices that are analytic, political, and cultural, that are at once relational, synergistic and generous.[52] Such practices are a necessity in any struggle for a loving freedom.

II

MAPS OF EMPIRE, OLD AND NEW

3

Whose New World Order?
Teaching for Justice

There is a task we have before us of understanding this apparently new geopolitical constellation of power, this "new world order." What knowledges of it can we derive at this juncture, in this place? Place and space are important sites in the processes of knowledge production. What kind of liberatory praxis can we engender at the meeting of these transnational practices? These are some of the central questions you have set for yourselves in juxtaposing the new world order to liberatory teaching practices, in your desire to draw a different kind of map, "to put forward," as Toni Morrison phrased it in the context of the necessary analytic task that awaited U.S. literature, "a wider landscape . . . to draw a map . . . of a critical geography . . . without the mandate for conquest."[1] This critical mapmaking is a gesture that makes of education an explicitly political project. It suggests that the analytic and pedagogical apparatuses we deploy to grapple with this "new" geopolitical constellation are themselves political practices, even as we engage the politics of constituency formation, which are at once analytic (textual and contextual) and pragmatic, if you will. Pedagogic projects are not simple mechanistic projects,

A version of this chapter was first delivered as the keynote address at the Great Lakes Colleges Women's Studies Association conference that was held in Indianapolis in 1994. The chapter's title bears the name of the conference.

for they derive from theoretical claims about the world and assumptions about how history is made, in other words, pedagogy and theory are mutually related.

I should like to proceed in light of this mutuality to make transparent a mode of thinking that can be engaged in a range of sites, only one of which is the classroom, whose architecture, of course, is shaped by the larger outlines of the academy. What is the role of the academy in this era of increased militarization? How can we be persuaded to take up the pedagogic imperative of teaching for justice, a project that is fundamentally at odds with the project of militarization, which always already imagines an enemy and acts accordingly to eliminate it. Teaching for justice is at odds with a hegemonic narrative that would foreground in a one-sided manner an ascendant corporate class as the sole agents of history. The ascendancy of this class is intimately linked, of course, to an exponential surge in global capital and the shift that has occurred from manufacturing to service, but this transformation would not have been possible without the corresponding mobility of a transnational workforce that services a wide range of technologies and people. What are the new workplaces that characterize globalization? What kinds of racial, gendered regimes of work are to be found within them? And since women have been mobilized into new circuits of production far more consistently and in far greater numbers than during the earlier period of conquest, we shall want to know how the collectivization of women's labor secures the very structures through which they understand the terms of their own exploitation. What do we now know from women about their experiences within this transnational empire? How do Mexican immigrant women workers, for instance, come to know that they are hungry for justice: "Tenemos hambre de jusiticia"?[2] As we confront our own pedagogical desire to teach for justice, what might we learn from women who have discovered a yearning for justice in their new work sites, which only *appear* to be different from the work site of the academy?

As we tackle these questions, we also need to understand where the major threats to freedom and democracy originate: how capitalism frustrates democracy; how free-market democracy might stand in the way of justice; how legacies of transformational struggles in the academy may not be reflected in the everyday life of an institution. Above all, we need to learn how to *practice* justice, for it is through practice that we come to envision new modes of living and new modes of being that support these visions. Where do our visions for justice originate? How do we inhabit them? Clearly our task is to reexamine and transform inherited practices that stand in the way of justice. The new world order is one such practice; this conference, a call for a possible transformation.

As we map the major outlines of this new world order, we should recall the crucial contours, "the signposts," as Gramsci calls them, of its progenitor, not because this past delineates the future in any deterministic, linear way, but because this moment of a new temporality, of a new discursive, which is to say political, economic, ideological, and cultural production, "had already appeared in some place." "It had already been inscribed," as Stuart Hall puts it, "in an earlier positioning."[3] That "earlier positioning" refers to a much longer history of colonialism that has undergone a series of metamorphoses but that, nonetheless, continues to traffic in this terrain that is being designated as "new." The persistence of continuities ought to give us a great deal of pause about announcing the premature end to things, as in the end of history; the "post" of things, as in postcolonialism, for history proceeds in a way that makes ruptures neither clean nor final.

Initially, we will rely on Hall's analysis to help us think about how this new world order has been discursively coded, recognizing that there are clear material effects to these political economic realignments. But we need to think the discursive and material together, particularly because the texts that the state used to mark this new invention were simultaneously diffused as public symbols to generate support for war and to uphold a preeminent place for the United States at the helm of an order it was still attempting to create. Thus, the texts of the new world order are constitutive, even to the point of being constitutive of the very relations they purport to create—relations of order.

Let us begin by charting this apparently new discursive invention of the new world order in the U.S. media, for it gives an indication of the symbols that were harnessed to generate consent for this new geopolitical arrangement. In December 1989, the *New York Times* ran an article with the auspicious headline "Destiny in Air, Leaders Arrive for Summit."[4]

The article describes how presidents Bush and Gorbachev of the (then) Soviet Union had arrived on the Mediterranean island of Malta for a summit conference, during which both had hoped to start the search for a new world order. The meeting had no formal agenda, but Bush, speaking aboard the aircraft carrier *Forrestal*, called his mission "a great and noble undertaking"—the same terms of the prayer that Dwight Eisenhower offered approximately four decades earlier on the eve of D-Day. The remainder of the article followed in the best style of colonial ethnography: *Times* readers were regaled with their psychic readiness for this "noble" undertaking: Gorbachev was reported to be in "ebullient form, cocky, determined and thoroughly in command," while Bush was "in high spirits, his mood seemingly unaffected by an attempted coup in the Philippines, or the long overnight flight." The article described where they were to sleep and gave details about their tour of the photogenic (not exotic) city of Valleta, the capital, and about other preoccupations: Bush took great delight as a former naval aviator in watching flight operations on the *Forrestal*, "trading old navy jokes with the crew and piling his mess tray high with lasagna and chicken legs doused in hot sauce." Of course, we cringe at the mention of the old navy jokes, in light of what women have revealed in the Tailhook investigations about a fraternity of army culture that promotes practices of sexual harassment.[5] The general mood, we are informed, was auspicious, yet casual—casual as the principal architects of this governing class mark the inscriptions for war in their ostensible search for a process that we are not told is well underway.

Less than a month later, this initial elusiveness gave way to a rapidly developing set of events. "History had suddenly picked up," Mr. Gorbachev announced. The *Washington Post* agreed, as it carried this headline: "New World Order, Galloping into Position."[6] But it was the Iraqi invasion of Kuwait that brought greater clarity of definition and brought Bush to testify before a joint session of Congress on the "troubled times" that required a "new world order." According to the president, "stability [was] not secure; interdependence [had] increased; the consequences of regional instability were global; and American interests [were] far reaching." And because "the world [was] still dangerous, it [was] no time to risk America's capacity to protect her vital interests." Following Bush's testimony, the *Christian Science Monitor* reported that expert opinion found Bush to be more comfortable, forthright, and even more dramatic than in his previous three prime-time televised addresses as president.[7] Marshall Ingwerson, staff writer for the *Monitor,* offered that one of Bush's noted weaknesses as president was his inability to address the nation directly in a persuasive and presidential style. He had difficulty finding his voice for presenting deeply felt values. Bush seemed to overcome this weakness, Ingwerson speculated, perhaps in the face of support from the joint session, perhaps because he may have been more comfortable than usual with the strength of his message. Imagine finding one's voice in the promotion of war! Imagine rising to the power of one's persuasion while announcing one's intended use of the technologies of killing!

Let us examine this narrative for its constitutive capacity; for what it organizes, defines, and attempts to solidify. What are the constituencies it summons in this task of assembly? One major aspect of this narrative is that the state is unable to do this task of assembling order on its own. It has to build an alliance. And it does so by making its interests consonant with those of a corporate class, which it feels obliged to protect through war and aggression. While this state-corporate alliance is quite formidable, the state cannot act without securing popular consent to legitimize its rule. It has to find a way to have popular interests dovetail with its own. In that sense, the designation of "troubled times" functioned also as an appeal, intended as much for the joint session and members of the corporate class as it was for the "American people," that amorphous, necessary grouping in whose name and on whose behalf a great deal has been undertaken. The American people would have to come to believe that their assistance was indispensable to the state's task of protecting the nation; that their "vital interests" were the same as the state's "vital interests"; that those interests would be secured by the state as it resorted to war and aggression to protect them in a "dangerous . . . interdependent world." But defense, aggression, and protection do not mean the same thing. Their meanings have to be made to cohere. In the context of war, the external enemy provides that coherence; the enemy could only be eliminated through violence; only violence could provide protection; only the state who owns the means of violence could provide that protection. Thus, protection from the enemy made the use of violence not only plausible but necessary. Ultimately, functionally, the U.S. state marked out a position for itself at the helm of this new world order as protector simultaneously of the interests of the world, the interests of U.S. capital, and the interests of the American people.

The triage of defense, aggression, and protection also relied on additional symbols to complete the task of manufacturing coherence and building patriotic support for the American nation. Two racialized, gendered symbols were deployed by the state as it made preparations to attack Iraq. One symbol was anchored in the notion of the superior might of a white Western masculinity that would vanquish traditional orientalist masculinity, the one defender of the globe, the other—in the figure of Saddam Hussein—enemy of the globe and of the American people. The other symbol was taken from the newly reconfigured gendered regime in soldiering: the American soldier woman.[8] She was chosen as the loyal marker of emancipated modernity, positioned against the "veiled" orientalist woman who, much like her masculine counterpart, was similarly bound by tradition. And although the job of soldiering was being increasingly overtaken by people of color, the marker of (white) modernity against (dark) tradition had to be made white. Overall, the strategy tapped this latent reservoir of older symbols of the dark Orient while stirring more contemporary mythologies of a treacherous and cruel Arab/Islam "character."[9] In other words, it offered up to the American people a population that became culturally legitimate to hate.[10]

An internal enemy had already been produced during the Bush campaign's war on crime in the figure of Willie Horton. The enemy was constructed as the threat that black masculinity posed to innocent white girlhood. The symbol, of course, was meant to establish a need for the state's protection. The effects were manifested as a series of profound contradictions, since the American people was not a homogeneous group but consisted also of Arab Americans. Mervat Hatem characterized the dilemma in these terms: "Public repudiation for the Arab 'other' meant that only crude choices and definitions were available. One could support the war and in this way prove one's nationalist credentials as an American. Or one could oppose the war and be identified as un-American/traitor/enemy/Iraqi/Arab . . . There was no place for the many Arab Americans who simultaneously disapproved of the Iraqi invasion of Kuwait and the U.S. military plans for its reversal."[11] Clearly, large processes are being reconfigured in the name of order: the meanings of defense, aggression, and protection; of loyalty, citizenship, and Americanness; of regimes of gender, race, and power, which are mobilized in their service; and of tradition and modernity, each positioned historically in a constant linear struggle for ascendancy. All of these processes were being mobilized in this project of constituting order.

The timing of the call for order is not coincidental. Indeed, the U.S. state was obliged to remake order precisely at a moment of crisis when its economic capacity to underwrite the terms of war was in serious jeopardy. The fact of the state's own instability is evident, in the first instance, in this gesture of re-creation, where it needs to develop economic capacity to undertake a project it is simply unable to do on its own. But it cannot position itself at the helm of the new world order and appear vulnerable at the same time. Thus, instability is made to originate from the outside, not from within. It is no coincidence, then, that the moment of identifying the global enemy of instability on the outside is the same moment for the unveiling of the vulnerability of the U.S. state on the inside.

At this point we need to dwell a bit more on the ways in which order is a gendered undertaking and how gendered militarization becomes crucial in securing the "vital interests" of the state as it aligns those interests with those of the American people. What particular gendered appeals are deployed in a moment of crisis? If securing the nation's "vital interests" is part of the project of nation-building, what kind of citizenship is required when militarization is collapsed into nation-building?

Cynthia Enloe's work has shown consistently that militarization is essential to the project of nation-state formation. But militarization cannot succeed without women's consent. Enloe argues that the U.S. state first sought that consent by building appeals to national unity through a specter of danger—the danger that U.S. citizen troops faced on enemy soil. But they were not only citizen troops, they were "*our* troops." Above all, they were troops of women's children, their daughters, two hundred thousand of whom had been recruited since 1973 to boost the decline stemming from the end of the mandatory male draft. "Our troops" were women's sons: their children, the nation's soldiers, were at risk. And their husbands were also at risk. At times, entire soldier families were at risk.[12] Thus, women could perform the task that the state required of them by supporting their endangered loved ones. They could support loved ones and support the war simultaneously. Both would be the natural, commonsensical, and, indeed, the patriotic thing to do—the mark of good citizenship.

A gendered imperative was also at work in the way in which the state moved to provide a greater rationale for war. It positioned itself as "benign patriarch" by generating what Enloe has called the "women-and-children-requiring-protection-by-the-statesman" script. It bypassed combat women soldiers and elite women in military decision-making positions in order to create one of militarism's major ideological symbols: the feminized victim.[13] Militarism relies on women, but with different intent and with a different settlement. Yet, in much the same way that colonial bureaucratic masculinity mobilized an identity of restraint that tended to mask the widespread practice of rape in colonial formations, this script of protection from the enemy by the statesman often masked the vulnerability of soldier women who were not being protected by the state or those in its employ. Some 64 percent of women in the military have reported that they have been sexually harassed. After the Gulf War, a number of American women testified to being "forcibly sodomized," or gave reports of being sexually abused by sergeants and fellow male soldiers in the desert, the same site on which "our troops" had been endangered.[14] Clearly violence against the outside is not so neatly cordoned off from violence that takes place on the inside.

At the same time that the U.S. state was engaged in the process of carving out a preeminent role for itself at the helm of the new world order, it was simultaneously presiding over a series of internal processes that reduced its historical role in a social settlement with the same American people it now mobilized in the interests of war. The set of social rights regarding the provision of welfare, social security, and minimum wage protection, which historically had been provided as part of an internal postwar settlement, were being revoked and replaced by a new arrangement that made ideological and material room for the ascendancy of the market and the plausibility of the state's own arguments about retrenchment.[15] Such rights were forfeited, no longer a part of the contract of citizenship.

Each text that the state generates has its own set of corresponding ideological symbols. In the case of the retrenchment of the social wage, otherwise known as privatization, the symbols were developed in the course of the struggle over welfare—one of the "cultural signposts" of restructuring. If in the Gulf War the figure of the white soldier woman-as-loyal-to-nation was diffused to anchor support for modernity, in the internal war against an unwieldy, costly state an opposing symbol—the African American woman as disloyal to nation—was diffused to anchor support for the market. Both symbols were used as markers of racial difference, yet the portraits worked as opposites: the one white, in the service of national sacrifice; the other black, in the service of national betrayal. The thick ideological layering of the welfare queen indicated how much was at stake in this project of restructuring. The formulations took the following forms: she occupied a throne as a result of ill-gotten gains, by dint of the hard work of others. Poor by choice, not through the permanence of capitalism's underside, she disproportionately consumed national resources better appropriated to the wider social good. As promiscuous mother, she had contravened the boundaries of moral community. She required rehabilitation, but faced with a moral vacuum only structured state intervention could transform her behavior. This is the context in which we can understand the significance of means testing, as mechanisms that attend not only to questions of need (although it is increasingly unable to do so) but also to formulations of the moral status of claimants.[16] These tests police women's behavior and monitor their living arrangements and their love attachments, the number of children they have, and their attendance at job skills courses, but they are also based on a set of assumptions about poor people: that the dignity of work is a rhetorical luxury; that the poor occupy a marginal matrix of citizenship, with no freedom to have the desires of taxpaying citizens—the desire for love, the dignity of work, or the desire to have and mother children. Thus, welfare, like war and militarization, is a terrain on which questions of citizenship are being fought out.

When we combine the scripts for militarization with those for welfare within this larger script of the privatized new world order, we see that they embody different meanings of citizenship. The "women-and-children-requiring-protection-by-the-statesman" script is in stark discursive disagreement with the "women-on-welfare-requiring-*no*-protection-by-the-state" script. Both rely on women, but women on welfare are not feminized victims, not victims at all by dint of their own failings. In these scripts, the loyal patriotic wartime family is upheld against the disloyal, decadent family. The loyal patriotic family is asked to come to the aid of the nation in crisis, to exhibit patriotism in the form of militarized sacrifice.[17] But when the patriotic wartime family is judged against the decadent "peacetime" family, there is an implicit call to a populist patriotism to support the war since it is good for the nation, but to oppose welfare and people on welfare since that, too, represents a gesture of loyalty to nation, loyalty to the citizen who is a tax-paying, morally conforming consumer, and loyalty to the government that has aligned itself with the people against an unwieldy state, as part of the new settlement.[18] Ultimately, people on welfare come to be characterized as one of the threats from within, another group that becomes culturally legitimate to despise. Feminism always needs vigilance around these contradictory state constructions, the cultural opposites that the state constructs as a way of maintaining hegemony. But that vigilance needs to travel within, since some of these very contradictions traffic within feminist political practices intended to be oppositional.

Thus far, our focus has been on the state, the cultural texts it has produced in this new world order, the texts and practices that are embedded in an ethos of war that upholds a version of nationalism premised in an enemy, an enemy on the outside whom the state has to eliminate, and an enemy on the inside whom it is culturally acceptable to hate. We should turn now to examine briefly this new global political economy and its requirements, so as to better understand how and where women are positioned within it and to understand the often contradictory practices that are made visible from these positions.

Global Boundaries, Global Markets, and the Making of Class

One of the distinguishing features of the new global arrangement is the shift it has produced from a manufacturing to a service economy. It is not that manufacturing no longer occurs—it is, rather, that a whole panoply of service has come to characterize this phase of capitalist development, ranging from financial and banking investment services on the high end of the profit scale, to food-processing plants, food service companies, electronic assembly, and various retail establishments on the lower end of the profit scale. A great deal of analytic work has explained this moment in terms of rapid business transactions among trading partners in New York, São Paulo, and Bombay, for instance; the accelerated use of cybernetic technologies that speeds up production all across the globe; and the hypermobility of capital as it crosses borders in a constant search for new markets. While these characterizations are important, I should like to think about this global economy in a way that allows us to examine the particular kinds of class relations that are reproduced at this moment, both for the ascendant corporate class and for the class that makes its ascendancy possible: large numbers of women who work in export processing zones and "free-trade" zones all across the globe. Let's look briefly at this corporate class and the kinds of requirements it has constructed.

At one level it requires, as we noted earlier, a set of rapid transactions that condense speed, space, and time to interact with other people in the circuit. It requires, as well, a range of services, including accounting, legal, financial, and cultural services. It has come to depend on a segregated workplace, in which workers mostly occupy jobs with members of their own racial-ethnic, gender, and class group.[19] But homogeneity at the bottom of the class structure is reflected by homogeneity at the top as well, since the reproduction of this corporate class coheres around its own racial-ethnic and gender affinities. Members of this class require a household in which reproductive labor is paid labor.[20] This labor is most often provided by the same class of immigrant women who perform service work at the bottom of the very firms this corporate class manages. It also requires relaxation, a clean environment, security, and protection. In other words, this class requires an extensive workforce—in local firms, in private households, and in business enterprises all over the world. It is a transnational class, the financial elements of which are in the forefront of managing the new political economy, of generating support for neo-liberal market ideologies that anchor privatization, the very strategies that neocolonial states are forced to adopt as they streamline their economies to be more in keeping with the imperatives of a global market. The evidence of the past thirty years indicates that skewed economic development in neocolonial formations is largely responsible for internal dislocations that trigger immigration. It is this immigrant workforce that constitutes the cheap labor on which this corporate class relies. It would not be excessive to argue, therefore, that this corporate class *requires* inequity as one of the terms on which it assists in the management of this new world order.[21]

If we retrace these routes of migration back to their "home" countries, we will understand something about the cross-cutting reach of the transnational empire and the vast territory over which this corporate class presides. We will also derive a clearer picture of the kinds of displacements that privatization has provoked. For neocolonial formations, the widespread adoption of Structural Adjustment Programs (sap) has had devastating consequences. In order to service a growing debt, these countries most often pursue a cycle of borrowing, which has ignored internal infrastructural development. In addition to retrenching the social wage, governments have devalued local currency and slashed wages in contexts where people's earning capacity had already been jeopardized. These conditions destabilize economies, producing dislocations that assist global capital in mobilizing workers for the new circuits of production in which women predominate. Variously named export processing zones (epzs), free trade zones (ftzs), or *maquilas,* they are the (relatively new) local circuits that secure transnational profits, but they are simultaneously the very places that collectivize women's labor and provide the contexts in which women come to understand the meaning of exploitation.

Recent activist scholarship has brought focus to the women who work in the sweatshops of these zones and in the nafta food chain—those who produce fresh fruits and vegetables in the South that are consumed in the North—in order to document how women come to exert control over their work lives; how they come to distinguish between the struggle for survival and the struggle for dignity and justice; how they come to know, as Mexican immigrant women have put it, "No tenemos hambre de comida; tenemos hambre de justicia!"—We are not hungry for food; we are hungry for justice. How do women come to know they hunger for justice?[22]

Genealogies of Consciousness:
"A Place on the Map Is Also a Place in History."[23]

A map of the new corporate South reveals a dense web of overlapping corporate interests that intersects with a constant movement of people, goods, and services over a vast terrain. In fact, the map reveals that North and South are neither as discrete, nor as separate, as they might appear. In the South, women are drawn into export zones in unprecedented numbers, in the borders between Haiti and the Dominican Republic and the two-thousand-mile border between the United States and Mexico that extends from El Paso to Los Angeles: the borderlands. In Haiti, women work for twelve cents an hour in the more than fifty firms producing "Mickey Mouse" and "Pocahontas" pajamas for Sears, J.C. Penny, and Wal-Mart, under license with the Walt Disney Corporation. Their counterparts in New York—Disney's cultural corporate center—are primarily Chinese women who work in apparel shops, 65 percent of which are sweatshops; or they work at hospitals where they join Filipina women as nurses' aids and cleaners. In Mexico, women work as pickers and packers at the Santa Anita Packers Corporation, a large export-oriented, tomato-packing business, or in the Del Monte ketchup processing plant in Ira-puato, Mexico. Their Chicana counterparts work assembling electronics in the Texas cities of El Paso and San Antonio, as do their counterparts in Silicon Valley. In Jamaica, women work in sweatshops and hotels in Kingston and Negril, while their counterparts work as home-care attendants and domestic workers in Queens, Staten Island, Long Island, Manhattan's midtown, and the Upper West Side. In another kind of export zone, such as *zona hotelera* in Cancún, women work as maids in the tourist economy that services as many as two million tourists a year, many of whom are North American students on spring break. Their counterparts work in other parts of the Caribbean at Four Seasons, Holiday Inn, and Sheraton hotels in Barbados, Anguilla, the Bahamas, or in Antigua as maids or as sex workers. They also work at home, producing garments for export, "privatized" work like their counterparts in the United States who do telemarketing.[24] In effect, this entire system relies on the mobility of labor, but capital also travels the former routes of empire in its search for markets that would ultimately reduce most of the costs of its production.[25]

In a fundamental sense, the pervasiveness and persistence of low-wage work—for women in export processing and free-trade zones; in the *maquilas*; in the "informal" economy; in the gaps left wide-open by the state; in flexible part-time work at McDonald's, Sears, Wal-Mart and J.C. Penny; or multiple food chains; in home work, not only in the North and South, but in Hong Kong and Korea, in Dublin and Gujarat, in Lagos and Dakar, in Eastern Europe, and in Kuwait and Jordan—is itself a consequence of asymmetrical gendering. While the ideologies about women's work identities vary from housewife/homemaker to temporary, supplemental worker, the notion of supplementary or incidental wages for women within an assumed heterosexual family both organizes and devalues women's work.[26] And since these service enterprises have been positioned as peripheral to those of financial and investment capital, the identities of women are hypermobilized in a way that substitutes "biological" attributes for work performance. Mythologies characterizing women as best suited for tedium, or as blessed with nimble fingers, both devalue women's skills and knowledge and erase the toll taken by routinization, excessive skill-segmentation, and overwork. Since women constitute the bulk of the workforce, they experience the daily force of these myths in gendered and classed terms. Their supervisors are most often men; and they least often experience a high degree of upward mobility. These are the very experiences that inform women's organizing strategies, enabling them to theorize exploitation—the gap between the value they produce and the remuneration they receive in contrast to the owners and managers of capital.[27] These experiences constitute the pedagogies through which women yearn for justice, through which they collectively come to know "tenemos hambre de justicia."

Critical consciousness developed at the borders or within these work zones bespeaks the different ways in which women have reinscribed work with dignity. This consciousness takes concrete shape as daily practice within organizations that brings both individual and collective self-definition to women as workers. Women's experiences of militarization with the border police, or of worker control in the form of sexual harassment, have given them insight into the twin operations of state and capitalist violence. When women laid off by Levi Strauss and Company walk from San Antonio, Texas, to their corporate headquarters in San Francisco to demand accountability, they challenge deep-seated corporate reliance on deregulation and corporate mobility without responsibility.[28] When action research enables the women who work at Santa Anita Packers in Mexico, at one end of the food chain, to trace the destination of their labor to the women who work at food stores in Canada, the other end of the chain, they become visible to one another and interrupt the corporate invisibility that has been placed on them. But there are also genealogies of critical consciousness that precede these more contemporaneous forms of organizing. Among women who work in sweatshops are the new revolutionaries, *las nuevas revolucionarias,* who identified a trajectory from the 1910 Mexican revolution to their struggles as young women workers on the global assembly line in northern Mexico, long before they crossed the border. They bring those histories with them as they learn with Chicana *maquilas* in El Paso the ways in which the internal colony joins the external colony at the borders. In these instances, women have chosen to replace the routinization of low-wage work with collective self-conscious definition.[29]

My aim here is neither to romanticize nor idealize exploitation. There are many instances in which conditions are severe enough to undermine or shut down organizational efforts altogether—instances where danger is borne out in lost lives. But I have underscored organizing here, for in spite of the histories of working-class and poor people's movements in the United States, a false opposition continues to circulate between the needs of survival and the demands of time, pitting individual survival against collective conscience. In such an opposition, there is presumably no time "left over" for political activity. When women say, "no tenemos hambre de comida, tenemos hambre de justicia," they reconcile this fictive split between the struggle for survival and the search for justice. When dignity and daily bread are brought together so that justice overtakes the (not unimportant) struggle for wages, in contexts where they are miniscule to begin with, women give voice to a deeper, existential yearning: the desire to make themselves intelligible to themselves and to each another, to make domination transparent, and to *practice* new and different ways of being. In this process there is no opposition between the demands of survival and the needs of time. Rather, the very force of existential necessity propels the desire to know, the desire to make sense of existence. Theorizing, therefore, becomes an existential necessity.

The Economy and the Academy: Education for Critical Consciousness

The various kinds of retrenchments we have witnessed in the "public" and "private" spheres have traveled into the academy with such a force that a collection by Becky Thompson and Sangeeta Tyagi, *A Dream Deferred,* characterized the period between the 1980s and the 1990s as "a mean time in the academy."[30] This was a time of drastic cuts in financial aid; a time of downsizing in which part-time and nontenure track faculty, in particular, felt the burden of lost jobs, benefits, and privileges. This was also a time in which multicultural education was attacked and blamed for the failure of the American economy to compete in the world market. Just as war and militarization became the terrain on which to contest definitions of citizenship and nation building, so, too, has education become a terrain on which to settle these very questions.

The academy is linked to the economy in at least three ways. First, universities, together with hospitals, make up one of the largest sectors of the service economy in this new transnational empire. Besides employing full-time and (mostly) part-time and adjunct faculty, it also employs vast numbers of service workers who share the same class location as service workers in corporate enterprises.[31] Second, in a most direct and related sense, universities provide workers for the economy. The ideological attack against multiculturalism as superfluous curriculum makes a corresponding statement about the kind of worker that the transnational empire requires—a worker who fits into an already assigned place within the productive process, without a critical examination of how she got there and who is there with her. Third, the economy requires a worker who naturalizes upward mobility, who attributes it to merit, an explanation that often masks inequity. As Paulo Freire has observed, corporatization requires a "banking concept of education," a mode of teaching in which knowledge is an investment, a set of received concepts that need not be subject to critical engagement or dialogic reflection.[32]

There are other knowledge formations that implicate the academy in the political economy. These formations are reflected in two interrelated contexts: first, in area studies, which owe their origin to the marriage between corporate (philanthropic) interests and state interests; and, second, a particular form of area studies that produced a way of thinking about the East as extreme alterity, a way of thinking that, as we saw earlier, was readily deployed during the Gulf War.[33] Orientalism assumed a certain form when it traveled within women's studies, particularly during the 1970s and 1980s, producing its own variant of alterity in the figure of the non-Western, tradition-bound woman. The work of Chandra Talpade Mohanty has shown clearly how the discursive imposition of "Western eyes" flattens the multiple experiences of a vast number of women over a vast terrain. Similarly, Marnia Lazreg's work has called attention to a certain gynocentrism governing the analytic relations between First World women and women in the Middle East.[34] Clearly not all feminist research or political mobilizations bear this content, but here again we are alerted to the ways in which dominant ideologies traffic in those spaces that intend to inhabit a different cartography.

What is the place of your own institution in this political economy? What is its debt to orientalism in the form of area studies, in its attachment to a Eurocentric identity of whiteness? How is that identity being rewritten in contemporary practices that dovetail with earlier forms of empire-building? It is to these questions that I now turn.

Teaching for Justice from a Hunger for Justice

We are all inhabitants of this world. The question we must pose is how do we inhabit this new world order? The processes I have outlined here have not all occurred at the same historical moment, but we can aim to understand them together because they constitute an ensemble.[35] We all have a relationship to them, although we are not all similarly positioned within them. Yet, we are all implicated in them. How do we contest these contradictions, even as we live and reproduce them, we, who are neither its creators nor its passive inheritors. "No one colonizes innocently," Aimé Césaire says.[36] There are no innocent spaces; thus, all spaces are fraught with interests, both conflicting and contradictory. As feminists, we are not immune to these contradictions. We cannot concede the operation of this new world order to the will of corporate restructuring. This is what you have expressed in your desire to draw a map without a mandate for conquest. You have expressed a will to teach for justice. *Las nuevas revolucionarias*, the new revolutionaries, have also expressed a yearning for justice: "tenemos hambre de justicia." You both want justice, and yet you are positioned differently—they as producers, you as thinkers. But we are all consumers and we consume what las nuevas revolucionarias produce. From what we now know about their political struggles we know that they are thinkers, for they have theorized the world from their own location within it. You share with las nuevas revolucionarias the existential imperative of making your lives intelligible and the moral agency to transform those lives. We can learn about integrity and dignity in the context of political struggle that is different from the struggle that occurs in the academy, but doing so would require that we not make dignity an enemy of material poverty, or make agency a matter of scarce resource. In this new critical geography, feminism would need to move beyond the old maps, which mandate a nationalist curriculum. Our project cannot be circumscribed with the borders of the American nation-state, which are themselves shifting in relation to global changes, but whose task of making insiders and outsiders remains the same. We are being required to travel in different ways than we have historically, to close the degrees of distance that inhere in corporate tourism and in the contradictions that are produced when pleasure thrives on inequity. Jamaica Kincaid offers a compelling insight here when she states:

> Every native of everywhere is a potential tourist. And every tourist is a
> native of somewhere. Every native would like a way out, every native

would like a rest. Every native would like a tour. But some natives, most natives in the world cannot go anywhere. They are too poor to escape the realities of their lives. And they are too poor to live properly in the place where they live, which is the very place the tourist wants to go. So when the native sees you, the tourist, they envy you. They envy your own ability to leave your banality and boredom. They envy your ability to turn their own banality and boredom into a source of pleasure for yourself.[37]

The kind of tense intersubjectivity to which Kincaid draws our attention is part of the double mirror that Marnia Lazreg holds up when she argues that Middle Eastern and North African women "have their own individuality"; they are "for themselves" instead of being "for us."[38] We need to conceptualize modes of being and ways of seeing that do not always already mobilize an "other," either in the service of our pleasure or in the service of knowledge. We need to enact strategies of reading and being that do not turn indispensability into victimhood. Collectivized "envy" is not the same as individual "envy." When collectivized, envy can ask important questions about how banality comes to be made into a source of pleasure, about who manufactures it, and about what can be done to transform it. It is what hambre de justicia propels collectivities to do. Without these understandings, we will be unable to map the lines between our own location—between where we are, what we see, and what we do. We would be left to render only incomplete, skewed accounts of history. There was a time we believed history to be incomplete, erroneous even, in its evisceration of feminist standpoints. We need to develop a similar urgency around relational curricular projects that put us in conversation, not domination, with a range of relational knowledges. There is something quite profound about not knowing, claiming not to know, or not gaining access to knowledge that enables us to know that we are not the sole (re)producers of our lives. But we would have to apprehend the loss that comes from not knowing and feel its absence in an immediate and palpable way in order to remake ourselves enough, so that our analyses might change. We have to learn how to intuit the consequences of not knowing, to experience their effects in order to reverse some of the deeply embedded deposits on which an imperial psyche rests—a psyche that still holds on to the idea of manifest destiny and the fiction of protection and safety from an enemy, who is either calculating on the borders outside or hovering on the margins within. We would have to visit the devastation of living segregated lives—the wrenching devastation that Pat Parker invokes in her poem "Sunday":

Each Sunday
   the people of   this town
would go to church
   eat dinner
     all at one table with their family
   the television silent
    & bless the food,
      father
        we thank
          THEE
  & their maids
off
    with their families
  & everyone rest
  until the Sunday
   when the rains
   began
     and crashed
     thru the wind
    moving away the dirt
    but somebody didn't
   stop it
    and the
 little river
    rose
     and
       rose
   till the cars

and televisions
and blankets
and people—all
washed thru the
    streets and past
    their neighbors'
    for blocks
      and blocks

The troops came on Wednesday
The water had
    stopped
  the wet
merged with the dirt
  mud
     was
  all over
    and
the troops shook their heads.

They could not
    bury
    the dead.

In the
    death murk

they couldn't tell
    the
    Black
    from
    the white.[39]

Feminism would have to travel deep within the innards of this cultural memory to wrestle with these segregated ghosts, these imperial ghosts, to devise the necessary ceremonies to placate them, so that they can return to continue the reconstructive work that the floods instigated. We can refuse the inheritance of the death murk, even as we know that there is a piece of this system within each of us. But there are some things that are simply not for sale. We simply cannot continue to substitute owning for being, privacy for intimacy, or substitute monogamies of the mind for the expansiveness of the Soul.

I began at the outset by arguing for a mode of thinking, a new conceptual map with an implied pedagogy. That thinking requires an ongoing piece of work on your part, the painstaking labor of reenvisioning curriculum, which at the very least does not reside within national and disciplinary borders; which takes account of the broad tempos and movements of history, while paying close attention to historical specificity; which demystifies the fictitious boundaries between the academy and the community, a division that leaves community work to particular disciplines, and worse, to particular bodies; which brings self-conscious positionality (a sense of place and space) to the knowledges we produce, the contradictory positions we occupy and the internal systems of rewards and privileges we derive from those very positions; which pays close attention to the questions we bring inside the classroom, as we instruct students in the delicate task of learning *how* to pose questions. And yet we confront a major difficulty in reconciling desire with practice, of teaching a vision we have not yet fully lived, of moving inside and across the outlines of a map, with no guarantees. Such work places a great demand on the imagination, on practice, on reconfiguring the relationship between practice and theory and on building solidarity with different communities, while remaining aware of the suspicion that academic knowledge bears.

How will the knowledges of this critical geography become the epistemic frameworks that inform your teaching? Your research? How will you engage the different regimes of knowing, some of their dominant paradigms, and the apparently neat separations that result? What political economies of competition have been spawned inside the academy in the scramble over resources, which have been made scarce at the bottom in order to better solidify the top? What kinds of interdisciplinary, cross-border conversations are you willing to engage? What is the relationship of women's studies to these knowledge systems? What frameworks are required to move beyond "Western eyes"? What might Morrison's *Bluest*

Eyes and Mohanty's "Western Eyes" teach us about the intent, directionality, and consequences of vision? How will students come to apprehend the deep significance of these questions? How will you engage a dialogic process where they might learn from las nuevas revolucionarias to recognize valences of earlier histories of working-class struggle in the United States, the student movement of the 1960s, or the more recent student mobilizations against the World Trade Organization? What dialogic practices do we perfect to develop a form of critical consciousness in which citizenship is never normativized?[40]

Since corporatization and downsizing have not escaped the academy, teaching for justice means that we examine the academy as a place of work with its own regimes of labor, its own internal economies. As a place of work, it has its own corporate system of inequities—a stratum of low-waged workers resembling women on the global assembly line, and a stratum of high-salaried managers. It has its own system of valorization, of disciplines, and of identities. What is the relationship between full-time, part-time, and adjunct women who work without many of the benefits of their full-time faculty colleagues—benefits such as access to medical care and research funds or opportunities for professional development? What is the relationship between the women in women's studies and the women who clean the dorms and classrooms, the women who serve us food?

The ideological motivations embedded in the idea of a free market are similarly ensconced in the ideas of the academy as a meritocracy. This is partly why the struggle over affirmative action becomes so fierce, and why, in those institutions where it does exist, allegiance to multiculturalism usually takes a form that evades an analysis of power, cathecting all difference onto the bodies of people of color in a way that avoids developing a commitment to antiracist practices. Sometimes even the language of multiculturalism is assimilated into the corporate system of governance, leaving the affirmative action office in these post-Bakke times to function largely as legal gatekeeper. How do we move from the pervasive race-neutral (ostensibly colorblind) practices of the academy to antiracist practices? Clearly, one of our tasks as committed feminist, antiracist intellectuals is to figure out how *not* to reproduce the racial regimes of the academy.

We have seen the ways in which the transnational empire has engendered the restructuring of the state, which has in turn moved to police the lives of impoverished women. All of these processes of restructuring and surveillance challenge both the idea of a disinterested state and the idea of a neat public/private binary. Teaching for justice means that state practices must figure far more prominently in our analyses and political organizing than they have historically.

Certain state imperatives have been stark in their intransigence. No one in charge of the (big) state apparatus in this country has advocated socialism. The state has an abiding interest in maintaining the geographies of capitalism. No one in charge of the state apparatus has refused allegiance to the technologies of killing. The state has an abiding investment in war, in owning and deploying the means of violence and coercion in the society. No one in charge of the state apparatus has challenged hegemonic heterosexuality in ways that legitimize lesbian and gay families. The state has an abiding interest in upholding the conjugal heterosexual family and in sexualizing morality so as to remove from the realm of moral debate its own ethics, as it pursues the mandates of war. No one in charge of the state apparatus has challenged an attachment to white race loyalty. No one in charge of the state apparatus has posed a serious challenge to the technologies of masculine rationality. The state has an interest in maintaining a hierarchical gender regime. Teaching for justice would not equate "disinterest" with benevolence.

Teaching for justice must interrogate whether feminism has perhaps bought into the script of an unwieldy state in its continued erasure of the political agendas of poor and working-class people's struggle. Does this practice travel into the classroom and erase those same histories and the histories of immigrant women from our syllabi? Do our analytic practices turn indispensability into victimhood, thereby reproducing the dominant script that rewrites citizenship in the names of members of the corporate class only? Do we shun socialist projects, or merely introduce them as a failure, merely to shore up a need for capitalism? How do class and privileges of different kinds operate within our own classrooms?

An examination of state practice would prompt us to rethink definitions of democracy—if by democracy we mean the political will of the state to provide the means for people to live with dignity; to reverse the idea that poverty is a permanent condition of identity and personality structure; to dismantle hierarchies of citizenship in order to remove the now-formidable crystallization of citizenship around the twin statuses of consumer and taxpayer.[41] Teaching for justice must examine how notions of free-market democracy seep into those ideologies of Western civilization that wander into the academy, latching on to the more recent debates about the defense of the canon and the fear of its displacement by "minority" discourses, which are still structurally marginalized. Teaching for justice would alert us to the fact that the state cannot be "democratic" at home and nobly interventionist abroad. We saw earlier that violence against "the enemy" in the Gulf was not neatly cordoned off from sexual violence against U.S. women soldiers. Teaching for justice would have us examine the contradictions of a civilization that, as Morrison put it, "has made it possible for children to bite their tongues off, to commit tongue suicide, and use bullets instead to iterate the voice of speechlessness."[42] Speech and voice have been intimate partners in our analytic preoccupations as feminists.

Colonialism is no stranger to feminism's political project, either elsewhere or here. Most people's lives, most women's lives, have been shaped by colonialism. Many women have come to feminist consciousness through anticolonial nationalist struggle. While we have devised modes of thinking that have enabled us to read back the effects of colonization and imperialism abroad onto populations at home, we must distinguish between the contemporary racisms of immigration that are knitted into the domestic economy and earlier processes of Jim Crow. All racisms do not behave in the same way. But there is another order of work that relates to the excavation of the psychic residues of the imperial project, an examination of the identities that this project has engendered and the costs that superiority wagers as it represses the extensive wealth of resources it utilizes, which are not of its making. This is the reconstructive work Pat Parker has bequeathed. It is the larger existential challenge we face as we "reverse the mad belief in separate thoughts and separate bodies, which lead separate lives and go their separate ways."[43] Yet, we must simultaneously pry open the fictions of race, even as we wrestle with racism's costly effects.

The desire to teach for justice can only come from a place of hunger, un hambre de justicia, a desire to enunciate a mode of being that we live, analyze, and practice in our teaching and undertake in our research, in as many ways and in as many places as possible, from a passion we are simply not willing to concede, from a passion that moves beyond the temporary comfort of demystification to anchor teaching practices that are at once theoretically informed, agile, and accountable. Teaching for justice must come, as well, from understandings of history, which are not ineluctably circumscribed by the academy, since our sojourn here is not only partial but also temporary. If each of us were to take on the most miniscule part of what we have outlined here, it would be sufficient to bring our work and our sensibilities to another register. Thinking justice, teaching for justice, and living justice means that we continually challenge each other to enunciate our vision of justice. Unlike the new world order with elite ownership for members only, we all have ownership in this new vision; no single one of us stands in a proprietary relationship to it, for it is to be collectively imagined, collectively guarded, collectively worked out.

As I close, I leave you a bequeathal from *The Marvelous Arithmetics of Distance,* Audre Lorde's posthumously published poetry collection. Having said all that she had come to say, she needed no preface. But, a bit before she had begun the shift to a different consciousness, Lorde was asked to reflect on her hopes for the book and the spirit in which she offered it. She had this to say: "Beyond the penchant for easy definitions, false exactitudes, we share a hunger for enduring value, relationships beyond hierarchy and outside reproach, a hunger for life's measures, complex, direct and flexible. I want this book to be filled with shards of light thrown off from the shifting tensions between the dissimilar, for that is the real stuff of creation and growth."[44] Audre Lorde: a vision for justice.

4

Anatomy of a Mobilization

Last night, winds howled; palm fronds thrashed against concrete slabs as they surrendered to insistent winds. As day broke, thunder roared its impatience. Threatening clouds hung close to the Ocean, readying themselves to dump their gift onto the land parched from months of neglect. As I sat before the expanse of vast turquoise jade, still pale from its night slumber, a small motor boat carrying six fishermen passed by. I watched as they slowly changed course, steering the tumultuous caress of waves still bent on carrying the memory of the night winds. I felt myself not wanting them to enter those waves, that part of the Ocean, far off, where there seems to be another shore. I felt myself not wanting them to enter those waves, those men who carry the imprint of the Ocean's vibrations on their Souls. As they receded, the place where I saw them last seemed to be overtaken by a pod of dolphins, except that the name I gave them was not dolphins but sharks. That startled me. Why danger? Then oh so slowly, as the soft of the morning sun made its gentle way through those threatening clouds, I began to sense that the danger did not belong to those men of the sea no longer in sight. It belonged to me. Preparing myself to reenter dangerous waters in which I swam five years earlier. Preparing to bring you to those waters so that you can travel with me, even to some still hidden places, so that you can better understand how I came to shore. Looking back as I walk forward.

We are committed to paying close attention to the histories which walk
and live with us within our personal and institutional lives, and to struggling
together around their effects.—THE MOBILIZATION FOR REAL DIVERSITY,
DEMOCRACY AND ECONOMIC JUSTICE, the New School University, 1997

Looking back, I realize that the words in the epigraph above serve as a call
to memory. These words call forth a relationship to history, knowledge,
and political struggle, a desire for an anchored commitment to being
attuned and attentive to the movement of embodied histories that breathe,
live, and walk with us. It designates an inheritance; delivers an injunctive
to remember, a debt owed, perhaps, for being accompanied, one that
could be paid through the active work of remembering. It suggests that
histories are not fixed in any predetermined way. Their multiple expressions are collectively worked out in the context of political struggle, the
conduit through which knowledge of the self and of institutional practices
is derived. Thus argued, the epigraph makes a claim about how people
work to make the world intelligible.

The "we" of the epigraph refers to members of the Mobilization for
Real Diversity, Democracy and Economic Justice (hereafter referred to as
the Mobilization) at the New School for Social Research located in New
York City (hereafter the School). Comprised of a broad coalition of
faculty, students, staff, and security guards, the Mobilization coalesced
over approximately a two-year period, from 1996 to 1998, to transform a
wide range of inequitable institutional practices in hiring, decision making, curricular and intellectual projects, and the unequal appropriation
of labor, all of which produced a culture of domination that stood in the
way of justice. Its vision was expressed in these terms: "We . . . share a
common vision of how communities of difference can work to abolish
structural inequalities of different kinds. This entails opening frank and
principled dialogues about our respective histories and different relationships to power and privilege. We share an ethical and intellectual commitment to understanding the histories and knowledges of particular
movements and struggles involving class, race, and decolonization; different feminisms; lesbian/gay/queer liberation and theory; and transnational and anti-imperialist perspectives and critiques."[1]

In a fundamental sense, the impulse for this vision ought not to have posed a threat to the School's cherished principles, at least not those that had constituted its official history or had otherwise traveled both nationally and internationally to announce its progressive legacy. Since their inception at the turn of the century, both the Graduate Faculty (formerly the University in Exile) and the New School (the Adult Education Division) had aligned themselves with the task of social reconstruction. For instance, the Adult Division was founded in 1919 by a group of men at Columbia University who had felt the pressing burden of the involvement of the United States in World War I, along with their own inability to generate a culture of conscience at Columbia. The New School was envisioned as a place for new pedagogic practices, interdisciplinarity, and as an experiment to place education in the service of transformation.[2] Thus, its reputation derived both from an alternative vision of education and from its outsider status—outside the Ivy League. The University in Exile gained its reputation not so much for its radical pedagogy but for the social composition of its faculty, which in 1934 was comprised almost entirely of German exiles fleeing fascism.[3] Had you visited or lived in New York City in 1996 and had reason to use its aging underground to ride the A train from Harlem to Christopher Street, a stone's throw from the Stonewall rebellion, you would have been greeted with billboards proclaiming the School a "world of ideas." The education it granted was a "passport" to that world. These billboards presented a contradictory display in an age of globalization and border enforcements, when passports demarcate insiders and outsiders. Yet, they worked as an implied testament to the School's continued commitment to an earlier "radical" history more than six decades later.

There is perhaps no institution in higher education today that has not resuscitated a visionary past in order to claim legitimacy in the present. What is different in the case of the School, however, is that its specific legacy of antifascism morphed into an institutional identity, which by the early 1990s had more in common with the imperatives of corporatization and downsizing than with a radical transformative project. When in the midst of the Mobilization, then-president Jonathan Fanton declared, "this is not a nation-state . . . This is a corporation, you will not get your civil-rights here," the statement and the practices it engendered signaled the reciprocal antagonism between corporate rationality expressed on the inside, and the apparent freedom the School conferred to traverse the world on the outside.[4] Securing a competitive edge for a School with a tuition-driven budget was indeed a challenge, thus making its reliance on a well-greased public relations machinery an absolute necessity. But it also provoked a profound contradiction, for while public relations worked externally in the service of liberalism, internally it plunged the School into a crisis of "managing diversity."[5] At stake was the very project of liberalism itself and the School's attachment to a version of progressivism in which Eurocentrism occupied the center. Ultimately, the president's statement struck at the heart of a moral emergency in which the School was engulfed, a multifaceted emergency whose elements the Mobilization exposed over the course of two years of work.

That emergency also wore a national face that manifested in a series of widespread cutbacks in both public and private institutions. As I describe in the previous chapter, colleges and universities in the late 1980s and early 1990s had become increasingly reliant on the labor of part-time and adjunct faculty and on a range of subcontracting arrangements that had become increasingly exploitative.[6] Questions pertaining to the processes of university hiring, the commodification of certain knowledges, and the marketing of difference were all being hotly contested, spilling outside of the academy into the courts and onto the streets through a series of culture wars, struggles over the canon, and attempts to "diversify" various populations as the backlash against affirmative action heightened and anti-immigrant sentiment rose. All across the country, the academy's invisible guidebooks were replete with student movements and union organizing efforts for workplace democracy; and ongoing struggles to undo Eurocentrism in curricular, pedagogic, and hiring practices. The bitter consequences of an unequal racial, gendered regime in the lives of women and men of color, and of progressive people more generally, were everywhere palpable.[7] Thus in 1996, the School's experience with the Mobilization may have been specific—particularly in light of its progressive, even radical, reputation—but it was by no means unique.

The story in this chapter is about speech and power, about voice and coming to voice, a process that has been indispensable to feminism's own intellectual and political project. It is a story about refusals, the yearning for justice, and the struggle to live that yearning. It is not a story about free speech, however, for speech is not free. As Stanley Fish reminds us, "there is no such thing as free (non-ideologically constrained) speech . . . because the shape in which (freedom of expression) is invoked will always be political, always . . . be the result of having drawn the relevant line between speech and action . . . in a way that is favorable to some interests and indifferent or hostile to others."[8] Speech can have grave consequences: people have been assassinated and imprisoned in the United States when their speech acts disrupted customary power alignments. And while no one in the Mobilization was killed in the context of exercising "academic speech" (in the words of Patricia Hill Collins), we shall nonetheless come to see that the lines the School drew between speech and action favored entrenched interests, which were hostile to those of the Mobilization.

The story in this chapter is not about the triumph of liberalism. Rather, it charts the failures of (Left) liberalism and the limits of its most treasured anchors: assimilation and diversity. Toni Morrison's elegant observation in the afterword of *The Bluest Eye* about the inelegance of racism's effects, of seeing oneself "preserved in the amber of disqualifying metaphors," is appropriate here.[9] At this moment of corporatization, diversity practices in the academy seem compelled to undertake such a preservation, not only in ways that supplant metaphors and practices of critical history, but also in ways that abrogate speech while ignoring the psychic, material, and spiritual costs of being put on display.[10] Still, if this aggressive response to the Mobilization could occur in what one of its administrator's called "a progressive icon," then it could occur anywhere. But crisis could have also provided a moment for a different imagination to emerge and, given the pervasiveness of inequity, it could have been a moment for the School to act as a catalyst, to exert a measure of national leadership on these questions of justice that are in sore need of critical engagement in the academy at this moment.

Justice and Truth

At the 2001 Women's Rights as Human Rights conference, Margaret Urban Walker delivered a speech about the rights to truth, a concept that she culled from the testimonies of survivors before various truth commissions.[11] At the center of Walker's schema was the idea that the "right to truth" was claimable—that indeed one had a moral right and legitimate claim to truth, particularly during periods of moral emergencies, such as those consonant with the violences of apartheid in South Africa, or with different periods of militarization in Argentina, Uruguay, Chile, and Haiti, for instance, which spawned their own truth commissions.[12] But while the "right to truth" is clothed in its own legitimacy, this right, like any other, can be subjected to distortion, particularly during periods of such moral emergency. Thus, rights become highly contingent and, as such, they need to be understood within those very contingencies. There are several such contingencies, including the fact that getting one's truth told is a matter of political will and a matter of justice; that one's will to speak might be crushed—indeed, that everyday oppressions prevent truth from emerging, which is why it becomes incumbent on liberation movements to enunciate truths about their experience of systemic violences, torture, and inequities; and that truth told is something that is put forward as claims about the world, both individual and collective. Yet, this putting forward of truth relies on other conditions: that one has to have the *will* to do it, the *means* to do it, the *opportunity* to do it, and the *standing* to have those claims accepted as credible. Ultimately, one's ability to be heard as saying what one is saying and what one intends to say is structured by one's social and legal status, one's *standing*. Put differently, to be recognized as a teller of truth requires basic authority, not only within oneself but, structurally, in contexts where both truth and credibility are not antagonistic.

The question of how one's truth comes to be socially authorized brings us closer to the crux of the considerations in this chapter. Of course, neither the will, the means, nor the opportunity to advance one's truth is a social given, and this, one might argue, is the reason that a moral emergency prevails in the first instance. In fact, the statement by the School's then-president, "you will not get your civil-rights here," seemed intent on ensuring that the *means* to advance truth would be foreclosed. Of course, it also provoked an opportunity to create alternative means. Who has authority, what is its source, who confers or denies it, and who struggles to gain ownership of it all became the highly fraught terrain on which the Mobilization was grounded.

We still need to understand, however, how one's ability to be heard as saying what one intends to say is linked to one's standing and power. In my effort to clarify this point, I will rely initially on Rae Langton's essay "Speech Acts and Unspeakable Acts," on whose suppositions Walker's own formulations rest.[13] Langton is interested in how speech acts subordinate and how they come to carry illocutionary force; how it is that actions that subordinate come to be constituted through them. For Langton, a speech act is an act of subordination when uttered by someone in power. Take, for instance, the utterance, "whites only." It has the effect of "ordering blacks away; it welcomes whites; it permits whites to act in discriminatory ways towards blacks and it subordinates blacks." Such speech acts "rank, legitimate, discriminate and deprive." Thus, (white) people understand their actions—of ranking, discriminating, depriving—to be legitimate because they have already been legitimated. Not only are actions constituted through these words, but such actions and words mark political power in their simultaneous capacity to silence. Here are the different ways in which silence operates: "If you are powerful, you sometimes have the ability to silence the speech of the powerless. One way might be to stop the powerless from speaking at all. Gag them. Threaten them. Condemn them to solitary confinement. But there is another, less dramatic, but equally effective way. Let them speak. Let them say whatever they like to whomever they like, but stop that speech from counting as the action it was intended to be." Some speech acts are unspeakable, Langton concludes: "Although the appropriate words can be uttered, *those utterances fail to count as the actions they were intended to be* [emphasis added]."[14]

To this kind of silencing Langton gives the name illocutionary disablement, where the speaking agent does not have the requisite social authority and is disabled from performing illocutionary acts in the relevant domain, the domain where they matter most. To understand the depth of this disablement, one must consider both the relevant domain within which that authority to disable is being exercised and the authoritative role of the speaker, for it is this role that "imbues the utterance with a force that would be otherwise absent were it made by someone who did not occupy that role." Subordinating speech acts are, therefore, authoritative speech acts when the speakers in question have authority and when, through that authority, *they can stop another's speech from counting as the action it was intended to be.*[15] Thus, unspeakable speech is not unspeakable by some mysterious naturalizing force, it is *made* unspeakable in the context of contestations over power and struggles over meaning, which and whose meaning would stand as truth and whether the standing of those who claimed to speak from the truth of a different epistemic history (different from the hegemonic story) would have what they say count for exactly what they mean.

Langton's formulations compelled me to return to two of Toni Morrison's essays: "Unspeakable Things Unspoken: The Afro-American Presence in American Literature" and "Friday on the Potomac," her meditation on the psychic costs of excising one's tongue.[16] In the former, she takes up the racial relations of unspeakability and their function in American literature. Specifically, she intended her analysis to apply to the rhetorical practices that enabled "America" to be constituted through whiteness only. For Morrison, the histories of race are unspeakable in the literary canon. But that unspeakability is imposed on individuals as well, since in the latter essay the character Friday was the one forced to excise his own tongue in order to make himself intelligible to the colonizer. In bringing Langton and Morrison into conversation with one another, we are able to understand excision of the tongue as a most severe form of disablement. Excision functions in much the same way as dominant knowledge frameworks that privilege themselves over others, ultimately silencing, disabling, and erasing. Such frameworks reside at the nexus of speech, power, and social authority, yet they are not simply about one's ability to speak.

The interpretations I offer above travel a long distance from the normative question of rights and freedom of expression that anchor political liberalism derived from European and Euro-American traditions. I stated earlier that a large part of what was at stake for the School was the very project of liberalism linked to social-democratic Left ideologies, which informed the dominant knowledge frameworks, and which also informed specific intellectual projects of members of the Graduate Faculty. The intellectual pedigree is quite instructive, for a significant part of the analytic work of this class of intellectuals proceeds from Habermasian understandings of harmonious, communicative interaction and the operation of "consensual norms."[17] Langton's formulation of speech outcomes is quite different from that of Habermas, however. Although they are both interested in the social power of speakers, Habermas privileges "consensual norms," thus leaving unexplored the very question of how power is exercised and maintained. It is Langton's formulation of *disablement* that subverts his formulation of harmonious communicative interaction and homogeneous publics, thereby allowing contestations over power to become transparent.[18] Precisely because the work of the Mobilization was not allowed to stand for what its members intended, we would need "disablement," not "consensual norms" as the analytic category to understand how entrenched knowledge/power interests performed the work of distortion. We can understand why Morrison equates canon-building with empire-building. Disablement helps us to understand how power resorts to various modes of silencing. Thus it aligns public communication not with harmony but with the kind of fear and danger that Audre Lorde has associated with "the transformation of silence into language and action. It is the danger of having what is spoken be[come] bruised or misunderstood."[19] Ultimately, disablement is not only a form of silencing, but a mode of violence and, as such, it remains existentially antagonistic to producing conditions of harmony.

The Mobilization: An Introduction

These are some of the frameworks I will utilize to contextualize the Mobilization, in which I was a full participant for approximately one year. I joined a political process that had already been in formation on my behalf, tying institutional racism to the permanent visiting status of most faculty of color, and to the exploitative conditions that security guards and part-time faculty and staff had experienced. What first began as a desire to secure a permanent contract for a single faculty member (myself) mushroomed within months into a larger public critique of institutional inequities of different kinds—the lived experience of everyday oppressions within the institution. In one respect, the issue of individuals illuminating contradictory social processes is neither new nor recent. It is through individuals that structures come to light. But structures themselves are never reducible to individuals.

Before proceeding further, let me briefly identify both the institutional mechanisms and the different actors who presided over them. The School is comprised of seven divisions: the Graduate Faculty (hereafter referred to as GF)—considered the flagship of the School—headed by then-dean Judith Friedlander; the New School (the Adult Division); the Milano School of Management and Urban Policy; Parsons School of Design; Mannes College of Music; Eugene Lang (undergraduate) College (hereafter Lang), headed by then-dean Beatrice Banu; and the School of Dramatic Arts. As a graduate degree-granting program, the Committee on Gender Studies and Feminist Theory (hereafter GSFT) was housed within the GF. Members of GSFT, along with representatives from various departments, served on the Executive and Budget Committee, which in 1996 considered a curriculum proposal aimed at transforming the dominant knowledge frameworks at the GF. The proposal, titled "Rethinking Europe in a Global Context: A Proposal for Diversifying the Graduate Faculty within an Intellectual Program of Study" (hereafter the Proposal), was rejected within weeks of its submission. The GF was also home to the organized opposition against the Mobilization. Members of that opposition comprised both students and faculty, some of whom were also signatories to "An Alternative," the counter-mobilization's public written document.

Each division of the School has its own administrative structure, including a diversity committee—members of which also serve on a university-wide diversity task force, chaired by then–associate provost, Barbara Emerson, who was also director of the University Diversity Initiative (hereafter UDI). Emerson's major responsibilities included the operation of the UDI and the monitoring of the Faculty Initiative for Diversity (hereafter FIND). These committees became the major focus of the student organizing efforts out of which Education Not Domination (hereafter END) was born.

The Mobilization was not allowed to occupy a disinterested public space. I will show, instead, how it was subjected to various contradictory distortions and disabled in several ways. Its intellectual and political agendas were not allowed to count for what we, its members, wanted them to mean. At times, there were claims that I stood for the Mobilization; at other times I was separated from it and from the conditions that spawned it; collapsed into it and turned into its mastermind as I pursued my "unbridled self-interest" in a job; and (almost) erased along with its demands for economic justice. Most often, the implication was that the conditions of which the Mobilization spoke had not been reproduced in the very fabric of the School but were specific to me. Because these distortions were publicly diffused, I need to say that I fully endorsed the political struggle for my own retention. When I signed on the dotted line of the dean's letter in July 1994 as she expressed her "very great pleasure to offer [me] a three-year (non-tenure track) appointment as visiting associate professor in the GF's Committee on Gender Studies and Feminist Theory" at Lang, it was an act to secure my individual interest in a job. We are all aware, however, that such letters of invitation, adhering as they must to conventions of politeness, never address the political contexts of one's hire. In my case, it never stated that my work focused on "race," a point that Dean Friedlander stressed later to students at the height of the Mobilization to underscore the School's commitment to "race." It did not address the long-standing contest between Lang and the GF that would have explained why mine was the "first" joint appointment, nor did it address the customary ways in which Lang had been criticized by members of the GF for an "inferior curriculum."[20] Nor did the letter state that the moral emergency in which the School had been engulfed had reared its head many times earlier, and that my hire might have been minimally intended to placate student and faculty interests because two black women fled the GF during the three years prior to my arrival. (Another woman of color would resign in the first year of my appointment, thus reducing our numbers to two "visitors.") There was no mention that students had consistently objected to "disappointing diversity efforts" at the GF and had voiced "deep dissatisfaction" and outrage that my appointment was yet another visiting appointment adding to the unspoken policy of a revolving door for faculty of color. Such politics are never divulged by those with power, yet they shape everyday behavior and everyday interaction in significant ways.

It is not unusual in higher education to attempt an extension of a short-term contract. Both Dean Friedlander and the GSFT faculty indicated it was a reasonable way to proceed—at least in face-to-face conversations with me. However, GSFT's own ambiguous position of pursuing a public strategy of placating students, who had begun to question the linearity of a still Western-centered curriculum by promising a successful reappointment while privately engaging me in condescending discussions about extending my contract, "advising . . . [me] that I would be crazy not to look for another job," led me to think that a certain politic of disingenuity had congealed rather early in the day, that I had long since been (re)evaluated outside of any formal terms of application, and that a pretext was being constructed to ensure my exclusion. The president created one such pretext in an early threat issued at a university-wide Diversity Committee meeting when he said: "Jacqui Alexander will not be the litmus test for diversity at the New School." If we are to understand the force of his statement, coming as it did from someone with control over centralized power—the power "to advance budgetary authority" for the appointment "of a qualified faculty member from an under-represented group"—it becomes clear that the statement authorized deans to act.[21] I will return later to the question of the very production of "diversity" in the terms "*qualified* faculty member from an under-represented group," but the point to be underscored for the moment is that the president's public statement constituted *action:* "Do not hire Jacqui Alexander." In that sense, it counted for precisely the action he intended it to be. The statement also indicated that I had been made a target in a very particular way. The later reversals and conflicting story lines were predictable. At times FIND required a national search, at other times it did not. After the president's mandate, Dean Friedlander once again shifted accountability from herself and placed it squarely on my shoulders. All I needed to do to secure a job, she informed students, was "to take one step forward to departments"—another expression of disingenuity that could placate students while being condescending to the position. Such condescension would be unimaginable had my faculty position been held by a senior white colleague—male or female. The contradictory reversals and displacements, and the extent to which a disingenuous bureaucracy could shift accountability and operate publicly to mask entrenched intellectual and political interests indicate how large a theoretical role we need to assign to the place the Mobilization held in the collective imaginary. It indicates how deeply entrenched the emergency had become.

A Mobilization had not existed prior to the work we began in 1996, and it would not have come into being had existing bureaucratic structures functioned as promised on paper.[22] It had to be *built*. I will rely here on Langton's schema, of *will, means,* and *opportunity* to discuss that building. But it is useful to remember that there is no compulsory, linear correspondence between the experience of domination and resistance, between identity and consciousness.[23] Yet, we can safely say that the will to political struggle emerges out of experiences of domination, which is why one would not want to simply concede one's will, even when—or perhaps particularly when—conditions are severe. Because the aggressive public relations strategy had climbed inside the School and attempted to veil itself, the routes of power were often hidden. Thus, a large part of the work of the Mobilization involved the job of demystification, what Cornel West describes as the process of keeping track of "the complex dynamics of institutional and other related power structures, in order to disclose options and alternatives for transformative praxis."[24] For the Mobilization, it involved tracking the ideological masks of the institution: the over-representation of "diversity" that substituted a discourse of assimilation and "the good record of affirmative action" for domination; "honor" and "privilege" for a living wage; "subcontracting" for the exploitation of security guards; and European heterodoxy for all progressive or radical frameworks. Demystification was indispensable as we engaged the interstices of power and simultaneously came to collective political consciousness.

How we, as a Mobilization, came to build the *will* to political struggle, how we came to consciousness as we fashioned a transformative praxis, is crucial to this story. In using the term "praxis" I want to foreground the different layers of a process: specific work undertaken during 1996–1997 that exposed the moral emergency that the School defined as "diversity"; the collective consciousness its members formed in that practice; the specific analyses of the complex dynamics of institutional power structures we had undertaken, including analyses of political interests embedded in knowledge claims; as well as the internal contradictions we experienced among ourselves. We ought not to have been surprised that the common interests of people of color had to be collectively imagined and shaped; that black people would not unquestioningly support the Mobilization; that some of the habits of whiteness would travel within; or that student architects of the Mobilization would have felt oppressed by faculty power. But all of these contradictions were exposed as we undertook our political work, and the confrontations were painful, the subject of long, torturous, almost all-night meetings. If in the microphysics of the School were woven the contradictions of the larger social formation, so too within the Mobilization were woven the contradictions of both. These were difficult moments of collective and individual self-confrontation as we realized we were not immune to some of the practices and behaviors we were attempting to transform. Yet, we sensed collectively a profound imperative in having to do, to learn, to practice, and to think justice all at once, as paradoxically incomplete and as liberatory as it turned out to be. All of this work of creating and re-creating ourselves is the work involved in figuring out a transformative praxis. It is never guaranteed before the fact.

In a fundamental sense, the work of the Mobilization was undertaken within one of the very arenas we were striving to transform—the arena of "diversity." Demystification was the means through which we came to understand that "diversity" documents were authoritative documents, an organizing schema within the School. Within them, people of color were classified, moved around, counted, recounted, and overcounted, our bodies extended across each of the School's seven divisions, each possessing its own mechanism of accountability and the nonconsensual agreement we had presumably made to remain within those proscriptions. It is within these discourses that people of color are simultaneously made invisible and hypervisible. I will trace how these discourses subordinate, rank, discriminate, and deprive, but I will also examine how "diversity" is manufactured, how it comes to be the dominant institutional common-sense reality for engaging people of color, how, in other words, diversity stands in the nexus of speech and power.

Refusals in the context of domination are seldom received kindly. And since one of the requirements of the kind of preservation of which Morrison spoke is silence, the combination of truth, speech, and refusal poses a threat to power. Once we refused the conscripted boxes of diversity discourses to become speaking agents, making claims that were diametrically opposed to those contained within them; once we ceased being mindless, spiritless bodies but rather became white faculty and students willing to interrogate privilege and to renege on the promise of white race loyalty, or became security guards who dared to insist on a living wage, or became students who felt the School's betrayal and declared ourselves at educational risk in the absence of certain knowledges, or became part-time and adjunct faculty who challenged the idea of the prestige we ostensibly enjoyed in the unequal exchange for low salaries, no status, and no say in decision-making, or became faculty of color refusing the permanent guest status of the revolving-door policies; once we argued that the external manufacture of progressivism had aggressive consequences on us as human beings, and that the university, once a haven for exiles, was actively producing its own; once we called attention to the very technologies of disciplining, the everyday oppressions that prevented truth from emerging and being acted upon, then—almost of necessity—the task and function of the counter-mobilization was simultaneously instigated.

What we shall see as this story progresses is that the primary function of the counter-mobilization was to obstruct our right to truth, to challenge the credibility of our analyses and threaten our authority and standing, to attempt to stop our speech from counting as the actions we intended them to be. Since part of its work had already been accomplished in the everyday life of the institution in what was business as usual, its limited tasks had already been defined and assigned, so it continued the work of contesting our claims and our authority with very little effort. Members of the counter-mobilization, moreover, believed their actions to be legitimate since they had already been legitimated by the president and the deans, and by everyday institutionalized acts of exclusion. They knew through practice that there were no institutional costs attached to the exercise of their privilege. On the contrary, such privilege had already been legitimated. Very little else could explain its meteoric ascendancy in the absence of advancing any vision of social justice whatsoever. It needed no such vision to legitimate itself. The sole task, therefore, of this counter-mobilization, variously comprised, was to achieve illocutionary disablement. Uppermost among our tasks was the goal of foregrounding the conditions we experienced at the School. But the counter-mobilization sought to displace these systemic inequities to focus on the authority and standing of the Mobilization, on our linkages to broader intellectual and feminist communities in and beyond the academy, and on my own authority. That strategy became the very nub through which official authority was exercised, the vise through which the counter-mobilization imagined and reinvented itself. Underneath it all, something far deeper was at stake in the continuation of particular knowledge frameworks and the avid defense of Europe and European thought.

Defending Europe: Defending Power/Knowledge

Comprised variously of several factions, the counter-mobilization constituted itself by temporarily putting aside earlier disagreements in favor of an (apparent) cohesion. We need to understand here how that cohesion was formed—how faculty interests at the GF became one with the administration's interests and the interests of some students, and, further, the catalytic role of specific actors, particularly the intellectual class that exercised a great deal of authority within the domain of the GF (the domain where it mattered most) and beyond, since the GF was commonly, or at least ideologically, positioned as the flagship of the School. The key mechanism I will use here is the level of authoritative overlap among the members of the counter-mobilization, the level of ventriloquism between and among them. Since the defense of Europe emerges relatively early in the life of the counter-mobilization in its rejection of the Proposal, we need to see how its premises stayed alive. When in one statement Dean Friedlander welcomes incoming students "to embrace the heterodox and foster the unfashionable," and in another applauds the European "market niche" of the School, she makes Europe the unspoken first term to authorize all (nonexisting) heterodoxies.[25] The GF's rejection of the Proposal seems to indicate that the unfashionable belongs only to a particular conception of Europe, and, as we shall see, it is a Europe supposedly devoid of histories of slavery and empire. Whose cultural memory, whose knowledge claims thread the institutional memory of the School in the face of the transience of people of color as knowledge producers? What broad agenda for economic justice might unhinge the moorings of the flagship? It would be difficult, indeed, to understand the Mobilization outside of the political struggle over knowledge claims and knowledge frameworks that occurred at the School.

In what follows, I first establish the ways in which "diversity" discourses built cohesion around various kinds of inequity. Because the Mobilization needs to be understood on its terms, as well as in relation to the counter-mobilization, I weave its formation into the gestures of refusal and disablement—the counter-mobilization's primary strategies. I allow myself moments for pause and reflection as I tell the story, and I end by examining the paradoxical ways in which GSFT both engaged and disengaged the major preoccupations of the Mobilization. And, not paradoxically, I begin again in one of the spaces that the Mobilization traveled —the New University in Exile[26]—in order to turn the soil for a new vision. Ending is the stuff of which beginnings are made.

The Manufacture of Cohesion:
"Diversity" as the Counting of Bodies of Color

Institutional claims made within "diversity" discourses become the claims within which people of color are understood. They represent people of color. But it is their centrality that helps us to understand the force of contestation and the reason why any challenge to them runs the risk of being discounted and silenced. Discourses, which on the surface appear benign, become quite aggressive in the context of an ideological struggle to transform the relations of representation, for the institution would want its definitions to stand as the only legitimate claims relating to the subjects of whom diversity is ostensibly about.

For my purposes here, I will conjoin several different but dependent documents (some of which are individual works, and others are in sets), and that, from the inception of the UDI in the 1990s, addressed the following goals: "To present multicultural perspectives to the university community and to reach out to the diverse communities of New York City for their participation." The first item is a document that contains census data from the Office of the Provost assembled for each of the divisions, which are also aggregated across the university. These data graph the School's hiring through the racialized categories of African American, Latino, Asian American, and Native American (a category in which Native Americans range from 0 to 1). These groupings are collected and placed into boxes as "minority totals." Women are collected and placed into another category without racial identification. There is no category bearing the label "white," nor are any white ethnic identifications assigned.[27]

The second item includes two documents—"Status Report on the Diversity Initiative" and "Affirmative Action Concept Paper"—that characterized the project of "diversity" as a series of phases. The third item includes two course handbooks, "A Handbook for Students of Color and Students Interested in Race, Ethnicity and Identity at the Graduate Faculty" and "Multiculturalism, Pluralism and Diversity and the New School: A Guide to Diverse Course Offerings," which were produced for the 1995–1996 academic year and for the fall 1996 term, respectively. Since these handbooks were produced under the auspices of the UDI, they automatically became the president's point of reference to applaud the existence of "more than 150 courses" that "explore race, gender and various cultures."[28] Except at Lang, neither the School nor the GF had engaged in a collective examination of curriculum under those rubrics. Thus, in the absence of such intellectual intentionality, we can understand these handbooks as rubrics that manufacture consent and coherence. In their attempt to do so, they can even be misleading. For instance, although there is a claim of a "focus on African-American, Native American and Latino scholarship" in "American U.S. Culture," there is no such name or collection of courses in the School's handbook. Similarly, the "focus on feminist, gay and lesbian scholarship" under "gender" does not appear as a focus in the GSFT course descriptions.

The fourth item is an elegant public relations document designed in muted polytones, thereby engaging the aesthetic of representation to make the point about national "under-represented" groups, the merits of international inclusion, and the desirability of an education in the urban oasis—the New School. The fifth item is a letter authored by the then-president's assistant, Josiah Brown, which appeared in the *Wall Street Journal* under the title "Engaging Diversity: America's Elusive Challenge" and which defines "diversity" as diverse opinions. The sixth item, an article titled "Seminar Series Examines Diversity, Other Issues," appeared in *The New School Observer* and featured the associate provost and director of the UDI amidst one hundred presentations over a two-year period, which attracted ten thousand people. The seventh item includes two presidential memoranda sent to the university community, dated 24 October 1996 and 3 February 1997, respectively.

All of these items were consolidated within a two-year time frame, so they will be positioned as contiguous and therefore related and dependent, since they draw from the same epistemic frame. They coincide with the phase identified in the "Affirmative Action Concept Paper" as the phase of "alignment," in which the institution moves "to effect structural changes so that diversity goals and functioning reality are congruent." According to this document, the alignment phase marked an important transition from the two earlier phases: first, "awareness," the moment when the university "recognize[d] that multiculturalism was in its interests"; and, second, "appreciation . . . where the University undertakes outreach and recruitment efforts to increase new staff and clients and educational activities that promote diversity."[29]

Neither the timing of these documents nor the rate of their production is incidental. When brought together, they can be seen as a gesture of consolidation and, as such, they enable us to understand how they perform ideologically—the role they play in the manufacture of cohesion. Their proximity enables them to produce an impression of *more* "diversity," *more* radicalism, than actually exists at the School. Thus, they constitute the ideological work of representing representation. Let me illustrate what I mean. On the elegant public relations document, which announces the UDI, there is a prominently displayed advertisement for the Diamond postdoctoral fellowship, a project to bring "young" scholars of color for temporary periods to the GF. In light of its prominence, it is surprising to learn that one fellowship recipient found its infrastructure to be almost nonexistent and more of a general "toss-them-in-and-see-if-they-sink-or-swim approach, a kind of neglect." From this participant's experience, Diamond fellows were used as "bodies for the color count, resources for use without cultivation."[30]

Superimposed on the face of the envelope of this same public relations document is a photograph of someone who appears to be Lani Guinier in a striking expository pose. Below the photo the caption reads, "Opportunities to work and study where W. E. B. Du Bois taught one of the first University courses on Black Culture and Race, and where the Mexican muralist José Clemente Orozco painted one of his first three fresco cycles completed in the U.S." Since Du Bois taught in the 1920s and Orozco completed his work a decade later, one might think that this contemporary invocation was a way of indicating that the School had surpassed its earlier avant-garde practice. It is surprising to learn, then, that in 1995, the same year in which the brochure was produced, there were 14 African American faculty members out of a total faculty of 147; and to learn that at the GF, where Du Bois taught, only one African American faculty had been tenured. One would not know from the current university data whether there are Mexicans or Chicanos at the School, since they are all under the category "Latino," of whom there were eight serving as faculty members and none holding managerial positions. One might then be curious to know what Orozco encountered while at the School and what he might have said to Stephanie Morgan, "a Mexican-American, a woman, a feminist, and a humanist" who, in 1996, addressed the School's moral emergency in these terms: "The central issue in all of this is honesty . . . that which is truthful, trustworthy, sincere or genuine. There is by definition no honesty, no trust, no sincerity when rhetoric does not match reality . . . I have now decided to give my money to another University, one which is perhaps more honest about the disparity between progressive ideals and their true interest in achieving those ideals."[31] Morgan had intended to pursue advanced degree work at the School.

Resting inside the envelope of the polytoned brochure are separate announcements and items about FIND, including: a photograph of Randall Robinson—director of TransAfrica and author of *The Debt*—receiving an honorary doctorate (presumably from the School); information on the Distinguished Visitors' Program; and photographs of Jayne Cortez of the Black Arts Movement and bell hooks, feminist teacher and writer. While many of the photographs capture the appearance of speech, we know nothing of what these visitors said, or how their speech might have influenced the university community. And since one of our main concerns is the right to truth, speech, and power, we should be curious to know how Robinson would have been received if, as a permanent faculty member, he had analyzed the debt owed African Americans in relation to the level of exploitation of security guards and clerical workers at the School. Would he have encountered the kind of illocutionary disablement directed against the Mobilization? Think how the School might have responded to bell hooks's understanding of both the threat and revolutionary possibilities of liberatory speech, as she stood in solidarity with END on 17 December 1996, the day the group Faculty of Color declared a state of emergency. What would have been the School's response to her words, had hooks not been merely a part of the Visitor program:

> When we dare to speak in a liberatory voice, we threaten even those who may initially claim to want our words. In the act of overcoming our fear of speech, of being seen as threatening, we engage in the process of learning to undo domination. When we end our silence, when we speak in a liberated voice, our words connect us with anyone anywhere, who lives in silence . . . This is an important historical moment. We are both speaking of our own volition, and out of our commitment to justice, to the revolutionary struggle to end domination.[32]

Why might hooks's words have posed a threat to "diversity" discourses? What definitions of "diversity" are deployed? What do these discourses do? And how are the structures they enable authorized to act? In addition to the documents listed above, we shall examine the President's memoranda, for together they codify particular definitions of "diversity," producing the very boundaries around which power resides. Here is the president's review of the School's accomplishments:

> The University began a diversity initiative in January 1990 intended to make *our* community more diverse and *comfortable* with diversity. Over time, the initiative broadened to involve recruitment of faculty, staff, students, Trustees, and Visiting Committee members of color, a curriculum which include[d] more than 150 courses on race, class, gender and *non-Western* countries, a richly textured co-curricular program *celebrating non-Western traditions,* concern for other forms of diversity including sexual orientation, protection against discriminatory harassment and active encouragement for *the expression of many points of view. Our* University pursued diversity in the belief that students educated in a multicultural environment would be better prepared for a world in which almost everything is internationalized . . . Our approach to diversity *values the contributions* that students and

faculty from other countries bring to *our* university. Students and faculty from India and Africa, from Asia and Latin America *enrich* the artistic and intellectual life of *our* University immeasurably. We also recognize the *contributions* that faculty, staff, and students of color, who are United States citizens, make to the quality and character of the University. And we should acknowledge a *special obligation* to over-come the effects of past discrimination by crafting a vigorous Affirma-tive Action program within our larger diversity initiative. Thus, our initiative pursues a balanced course, *welcoming* international students and faculty, while making an *extra effort* to meet the needs of under-represented groups in the United States. [emphasis added][33]

Much like its surrounding documents, this memorandum defines "diver-sity" as a plurality of perspectives. It provides a link to another part of the document in which the president anchors diversity in "the free exchange of ideas" and "the freedom of artistic expression." And it is simulta-neously a recognition of the university's "interests," that important first step in the phased-in approach to diversity. We can understand these interests as linked to the manufacture of a particular multicultural iden-tity for marketing in an urban environment, in an internationalized world. This is the context in which we can situate the aggregation of course booklets that advertise "multiculturalism, pluralism and diver-sity," which, when assembled, make it *appear* that there is more diversity and radicalism than is actually the case.

In his repeated use of the self-referential "our" and the privileging of the "West" as in "*non*-Western," which we shall take to mean "people of color," the president simultaneously produces a discourse on what *we* are doing for *them*. "*We*" who belong have to be made more "diverse" and "comfortable." "*We* recruit," "outreach," "welcome," "celebrate," "in-clude," "support," and "aid" *them*, the multicultural and the interna-tional. *They* anchor "the richly textured co-curricular programs." *They* make "contributions." Once welcomed, *they* can "enrich" us with "*non*-European traditions."

As these categories stand, they bleed into those in the "Affirmative Action Concept Paper." *They* become "projections," "target numbers," "role models," "critical incident[s] of importance to the community," "recruited in the interest of the organization and its constituents," and the result of "accelerated inclusion." *They* bring "originality," enable the institution in its "alignment"; provide evidence of "tangible progress"; and demonstrate the need to "implement" programs or otherwise affirm "the good record of Affirmative Action." Their presence confirms that the School is a "good place" for them. And perhaps most important in the language of capital, they are "the value-added dimension in salary negotiations." Ultimately, "diversity" is an additive to "*our* community," which is always already the first and privileged term, but it is an additive while still remaining *non*-Western, *non*-European, marginal, and subordinate to the project—that is, positioned with no agency, since *we* "welcome," celebrate, include, support, and "aid" them. These are stubborn hierarchies of belonging in the cultural relativist syntax of "us" and "them"; they are hierarchies of alienation, which when internalized can become deadly fossils—the disqualifying metaphors noted by Morrison.

There are no commensurate discursive structures that spectacularize or rank whiteness in the way in which people of color are ranked and spectacularized. Further, in the absence of any white ethnic differentiation, whiteness becomes homogenized. Although apparently absent, it nonetheless orders the hierarchy, establishing itself while disappearing at the same time. It would seem that white managerial masculinity travels everywhere, with the ability to normativize itself in its apparently silent movement as lawful benefactor in "*our* community." White women are placed within the boundaries of affirmative action as well, but there is a significant class disparity between managerial femininity and the disproportionate numbers of women who work as adjunct and part-time faculty. Black people and people of color always already exist or are to be found within the university—in the FIND program; the Diamond postdoctoral fellowships; the Diamond graduate fellows programs; visiting appointments; adjunct vitae reserves, which also house the majority of white women; distinguished visitors' programs; curriculum development grants; MAP (Multicultural Awareness Projects; university scholars awards (partial tuition waivers for incoming black and Latino students); and university faculty fellows seminars—as well as within *non*-Western traditions; *non*-European parts of the world; and disproportionately, unequally, within service, this time over-represented as security guards, food-service workers, and clerical staff. In practice, the "special obligation . . . to under-represented groups in the United States" resulted in a "special obligation" to anchor serviceability, since it is there, and not in the faculty and student body, that people of color predominate. "The balanced course between welcoming international students" and the "extra effort to meet the needs of under-represented groups in the U.S." resulted in a "fourteen percent increase in international students from *non*-European parts of the world," in stark contrast to a mere "two percent growth in the student of color (U.S.) population." Indeed, the juxtaposition between a "good record" and its effects marks the kinds of inequities that are produced, the specific ways in which "diversity" overcounts while it subordinates.

Overall, the School's definitions of "diversity" do not emanate from a historical reading of racialization—the historical collective aspects of debt to which black people and people of color are entitled, as Randall Robinson frames it. Rather, they attenuate history into notions of individual rehabilitation and individual remuneration. The institution would want to attempt such a revision of history in the absence of any discourse about the mythologies of race and the creation of racism, hence the substitution of "diversity," racially preferring race-neutrality, meaning presumably that white people can never acknowledge the privilege they derive from the hierarchies of race; people of color and black people can never talk about racism; and progressive coalitions of white people and people of color could never undertake fruitful discussions about the ways in which privilege and disinheritance mutually imbricate each other. These discourses establish, in effect, a system of segregation that absents white men in power, even while they rule. While racialization operates on white bodies differently, these bodies are nonetheless being conscripted to perform an important ideological function. White women's bodies are disproportionately found in part-time and adjunct teaching positions in these discourses; and within the larger institutional practice they are expected to maintain white race loyalty, even while being subordinated to white men (both managers and faculty) in status and decision-making power. It is for these reasons that in working to demystify institutional practices of domination, the Mobilization simultaneously engaged the demystification of whiteness, constituting itself, as well, through coalition with progressive white constituencies that refused the ideological mandate of race loyalty.

Discourses of subordination produce practices of subordination and such practices are refracted in discursive arrangements. The Mobilization showed them to be differential yet complementary, for different populations bore the brunt of "diversity" in different ways: in the wages and benefits for security guards; in the gendered economy of the School; in the organization of curriculum; and in the organization of financial aid. But perhaps more important, these practices are significant for the kinds of cultures of inequities that are legitimized and, in Langton's and Morrison's terms, the cultures of silencing that are produced. Systems of classification, such as those of "diversity," enact a form of symbolic violence. To use Stanley Fish's words, "It is not only that the class you take determines what class you get into. It is that in classes we *learn* to class, that is, learn to draw lines, establish boundaries, set up hierarchies. Classification . . . forcefully excludes what it does not embrace."[34] But there are also different kinds of violence. In addition to the violence of excessive categorization and disciplining, there is the violence of the appropriation of one's labor; the violence of imposed silence; the violence of being forced to struggle for the right to have a right; the violence of simultaneous erasure and overexposure; the violence of not being able to register one's own claims about the world; and, ultimately, the violence of being required to behave as if democracy and reasonableness truly existed, when in truth they do not.

The Mobilization determined that security guards, 90 percent of whom were black and Latino men, were exploited by the School at a rate of 95.6 percent. Put differently, the subcontractor made 96 cents for every dollar a security guard earned. That rate was derived by taking the hourly wage that the School paid the subcontractor ($11.25 per hour) and then subtracting out the average hourly rate that guards received ($5.75 per hour). The difference paid to the subcontractor amounted to $5.50 for every hour worked by the guards. When the subcontractor's "pay" was divided by that of the security guards, the rate of exploitation was exposed in the percentage above. Thus the rate of exploitation pertains to the disproportionate value generated from the guards' labor. Exploitation means that they are producing more value for the subcontractor than for themselves in a situation in which neither the School nor the subcontractor assumed the cost of providing them with health benefits, sick leave, and the like. Similar calculations can be done for part-time and adjunct faculty (with the School itself the contractor, so to speak) by estimating the revenue that each faculty member generates through the average number of students enrolled in each course, then subtracting the wages that she or he receives. Given the fact that part-time and adjunct faculty did 88 percent of all teaching duties, the rate of exploitation would be substantial.

Full-time faculty were not immune to these patterns, particularly full-time female faculty. In the course of a lawsuit that GF faculty member Adamantia Pollis brought against the School in 1993, it was revealed that "for at least two decades the University systematically paid female professors substantially lower salaries than male professors." The court ruled that the university "*knew* that it was violating Title 7 of the Equal Pay Act."[35]

Students on financial aid often expressed their own alienation as non-paying students. Many reported on the practice of being singled out and blamed for being on financial aid, a situation not mentioned in the president's memorandum. There, the picture seemed rosy: "fifty-six percent of University Scholars received awards totaling $1.7m." When the Mobilization did the calculations for a six-year period, however, it meant that each student would have received on average a total of $2,211 toward graduate school tuition and fees that actually cost upward of $9,000. For a woman of color at the GF, it would have meant receiving assistance for approximately two and a half credits of coursework.

Taken together, all of these practices need not say "White Men for Managers and Permanent Thinkers Only," "White Women for Part-time and Adjuncts Only," "Bodies of People of Color for Service Only," as in Langton's blatant utterances of South African apartheid. At times, the assault that expresses the will to colonize in such stark terms can simultaneously make ideological room for notions of "free speech," "freedom of expression," and even appeals to "civility," as President Fanton did. Practicing only the former would simply be too crude to sustain itself in a liberal institution, even with the local and national assistance of neoconservatism. This is not to say, however, that it can never be the case, for there is never an absence of contradiction in this symbolic universe, which governs the will to power. At certain moments, it is far more effective ideologically to do precisely what the administration did—that is, to publicly uphold community visions of "free speech" and "civility," while in practice obstructing legitimate dissent; or to extend a "welcome" as it pursued a set of de facto revolving-door policies with regard to faculty of color, which guaranteed that "whites only" would be the permanent guardians of knowledge and that men and women of color would be assigned the permanent work of service. At other moments, the work of the blatant assault was entrusted to the counter-mobilization and, as we shall see later, it was a task it assumed with a great deal of vigor.

It is now time to go back in order to move forward, to consider the work of the Mobilization in the terms we outlined earlier: its specific work undertaken during 1996–1997, which exposed the moral emergency the School had been experiencing, but which was defined as "diversity"; the particular self-consciousness that was formed in that practice; the specific analyses of the complex dynamics of institutional power structures, including analyses of political interests embedded in knowledge claims, that we brought to bear on the conditions of our lives. What *means* were at our disposal to engage this work? In what I have presented thus far, I have revealed what our work of demystification uncovered, what it meant to travel within the interstices of power and to peel away the deposits that coagulated along the way. In light of the extensive work of the Mobilization, I shall only examine here the particular watersheds that marked the collectivization of vision.

Here I conceive of *will, means, opportunity,* and *standing* as interactive rather than as discrete political processes, operating at both individual and collective levels simultaneously. *Will* can be taken to mean determination, resolve, and agency, but it does not necessarily have an inherently radical character, since there exists not only a will to radical political struggle but also a will to domination or to segregation (in the words of Howard Thurman). Both have to do with the interior and the exterior. *Means* pertain to the set of strategies and resources that are utilized to produce an intended outcome. *Opportunity* has to do with the moment of possibility, which often has to be provoked. In situations where neither means nor opportunity exists, *will* can act as an instigator to produce them both. Like opportunity, *standing* appears to be external, rendered only from the outside, but it also carries an interior quality that is akin to the quality of self-possession. One's standing in one's own eyes, particularly in the context of domination, is the quality that propels *will*, and in this sense they both pertain to a process of interior decolonization. They interact through a set of delicate yet persistent negotiations between one's interior and exterior. And while these processes are important for both the individual and the collective, not all members of a collective translate the process of coming to consciousness in the same way, even as they occupy a similar location. It is these questions that I address in the following sections.

Building Ground: Planning the END to Domination

The earliest phases of the work of the Mobilization, which began in spring 1996, involved learning the lines of institutional power. There were a number of positions of authority, which made it appear that power was diffuse, but while authority was diffuse, power and decision-making remained centralized. Approaching the deans and various "diversity" committees was the focus of the early organizational activities of the students. As they worked to understand the workings of "diversity," they saw that those very committees had no power to make crucial decisions. In the absence of student representation, one of their first jobs was to secure their presence, to establish some measure of standing. In coalition with the faculty of color at Lang, the students won "permission" to attend their first "diversity" meeting on 9 May 1996. During this meeting, they were asked to explain their presence and their purpose, which they stated in these terms: "We are bringing the issue of the retention of Professor Alexander, as well as greater issues of recruitment and retention of faculty of color, before the Committee," which exists "to generate ideas on the implementation of the University's Affirmative Action policy and plans, and to *recommend* strategies that would improve the recruitment of faculty, students and staff." We feel, they said, that "such improved strategies are vital . . . at this time."[36]

Using as resources their newly culled knowledge and the power of experience, they dramatized the School's revolving-door policy for faculty of color, which made a mockery of faculty retention. Students were simply not being taught the courses they had been promised. They addressed the structure of FIND and the widespread presumptions that FIND compromised quality and posed a threat to "regular faculty positions," and hence the overall departmental reluctance to utilize it. Voicing the suspicion that racism and sexism had attached themselves to bad faith on the part of the administration, they questioned the timing of opening a faculty line in fall 1997 (after my impending departure) to engage the very analytical issues I had been hired to teach. For students, it conveyed the message that there could be "only one female feminist Professor of Color at the Graduate Faculty at one time." They acknowledged the efforts of the committee in creating "diversity" and concluded by demanding an open "written" process for faculty searches. In order to dramatize the practice of overcounting, they demanded an investigation into the methodological strategies used to assemble the School's population and the disbursements under FIND, and they asked for assurance from the president that FIND would not create a two-tier system or in effect jeopardize lines, which had been authorized to departments under "other" fiscal arrangements. Outrage and betrayal provoked them to demand accountability both of the committee and of the university's administration in general.

Underlying it all was deep-seated concern about the culture of inequity and its accompanying ideologies: the absence of democratic, participatory processes of decision-making for students within the very committees that were understood to have authority, and the exclusion of part-time and adjunct faculty. Although the imminent termination of my contract opened an opportunity for the gathering of a collective will, students had to prepare their own soil. They had to become determined agents on their own behalf, which initially required them to speak from a place of authority garnered from the fruits of their own labor, from their own yearning for justice. The administration's practices provided ample evidence: short-term contracts were part of an ongoing practice for faculty of color and the exclusion of faculty was also related to their own. As one white student aptly put it on the night of 17 December 1996: "If this place is not a place for faculty of color, it cannot be a place for me. And I was led to believe it could be a place for me."[37] Building ground. Dangerous conclusions. Politicizing moment.

Holding those with power accountable for their actions is an important and necessary dimension of political work.[38] Those with authority who have no power also need to be held accountable, for even without power they occupy a critical role in the power hierarchy, since they guard the gates of, and for, those designated with official power. In their participation in "diversity" committees, students were attempting to expand the boundaries of participation, having a voice and having it count, but they were also holding administrators accountable for the existing inequities. But one of the truths of power is its habitual distaste for accountability, a distaste it exhibits through deflection and distortion. In the early days of grounding, mistrust and betrayal fueled students' demands for accountability since they lived the discomforting truth that truth was often masked. By placing accountability for FIND with the administration (notably with the president) even as faculty ignored it (in 1996, five FIND appointments were returned unfilled), students were opening an opportunity for solidarity with faculty, particularly faculty at the GF from which the bulk of the refusals to utilize FIND had originated.

The Mobilization was never able to ascertain whether FIND lines actually usurped (imaginary) authorized lines. Still, it need not necessarily have been the case that departmental interests had to collide with the interests of FIND, and they would not have collided had departments understood FIND to be in sync with their "regular" positions. Rather, it collided because of a hierarchy of knowledge claims that pitted FIND (read embodied knowledge through affirmative action) against quality. As the Mobilization argued later in its letter of 2 February 1997, "many departments simply [did] not see the intellectual pursuits of people of color as central to what they [did]." At that early point, however, the irony stood as one of the unanticipated consequences of FIND. We had hoped perhaps that in holding the president and the administration accountable, a positive political will around faculty interests would have prevailed to advance a position that would uphold both FIND *and* the promised "regular" faculty lines. Within a year of the Mobilization's work, however, faculty interests at the GF coalesced in an entirely opposite direction, positioning the GF at the center of the counter-mobilization.

By summer 1996 it had become clear to the administration that student questions were neither idiosyncratic nor individual; they could no longer continue to ignore student demands for accountability and deflect them through doublespeak by calling my hiring "an individual personnel issue," or by attempting to demonize me, a strategy that students refused. In the heat of New York's summer, and with the fictive advantage of a campus lull, administrators were forced to call a series of meetings to discuss FIND, faculty retention, and my hiring, so as to set the record straight—the hope perhaps being once and for all. By this time students had become adept at unravelling the School's doublespeak—a strategy that rested at the heart of the job of demystification and also at the heart of the administration's own vulnerability. It is this vulnerability that enabled us to understand why there was a concerted attempt to cover the rupture—to redefine, as we saw earlier, "diversity" as diverse opinions; to produce more of it in order to establish, in the president's words, the School's "good record of Affirmative Action." Student presence on campus made it possible to keep abreast of the developments in the Proposal, the potential success of which they were largely skeptical. Yet, the Lang students understood early the strategic importance of a dual organizing strategy and of building a coalition with GF students more widely, since a few GF students had formed a bridge with what would blossom into the student coalition, END. Such reciprocal organizing would also build, legitimize, and enhance the standing of the nascent Mobilization, which at that point was keenly aware of the pitfalls of representation. It could not speak for GF students, who came later to articulate their own conditions in their own terms.

In fall 1996 the autonomous student organizing had become increasingly visible, and it aimed ultimately to consolidate student interests and formulate independent channels of dissent in light of ineffectual bureaucratic channels of redress. As END later stated: "The Mobilization . . . exists precisely because the structures that have been established by the University to address persistent racism, (hetero)sexism, and class exploitation do not work. We know, because we have attempted to work within these structures."[39] The rejection of the Proposal within the GF in September 1996 fueled the organization of a large public meeting on 6 November 1996. Coming as it did on the heels of two solid months of what we can euphemistically call "heightened discursive production" on the part of the administration, it gave ample evidence that the strategies employed thus far were taking root. By this time empty walls, elevators, notice boards designated for the School's official business, and even sidewalks all conspired to make public that which had to be made public. It was one of the ways to build support in a context of alienation, in the absence of public cultures of dissent. As the students laid the ground for an autonomous organization, they simultaneously were laying the ground for building conceptual communities (to use a term developed by Yvonne Yarbro-Bejarano). As 1996 came to a close, END emerged as one of the primary mechanisms working to dismantle domination, including the dominance of European knowledge frameworks.

Rethink Europe? Not Here! Elsewhere!

END's suspicions regarding the slim chances for the success of the Proposal were, unfortunately, not unfounded. Jointly authored by a group of faculty from Lang and the GF (including myself) the Proposal's aim was to recruit a small group of scholars of color, whose intellectual work engaged Europe by placing it in a visibly global context as opposed to the isolationist perspective that reinforces the idea that everything pertaining to Europe was always already contained within it. Noting the GF's lapses in hiring and retaining faculty of color in permanent positions, the Proposal sought to launch an intellectual project that would simultaneously facilitate the hiring of scholars of color. Its dual purpose was indicated in its suggestion "that the University recruit scholars of color with expertise in the trans-Atlantic and its diasporas."[40]

The Proposal further called on a vigorous, interdisciplinary literature to examine the different kinds of power relations responsible for the transnational distribution of people, systems of governance, cultural forms, and intellectual approaches. The aim was to understand the re-inscription of Europe—not its disappearance—into multiple transnational sites with its technologies and power. No intellectual feats could be performed to erase histories of colonialism and empire.

The Proposal acknowledged that "European studies [had] always been the strong point of the Graduate Faculty," and it explained its intent to "enrich and engage these strengths by adding another set of intellectual resources" such that "traditionally held notions of Europe and the West [could] be further engaged." Intellectual projects at the GF had in fact intervened in reformulations of democratic theory and practice and questions of ethnic resurgence in the context of nationalism, but these interventions absented the still-intransigent legacies of colonialism and racism. Here was a moment for fruitful intellectual collaboration that might have reformulated democratic theory on different terms. For instance, how might national sovereignty and the formation of new ethnic alignments be understood in a time of cultural, political, and economic recolonization of the globe by transnational flows of capital, information, technologies, art, labor, and identities? How does recolonization intersect with interests that promote free-market democracy? How might European democracy be rethought in terms of these newly revised projects of empire-building? To date, there had been no theoretical room within the heterodoxies of Europe at the GF to position black and migrant Europe and its histories of colonization, displacement, and exile, its "ethnic resurgence." The Proposal presented an opportunity to link the rise of fascism to colonialism and racism. But, as stated earlier, the histories of anti-fascist theorizing had long since been folded into the fiscal strictures of downsizing. Predictably, the resulting antagonisms wove themselves into a vocabulary of sacrifice pitting the GF's overall intellectual project against the intent of the Proposal (read FIND), as expressed in these terms: "It is completely unrealistic to think that such an ambitious program . . . will not have the most negative consequences in funding positions that had been promised and which are essential for the integrity of existing programs . . . What precisely are the priorities for cuts, and for reneging on firm promises that already have been made? And what is to be sacrificed to institute your proposal?"[41] Here we find ample evidence of fiscal conservatism acting in staunch defense of curricular conservatism.

Both the manner and character of the Proposal's rejection are important for our considerations. The powerful Executive and Budget Committee, to whom the Proposal was submitted, never provided a formal response. Instead, the chair of the department of Philosophy, Richard Bernstein, assumed the responsibility of speaking "as a citizen of the GF community . . . passionately interested in [its] intellectual future." He entirely ignored me and the faculty at Lang who had been involved in the crafting of the Proposal, choosing instead to address his objections to

Rayna Rapp, chair of GSFT (with copies to other GF faculty) as if she were its singular author. The tone of gendered and racial scolding is quite palpable: "It was poor judgment," he said, "to submit this document to President Fanton before it was discussed . . . It violates a basic courtesy that you owe to your colleagues." And, he added, "I hope you have the generosity to realize that I am not speaking from the perspective of the Philosophy Department." Poor judgment and lack of courtesy then finally combined with irresponsibility: "The failure to address squarely the financial and structural consequences of this proposal is irresponsible on your part." In positioning himself as a citizen of the GF, one passionate about its future and responsible enough to share the concern about "diversifying" while responsibly rejecting a document that lacked "the substantive content of an important intellectual project," Richard Bernstein conveyed another message, a disciplining message: "Have you lost your mind to align yourself with this Proposal"? Recalling that part of the intent of "diversity" discourses is to keep everyone in an already assigned racialized place, within this gesture of rejection also resides a gesture of keeping women in their place, and, in the context of a cross-racial grouping, an attempt to keep white women in their place as well.

To Richard Bernstein, the Proposal simply had no merit. Its trans-Atlantic center was "provincial and narrow." There was "substantive confusion running throughout . . . constant slippage from "diversity" to "scholars of color," "without any critical reflection." And in what lay at the core of his objection—its alignment with the thrust of the School's overall approach to "diversity" as diverse opinions—he argued, "by the implicit criteria of this document, a department such as . . . Philosophy . . . which consists of a Russian, an Israeli, a Hungarian, Germans, Americans and a regular Algerian-born French visitor (referring to Jacques Derrida) with radically different intellectual backgrounds and life experiences, is not really diverse." The Proposal was "not really about diversity, but rather about how to get more persons with the 'right' skin color on *our* faculty." And, with the parting hand of Bakke, he found the Proposal discriminatory, since "white" persons, whose research interests were consonant with the interests of the Proposal, would have been excluded "from serious consideration." In the end, his "most generous reaction" was that the Proposal was "just pure PC sloganeering and claptrap." In the words of one of its authors who witnessed the faculty's swift (dis)engagement with the idea of rethinking Europe, the Proposal was "collectively murdered" at the GF.

For the moment, I simply want to mark the anxiety that presumes a sinister tension between identity and knowledge. Recall that this chapter's epigraph called attention to this relationship, which the Mobilization positioned as mediated through political struggle. As such, they need not be antagonistic to one another. Within the more general terms of disablement, the refusal to rethink Europe carries additional weight. In much the same way that the president's statement that "Jacqui Alexander will not be the litmus test for diversity at the New School" transferred authority to the deans in the sense of "do not hire Jacqui Alexander," the refusal to rethink Europe constituted authoritative action: "Not here! Elsewhere!" Thereafter, the GF began an official assertion of itself as an institution for European studies. Dean Friedlander was now authorized to take a public stance invoking a proud defense of the GF's "market niche" for European studies and to use the second-year classroom of GSFT as an arena to subordinate the intellectual imperatives involved in rethinking Europe. This new posturing stood in contradiction to the dean's own statements to incoming students of color in fall 1996, where she positioned the GF as committed to their interests in studying the effects of race, class, and gender in the social and political sciences. Possessed with additional authority, the dean urged students who were "dissatisfied" with their education to go "elsewhere,"[42] a position that provoked a deep sense of betrayal. As a graduate student of philosophy noted, "We were recruited under the assumption that our theoretical interests would be welcomed and engaged."[43] And, as further surmised by the student co-chair of the GSFT Subcommittee on Curriculum, "I guess we might conclude that we should have never come here, that we shouldn't have imagined we belonged here in the first place."[44] Thus the newly purported "market niche" for self-contained European studies in the face of "diversity" held its own dire contradictions.

When things suffer premature death, they never concede to being put to rest. And so it was that the analytical issues that framed rethinking Europe began to travel within GSFT, circulating with the internal curricular and analytic conundrums that it, too, had begun to experience. Reading the pulse of the moment, the Lang faculty with a long-standing critical attention to cultural studies decided to part company with their colleagues at the GF who jettisoned the opportunity to rethink Europe, deciding instead to advance a proposal that centered the theoretical work of race, gender, and transnationalization within the entire project of cultural studies. Still, the rejection of the Proposal emboldened the will to struggle. A coalition in formation among students, clerical staff, and faculty with full-time, part-time, or adjunct status became a palpable manifestation of that quickening. At the culmination of almost a year of work in 1996, we shifted into a combined politic of celebration, confrontation, and stock-taking, the starting point of which was the declaration of a state of emergency on the part of faculty of color.

A Movement on Many Fronts:
The Faculty of Color Declare a State of Emergency

At dawn on Tuesday, 17 December 1996, members of END along with other student groups put the finishing touches on placards and posters: "If you are sick of the New School's hollow commitment to diversity, MOBILIZE." They drew maps outlining the geographies of power, which they then turned into points of protest. As WBAI aired public service announcements, faculty of color as well as part-time and visiting faculty were making final preparations for their report. Letters of support poured in from poets and writers, public intellectuals, and people of conscience in the academy, as well as from organizations such as the Latino Workers Organization and the National Labor Committee, urging the School to respect and honor the rights of workers; to take advantage of the opportunity for self-critique and transformation; and to be accountable to different publics who believed in the School's progressive legacy. By evening, the Wolff Conference Room of the GF was packed. Faculty of color reported on the state of emergency at the School, while students read letters of solidarity that described similar conditions at other universities—thus linking the Moblilization to similar struggles elsewhere. We were being situated within a larger critical community— carrying part of the "force of history with us," as James Baldwin put it—

thereby creating the sense that we had not arrived at the School by ourselves, but that we were indeed living the different "histories that walked and lived with us." All the means at our disposal, both internal and external, were brought to bear on that day of declaration, a moment of confrontation and profound hope. The struggle that day arose from the conviction that dignity is rooted in self-accountability. Knowing this, we could celebrate our collective will to dissent—a move from silence to voice in the face of rejection. And self-accountability also meant that we were obliged to keep counsel with our inner selves, to come to the point of speaking the unspeakable.

How does it feel to "see oneself preserved in the amber of disqualifying metaphors"? To be made both hypervisible and invisible at the same time? One of the points of organizing was to underscore the dangers of preservation and the costs of complicity. For almost a year, I had experienced that odd kind of alienation that results from being positioned as onlooker in the usurpation of my own identity. For almost a year, rumor and gossip about me patrolled the corridors and elevators of various parts of the School, arresting all usual norms of conduct. Deans, both at Lang and the GF, had drawn students into the rumor mill, giving them information from my curriculum vita in order that they might construct a makeshift structure for my evaluation. The paradox was that they were being drawn into the rumor mill while being placed outside the structures of decision-making. It was only four days before the School's Women and Philosophy Conference that, in a conversation in the elevator, I was asked to participate (with a letter slid under my office door, perhaps at that same moment). In the wake of the conference, the dean of the GF assured the GSFT students in her class that I had been invited at the outset, along with Patricia Williams. I was one of two black women out of a faculty body of sixty at the GF, occupying the contradictory gap between the management of "diversity" and its effects: two black women being called on to "diversify" an entire division. Meetings in GSFT began drawing faculty whom I had never seen at the numerous program meetings that I had attended two years prior, meetings in which I would be spoken about in the third person, as if I were absent. I would listen to endless repetitions about the forward thinking that prompted my hire. I lived all of the discomfort of this tight space as I did the foundational labor for GSFT and the identity work for the School. I came to realize, however, that the same tight space carried the greatest potential for dissent, paradoxically assuming at the same time the greatest risk of being policed. Rumored as being "behind the students," I felt no longer able to appear to be complicit in speechlessness, one of the major requirements of preservation. Nor could I choose complicity in conceding the collective will to struggle. Preservation was a demand to concede that will and renege on the promise I had made to myself about self-possession, not self-absorption, or self-aggrandizement, but self-possession. Taking ownership of myself. All of these things combined figured in my decision to speak publicly on 17 December 1996, that Day of Struggle and Celebration.

And yet, risk and responsibility came to reside together at these very crossroads of disclosure. Things would never be the same again. The night of 17 December was perhaps the last time we secured a building for an event without general harassment or the demand for multiple signatures, countersignatures, and proven departmental sponsorship. We felt a collective power of having worked, of having organized, of creating a space that affirmed that our lives mattered, of having represented ourselves to ourselves: a mobile space for the aesthetic, the poetic, the analytic, the critic, the prophetic to live all at the same time. All relations in the same dreaming. Coming into our own.

Crafting the Vision: "Diversity," Democracy, and Economic Justice—Linking the Issues, Making Community

The political work of constituency-building that brought 1996 to a close and inaugurated 1997 anchored the letter-writing strategy of 2 February and a large forum on 18 February, which linked all seven divisions of the School, (students who were isolated from one another but who shared similar experiences of exclusion and inequity) as well as security guards and additional clerical workers. Multiple constituencies provided the leverage we needed to demand negotiations with the administration. In all, the period from February to May of 1997 compressed and intensified the activity of the Mobilization. Strongly attached to the myth of time, we worked overtime teaching, organizing, going hungry, negotiating, confronting, living, and dreaming, aware that as the resistance of the central administration crystallized, the counter-mobilization at the GF was active and on alert.

The purpose of the letter of 2 February 1997 was twofold: to focus our critique on, and our set of demands of, central administration, and, with wide distribution, to leave the effects of the emergency and the possibilities for transformation in everyone's hands. But the latter goal would have been infinitely more difficult to achieve without solidifying constituency work—the important political work of building a base—to broaden support for what we had begun, and, frankly, to narrow the possibilities of racial co-optation. To critique white power in a predominantly white, Left-identified institution—to guide the delicate undertaking of implicating structures, as well as people, in the culture of whiteness, while at the same time disentangling a politics of accountability from a politics of blame—required a great deal of vigilance, a great deal of sensitivity, and a great deal of time. As a multiracial grouping we had detached race from its dominant, historic black/white moorings and shifted the racial terms of struggle, but we risked, at the same time, alienating the people who had understood the world in those terms and had engaged political struggle on that basis. Yet we could not move forward without a broadened base of support. After all, whom were "we" representing? And who comprised that "we"?

Constituency-building had illustrated that something quite profound had begun to take hold at the School: a moment of awakening, in the sense that the knowledge about our lived experiences had inspired points of identification. We were approached by food service workers who, like security guards and clerical workers, also felt exploited; by women who had been sexually harassed, but who had not been protected by the School's sexual harassment grievance procedures; by students who were endangered in field placement settings, but whose complaints had been consistently ignored; and by clerical staff who had experienced the use of disciplinary action against them. The Mobilization was being perceived as a safe place to be, and this was possible because people had their own experiences, which were awaiting another moment to become collectivized, to be put into a larger framework and made intelligible, to broaden a space outside of the dominant to express themselves, to create the means through which we could begin to articulate a radical vision—a transformative praxis—a sense of freedom.

Five internal developments distinguished this period from earlier moments. First, it was now possible to define a "we," to reverse the will to objectification and to specify the different social locations from which we made claims about the world. Part-time faculty—often women, mostly white, some of color, lesbians and gay men, many having worked for over a decade with reduced benefits—brought vision and labor to the work of the institution. Yet, their attempts to build genuine community with their full-time colleagues had been blocked. As stated in the letter of 2 February: "All part-time faculty [were] excluded from the venues in which full-time faculty and administrators made decisions." Students—some of color, some gay and lesbian, some of whom were white, and most of whom had very little money—worked two and sometimes three jobs as well as secured loans to make ends meet and pay ever-increasing tuition. Yet, they were consistently being placed at educational risk. Security guards—the majority of whom were black and Latino men—had in many cases served the institution for twenty years and more yet continued to work without a living wage, and without sick leave or health benefits. Scholars of color—women and men, gays and lesbians—taught four or five courses to fill curriculum gaps while still being expected to serve on innumerable committees, thereby frantically overextending themselves. These were the men and women whose work anchored the work of the institution.

Second, the work of demystification brought us face to face with the interstices of power. As we used "race" to understand how power worked, "it became difficult to separate the production of diversity from the internal project of racialization and other hierarchies."[45] Leaving aside what we termed "the laundry list approach to diversity," we employed an intersectional analysis that enabled us to attend to the fact that "race is always gendered, class is always racialized, sexuality is always experienced through race, and so on." We, moreover, were the ones who occupied those intersections.

Third, the shared stories of students, staff, and faculty exposed a "top-down management structure" absent of "a system of committees governed by faculty senates." When whiteness wove itself into such management, the refusals around FIND assumed a more insidious cast: FIND had "become hostage in departmental battles over autonomy with the Administration," but it also enabled "white-dominated departments" to retain their own interests in "maintaining racial homogeneity." Our hopes in spring 1996 that faculty interests, particularly at the GF, would coalesce around the support of FIND had proven to be entirely unfounded.

Fourth, practice made it possible to define a collective vision of self-determination, to "live free of discrimination; to receive equal pay for equal work; a decent job and income; quality health care; quality education; and the right to organize and maintain unions." We placed ourselves within new visions of scholarship that fused "traditions of radical engagement, traditions of decolonization, anti-sexism, anti-racism, gay and lesbian liberation, with transnational feminist critiques."

Fifth, we had created the mechanisms to leverage an interrelated set of demands, each of which also specified the particular mechanisms for redress. We posted them widely, as well as photocopied and distributed them along the streets of New York to anyone who would accept them. We demanded a response from central administration by 11 February, followed by a meeting on 24 February. The demands included the following:

1. That the university . . . take immediate steps to dismantle the practices of institutionalized white supremacy, white hegemony, and white power in its curriculum, hiring practices, and in the New School's general social and intellectual environment.

2. That the university respect the rights of workers . . . cease immediately all forms of class and labor exploitation condemned by the National Labor Relations Board . . . and account for the exploitative labor practices that it engaged in and condoned.

3. That the university promptly cease its discriminatory practices against female employees.

4. That the university immediately end the proliferation of a social and intellectual environment in which heterosexuality is an enforced norm and where the lives of lesbian, gay, bisexual, and transgendered people are marginalized and viewed merely as a reflection of "alternative" lifestyles.

5. That the university dismantle decision-making processes that do

not fully incorporate the participation of a variety of constituencies from the university community . . . and that it adopt a process for a comprehensive, democratic, and participatory structure.

6. That the university begin the process of rethinking curriculum in all divisions by offering a senior faculty position to Jacqui Alexander.

The demands consisted of multiple elements and stood simultaneously as "an articulation by different communities of the conditions under which we worked and lived." Early on, we had to resist attempts that pushed us to prioritize and to disaggregate, which meant, in our view, pulling apart our analysis, relinquishing communities, and separating issues and people from one another. Disaggregation would have meant abandoning an intersectional analysis, so we adopted the motto of the part-time faculty for concretizing overlapping constituencies: every issue was "our issue." We knew internally that new cultural democratic processes could not be legislated, but we also knew that we had to remain steadfast in putting forward the terms of our opposition as well as a vision of the new structures we wished to call forth. Later, there were heated internal discussions about the wisdom of putting forward demands as a step in negotiations as opposed to more radical action that might have forced negotiations. Neither strategy, however, would have avoided the inevitable contradiction of having to rely on the very structures of domination to bring about transformation, of "demanding" democracy when the structures to support it were nonexistent.

We made almost no move without encountering the administration's intransigence. The president continued to build pressure against us by issuing another memorandum to the university that challenged the standing of the Mobilization—this time in the form of a call for grassroots consensus. His call incited the counter-mobilization to begin a more public rally of its forces at the GF, with the public support of Dean Friedlander, who, by that time, had visibly aligned herself with it. Central administration, on the other hand, experimented with a more reasoned, balanced course of gaining grass-roots consensus by identifying us, in the president's words, as "barriers to progress" that needed to be "re-mov[ed]."[46] Its course was silence: "diversity" was no longer the existence of diverse opinions; no longer the exercise of free speech.

Of course, one way to attempt illocutionary disablement is to pretend that there was never any locution and to behave as if what was said carried no weight. The phrase "barriers to progress" provided the rationale for dismissal. "Identification and removal" occurred later—in the midst of negotiations at the height of the hunger strike—through the stationing of armed guards, surveillance, harassment, and intimidation. Students reported being searched and frisked by plain-clothes guards. Those in the Mobilization were under constant surveillance. Clerical workers who were also students were being harassed about their "time on the job." Yet, the distribution of the Mobilization's letter of 3 February immediately following the president's call for consensus on the following day made it appear that we were quick on the uptake and gave us some more ground. Additionally, a meeting, which the administration hastily called with the union for the security guards on 19 February—right on the heels of the forum of 18 February in which the union representative spoke to the School's possible violation of regulations of the National Labor Relations Board—impressed on us the threat posed by linking racism and sexism to workers' rights, those of security guards, clerical workers, and adjunct, full-time, and part-time faculty. It also signaled to us the threat posed by our coalitional work and the absolute necessity of sustaining it. And it was this sense of absolute necessity that propelled the Mobilization into yet another stage of organizing.

Feeding Many Hungers . . .
Healing the Wounds of Exile

The decision of nine students (initially seven from the GF and two from Lang) to launch a hunger strike on 10 April indicates the extent to which the administration had become increasingly duplicitous as it continued to challenge the standing of the Mobilization, while at times voicing a public sentiment about a willingness to be reasonable and enable free speech. Its underlying anxieties were, however, palpable: disbanding existing "diversity" committees and creating new ones; attempting to co-opt graduate students who criticized "diversity"; and cautioning ASELA, the Latin American Students Alliance, to stay out of the Mobilization because of their ignorance of "the racial terrain." Lang's dean, Beatrice

Banu, remained loyal to the president's unspoken edict, "Do not hire Jacqui Alexander," by allowing the cultural studies proposal to languish on her desk. But it was the refusal of the administration to negotiate that dealt the greatest psychic blow to the Mobilization. Although it propelled the students' decision to strike, it also authorized two factions of the counter-mobilization to come into being. Further, not even the hunger strike was sufficient to initiate serious negotiations. More than sixty days had elapsed since the letter of 2 February, in which the Mobilization had formulated its demands and presented them to the president and the School's community. The deadline of 22 February for meeting with the administration had come and gone. In several negotiations, responses were elusive, of the kind students had encountered early in 1996. We were finally forced to admit that the counter-mobilization's strategy of collapsing me into the Mobilization had begun to take effect. On 22 April, twelve days into the strike, the administration finally provided an official response to the demands of 2 February.

It is a serious matter to choose to starve oneself intentionally, to use one's body as metaphor for a truth that was not only not being listened to but dismissed, canceled out, and written out of the place where one believed, however fleetingly, one had made a claim and had a right to belong. In a profound sense, students believed in the validity of their claims, the validity of their demands, and in the idea that power had a duty to act responsibly. They believed, too, that reasonable arguments mattered, and they devoted hours and hours to researching, archiving, preparing for negotiations so as to be equipped with facts and figures. But more fundamentally, students believed that they would be listened to, trusting that their trust had been well entrusted—to deans, more immediately, and their teachers—who would see these demands as just, would honor them as just, and would exert a level of political will *because* they were just. Betrayal and a sense of justice turned into careful work, the work of preparing their whole selves—body, mind, and spirit—to remind the body that what it had ingested for sustenance for whatever number of years would be withheld for an indeterminate period of time; that it would have to accustom itself to being sustained in other ways, since a deeper hunger, not satisfied by food, needed to take precedence. And yet we were privileged, in the sense that we could *choose* to go hungry, unlike many for whom material hunger was a way of living.

The hunger strike brought another center, another dynamic, to the Mobilization, a quality of responsibility of one person for another. It was a way of saying, "I am placing my life in your hands," a gesture of handing over, a quality of combined power, courage, outrage, vulnerability, and intimacy, whose nuance I can only now fully appreciate. Then, we managed the full gestalt through the hunger strike support team who worked virtually around the clock—looking after material needs, the proper balance of cayenne, lemon juice, and electrolytes in water, and pro-bono medical support.

The strike shifted the tone of the Mobilization, prompting the pace to quicken for humane reasons. Deteriorating physical signs of those on strike, the fact that the mobility and reflexes of strikers had been compromised and the presence of emergency medical technicians had, for some, the impact that words failed. Their visibility made innocence impossible. And so there was genuine concern for the well-being of the strikers. Professors "who initially saw no particular problem with rehiring a Visiting Faculty" now began to examine more closely the university's actions. The strike also raised the stakes regarding the School's accountability, since parents had begun to voice charges of insensitivity. In response, the administration developed a dual strategy: internally it argued that students had opted for an unreasoned choice, while externally it informed parents that the strike had ended, when actually it was still in full force. Overall, the administration still believed it could ignore the Mobilization, hoping, perhaps, that its allies within the counter-mobilization at the GF would assume the task.

It was now April. Both the administration and the counter-mobilization knew that time was on their side, so they amplified their discursive attacks about my involvement in the Mobilization—that is, that I was acting only out of unbridled self-interest. It was a deflective strategy to undo the extensive analytical and organizing work of the Mobilization, yet we could do little to unhinge it. And so it stuck, following us almost everywhere.

Before embarking on the hunger strike with the students, I kept a long, silent vigil with myself, along with the counsel of some close friends. Days seemed to be made only of nights, with dawn fleeting. The sky assumed a protective, yet ominous, royal blue color. These were dark times. Already five days into the strike, students had begun to experience dramatic loss of weight, in spite of their efforts to follow the meticulous instructions of fasting. Rounded bellies slackened into concave discs. Faces began to fall with the collapse of muscle. The heart, still in its usual place, lost its rhythm and increased its pace as if wanting to flee the body to take residence elsewhere. During those nights of royal blue, I felt the weight of the growing weightlessness of the hunger strikers press up against the delicate edge of life; their lives now a nagging sacrifice for ours. But I also felt the weight of the School's objectification and the contradiction that seemed impossible to reconcile: that the struggle for my retention had indeed unmasked apparently neutral hiring procedures that thus prompted the administration to create channels of deflection that were all directed to the charge of self-interest. In joining the hunger strike and requesting that the Mobilization remove the demand for my retention from its collective set of demands, I had hoped to diffuse the administration's deflection strategy and in so doing press them into confronting their own spoken commitment to diversity.[47] I had hoped that the Mobilization would secure some modicum of change from the work we had undertaken.

Paradoxically, the body that had been multiply mobilized by the School in its own service was now the same body that had to be reclaimed. It was now being called on to bear the brunt of a different kind in this moment of reclamation, a simultaneous moment of its own undoing. For there comes a moment in starvation when messages to the body lose their urgency, when the mind begins to wear a veil that thickens as the body begins to nourish itself with itself. Memory falters. Desire narrows, its expansive charge transforming itself into points of decision—the decision to open one's eyes; to wash; to dress; to get to one's destination, but destination not as in taking the A train from Harlem to Christopher Street, but as in deciding to walk from the dining room to the kitchen; from the front door to the gate; the elevator to the second floor. In these moments, only water can rescue the intent of the will—only water and love. These moments of starvation were the very moments when those who lived and walked with us did the walking for us, since we had become temporarily unable to do so for ourselves.

While the strike shifted the tone of the Mobilization, we continued to work nonetheless. The day after I joined the strike, the president canceled a scheduled meeting with the constituencies of the Mobilization. Amid threats that he would meet only in a location outside of the university, it took five hours of negotiation (including a group intending to mediate both sides) for the president to meet with representatives of the Mobilization in the company of his newly hired private security guards and the School's attorney. Thereafter, we simply kept up the pressure with rallies and teach-ins. The hunger strikers continued to place responsibility for ending the strike squarely at the door of the administrators by refusing to eat until the administration began serious negotiations. We kept an all-night vigil on 21 April and declared 22 April—the day on which the administration was due to provide a formal response to demands—a day of solidarity.

A week later, the event of the opening of the New University in Exile gave us a moment to pause—to take stock of where we had been and to assess the results of struggle. We marked ourselves as exiles within the School, a status to which we had not consented but to which we were now giving both name and voice. We assessed the promised results: five faculty-of-color appointments at the GF over a three-year period; curriculum review within each division of the School; an investigation into the School's direct hiring of security guards; and the hiring of an official to oversee structures of redress. As we urged, a range of people brought their inspiration to the lobby of the GF in order to create an ample space where the texts of our new understandings displaced the old.

Thus far I have discussed the Mobilization on its own terms. This choice was both methodologically and spiritually necessary since the work of the counter-mobilization was to ensure distortion—to ensure that what we said would not count for what we meant it to say. Now, as I did earlier with the "diversity" documents, I wish to examine more closely the work of the counter-mobilization to see how that grouping came to manufacture cohesion and how it was that different interests coalesced into one and spoke as one.

For my purposes here, I will focus on particular moments in the configuration of the counter-mobilization: on the efforts of the group called "An Alternative," both the document it produced (circa 12 April) and the public consolidation of its forces in the forum of 6 May; on the continued circulation of the premises on which the proposal to rethink Europe was rejected; on the paths of ventriloquism and the mechanisms on which members of the counter-mobilization relied to manufacture cohesion and their close resemblance to the rhetorics of the School's "diversity" discourses. Of importance here are the specific ways in which the counter-mobilization directed its power toward its primary task of illocutionary disablement: that of challenging the standing of the Mobilization and of attempting to have our analyses not count for the actions we intended by substituting narratives that threatened to take their place.

The counter-mobilization comprised different factions and interests, including those of the Board of Trustees; the central administration; the deans, in particular those of Lang, the GF, the Adult Division, and the Milano School; the members of a differentiated intellectual class at the GF and their networks on the outside; some students at the GF, many of whom were signatories of "An Alternative"; an unidentifiable group that identified itself as the "Loyalists"; and segments of the media, such as the *Chronicle of Higher Education, Lingua Franca*, and the *New York Post*, whose writers endorsed the racially dismissive terms of the counter-mobilization as they attempted to subject my scholarship to national review and represent the Mobilization as a lunatic, exotic fringe. Eyal Press's account in *Lingua Franca* was particularly incendiary.[48]

The counter-mobilization was not all located in the same place, but the GF, the flagship of the School, housed its center. That was the location of part of its authority, but that authority also traveled, as it was simultaneously housed within different interests at different times. Prior to constituting itself as such, its different interests had collided. For instance, there had been an ongoing struggle between pragmatism (in the work of a new guard of American-born social scientists) and theory (in the work of the founders of the University in Exile) that had never been resolved. The GF had been notorious for disregarding FIND and had been issued a series of warning letters from Barbara Emerson, the associate provost and director of UDI, about GF compliance. But it was not only FIND that stuck as a bone of contention between faculty and administrators. A far more serious point of antagonism from the School's vantage point was the falling enrollment of the GF and the grave consequences that the decrease posed for the School, which relied heavily on tuition. All of these living antagonisms were temporarily buried to constitute the counter-mobilization: faculty conceded their interests and began speaking the same words as the president, and the students caught in the trenches of professionalization suspended their own passion for democracy and the cultural feel of its absence. But a number of other conditions had to be fulfilled.

First, the counter-mobilization had to announce its relative autonomy from the administration. Its members did so by agreeing with the Mobilization about the conditions that had been described, and they acknowledged that "the New School's Administration had been procedurally inept and improperly complacent in addressing the gross structural inequalities which persist[ed] within [the] institution."[49] Second, in the face of the confrontation posed by the Mobilization, members of the counter-mobilization had to hold on to a commonly purveyed ideology—that of progressivism. Indeed, they held on to this ideology (even in the midst of a profound silence on the question of a living wage for security guards) with a familiar strategy centered on agreeing with the Mobilization's "ends" but not its "means." This stance cleared the way for the counter-mobilization to meet the third condition, which was to decide, although not necessarily consciously, that they had more to gain in temporarily burying their long-standing antagonisms, which we can reasonably assume reemerged with the force that only buried things can.

The fourth condition, alluded to earlier, was that its members had to become adept at ventriloquism—that is, at adopting each others' speech —and they needed to do so as if they were its authentic authors, particularly because they had been unable to construct any collectively shared vision of social justice to contest that of the Mobilization's. Fifth, at the moment of self-confrontation, they needed to rely on certain affinities, some visible, some not so visible, including affinities of class and race. It is not that all members of the counter-mobilization occupied the same racial and class positions; rather, it was more the case that such positions overlapped for its most dominant representatives. And perhaps there was also a sixth condition—legitimacy—which it already possessed and, therefore, did not need to secure. Legitimacy had already been authorized within the routine, ordinary practices of the School, assured within the technologies of power and exercised through longevity.

What were the shared epistemic claims of members of the counter-mobilization? As expressed, they shared the School's definition of "diversity" as diverse opinions, emptied of any history of race. The signatories of "An Alternative" saw themselves as "a positive alternative to unproductive harangues," as agents of "democracy and representation," and as a reasoned alternative to the fringe—all in much the same way that the president had positioned himself during the early period of the Mobilization as the center of calm reason in the eye of the storm.[50] So much for relative autonomy.

The (apparent) evisceration of race on the part of the counter-mobilization is particularly evident in its consideration of curriculum and in the grounds on which it continued to defend the rejection of the Proposal. According to "An Alternative," "issues of faculty hiring and curriculum development [were to] be disaggregated. An individual's racial, gender, or sexual identity [was] relevant to, but not [to] be conflated with, that person's intellectual and academic interests." But how is it possible to disaggregate faculty hiring from curriculum development? The Mobilization had not argued for an unmediated relationship between identity and knowledge, or identity and politics, or curriculum and affirmative action. It refused the collapse of identities into mindless bodies, whose only position was to "enrich" and "contribute" to a project that had always already been conceptualized. Its different threads argued for a way to think about the relationship between cultural identity and knowledge, as well as for particular faculty who could bring certain modes of theorizing to the knowledge project. In other words, the Mobilization called for a theoretical engagement of particular knowledges, which were linked to the intellectual projects of scholars of color, not ritual inclusion of either bodies or texts. In its line of argument, the counter-mobilization would have no way of understanding how the formulations of intersectionality and the simultaneity of oppression originated with feminist women of color. Thus, the questions remained: How relevant is identity and social location to the production of knowledge?

What is the degree of relationality between one's social location and the subject of one's theory?

The work of disablement continued in the refusal of the counter-mobilization to engage any of the demands for economic justice. Its members labeled the demands "intransigent," thus confusing the directionality of power (the Mobilization had underscored the administration's intransigence) and dismissing their validity. No document in its brief life ever made explicit reference to the struggle of security guards and staff for a living wage; of the subordinated positions of the predominantly female, part-time faculty; or of the unequal pay scales between male faculty and all female faculty. It was as if these class dimensions of the political struggle never existed. Once these erasures were put in place, however, it became possible for the counter-mobilization to substitute personality discourses for the inequities of structure. "I have witnessed hunger strikes before, in the 1960s," James Miller, chair of the Program in Liberal Studies, proclaimed during the forum on 6 May and in a written statement circulated throughout the GF: "I met César Chavez, a great activist of genuine spirituality. Jacqui Alexander is no César Chavez."[51] As if such were the terms upon which the Mobilization had argued for structural change.

Distortion and disablement continued to operate within the racial perceptions held by the counter-mobilization. Its members behaved as if the subjects of the Mobilization were homogeneously black, as if people of color of various backgrounds did not exist, and as if progressive white people had not also undertaken a critique of whiteness. Within the race neutrality framework of "diversity" discourses and institutionalized practice, the place of white people was to uphold white race loyalty above class interests, above coalitions that crossed racial lines. When Andrew Arato, a senior faculty member in the department of Sociology and a signatory to "An Alternative," declared at the forum on 6 May, "Your halcyon days are over! Negotiations are stopping now . . . The faculty is not going to sit down with you!" he framed his address as if he were speaking primarily to black people, while reminding white progressives of the loyalty they presumably swore to uphold the race. He had already received authorization from the unspoken injunctive of the "diversity" discourses, "white bodies only as permanent thinkers," "(black) bodies only for permanent service," yet he adopted it with force, as if he were its authentic author.[52] So much, then, for the expression of "democracy and representation" that he endorsed as part of "An Alternative," or for the Habermasian model of "consensual norms" that informed some of the intellectual projects at the Graduate Faculty.

The conflations and collapses described above should not be taken to mean that the counter-mobilization was confused about my location in its overall strategy of illocutionary disablement. Its intent was reflected in its vociferous claims about a national search. The multiple ways in which national search engines operate were suddenly rewritten in terms that were unitary and singular, as if another form of affirmative action, one that ensures like-mindedness (hiring faculty who are most like those already on the inside), did not operate. The hasty contrivance of consensus in the midst of ambiguity betrayed transparency. Most of it was manufactured by word of mouth, but Dean Friedlander's authority gave it the signature it required when, in a letter to students of GSFT, she made my hiring seem like an aberration far removed from the "very great pleasure" it had elicited earlier. Indeed, she expressed my hire in these terms: "When entering into temporary commitments . . . we do not necessarily follow the strict set of procedures used to select faculty members for regular appointments."[53] The absence of "strict procedures" invoked the specter of a relaxation of rules in the face of questionable scholarship, and since the rethinking Europe proposal had already been rejected as "PC sloganeering and claptrap," and as "lacking . . . the substantive content of an important intellectual project," this strategy could hold. Once the internal work was done, the counter-mobilization began to work nationally through articles in the *Chronicle of Higher Education*, *Lingua Franca*, and the *New York Post*. If other strategies ran the risk of failure, this attack on scholarship was foolproof. If my scholarship were legitimated, then I, too, would have to be legitimated. If I were legitimated, then the struggle to retain me would have to be legitimated, as well as the Mobilization and its demands. There could, of course, be reasonable disagreement over the demands, if all things were equal. But all things were not equal. Thus, the underlying suppositions could not be allowed to stand: not the Mobilization and the intersectional terms on which it had argued; not the demands and their links with constituencies;

not the terms of my hire; (*especially*) not FIND; not transnational analytic and theoretical frameworks; not my scholarship; not my work within GSFT. All of those positions had to be dissolved in order to clear the way for demonization to complete the remainder of the ideological work that the president's earlier edict had begun.

Symbols of demonization were only a part of the mixed universe from which members of the counter-mobilization drew. To the writers in *Lingua Franca* and the *Chronicle,* the Mobilization produced "A Nightmare on Twelfth Street," "A bizarre battle over Faculty Diversity." Internally the strategies of the Mobilization were deemed "uncivil" and "authoritarian," although there was some confusion about which ideology informed such authoritarianism: at times it was unqualified authoritarianism, at times Leninist, at times Stalinist, at times Maoist or "vanguard," and at other times simply narrowly "essentialist." To "An Alternative," the demands were "intransigent" and our tactics were "archaic, offensive and ineffective." To the president, the Mobilization had more in common with an extremist fringe that resisted change "by any means necessary," "by shouting down speakers on a college campus, bombing abortion clinics, burning black churches, harassing gays and lesbians, vandalizing Jewish cemeteries."[54] James Miller saw a "cult" performing odd rituals, using "pseudo-religious mumbo-jumbo."[55] Not only was our speech unable to count for the actions we intended, it was now simply unintelligible. Once "pseudo-religious mumbo-jumbo" was invoked, its surrounding symbolic associations of magic, terror, evil, and the grotesque were brought to its aid. As James Miller stated, "I thought Jacqui Alexander to be a force of great evil," and apparently the writer for the *Chronicle* agreed, since she devoted an entire section of her article to the theme "a force of great evil." In the end, the salience of this entire strategy was brought home in the cry of victory voiced by one member of the counter-mobilization on reading the article in *Lingua Franca*: "We won!" The extent of the "victory" remained questionable, however, in light of the challenge posed to the *Chronicle*'s formulation by scholars and activists.[56]

Part of the later strength of the counter-mobilization derived from its early refusal to engage new knowledge frameworks as presented in the rethinking Europe proposal and as evident in the expanding scholarly terrain of gender studies and feminist theory. But in a fundamental sense the Mobilization had become a place to formulate a new set of pedagogies that would have had relevance both inside and outside the classroom, had they been allowed to travel in that way. It is an irony that in these moments of crisis, those projects, which have moved away from the dominant mode, become more vulnerable to critique. The Gender Studies and Feminist Theory program was no exception. In what follows, I examine how the analytical issues raised by the Mobilization began to travel within GSFT itself, and how it sharpened the very conundrums GSFT had been experiencing.

Gender Studies and Feminist Theory: The Failure to Transform

To engage the theoretical implications rather than the mere textual inclusion of these feminisms, would prompt a fundamental revisioning of what constitutes feminist theory and would enrich the conversations and terrains upon which feminist scholars of all stripes could research and theorize. To account for, yet simultaneously de-center European and European-American feminist thought, to wholeheartedly incorporate theoretically and textually the work of Third World, U.S. women of color, and a body of work labeled transnational feminism, and to put all of these feminisms in conversation with each other could prove to be an exciting and intellectually stimulating project. These processes of foregrounding, de-centering and enabling conversations to engender rethinking of all sorts of curricular configurations, shifting the feminist canon traditionally utilized in the program's foundational courses, are precisely what students and some marginalized faculty have attempted and, are precisely, from my perspective, what have become delegitimized and erased at the GF.
—CO-CHAIR OF THE SUB-COMMITTEE ON CURRICULUM,
GENDER STUDIES AND FEMINIST THEORY, letter to GSFT

The terms on which the Mobilization examined the relationships between knowledge and power, and between knowledge and identity, challenged the foundations of GSFT and its own self-conscious mission of producing a body of knowledge called gender studies and feminist theory amidst contentious discussions in the field. Although the committee was first organized in 1991, well after these debates had gained widespread international currency, the foundational, interdisciplinary year-long course, one of two requirements housed within GSFT for the master's degree, anchored a feminist epistemic center that remained white and European. "Foundations included western social theory," faculty explained, "because students demanded it; they couldn't understand critical race theory and postmodernism without seeing what had come before. We can't understand the intersections without understanding the basics. We do need some basics. We can't get to liberalism and rights without John Locke, but we can watch him as he gazes at Indians in America."[57] In other words, European liberalism anchored the basics and apparently never lost its hold—in the statement above it is still Locke who gazes at Indians in America with no apprehension that "Indians" gaze back, refuse his gaze, or oppose it entirely. GSFT students argued about the limits of liberalism since it separated "the basics" from "transnational approaches." For them, the "first semester [was] devoted to 'white women's feminism,' " while the second semester course, which I co-taught with Donald Scott, presented the alternative of "transnational and people of color texts." Their central question could be understood in terms of the constitution of the center: "Why," they asked, "do we have to start with Aristotle or Locke? Can we not learn rights from Audre Lorde and Frederick Douglass?"

These were not new questions, nor were they misplaced, but they were being raised by a new group of women, some of whom had assumed the political identity of women of color, some white, some working class and lesbian, who, particularly in the case of eight women of color, were vigorously recruited with the understanding that their overlapping intellectual interests would be taken seriously. Their projects corresponded with some of the textual inclusions of the foundational course, but were believed to be disruptive, not oppositional. Yet it is this oppositionality to the center that provoked an ostensible split in the classroom between definitions of "feminist theory" and "women's studies" and between theorizing and consciousness-raising/activism. As played out in the classroom, women of color were automatically collapsed into "women's studies," thus making their preoccupations subordinate to theory—a gesture, of course, that exposes another genealogy.

In one sense, this collapse of women of color into "women's studies" meant that white women were always already positioned in theory, while women of color were always already in women's studies. But the split spoke, as well, to a deeper, more vexed element in one strand of the postmodernist project that has textually erased difference even while (mis)reading, as Paula Moya has shown, the work of women of color. One of the effects of this erasure is that cultural identity, the very category around which some women of color have theorized and mobilized, is shorn of any theoretical or epistemic significance. It is not only that identity is eviscerated, but also what its understanding enables. In Moya's words, "identities are theoretical constructions which enable individuals and communities to read the world in specific ways. These identities are grounded in a social historical location in which there are social, political, economic and epistemic consequences to that very location, a location which is constitutively defined by relations of domination."[58] As was the case with the formulations of "An Alternative" and the premises in the rejection of the Proposal, the problem that GSFT faculty faced was precisely the problem of the status of cultural/racial identity and its constructed and lived implications, which could be interrogated from a broader engagement with the colonial histories of Europe and Euro-America, with hegemonic European thought, and with social thought emerging from communities and geographies of color. But in order to engage its "theoretical" emendations, cultural identity would have had to have been ascribed theoretical import, so that the knowledge that women of color derived from their experience of the world would be brought into tension, argumentation, and engagement with formulations of subjectivity and agency derived from this alternative reading of cultural identity. That knowledge need not have been "delegitimized," since it was not taken to be knowledge; and not "erased," since the extensive labor of the students on that subcommittee never saw the light of day. Ultimately, these questions and the answers they received catapulted faculty and students squarely into a larger quarrel about the status of experience and differing realist and postmodernist accounts of cultural identity, and simultaneously brought GSFT to the center of a political contradiction, which I describe below.

The story of this confrontation is instructive both in terms of the additional material limitations of a textual erasure of difference—what happens when theory splits off from practice and is forced to encounter other material conditions—and of the already subordinated position of GSFT within the Graduate Faculty. I will address the material limitations first. The categories, which for some postmodernists are textually irrelevant for cultural identity, the constructions of race, class, gender, sexuality, and nationality, are the very categories around which power coheres in social relations. They are the very categories through which material life is organized, the very categories in which "diversity" discourses are premised, discourses that, as we saw earlier, collapsed identities into bodies and placed them into fixed positions. The work of the Mobilization divulged the fact that the material consequences of all of this collapsing, moving, and fixing were both severe and unequal and that the social location of the "we" was constituted through these very inequities. The majority of women of color worked as clerical staff and food service workers, not as teachers; most of the black and Latino men worked as security guards, not as faculty; and the bulk of teaching was done by part-time faculty whose remuneration was disproportionate to the value they generated for the School. Remember Adamantia Pollis's lawsuit, in which the court ruled that all female professors were paid substantially lower salaries than male professors. The GSFT committee remained unable to intervene in the School's discursive mobilization of bodies, both of white women and of people of color, since the textual erasure prematurely closed off another political space that might have understood that the different locations we occupied were produced through relations of domination and subordination, and that we indeed inhabited those very interstices of race, gender, class, sexuality, and nationality, which were found in texts. Such an intervention would have enabled a reading of communities as both political and conceptual, of a moment of political mobilization as conjunctural and, therefore, begging theorization, a moment to conjoin theoretical and political allies.

There is an additional implication here that also needs to be addressed—the notion of the textual absence of identity in apparently de-racialized texts. I want to suggest that within such epistemological frame-works are embedded (auto)biographical accounts of (white) identities, most often identities of privilege, thereby reinforcing Paul Valéry's obser-vation that "there is no theory that is not a fragment . . . of autobiogra-phy."[59] It seems, then, that the habits of privilege to which teachers are attached turn on their own solipsism and disable white teachers from seeing the reinscriptions of their own identities within texts. Such habits explain why, for instance, questions about the epistemological founda-tions of the GSFT core course—which were raised by students who named themselves women of color, white, working class, and lesbian—produced such an incendiary response in the classroom: "You racially stigmatized people have no right to oppress others." Such habits also explain why Dean Friedlander, who taught one of the two requirements within GSFT, informed one student that the study of whiteness was not a viable project. Far from being the response of the disinterested theorist involved in texts, not politics, these statements dovetail with the visceral confrontations that are more characteristic of consciousness-raising groups of second-wave feminism in which white women would deny privilege (the episte-mic consequences of their own location), and instead feel personally attacked (not textually accused) by women of color. The "pain when GSFT becomes such a battleground" is palpable, as the co-chair said later in her letter of 1997, feeling "the erasure of hard work, a disregard of our at-tempts to dialogue and to make collaborative decisions in this program, an erasure of imagination, of a passion for knowledge and for feminism . . . I never imagined that the kind of battles that go on inside of gender studies would be waged at this moment in history." Given these com-ments, it would seem that "we are back to where we were," as Cherríe Moraga states, "bodies to be thrown into a river of tormented history, to bridge the gap between white women and Third World women. Are we back to square one again"?[60] We need not return to square one, but we can only preempt that return when we grapple with analyses that sub-stantiate the fact that "important knowledge" is amassed at the con-juncture of the very intersections—of class, race, gender, sexuality, and nationality—that people inhabit, and that women of color, as Moya says, "possess knowledge—knowledge that is not only important for ourselves, but also for all who wish to understand accurately the world. We possess that knowledge partly as a result of the fact that we are women of color."[61]

Now to the second lesson of the confrontation. As I have already indicated, GSFT functioned as a committee within the GF. Its committee status spoke, of course, to the historical subordination to which women's studies and gender studies have been subjected, and to the double shift that women often undertake as they labor in their home departments and in women's studies simultaneously. The fact that a number of GSFT students and myself were active members of the Mobilization provoked a political problem for GSFT, particularly because the opposition to the Mobilization was housed within the GF, the very home of GSFT. The problem is symbolized in the GSFT chair's statement, "I want Jacqui, but I will not *delegitimize* my line or the Committee."[62] The tenor of this statement is at odds with an earlier one aimed at staving off student discontent: "It is too late," she said, "to have a white women's program; that's why Jacqui Alexander was hired."[63] At one moment, Jacqui Alexander can be employed to save whiteness from itself and, at another moment, exist as a stain requiring removal. Clearly, the Mobilization brought GSFT in confrontation with itself, but the committee read that confrontation in personal terms ("*my* line") invoking individual ownership of a collective project undertaken through collective labor—the feminist work of U.S. women of color, Third World women, and the scholarly projects of transnational feminism—including my own. At that moment, GSFT would have had to make explicit political choices, explicit antiracist choices, that would have made women of color into theoretical and political allies, not antagonists; that would not have collapsed legitimacy into white feminist knowledge claims in order to subordinate the epistemic claims of women of color, white, working-class, and lesbian students; that would, therefore, not have seen women of color as stain to be removed, or collapsed into what the chair later referred to as "the contaminated past" of the now defunct program.[64] GSFT saw itself as having to "sacrifice" too much, the same unfortunate terms in which the proposal to rethink Europe was rejected (to echo Richard Bernstein's question cited earlier: "What is to be sacrificed to institute your proposal"?). There is no end of paradoxes at the crossroads. These personalized, ultimately patronizing, renditions continued to operate, as seen in 1997 when a moratorium on the study of GSFT at the GF was imposed, shortly after a historically unprecedented number of women of color had been recruited into the program and found affinity with the scholarly work in transnational feminism and, not coincidentally, with the analyses of the Mobilization. "That's what *they* have always wanted," one GSFT faculty member who was active in the counter-mobilization said regarding the decision to suspend admissions to the GSFT program, "*they* have not appreciated what *I* have done for *them*." Rather than fight to continue a GSFT program that would incorporate the knowledges and presence of women of color, white feminist faculty would concede to its closure.

It is a long and arduous distance between the will to power and the will to reconciliation. The School's lack of vision regarding a renewed, contemporary commitment to its progressive intellectual tradition shows how political liberalism—without comprehensive antiracist, profeminist, proworker, and transnational ethical and scholarly commitments—remains ill-equipped to undertake the journey.[65]

Emotion played a large role in this story I have told. Members of the counter-mobilization no doubt felt attacked in the politics of confrontation, feeling that they needed to defend something. It was not the institution, since few faculty or students of the counter-mobilization could rush to an unambivalent defense of it. Few could say that the record on "diversity" was impeccable, or that the passion for democracy was lived. It seems that, underneath it all, members of the counter-mobilization felt compelled to defend themselves as individuals and as a collective. In critiquing the School's brand of "diversity," the Mobilization was also saying something about the individuals who upheld it—not in terms that expressed gratitude for the normative but in terms that called good intentions to account for the reproduction of inequity. FIND is a discursive invention with material effects, but it iterates its own emotional requirements: gratefulness for being rescued. If we recall Friday's dilemma, we will remember that the debt he paid for being rescued was to forget his speech, to discard the terms of his own truth and speak the language that he had been assigned. When one refuses to pay the debt by seeming ungrateful, by calling for accountability, by presuming belonging, and by insisting on the right to truth and to knowledge derived from one's social historical location, the existing emotional cart is upset by the prospect of no longer being able to rely on the same terms for balance. If the cognitive mediates the relationship between knowledge and experience, the emotional is no less an important mediator. Emotional interests are simultaneously embedded within knowledge interests and in the organization and distribution of resources, both material and psychic. In part this explains why questions about the reorganization of knowledge resources are experienced as threat, loss, and displacement. But in the context of asymmetries of power, such feelings can be a simultaneous exercise in the power of privilege, particularly since power has the privilege of reasserting itself and of reconsolidating its interests, even in moments of perceived loss.

There is, as well, something more subtle at work in the virulent emotion that accompanied the defense of Europe and European thought as the center of the GF's intellectual mandate and its professed progressive identity. This subtlety occurred to me later when I compared the early mission of the GF (then the University in Exile) with the objection to the Proposal stated in "An Alternative." The bylaws of the University in Exile stated its mission in the following way: "To be guided solely by considerations of scholarly achievement, competence and integrity, giving no weight whatsoever to scientifically irrelevant considerations such as race, sex, religion or such political beliefs as bear upon individual freedom of thought, inquiry, teaching and publication."[66] "An Alternative" framed its objections to the Proposal in *apparently* opposite terms: "An individual's racial, gender, or sexual identity is relevant to, but must not be conflated with, that person's intellectual and academic interests." But both constituencies share a deep anxiety about identity and its potential to disrupt knowledge. The force of both of these declarations alerts us to what lies behind them. Histories of antifascist movements may have been obscured within the fiscal conservatism of the School, but the collective memory of fascism has not been erased—the memory of trauma, of the perverse use of the facts of one's identity in the service of mass genocide and destruction. The force of refusal seems anchored in the sentiment: better make the facts of identity irrelevant than allow anyone to assert them or to succumb to the pain of figuring out their usefulness and the possibilities of living a mutual knowing, an understanding of parallel histories, an interlocking set of alliances, and an affirmed solidarity with each other's struggles.

On Endings, Beginnings, and the Changing of Seasons

By mid-May 1997 the Mobilization began to assemble certain things that kept its members company on the journey—flowers from the corner grocery; candlelight as a symbol and request to see our footprints and to know the direction in which they were heading; and water to help carry the reflection of the people we wanted to become. And ourselves. The space created in the lobby of the GF at 65 Fifth Avenue was ample, since it was one of the places we had entrusted with a year and a half of dreaming. It preserved the imprint of our yearning. If you visit New York, you will feel that yearning still etched in those walls and in those tiny crevices that make a habit of hoarding things. On 12 May we held the commencement celebration of the New University in Exile, with testimonials and the bittersweet feelings of which endings are made.[67] We sang freedom songs and redemption songs, "We who believe in Freedom shall not rest." We looked back: "This School will take my TAP or my PELL, but it will never take my voice."[68] "Those of us who speak out are moved by a deep sense of the fragility of our self-worth. It is the determination to protect our sense of who we are, to risk criticism, alienation and serious loss, while most others, similarly harmed, remain silent." "How will you be engaged in the struggle? What will you stand for and what will you be silent about"? "If I am not for myself, who will be for me? But if I am *only* for myself, then what am I?" Looking back in order to walk forward.

We had come this far having sung of things we most needed to learn: "So let the words of my mouth and the meditation of my heart be acceptable in thy sight." Looking back in order to move forward: "Be creative. Ingenious. Pursue excellence. But remember scholarship isn't just about books. Scholarship is about how to create the tools that will free us from oppression." "Always seek to disconnect truth from the will to power." Amid tears, we struggled with the pain of separation. For each thought that dared not be uttered a tear was shed. "The New University in Exile hereby acknowledges you as a warrior who has steadfastly battled

Racism, Sexism, Homophobia, Anti-Semitism and all forms of exclusionary, discriminatory, exploitative practices that pervade our planet."[69] "So let the words of my mouth and the meditation of our heart be acceptable in thy sight."

Coda

The moments of truth that the Mobilization generated and the opposition that was encountered speak to a continued contestation at the School and beyond. Jonathan Fanton was replaced by the controversial former U.S. senator Robert Kerry, whose role in the horrors of the Vietnam War provoked continued contestation between the School's progressive identity and its actual practices, its contradictory associations with the disturbing geopolitics of the U.S. national security state, the imperatives of empire-building, and its determination to institutionalize instrumental diversity in the service of the latter.[70] Security guards were successful in securing the university as their employer, in securing a living wage, and in winning health and sick leave benefits. Another stage of the Mobilization continues at this very moment, since these practices of empire are not divorced from the very process of knowledge production. And the story continues: Which truth will prevail, which dreams will be enacted?

> The rainy season came as abruptly as the dry season left. Unannounced. Clouds and Ocean prepared for the change as Thunder persisted its roaring impatience, occasionally softening its clamor. Who would know that the companion of a force with the power to dislodge the heart from its usual resting place could fleck such delicacy into platinum pink? The night sky adorned itself with a veil of stars that opened to honor the goddess, the moon goddess, who had taken station there before time. Legend says she was seen by Cortés as he made his first foray into forest. She seemed to him to keep watch over the island peopled by women, which, to this day, bears the name Isla de Mujeres. Wind had whispered a message of the change of season to fishermen in their dreams. By morning, they were nowhere in sight.
>
> There were no rocks rising from this Ocean floor with the memory of

another time, distant. No fossil to pay homage to their age, ingrained, steadfast. The vastness was hers alone. Turquoise jade announcing the change of season with moving bands of forest green and ebony brought from the second shore and from the deep below. Sargasso. Thick. Sluggish. Clouds opened and drenched everything in sight. Although the rocks had long since taken root in a different time, their memory lingered. Swollen waves climbed on them, laden with forest green, dancing shapes, broken fishnets, sea fans, and glass, called sea glass. Riding the waves. Day and night, the Ocean raged, thrashing against rocks in her haste to shore, colliding as she retreated into the one advancing, until they both surrendered. To oneness. Day and night, forest green piled high took the place of the shore. Jade lost its luster, becoming sullen. Day and night, she vomited all that had been dumped there from another time, for she had awaited this water which humans called rain to join hers. Ocean. She would not be satisfied until the shore became impassable; no human could mistake the extent of her labor, could pretend not to see the fruits of her travail. On the seventh day exhaustion set in; waves no longer climbed the rocks; no thrashing sound; no backward, forward tumbling. Just endless miles of sludge. Everything riding the waves. Three days later. Another mystery. Forest green and ebony piled high on shore succumbed to another tide running deep beneath the surface. They disappeared back into the place whence they came, to await another season. Bearing the memory of riding the waves. At day's end, dusk sprayed a film of pink violet cupped with a tinge of orange. Another time. In the distance, the echo of a pod of dolphins. The sharks had been put to rest.

5

Transnationalism, Sexuality, and the State: Modernity's Traditions at the Height of Empire

I offer this chapter as a way to think through the methodological layerings of an approach to feminist praxis that addresses state investments in sexuality within formulations of transnationalism. Building on chapter 1, here I explore whether the processes of the neocolonial state's investments in heterosexualizing the nation are perhaps not unique at all (of course, they can be particular while not being unique), but rather have import for other kinds of state formations—more specifically those moments that have been characterized as colonial and neo-imperial. My purpose in this chapter is to establish the terms for the transnational by taking a set of disciplining and otherwise regulatory heterosexual practices both within and across three social formations—the colonial, the neocolonial, and the neo-imperial. I hope that it will teach us about the deployment of sexuality in nation-state formation: notably the complicity of state and corporate processes in the manufacture of citizenship normativized within the prism of heterosexuality, and the indispensability of both processes to the project of nation building, which often inaccurately is assumed to be a completed project within neo-imperial social formations yet assumed to be always ongoing within the neocolonial. Here I view colonialism in multiple ways: as those practices that attempt to foreclose self-determination, and thus a political category; as a set of social relations inaugurated at the height of European imperialism,

which involved the annexation of land and the subordination of resources to European interests; and as ideological practices that draw their
epistemic fodder from these forms. I also view colonialism as a metaphor,
both in its capacity to travel and in its capacity to stay put—in the form,
for instance, of indigenous American colonization. As we shall see, different colonialisms operate in different places at the same time, and also
in the same place at the same time.

As an empirical point of reference for the neocolonial I use the Anglophone Caribbean, particularly Trinidad and Tobago, and the Bahamas,
following the terms I established in chapter 1.[1] This designation is intended to encompass the specific class that took hold of the reigns of the
state apparatus at the moment of organized anticolonial struggle in the
1950s and 1960s. I use the word *organized* for two reasons: first, the
anticolonial always already existed within the colonial; and, second, different epistemological, political, and cultural practices continued to operate outside of colonial time. The term *neocolonial* is also meant to
describe the class that has forfeited nationalist claims to sovereignty since
it also manages the global neoliberal imperial project. On the ground,
this project is interpreted as one of imperialism (instigated by the United
States operating in close concert with corporate financial interests) and of
recolonization simultaneously, suggesting that within the neocolonial
also resides the imperial.[2]

Operating both alongside and within the neocolonial is a new set of
imperial relations. Characterized by several interrelated practices, these
new relations derive from the organization of a global capitalist class that
also functions as the dominant partner in a now uneasy alliance between
the group of nations called the G8 countries and the multinational corporations that govern through a series of population displacements, the
uneven dispersal of resources, and gendered and racialized class hierarchies.[3] One of its most visible manifestations at the seat of its empire in
the United States is the entanglement between state and corporate power.
Given that the empirical focus here is the United States of North America, I shall also take neo-imperialism to mean the extension of the territorial interests of the U.S. national security state through war and militarization, procured both externally and internally.

The pertinent geopolitical sites of my analysis, then, are as follows:

first, the moment of Spanish colonization of the Americas in 1513, in which the invading army led by Balboa massacred over forty Indian "cross-dressers" and fed them to dogs; second, the moment of the neo-colonial state's legislating of heterosexuality by criminalizing lesbian and gay sex in Trinidad and Tobago (1986 and 1991, respectively) and in the Bahamas (1991); and, finally, the contemporary moment of neo-imperialist militarization within the United States, which is characterized by a new phase of empire-building in which hegemonic heterosexual masculinity wishes to assert a Pax Americana through imperial violence undertaken within its own borders as well as in different parts of the world. In my examination of all three sites, I will foreground processes of heterosexualization as a way of narrating these simultaneous histories that are often positioned as distant and separate, occupying a linear temporality in which tradition ostensibly displaces the neocolonial and modernity displaces the neo-imperial as preferred terms.

My aim in this chapter, therefore, is twofold: first, to bring sexuality studies into a political conversation with transnational feminism in a way that cuts a path through an existing disciplinary segregation; and, second, to put forward a methodology that can potentially disrupt the vestiges of a form of (cultural) relativism in which modernity is used as an alibi to circumvent some of the most egregious practices of violence that colonialism and imperialism expose. Before addressing these aims, however, I need to clear some analytic ground as a way of proceeding with the terms of my argument, because the itineraries of transnational feminism and sexuality studies have been plotted largely along divergent paths, and because the very category of the transnational—which has itself been put to multiple uses—continues to be haunted by relativist claims that effectively reinscribe dysfunctional hierarchies and obscure the ways in which national and transnational processes are mutually, although unequally, imbricated.[4]

Much of the urgency for this chapter derives from what I perceive as a latent absolutism within (cultural) relativist knowledge frameworks and political projects bearing the word "transnational." While it is not possible to provide an exhaustive itinerary of relativism's multiple deployments, or those of its absolutist predecessor against which it is often positioned as an analytic advance, let me specify its usage here. By cultural relativism I mean an apparently neutral rendering of the practices within different social formations based on simple observations of difference, and ostensibly not based on hierarchies of moral judgment or cultural handicap. The analytic struggle over neutrality has been more customarily fought out between the territorial claims of those within moral philosophy and anthropology desirous of staking out some clear ground between "neutrality" and "objectivity."[5] Without venturing too far into that territory, let me begin with two illustrations of the political and epistemic consequences that result when absolutist claims traffic within relativism. The first is the contemporaneous alignment between a liberal feminist political organization, Feminist Majority, and U.S. state imperialism that makes war and militarization not only plausible but also desirable. If vestiges of cultural absolutism had not lingered within cultural relativism, there would be no need for imperial rescue narratives to circulate at this conjuncture where presumably only cultural relativism exists. Of course some of the most cynical deployments of cultural absolutism have been rendered by U.S. state narratives constructing the "axis of evil," the most contemporaneous template for the construction of absolute alterity. The second example is a pedagogical one from a fairly persistent U.S. classroom response that indeed presumes an absolute alterity in the reading of "Third World" texts.

Rescue Narrative One: The Feminist Majority and the Women of Afghanistan

For more than a decade the Feminist Majority organization consolidated its representation around "majority" status and a variant of geographical, racial, and cultural hierarchy that affixed patriarchal violence in Afghanistan to traditional fundamentalism. Operating within a modernist continuum, the organization's epistemic focus left little analytic room for matching the contours of U.S. patriarchal state violence with Afghani state violence; for linking American patriarchal fundamentalism to its Afghani counterpart; or for understanding the "contextual asymmetries" (to use Uma Narayan's formulation)[6] of U.S. and Afghani women's engagement with fundamentalism, patriarchy, or their various collusions.[7]

In the absence of plotting the routes of traffic between Islamic patriarchy and Christian patriarchy, for instance, Feminist Majority's mobilizations assisted in anchoring a set of implicit and explicit assumptions that located violence in tradition only, demarcating "primitive" and "modern" patriarchy in a way that gave modernity the power to automatically dissolve traditional patriarchy—whose source was singular and archaic— since modernity presumably had no patriarchal requirements of its own.[8] The singular manifest task of modern Western feminism, then, was to save Afghani women from Afghani men, to save them from tradition, and ultimately, to save them from themselves.[9]

In "An Open Letter to the Editors of *Ms Magazine*" the Revolutionary Association of the Women of Afghanistan (RAWA) credited Feminist Majority for its early recognition and diffusion of the dangers that Afghani women faced under the Taliban, but pointed to the very erasure that can ensue when, in this case, a particular American feminism adopts the role of savior. In their challenge to the magazine's obliteration of Afghani struggle that was presented in an article, "A Coalition of Hope," published in 2002, RAWA noted, "What is missing from this telling of the 'Feminist Majority Story' is any credit to the independent Afghan women who stayed in Afghanistan and Pakistan throughout the 23 year (and counting) crisis in Afghanistan and provided relief, education, resistance and hope to the women and men of their country."[10] But this discursive power rides on another set of social relations through which "majority" status has been constituted, and those rest with the organization's relationship to the U.S. state.

The very category of state-sponsored terror, which the Feminist Majority organization foregrounds in examining the operations of the Taliban, disappears in relation to the practices of the American state. One of the results of this hypervisibility and erasure is that the denunciation of the Taliban comes to inhabit a political space that simultaneously supports the act of the U.S.-led invasion of Iraq in 2003. Indeed, there is the performance of a customary ideological feat that positions democracy as a set of practices devoid of the violences of capital's imperialisms, thereby underscoring a politic in which neoliberal streams of feminism succeed in melding their interests with those of the neoliberal state. This move reveals why the state can deflect radical (feminist) opposition to it by universalizing liberal feminist political agendas that dovetail neatly with its own expansionist practices. Imperial rescue narratives are neutral neither in intent nor in design.

But it is not only because of the Feminist Majority's access to the state that we need to be attentive to its discursive political genealogy. The organization continues to generate wide appeal by virtue of its massive political mobilization on college campuses throughout the country and its more popular diffusion through its corporate arm, *Ms Magazine*. Its vigorous campus program, founded in 1997, organized student members on more than 650 colleges and universities in the United States and on 79 campuses in 56 other countries throughout the world. Admittedly, Feminist Majority is not the only avenue through which liberal feminist claims travel, but there is a great deal of correspondence between its organizational brand of cultural relativism and a concomitant expression in women studies classrooms, which I address below. At a fundamental level, the long-standing challenge for imperialism to be made integral to the political and cultural lexicon of U.S. feminism is still very much in place.

The Transnational Feminist Classroom: The Familiar, the Foreign, and the Distant

In the introductory course on transnational feminism that I taught at Connecticut College, which forms one of the capstone courses of the major in Gender and Women's Studies, students consistently claimed an absolute alterity—too much difference—when they confronted Third World texts. That is, in books such as Edwidge Danticat's *A Farming of Bones* and Tsitsi Dangarembga's *Nervous Conditions,* for instance, students positioned themselves as predominantly white readers at odds with the population of the text. Indeed, these students believed they had better access to understanding the U.S. missionary colonization of the Kôngo kingdom when guided by a white American narrator, as in Barbara Kingsolver's *Poisonwood Bible,* and they believed that sexuality was intelligible —more intelligible than "race" or "culture"—in their reading of Shyam Selvadurai's *Funny Boy.* The issue, then, is not simply about Third World texts. These multiple positions stood in stark contrast to the palpable desire to flatten out difference—"we are all the same"—when students confronted First World texts, such as Cherríe Moraga and Gloria Anzaldúa's *This Bridge Called My Back: Writings by Radical Women of Color* and Audre Lorde's *Sister Outsider,* that contest racism and xenophobia within U.S. feminism. When I requested that they provide the most immediate images (as opposed to the more studied, politically correct ones) that came to mind in the constructs of the terms First World and Third World, their responses came usually in the form of "too much difference." The adjectival narratives worked in fierce opposition to one another: illiteracy, disease, and poverty in the Third World; wealth, class mobility, and technological advancement in the First World. When asked how a homogeneously illiterate, disease-ridden, and poverty-stricken population would be able to produce the bulk of the clothing they wore and the technical equipment on which they relied (such as computers, recorders, etc. that most often are associated with civilization and progress), a customary, apparently concluding/conclusive response was offered in these terms: "They have their culture, we have ours." How do we understand this paradoxical gesture of flattening out and assimilating difference on the one hand, while freezing and reifying it on the other?[11]

Of course, the larger epistemological universe from which students make these normative claims is constructed within the contours of liberal academic feminism, whose own analytic paralysis in relation to questions of difference, power, class, and racial and sexual privilege gave rise to the "add and stir feminism" in which the intellectual and political agendas of white middle-class women were grounded. These were the very terms of critique made in the texts that students were reading. What these texts showed is that, when diffused globally, local analyses of the United States re-centered the local as universal and the West, more generally, as feminism's epistemic center, evidence once again that curricular projects are profoundly political projects. "Add and stir feminism" continues to frame the dominant curricular imperatives in far too many women's studies classrooms. Chandra Talpade Mohanty has identified its contemporary pedagogical variant as the "feminist as tourist," or "feminist as international consumer."[12] According to Mohanty, the effects of this strategy are that students and teachers are left with a clear sense of the difference and distance between the local and the global.[13] Indeed, geography and race become proxy for distance, difference, and ultimately, cultural incommensurability.

In terms of the students' claims, it seemed initially that while "culture" was the presumed point of comparison in both parts of the equation—"they have their culture, we have ours"—it was reified in the context of the Third World and rendered absent in that of the First World. But it is perhaps more accurate to say that "culture" was overdetermined in the former and effectively absent in the latter, a situation that amplifies Uma Narayan's claim that cultural explanations are proffered more readily to "problems" in Third World contexts than they are in Western contexts. One effect is the muting or evisceration of political and ideological processes.[14] In the case of the Third World, "culture" stood in for values, which almost arithmetically added up to tradition, whereas in the case of the First World, "culture" operated as proxy, not for values but for constructs such as class, wealth, and intelligence, the very constructs that produced "too much difference." Values, often difficult to define in these discussions, were understood tautologically as beliefs in, and adherence to, tradition and a resistance to change—an odd, perhaps unnatural, evisceration of the superior benefits of the West, naturally and homogeneously imbued with wealth, intelligence, and class mobility. These values undergirded traditional patriarchy that subordinated women, subjecting them to practices such as female genital mutilation and thereby ridding them of any claims to agency such as those conferred on their distant counterparts in the West. Again the regnant but implicit assumptions in the work of Feminist Majority were being replicated here: that patriarchy was irrelevant to modernity and that "traditional patriarchy" had only a single archaic source, which Western modernity automatically dissolved. Ultimately, it seemed that ascriptions were being made selectively in the service of "culture" in a way that suggested the working of a forbidden, unspoken clause that completed the phrase "They have their culture and we have ours": "never the twain shall meet." Thus, there were two important elements in these generative protestations. First, they unmasked a latent judgment residing in that apparently neutral, relativist claim of the first part of the equation. Second, there was something instructive in this ideological formulation of distance: geographic distance produced analytic and experiential distance that is perennially inaccessible. It signaled a move from a "local" that was problematic but familiar to a "global" that was problematic and foreign—a similar unmasking of latent hierarchy.[15] It is in this slippage from local familiarity to global foreignness that latent hierarchical assumptions reside—assumptions that seemingly mark their difference from one another. An apparently neutral cultural relativism is not free, then, of absolutist claims.

"Time and the 'Other' ": The Adventures of Anthropology and Other Sightings[16]

There are, as well, other important symbols that circulate within these cultural gestures that collapse distance into difference. These symbols need to be summoned here as a way of marking the epistemic universe from which those apparently concluding/conclusive statements are drawn. Cultural relativism does not live alone. As Ella Shohat has shown, the modernization discourses and practices it infuses "stretch across geographic and national borders."[17] In the process, they collapse divergent histories and temporalities into these apparently irreconcilable binaries of tradition and modernity, and produce other accompanying corollaries around religion and secular reason, stasis and change, and science and the nonrational. In so doing, they also territorialize their own distance, ultimately placing their claims within an ideological universe, whose analytic and material boundaries dovetail with imperatives that are most closely aligned with those of colonization. Cultural relativism's livelihood within anthropology—a discipline that, like others, butts out other knowledge paradigms in favor of its own and legitimizes its methodologies and chosen "objects" of study—worked to facilitate the installation of colonial knowledges while furthering anthropology's own colonizing mission.[18]

Implicit within this tradition/modernity opposition is a conception of time that is, paradoxically, constrictively linear and resolutely hierarchical. Indeed, this formulation of time is itself ideological in that it props up investments in the political and psychic economies of capitalism, which ground modernization and provide the conditions in which it thrives. This paradox of linearity and hierarchy within time demarcated as tradition, ostensibly distanced from and subordinated to time demarcated as modernity, is rendered in a way that produces the very distance and difference that students replicated. Johannes Fabian's critique of this dualism is instructive here, for he shows how tradition is ostensibly placed in another time, one that is not contemporaneous with "our" own. The West is presumably "here and now," while the Third World is "then and there," apparently exclusive of the "here and now."[19] Both time and distance, then, are ineluctably circumscribed.

Within this chapter's framing of the transnational, time is neither vertically accumulated nor horizontally teleological. Nor is it simply a thing ordered by the mechanics of another, outside, thing—the clock (a point I engage more fully in the final chapter). Rather than deploy the linear evolutionary narrative of a horizontal telos, I propose that we consider time in terms that conjoin Shohat and Fabian with those of Stuart Hall. For Shohat, time is "scrambled and palimpsestic, in all the Worlds, with the premodern, the modern, the postmodern and the para-modern coexisting globally."[20] But it is not only the global coexistence of different technologies of time telling that is of concern to us here. The central idea is that of the palimpsest—a parchment that has been in-scribed two or three times, the previous text having been imperfectly erased and remaining therefore still partly visible. This understanding of the imperfect erasure, hence visibility, of a "past" bears close analytic resemblance to Stuart Hall's formulation that I used to signal the ways in which the new world order, inaugurated through the political economies of the 1991 Gulf War, "had already been inscribed in an earlier position-ing."[21] The idea of the "new" structured through the "old" scrambled, palimpsestic character of time, both jettisons the truncated distance of linear time and dislodges the impulse for incommensurability, which the ideology of distance creates. It thus rescrambles the "here and now" and the "then and there" to a "here and there" and a "then and now," and makes visible what Payal Banerjee calls the ideological traffic between and among formations that are otherwise positioned as dissimilar.

Using the social formations we have designated as colonial, neo-colonial, and neo-imperial is not to suggest a logical teleology in which one form of state morphs into the other. Instead, we want to hold on to the historical specificity through which those various social relations are constituted at the same time that we examine the continuity and disjunctures of practices within and among various state formations. These practices are neither frozen nor neatly circumscribed within temporalities that never collide or even meet. Colonialism's multiple projects, often normalized through hypervisible practices of racialization and (hetero)-sexualization, cannot be seen simply in terms of having been past, and thus no longer constitutive of the (post)modern. Not only is there no fixed past, but various technologies of timekeeping and various narrations of time can exist within the same temporality, thereby provoking important disturbances to the hegemonic financial market time of modernity, for instance, whose passage is contemporaneously marked by militarized war time.[22] These different narrations of time, these "perverse modernities" (to use Lisa Lowe and Judith Halberstam's felicitous phrase)[23] unravel that which has been normalized and normativized in modernity's desire to be seen as a single homogeneous project.

Deploying this notion of time is not only about urging future pedagogical and analytic frameworks to become palimpsestic. Modernity itself as a conceptual apparatus needs to be scrambled; the ideological traffic between cultural absolutism and cultural relativism would have to be made visible. In addition, linearity would not be constituted solely on the outside—that is, operating elsewhere. Scrambling time would mean that there is no neat, discrete demarcation between and among state or heterosexualizing processes on the inside and those undertaken on the outside, among conceptual categories and historical processes. Spanish imperialism, as a set of processes, inaugurated the colonization of the Americas, but these processes did not simply install themselves elsewhere without constituting and legitimating a set of practices of rule within the geographical borders signifying as Spain. Thus, the practices of Balboa had to have been already contained within that formation, having set up their own structures and mechanisms of distance and difference, having marked their own structures of negation. Since the ideological traffic is not merely one sided, there is, as well, another route from colony to metropolis.[24] Thus, one crucial question in our analysis pertains to whether those psychic economies, produced at an earlier colonial moment, as in Balboa's carnage, continue to operate in the global mobilization of a particular brand of white warfare (hetero)patriarchy, which utilizes modernity to legitimize itself.

It is not my intent, however, to collapse historical moments and conceptual categories into one another, nor to collude in an unwitting gesture of homogenization. In focusing on these three historical formations in which heterosexuality works as a mechanism to normativize and discipline, the practices that structure and mediate heterosexuality become crucial to show how these formations are indeed mutually, though unequally, entwined. The multiple sites in which heterosexuality is made to matter will also be made visible. The practices—the very mechanisms through which state and nation are mediated—would have different effects that bear on the contextual arrangements in which they find themselves, which in turn shape their capacity to travel, to overlap, and circulate within and among these formations. This layered complex thickens our understanding of the multiple sites in which state and corporate neoliberalism re-enact heterosexual coercions at this contemporary moment. Methodologically, all those sites that appear not to be (hetero)sexualized—welfare, militarism, the patriot, the citizen, the immigrant, the tourist, the soldier, the enemy—will be made to carry heterosexual freight. We will conjoin practices that appear bounded by binary, materialized temporalities and spaces so that they constitute an ensemble and work in mutually paradoxical ways. In addition, we will destabilize that which hegemony has rendered coherent or fixed; reassemble that which appears to be disparate, scattered, or otherwise idiosyncratic; foreground that which is latent and therefore powerful in its apparent absence; and analyze that which is apparently self-evident, which hegemony casts as commonsensical and natural, but which we shall read as gestures of power that deploy violence to normalize and discipline.

This ideological reassembly is not simply a textual or methodological innovation but rather an instance of how ideologies actually traffic across multiple sites. How is it, for instance, that the ideological scaffolding that bolstered the sixteenth-century massacre by Balboa, undertaken "then and there" in an apparently "distant" geography, shows up in the "here and now" in the United States as the Military Working Group convened in 1993 to consider whether "homosexuality was compatible with military service"? How is it that the neocolonial Caribbean state's recodification of domestic violence in terms of familial property relations imports a specifically colonial collocation that defines women as property with ostensibly little erotic space outside the boundaries of domestic patriarchy? How is tradition reworked in the modern in ways that make it worthy of upholding rather than impeding progress?

I will use tradition and modernity as shifting ideological authorizations because they have been either intentionally invoked, disavowed, or muted as part of the repertoire of strategies deployed by different interests within or related to the state. Put differently, tradition and modernity have been used to designate specific temporalities, but they are themselves practices that are constituted through social relations that are interested in their purchase, and thus in that process move them into ideological proximity to, or distance from, one another. Since they do not operate simply as linear designations neatly demarcating a transition from one historical moment to another, or as categories that are merely fixed and inert, the question is not so much whether they matter but *how* they have been made to matter in matters sexual, what meanings have been affixed to them, who deploys them, and to what ends. When do "traditional" (hetero)sexual discourses get valorized within "modern" neo-imperial formations, and why? How do they come to be positioned as critical to the project of modernity? Does heterosexualization occupy a civilizing nexus in the neocolonial state's imperative of distancing itself from tradition in order to be counted as modern, that is, "civilized," and accorded the "benefits" of modernity? Does heterosexuality sit at the nexus between fundamentalism and militarism within the neo-imperial national security state? What are the ways in which heterosexual tradition becomes differentially, yet mutually, constitutive of both formations? And how do hierarchies, which apparently mark their difference from each other, get mobilized? How is tradition deployed within a hierarchically ordered West and its Others to construct a good democratic tradition— one that accepts the ostensibly progressive character of the imperatives of global, neoliberal capital by muting its uneven hierarchical dispersals—as over and against a bad barbaric tradition, whose agents require schooling or coercion to recognize its benefits? What kinds of patriarchies do different modernities require?[25] I do not take up all of these questions in the context of this chapter, but one of the major analytic implications of bringing these three historical formations into a universe in which they share palimpsestic time is that we are able to plot the routes of ideological traffic and proximity within and among them. Thus, neo-imperial modernity, understood as democracy, can no longer be positioned in a hierarchical, superior relationship to neocolonial tradition understood as underdevelopment, and therefore of no relevance to modernity.

Since there is, analytically at least, no good heterosexual democratic tradition and no bad heterosexual primitive tradition, there can be no false deduction that democratic heterosexualization is simply more benign in its alignment with modernity than traditional heterosexualization which, in its alignment with backwardness, is simply more pernicious. (I would say "perverse," except that we want to hold on to the felicitous designation to which I alluded earlier.) Put differently, democracy and neo-imperial modernity can no longer be positioned to circumvent the nexus of violence—neither the violence through which they are constituted nor the regulatory disciplining practices that they animate. Particularly at this moment of the bald exercise of empire—when practices of violence have compromised democracy—analytical, political, and ethical claims to it cannot easily or disinterestedly free themselves from such compromise. Given how impossible it is for any system of regulation to operate outside of a series of coercions and violence, it is not, as I stated earlier, simply a question of foregrounding heterosexualization in these formations, but rather foregrounding the shared violence of heterosexualization so as to provide the connective web within and among colonial, neocolonial, and neo-imperial social formations.

Thinking about these geopolitical histories of colonialism, neocolonialism, and neo-imperialism together is also a way of thinking about the various ways in which racialization and colonization are being consistently written into modernity's different projects. These different projects are occasioned by the uneven class relations and differentiations produced by neo-liberal capital's dispersions. We now have ample archaeologies of the gendered, sexualized investments in colonialism's racial project. Remember that in the linear technology of time, tradition displaces the neocolonial and modernity displaces the neo-imperial as preferred terms. Since both neocolonial and neo-imperial states work, albeit asymmetrically, through colonial time and simultaneously through Christian neoliberal financial time—organized under the auspices of global capital interests and lending agencies such as the International Monetary Fund and the World Bank—our task is to move practices of neocolonialism within the ambit of modernity, and to move those of colonialism into neo-imperialism, reckoning, in other words, with pa-limpsestic time.[26] We shall use heteropatriarchy as the pivot on which to make these moves, the chart to help us navigate the various ways in which it is at once intimate to modernity and its intersecting practices—the very practices through which nation and state are mediated and produced. But it does not mean that patriarchy operates transhistorically. The fact that the project of heterosexualization is formative of state conduct in all three historical instances means that it is not unique, but it does not mean that everywhere it operates the same. There are particular codices through which state conduct unfolds, and those codices are grounded in particular configurations of class, gender, racial and sexual antagonisms. They assist or frustrate the imperatives that promote nation building, break apart the ideologies of a seamless nation that serve imperial/interventionist ends, and demystify those moments when the project of nation-building and the project of empire-building become coincident.

The assumed tasks of heterosexualization, always governed simultaneously by and through gendered, racial, class, and sexual formations, will tell us something about how specific states govern and about their practices of rule. We will think of "state" as a set of contradictory and uneven locations, institutions, personnel, managerial practices, and imperatives; and as a gendered, classed, racialized, and sexualized ensemble.[27] Although connected, the particularities of governmentality will no doubt differ. Thus, the difference between the particular and the unique will be used to mediate the transhistoric.

Patriarchal state-building practices are multiple, and, as stated earlier, are paradoxically constitutive of nation-building. Among these practices are heteromasculine soldiering; the territorial marking of land and property coincident with the territorial marking of whiteness; inscribing particular gendered and sexualized bodies and communities (same-sex and sex workers) with the consummate power to disrupt the conjugal household; positioning the nonpatriot terrorist with the power to undo the secure borders of the nation; rendering heterosexuality, consumerism, and citizenship mutually contingent; folding Judeo-Christian conjugal tradition into the regimes of rule; and aligning corporate and state interests in ways that benefit imperialism but also render the neocolonial class as complicit in global capital's project of recolonization.

At this point, as we move toward thinking about these histories together and separately, let me resummarize my methodological approach. First, I will bring segregated (discursive) practices into greater ideological proximity with one another in order to make visible the extent of ideological traffic that takes place between and among them. Put differently, I aim to render any single practice unintelligible in the absence of its ideological cohorts. Second, I will bring into greater ideological proximity segregated (discursive) practices across and between these overlapping histories and geopolitical sites in order that the extent of ideological traffic between and among them might be made visible. Third, I will foreground those spaces where "hidden hegemonies" reside (in the words of Jakobsen and Pelligrini),[28] such as in the notion of the "secular" neo-imperial state, which not only mutes Judeo-Christian claims on it but also enables it to function, in general, as the quintessential marker of (post)modernity's triumph, or in the figure of the "patriot," who bears the ideological mark of the originary heterosexual citizen.

Rescue Narrative Two: Sodomies Old and New

During the course of his travels of conquest in 1513, Balboa came upon the Panamanian village of Quarequa. In an act of carnage intended to establish Spanish imperial rule, Balboa and his men killed the leader of the village along with six hundred of his warriors. Balboa killed and then fed to his dogs forty more Indians, whom he found dressed in "women's apparel." What follows is the scene as described in one of the few primary accounts, which I take from the work cited by Jonathan Goldberg in his essay "Sodomy in the New World":

> [Balboa] founde the house of this kynge infected with the most abominable and unnatural lechery. For he founde the kynges brother and many other younge men in womens apparel, smoth and effeminately

decked, which by the report of such as dwelle abowt hym, he abused with preposterous venus. Of these abowte the number of fortie, he commaunded to bee gyven for a pray to his dogges.[29]

As in the case of the texts I assembled in chapter 3 for the ideological production of the new world order, I will use this moment as constituting the very relations it describes. Goldberg rightly points out that sodomy is neither mentioned in these lines nor found in the text surrounding it,[30] nor, I might add, is Balboa's heterosexuality declared. The text, however, forcefully presumes it. Its substitutes—"preposterous venus," "abominable and unnatural lechery," and "infection"—carry sodomy's weight, and carry, as well, the threat of contamination that ultimately justifies its evisceration. We can only presume that the power of heterosexuality, which operates without definition, is asserted through this act of carnage, which welds imperial and heterosexual interests together. In the course of only five lines of text, the horror of this act is further normativized by being positioned as the only civilized response to the scene; as the conclusive response to the "preposterous venus." I use the word "further" here because within the terms of imperial carnage there is apparently no need to explain why six hundred Indians had to be killed by Balboa. But there is a great deal that is being inaugurated in this narrative economy.

First, there is the suggestion that the king's brother and those around him substituted cross-dressing and sexual indulgence for responsible warriorship, although, as the imperial paradox would have it, the reward for both is death. Yet, the coupling of sexual indulgence and the presumed infraction—wanton inattention to the business of the state and the business of defense—cathect a certain suspicion unto cross-dressers and those engaged in abominable lechery. The result is that heterosexuality animates militarism.

Second, militarism requires such staunch adherence to heterosexual masculinity that it resorts to violence in excess even of its own norms of killing. What threat, we might ask, did Balboa and his entourage confront that they needed to redress (reclothe) themselves through such a spectacular, grotesque act of terror that required the sight of prolonged agony and mangled flesh to seal its authority?

Third, it would seem that given the swiftness of Balboa's response (the event occurred only two days after his army invaded Panama) heterosexuality was required to constitute those early moments of imperial incursion. Neither secondary nor marginal to imperial conduct, then, it seemed crucial to the ways in which that army imagined itself. Here there is evidence of an incipient colonial state apparatus moving to supplant an indigenous state as it sought to anchor heterosexual sexuality as the official sexual story, while turning homosexuality into violent spectacle. While it is indeed too early here to speak in terms of a state apparatus per se, we can safely presume that imperial intent hinges on the establishment of heterosexual relations of rule.

Fourth, the racialized right to European rule is, in the conquest of the "savage" Indian and resulting genocide, simultaneously a racialized right to European heterosexual rule, subordinating indigenous heterosexual interests to imperial ones; marking boundaries around which imperial power coheres not only for sexual difference but for racial superiority as well. In the psychic map of imperialism, its ideal typical heterosexuality is simply superior to all others.

Finally, in this somewhat classic struggle between (heterosexual) civilization and (sodomitic) savagery, indigenous heterosexual interests needed to be rescued from themselves. Only an outside power could perform that act of rescue and invest in the heterosexual the presumed power of restoring order out of chaos, of sexually cleansing the newly conquered body politic from its own internal infection. The spectacle of war and the spectacle of sexual cleansing meet on territorial grounds so that territorial claims around the body politic might be secured. The slaughter of enemy cross-dressing Indians and heterosexual Indians clears the way for the white, presumedly heterosexual, soldier to claim citizenship. Thus territorial claims and citizenship claims work hand in hand, and both are racialized and gendered. It is not only that the colony is not worth having unless it can be made heterosexual, it is also that the violent assertion of white citizenship reserves personhood for white masculinity alone.[31] What Spain could no longer eliminate as the undesirable through massacre was installed within a more elaborate apparatus for colonial governance, folding criminality into a civilizing mandate through law that transferred the cathected suspicion from cross-dressers to sodomites, the latter still bearing the status of outlaw. Nor was Balboa simply "then and

Ch. 3 → Hungia

there," occupying the bounded space of Panama. The invading army was well familiar with the set of Iberian practices that either executed "sodomites" or burned them at the stake.[32]

What kind of sexuality befits responsible soldiering? In what sexual garb does the white manly citizen soldier wish to be clothed as an invading army brings sovereign nation-states within an imperial ambit? Which bodies are made to bear the violence of heterosexuality's colonizing mission? These questions posed in terms of one geography will now be revisited in another.

All Homosexuality Is Incompatible with Military Service! Heterosexual Loyalty as the Moral Imperative of the Imperial Fighting Force

It appears that we have traveled a long distance from the sixteenth-century Balboan carnage to twenty-first century imperial militarization in the United States, in both its external and internal manifestations. It was 1993—on the heels of the end of the first Gulf War and a decade before this more recent round of imperial violence in the Middle East; seven years after the Supreme Court ruling in *Bowers v. Hardwick*;[33] and five centuries after Balboa's invading army salvaged Quarequa—when senators and members of congress in Washington, D.C., convened for hearings that would spectacularize, yet again, heterosexual anxiety in a manner that put homosexuality on display. Much had intervened in the traffic between geographies and time, but the distance from Balboa was substantially narrowed. Of course, the proposals did not specify heterosexual anxiety but rather a rhetorical preference for titles such as, "Public Debate over Homosexuals in the Military," or the thoroughly sanitized version by the Military Working Group: "Summary Report of the Military Working Group." Members of this group defined their task in terms of a dehistoricized presidential mandate that directed then-secretary of defense Les Aspen to develop a policy "ending discrimination on the basis of sexual orientation in determining who may serve in the Armed Forces of the United States."[34] President Clinton had further directed that the policy be implemented in a manner that was "practical, realistic, and consistent with the high standards of combat effectiveness and unit cohesion our Armed Forces must maintain."[35] But the mode of address, the narrative solipsisms, and the rhetorical sleights of hand all helped to fashion a particular regime of truth that can most accurately be understood as quintessentially Balboan.

The Military Working Group was only one of the major constituencies charged with instituting a shift from the then-existing policy that discharged military service personnel for their status. But since its members presided over the very domain that was the object of possible transformation[36] (thus privileging military dominance over its own restructuring)[37] and since the report almost forms the entire content of the final statute, it is appropriate to utilize it as the focal point of my analysis here. Specifically, I want to travel deep inside its symbolic universe to map the specific ways in which it positions homosexuality as incompatible with military service and imagines it as threat to national security; and how it is, in this presumed shift from old policy to new, that it charts a continuous course with the racialized psychic economies of heterosexuality and the exigencies that constitute its regimes. Lest we are tempted to view the most recent war rumblings of ignoring homosexuality in military service as the actions of a benign state, we need only to examine the multiple ways in which other of its related heterosexualizing projects, particularly those related to the production of the enemy, are continually being undertaken.[38] Moreover, the new statute, which Janet Halley describes as even more discriminatory than its predecessor, is being avidly fought out in courts, thus showing that the regulatory violence it exerts continues to have effect.

There is, of course, historical precedent for moments in which exigency overrides ideology. The massive mobilization of women to produce military hardware—to perform the public feminized work of allegiance to the nation-state by supporting the troops through (segregated) employment during the Second World War, in the context of an ideology that defined a woman's place as in the home—is one such exigency, as is the mobilization of Indian nations in the Second World War[39] and the use of black troops to fight the Civil War and subsequent wars in the context of an ideology of white racial superiority.[40]

In its deliberations, the Military Working Group invented its own sexual taxonomy that was not entirely independently conceived (although it seemed to claim it as its own), in the sense that it drew from normative definitions of homosexuality that collapsed identity into sex and the satisfaction of sexual desire. As was the case with the Caribbean state managers discussed in chapter 1, the implicit dictum relied on a reification of sex: sex was all of what we did; it therefore constituted all of who we are. "For clarity," it provided (very abbreviated) definitions for terms such as "bisexual," "homosexual," "homosexual act," "homosexual conduct," "homosexual marriage," "homosexual statement," "homosexuality," and "sexual orientation."[41] A homosexual was a "person, regardless of sex, who engage[d], desire[d] to engage in or intended to engage in homosexual acts," such as "bodily contact actively undertaken or passively permitted between members of the same sex for the purpose of satisfying sexual desires." Such acts included "sodomy and acts other than sodomy such as kissing and dancing between members of the same sex for the purpose of satisfying sexual desires." Together with these "homosexual acts," "attempts or solicitations to engage in them," "homosexual marriage" or "attempted homosexual marriage," as well as "homosexual statements by a member that he or she is homosexual or bisexual," constitute "homosexual conduct." Homosexuality was "the quality, condition, or fact of being homosexual," while sexual orientation was defined as "a sexual attraction to individuals or a particular gender." Within this bounded system that turns inward on itself, particularly in its definitions of acts and conduct, sex (by which is meant sodomy), sexual desire, and sexual attraction turn into homosexual persons. They become, in Janet Halley's terms, "metonyms of one another."[42]

Once this hermetic system was sealed as truth, the next task of the Military Working Group was to delineate the unique character of the military: its singular mission, its moral imperatives, and its institutional and environmental climate, all of which carved out a superordinate role for militarized heterosexuality. The armed forces' purpose was to further the "national interests [of the United States] abroad, to defend [its] borders and [to protect] the American way of life."[43] This was a unique mission that required equally unique moral prescriptions in that the "military's mission to fight and win wars" necessitated that "citizen soldiers" both give their lives, "as the ultimate sacrifice in service to . . . country," as well as take lives: "to kill and destroy" in honor of "the nation's call." Recognizing that this moral mandate to kill was in specific, not generalized, terms, it distinguished these "citizen soldiers" from the "mercenaries" who killed indiscriminately. The former, "a professional armed force," "privileged" and "qualified" to serve, had ceded their "individual rights . . . for military necessity." Its members were often not able to "separate their private lives from their working environment." They were required "to work, eat, recreate, sleep and bathe in cramped spaces for prolonged periods of time, sometimes in the most remote parts of the world." "Separation of the sexes [was] often the only concession to privacy." In addition, these "citizen soldiers" brought their values with them, values and beliefs that were strongly held and not amenable to change. Leadership and discipline, the Military Working Group concluded, "should not attempt to counter the basic values which parents and society have taught." Heterosexual homosociality, then, needed to be protected at all costs.

We must bear in mind that such narrative logic has already been established and that the various solipsisms need to cohere ideologically around a conclusion that had actually been formulated before the fact, namely, that "all homosexuality is incompatible with military service." Nonetheless, we need to trace the particular set of perfidious threats through which homosexuality is imagined. How specifically is it positioned to undermine "national interests abroad," instead of "furthering" them? How does homosexuality undo that "synergistic mix" of "unit cohesion . . . and readiness," the "sine qua non" of "combat effectiveness"? From the definitional choices that produced the taxonomy above, one might conclude that "acts," statements, and conduct alone would constitute such perfidy, but this is not what occurred. For the metonymic structure to function fully no act or conduct alone could fulfill this task of perfidy. Only homosexual persons themselves could satisfy the underside of a mandate so large. Thus, the Military Working Group presented its verdict not through acts alone, but through presence and identity— that is, it made the mere presence of homosexuality sufficient to undo heterosexuality. Here is how the argument was rendered:

> The essence of unit cohesion is the bonding between members of a
> unit which holds them together, sustains their will to support each

other, and enables them to fight together under the stress and chaos of war. The MWG found that the presence of open homosexuals in a unit would, in general, polarize and fragment the unit and destroy the bonding and singleness of purpose required for effective military operations. This phenomenon occurs whether or not homosexual acts are invoked. By simply stating that he or she is a homosexual, the individual becomes isolated from the group and combat effectiveness suffers.

And, thereafter, only chaos could ensue. Heterosexuality continued to mobilize heterosexism to defend itself: it would be "extremely difficult for an open homosexual to exercise authority as a leader in the Armed Forces of the United States." "Perceptions of unfairness and fraternization" would impair their ability to generate "mutual respect, fairness and concern for the well-being of subordinates"; "leadership priorities would be reoriented from training and combat to prevent internal discord." But, ultimately, it was the "privacy principle," to use Kendall Thomas's apt phrase, that put the proverbial (heterosexual) nail in the coffin, or, perhaps, in the door of the closet.

Homosexual privacy thus came to be positioned as the primary mechanism for protecting heterosexual homosociality. Leaving untouched the question of how institutionalization normalized heterosexual privacy (what was made homosexually private was heterosexually public), sexual orientation was affixed onto homosexuality alone (the same way that in *Bowers v. Hardwick* sodomy was affixed onto homosexuality alone, in spite of the criminalization of heterosexual sodomy), and was defined as private and policed in order that it remain as such. Once it climbed out of the closet, it threatened heterosexual privacy—the collective, public "personal sanctuary," constituting "a major and unacceptable invasion" into the little privacy that heterosexuals enjoyed. But it is not sexual orientation alone that is operative here; rather, it is a reified sexual orientation that comes already armed with the apparently uncontrollable desire to seduce, and it is the power of this seduction that invades the personal sanctuary of heterosexual service members, those spaces where individuals "relax, bathe and sleep together" that propel homosexuals to engage in "high risk . . . unhealthy behavior" and propel them to form "sub-cultures" outside the formal chain of military command, thereby sub-stituting military authority with their own sexual authority—the very propensity of the Indian cross-dressers massacred by Balboa. Ultimately, the perfidy is not even homosexual "presence" but character, a secret, suspect homosexual character, perverted and sex-operating, as an "en-emy within," bringing harm, undoing collectivity, and corrupting hetero-sexuality ("even non-practicing homosexuals either intend to engage in homosexual acts or desire to engage in homosexual acts") by forming "sub-cultures" loyal to sex alone. In the same way in which "the house of the kynge" became the object of irresponsible soldiering, these "citizen soldiers" are positioned with the proclivity to forego allegiance to com-bat, the allegiance to "fight and win wars"—the imperial imperative—and substitute in its stead allegiance to their own narrow sexual interests.

Thus far I have focused on the extent of the narrative regulatory violence through which military masculinity constituted the soldier citizen. Clearly, violence operates not only on the narrative level, since the effect of this statute rests both in its power to discharge service members and to exclude them. Homosexual orientation alone does not constitute grounds for dis-missal. Homosexuals can continue to be part of the imperial fighting force insofar as they do not confess or do not "tell" that they are homosexual or bisexual. The structure of this framework brings us to yet another dimen-sion in our understanding of state homophobic violence and its quotidian effects: the fact that the pretext for discharge from military service inheres within the very interstices of the regulation. That pretext is established in the manipulation of the dual axes of status and conduct that hinge on a set of "propensity" clauses embedded in the final statute that crafts a singular role for a "reasonable" (and I would add, heterosexual) person to determine their interface. More to the point, the policy prohibited statements that "demonstrat[ed] a propensity to engage in homosexual acts," prohibited conduct that "a reasonable person would understand to demonstrate a propensity or intent to engage in homosexual acts,"[44] and allowed ser-vice members who acknowledged themselves as gay and engaged in homo-sexual acts not to be subject to discharge if they proved that they did not "engage in homosexual acts" or had a "propensity" to do so. Put differ-ently, instead of shifting the locus of guilt from status to conduct, the policy defined status as conduct then made conduct into a propensity that needed to be disproved so as not to be believed to constitute status. In the end it invested military personnel with the ultimate power of reasonableness to judge the extent to which, and the success with which, homosexuals and bisexuals rebutted the regnant presumptions. We can grapple with the colossal scope of what is being undertaken, in spite of its "irrationality," by relying once again on Halley's insight:

> Having created the propensity apparatus in order to justify discharge based on coming-out statements, the policy vastly expanded the conduct grounds for discharge. Commanders have unreviewable discretion to initiate proceedings against service-members who have engaged in any acts that a "reasonable person" would think manifests a propensity to engage in same-sex sexual conduct. Because this decision cannot be reviewed, the commander has the ultimate call on what a "reasonable person" would think. And because it is tied to the norms of sexual performativity in the commander's unit, there can be no law on this subject: anything could be conduct that manifests propensity.[45]

And it was not only Balboa who had come to sojourn in the court but also *Bowers v. Hardwick*, which had provided an earlier metonym that divorced sodomy from heterosexuality and married it to homosexuality alone.[46] The Supreme Court's decision to reverse *Bowers v. Hardwick* in 2003 and grant a broad constitutional right to sexual privacy is being brought into contest in the 2004 bid on the part of traditionalists and neoconservatives, spearheaded by President George W. Bush, to call for a constitutional ban on gay marriage.[47] As I discuss later, the Defense of Marriage Act is apparently insufficient to solidify these psychic associations that have collapsed perfidy into homosexual personhood. Heterosexual anxiety seems bent on continuing to be imprisoned in this violent genealogy.

When the Region Is a Closet: Disciplinary Time and the Morality of Heterosexual Tradition

In foregrounding the idea of the region as a closet, I want to signal the ways in which the imperatives of heterosexualization share a disciplining imperative that crosses the fictive boundaries of the nation-state to encompass the region that is signaled as the Americas. The title is a play on Tana Alturi's "When the Closet Is a Region," which examines the various ways in which heterosexuality operates in the Commonwealth Caribbean region in favor of what she terms a "homophobic exclusionary nationalism."[48] Here, I intend the idea of region to move beyond the geography of the Caribbean and into the United States, a move that positions both the neocolonial and the neo-imperial within a shared, though unequal, frame of disciplinary time. My empirical referents here will be drawn from the Bahamian legislative codes I discussed in chapter 1, namely the Sexual Offences and Domestic Violence Act of 1986, which was installed by the neocolonial state managers in Trinidad and Tobago (the very year in which *Bowers v. Hardwick* was passed) as a way "to bring back morality within the fabric of society,"[49] and the 1993 Defense of Marriage Act in which neo-imperial state managers in the United States felt compelled to "define and protect the institution of marriage."[50]

The heterosexualization of morality and the reinvention of a heterosexual-only tradition, whose pedigree ostensibly harkens back to an ancient religious mandate along with an equally ancient secular mandate based in Western civilization, traverse the region via multiple, interrelated routes: a set of legal codes that reanchor the perimeters of heterosexuality, and interests that are organized through the globalization of the Christian Right, which as early as 1975 in Mexico City had already exerted its power to shape explicitly feminist political agendas that refused the collapse of woman into wife and motherhood. In the United States these interests coalesced, as Sara Diamond has shown, in a coalition of moral traditionalists and capitalists who support empire-building.[51] And while Trinidad and Tobago was one of the countries at the forefront of contesting the importation of American televangelism as "off-shore religious banking,"[52] local (indeed, regional) patriarchal interests did not need American imperial assistance to solidify Judeo-Christian patriarchal imperatives or, more ambivalently, those of Islam. While both tradition and morality are made to function in heterosexual garb, they have different symbolic meanings for neo-imperial and neocolonial state managers. While the former believe themselves always already equipped as the originary heirs to civilization and its accompanying heterosexual mandates, the latter can make no such claim. By participating in the West, not as heirs, but through a truncated colonial memory, as if they possessed no genealogies of their own, neocolonial state managers, much like middle-class black women in the Club Movement in the United States and middle-class black women of the early nationalist movement in the Caribbean, are forced to comport with a heterosexualized morality that seems somehow devoid of sex—but only in certain domains.[53] That is, for instance, not in the domain of the globally driven sexual economy of tourist desire, which relies heavily on the "hypersexed bodies" (the term is Tracy Robinson's) of heterosexual women.[54] Ultimately, however, tradition, morality, law, Judeo-Christian religion, the natural, and the heterosexual are multiply constitutive, policing various texts through various forms of masculinity and respectability while purporting to signal lesbians, gay men, and marginalized constituencies.

As neither a stable ontological identity nor a fixed process, heterosexuality resorts to makeshift signs through which it is registered and through which it creates and legitimizes idiosyncratic boundaries. Operating visibly (or even hypervisibly), I will trace just how the state makes its investments in tradition and morality known by positioning lesbian and gay bodies as an ideological foil in its service. But there is a thick nexus of contradiction operating here as well—that is, of criminalizing some women while "protecting" others; of making property relations the basis of protecting middle-class women against patriarchal violence in the home, while undermining the material base for the social reproduction of the working class in ways that would legitimize the refusal of state "protection" and uphold privatization; of claiming a moral ground on the basis of what heterosexuality is not (that is, not homosexuality), which of necessity eviscerates the state's own complicity in bringing violence into being; of legalizing a putative heterosexual conjugal household while making it impossible for recipients of Aid to Families with Dependent Children (AFDC) to live as family. I now turn to the specific elaborations within neocolonial formations and the precise articulations of the heterosexual, the moral, and the natural through a close reading of the manipulation of the category of "consent"—that category that hints at adulthood, or at the very least at autonomy, but that ultimately eviscerates it.[55]

Negotiating and Suspending "Consent":
The Law as Moral Arbiter[56]

In an internal note written prior to the passage of the Sexual Offences and Domestic Violence Act, law commissioners in Trinidad and Tobago stated explicitly that the bill's aim was to "bring back morality within the fabric of society."[57] But who were the culprits responsible for such moral destruction, and what guarantees could the law provide to attend to the reversals that such moral destruction had produced: a society overtaken by all the signs of Western decadence including AIDS, promiscuity, prostitution, lesbian and gay sex, and simple overall sexual intemperance? Perhaps the law needed to provide no guarantees, in the sense that as a disciplining mechanism morality's entanglement with the punishment practices of power means that it requires no prior proof of potential effectiveness.

The significance of the Sexual Offences and Domestic Violence Act is that within it lie two sets of provisions that are apparently unrelated: the criminalization of lesbian sex (and the recriminalization of gay sex) and the criminalization of rape in marriage. Bringing these provisions into ideological proximity with each other enables us to track the discursive production of morality and to demonstrate that state managers reinscribe sex (albeit forbidden, "amoral," and "unnatural" sex) as the basic relationship between women, between men, between men and women, and between adults and "minors." Maleness and femaleness are sexualized. But this sexual reinscription is not based on relationships of equivalency. A hierarchy is established within the discourse that manifests itself in two simultaneous gestures: one that draws boundaries around licit sex (boundaries that become isomorphic with the right morality) and the other that creates a category of illicit or criminalized sex to enforce licit sex. The right morality cannot be established without what state managers construct as illicit. Clearly, eroticized domination in the form of marital rape is not the same as sex between lesbians, but their location within this legal frame is necessarily heteropatriarchal. Their proximity, moreover, derives from the force of a constructed morality that resides in nature, where the only sanctioned form of sex is identified as procreative. Biology and procreation sanction nature and morality to such an extent that when eroticized violence threatens to dissolve hetero-sexual conjugal marriage through rape, a textual restoration is enacted by criminalizing lesbian and gay sex and sex among gay men—an act of reasserting the conjugal bed. Indeed, the reinscription of the conjugal bed occurs precisely because no alternative sexualities are permissible.

A close reading of the constitutive elements of the legal text and its interpretations indicates that it took shape within an established hier-archy of punishments, stipulations, and injunctions. It is through this schedule that state managers established what they deemed to be an appropriate morality and, correspondingly, the set of practices that fall outside its purview, which required policing of some kind. But what are the ways in which the text functions as moral authority, as the definitive moral arbiter of sexual practices?

Textually, morality is codified through the enactment of three simulta-neous gestures: first, the central positioning of legitimate, naturalized sex within the conjugal arena, and with it particular notions of procreative sex; second, the establishment of a sexual standoff, as it were, between that form of naturalized sex and other forms of amoral, forbidden sex: incest, prostitution, sex with "minors," and lesbian and gay sex; and, third, the construction of an unnatural underworld of lesbian and gay sex by a textual association with bestiality. These textual strategies must be read simultaneously because there is no absolute set of commonly under-stood or accepted principles called "the natural" that can be invoked except as they relate to what is labeled "unnatural." Heterosexual sex, even while dysfunctional such as rape in marriage, assumes the power of natural law only in relation to sex that is defined in negation to it (what natural sexual intercourse is not) and in those instances where desire presumably becomes so corrupt that it expresses itself as bestiality. Here is the definition of sexual intercourse that was attached as a supplemen-tary note to the Sexual Offences and Domestic Violence Act: "[The Clauses] do not necessarily define 'sexual intercourse' but give a charac-teristic of it. 'Sexual intercourse' means natural sexual intercourse in the clauses relating to rape and other offences of sexual intercourse with women, whereas the clause concerned with buggery relates to unnatural sexual intercourse." Put differently, heterosexual practices carry the weight of the natural only in relational terms and—ultimately, one might argue—only in its power to designate as amoral and unnatural those practices that disrupt marriage and certain hegemonic notions of family. What is fundamentally at stake, therefore, in consolidating these moral claims is the institution of marriage and its patriarchal correlates: hegemonic masculinity, procreative sex, subordinated femininity, and vague, but powerful notions of "consent."

In laying out the terms of "serious indecency" that criminalized lesbian sex, legislators faced quite a dilemma about language. The first clause stated broadly: "A person who commits an act of serious indecency on or toward another is guilty of an offence." It is unclear at this point for whom the penalties are intended, except that in the second clause it is noted that a "husband," a "wife," or a "male or female" who is "sixteen years of age or more" is exempt. The definition becomes somewhat more explicit in the final clause: "An act of serious indecency is an act other than sexual intercourse (whether natural or unnatural) by a person involving the use of the genital organs for the purpose of arousing sexual desire." Clearly the definition of what is natural or unnatural is predicated on a heterosexual conjugal contract; by default, an act other than sexual intercourse between men and women defines lesbian sex! State managers are thus unable to draw on any widely understood category to describe lesbian sex. Instead, they seize on the notion of the body, of women's sexual organs, which are constructed and essentialized as an autonomous force, insensitive to all morality and in single-minded pursuit of arousing and gratifying sexual desire.[58] This is what is to be curbed and placed within the confines of a prison. So, unlike religious discourse, which gives no room to experience sexual desire, this apparently secularized discourse acknowledges desire, but it is the form of that unnameable desire and presumably the objectionable ways in which it is expressed that must be outlawed. In addition, "buggery," "bestiality," and "serious indecency" occupy contiguous spaces in the unnatural world of the illegal. The term buggery itself supersedes the term sodomy, which evokes the scriptural metaphor in which God and nature punish sexual deviation and restore order.

Taken together, the set of practices that were legally defined as sexual crimes and kindred offenses are offset by a notion of consent and a schedule of punishments that operate in sometimes unclear, sometimes idiosyncratic, and sometimes even contradictory ways. And even within these spheres of consent, hierarchies operate. Certain types of consent are more legitimate than others; at times adulthood serves as proxy for consent, while at other times it is suspended and infantilized, especially when it operates within the arena of forbidden sex. Consent here has also been transferred from the domestic to the public sphere, where it was defined as the power of the state apparatus to prosecute. Within the legislation, the terrain of consent and distributive justice is uneven—indeed complicated. In what follows, I examine the contradictory nature of this terrain and its intersection with the definitions of morality framed earlier.

The legislative provision on rape draws a distinction between marital rape ("sexual assault"), which can be committed only by "husbands" and for which the penalty is fifteen years of imprisonment, and real rape, which can be committed only by men—ostensibly strangers—for which the penalty is imprisonment for life. The defining element here is that a husband "forcefully has sexual intercourse with [his wife] without her consent." But if it is the violence attendant with sex and the protection of women that state managers insist is the focus of the rape penalty, then there is really no compelling reason for the law to distinguish between marital rape and other forms of rape. In this legal sphere, however, the horror of rape rests not so much in its violence as in the moment where a wife withholds her consent. Consent works, therefore, to obscure the actuality of violence. In contrast, a woman's consent, which presumably acts to prevent rape within "normal" marital relations, is eclipsed when she is actually raped. Thereafter, consent resides in an official of the state, whose authority determines the admissibility of the charge for trial. According to the legislation, "No proceedings shall be instituted except by or with the consent of the director of Public Prosecutions," a move that underscores Tracy Robinson's argument that women continue to be the "object" of rights even as these rights are being abrogated.[59]

Further, the state's notion of consent is ideologically bound to the enforcement of morality and permissible, procreative sex, and is exemplified in the case of prostitution and lesbian and gay sex. In the case of the former, the provision reads: "A person who, (a) knowingly lives wholly on or in part on the earnings of prostitution, or (b) in any place solicits for immoral purposes is guilty of an offence and is liable on conviction to imprisonment for five years." That an adult woman consents to earn her livelihood by exchanging sex for money is defined as "immoral" and abrogates her rights to give consent. A similar suspension of consent operates in the case of lesbian and gay sex, which are simultaneously stigmatized and criminalized. "Buggery" between "consenting" adults carries with it a sentence of ten years. It is presumably as serious a sexual infraction as heterosexual incest between adults and nonconsenting heterosexual sex either with "minors" in the workplace or with "mentally subnormal" women. Gay sex between minors appears more serious than incest between minors, and it carries the same five-year penalty as does lesbian sex. "Mentally subnormal" women and girls are deemed incapable of providing consent. (Ironically, the text eroticizes girls from the outside by sexualizing them and constructing them as untouchable, but criminalizes them for any expression of sexual agency.) In all instances, however, morality acts to regulate consent, and, in keeping with its position of power within the text, it can either dispense consent or revoke it. Morality acts to penalize women who consent to intercourse with anyone except their husbands, to suppress the sexual agency of women (particularly prostitutes and lesbians), girls, and gay men who stand outside conjugal marriage. Ultimately, conjugal heterosexuality establishes, polices, and guards the moral. No other guarantees about moral restoration are necessary.

One decade later, the pivotal terms of the Sexual Offences and Domestic Violence Act traveled into the U.S. Congress with a different set of indigenous class interests. The immediate instigator also appears to be different —the proximity of a nation of queer Hawaiians in a "colony" that mainland congressional leaders believed still belonged to them. Yet, to the same extent that the feminist movement in the Caribbean is coded as lesbian, and much like queer is made to function outside of, and as threat to, the conjugal heterosexual, these apparently different instigations can be imagined and positioned in ideological proximity to one another. In both instances, the threat to heteropatriarchy comes from that which is already contained within it. I will examine here just how neo-imperial state managers premised the fragility of marriage, as well as the guarantees they believed could "defend" and "protect" it. We can imagine that the fact of its fragility could mean that tradition itself had been repudi-ated—hence the need to legislate it. Just how the power of law established tradition as power is the theme I turn to next.

Fear of a Queer Nation:[60]
Heterosexual Marriage under Siege

The Defense of Marriage Act of the United States was passed on 21 September 1996 in order to preempt the success of a lawsuit that aimed to legalize same-sex marriage in Hawai'i. It marked new historical ground in that it was the first time that state managers were propelled to "define" the terms of marriage, and to "protect" it. Public Law 104–199, "An Act to Define and Protect the Institution of Marriage," defined marriage as "only a legal union between one man and one woman as husband and wife." As a way of producing and maintaining its own tautology regard-ing sexual difference, the law reserved the term spouse to refer "only to a person of the opposite sex who is a husband or wife." Once defined, the architects of the law believed they could "protect" this endangered in-stitution by forbidding any "state, territory or possession of the U.S. or any Indian tribe" from legitimizing "a relationship between persons of the same-sex that is treated as a marriage" under the laws of another state. Thus, the disappearance of conjugal heterosexuality would derive not from its own internally constituted set of threats or fissures (such as divorce, "infertility," or the sexual revolution) but rather as dangers ema-nating from the outside, the most notable of which being same-sex rela-tionships that are "*treated* as a marriage [emphasis added]."[61]

Of course, I would be remiss in not noting that this narrative shares with the carnage by Balboa a sparse economy that effectively belies the massive scope of the formations that were to be transformed: rewriting early constitutional arrangements in which states were required to give "full faith and credit," that mainland U.S. states would be legally bound to honor the same-sex marriage lesgislation passed in Hawai'i;[62] usurping by the federal government of a function that had historically been estab-lished within the prerogatives of state law; rewriting the interpretive framework of more than a thousand federal laws that relied on the cate-gory "marital status" as a basis on which to disburse benefits; attempting to deal an immediate blow to, and therefore halt, a political movement that instigated the legal mandate to begin with; and, finally, attempting to reconfigure a cultural imaginary in terms that were large and forceful enough to position same-sex coupling as unimaginable, to divest it of any legal and cultural—which is to say, moral—authority. On no account could a queer nation be allowed to exist, nor could its intimate attachments ever be made to assume a position commensurate with the "holy" union of "husband" and "wife." We need, however, to examine the surrounding texts, in particular the congressional hearings, to be able to outline how the investments in heterosexuality were fully animated.

The state managers in the congressional Committee on the Judiciary were not the least bit reticent about delineating what was at stake in advancing the legislative mandates codified in HR 3396 (the congressional variant of the public law). They identified the four most significant investments as follows: first, defending and nurturing the institution of traditional heterosexual marriage; second, defending traditional notions of morality; third, protecting state sovereignty and democratic self-governance; and fourth, preserving scarce government resources. For the purpose of my argument, I want to make particular note of the first two investments since they form the ideological scaffolding in which the latter two are housed. They are important because they embed the very interests that need to be demystified: "tradition," which I shall read as a normalizing force; and "morality," which I shall read as an idealized type of the heterosexual by which the homosexual is disciplined, since by the congressional committee's own defensive admission heterosexuality had, indeed, become a fragile institution. According to one member of the committee, "the fact that marriage was embattled was surely no argument for opening a new front in the war." These two simultaneous gestures work to produce and maintain the very category of "tradition" in such a way that that which is "moral" is always already contained within tradition. Within these mutually constitutive boundaries, power fractures into multiple anxieties about the extinction of the human race, misplaced desire, and violent repression all at once. But it was not only "tradition" and "morality" that were positioned to displace homosexuality. Love had to be assailed. And it had to be assailed because the idea of bringing same-sex marriage on par with heterosexual marriage was so "offensive" that the very tissue that connected Western romantic attachments had to be made homosexually suspect. We can only make sense of the level of violence it takes to foreclose these boundaries and reinvent them as if they were hermetically sealed in relation to the extent of the disruption that would be unleashed if the boundaries were no longer policed. Let us now turn to examine the set of technologies through which these categories of "tradition," "morality," and "not love" were produced, bearing in mind the earlier idea of an ideological scaffolding.

The congressional hearings were disturbed by a dense current of righteous outrage and cosmic injury. Homosexual sodomy was an offense to be sure, but same-sex marriage was an act that offended "moral" sensibilities—that is, it was offensive and its offensiveness inhered in the "idea" that it wished to be *treated* the same as heterosexual marriage. One of the ways it would be treated the same was if it shared that emotion that only heterosexual romantic attachments were presumed to have: love. But committee members did not know quite what to do with love when its presence was introduced by the dissenting opinion as the very thing that made both homosexual and heterosexual romantic attachments the same. At first they offered that there were indeed different kinds of love— filial love, for instance—that were different from romantic love. It was not the former, however, that was the object of same-sex intention. They then recognized that marriage was not needed to mark the presence of love. But if love did not need heterosexual marriage to express itself, where else could it reside? Of course, it is the answer to this question that remains unspeakable. Thus, in the end, they detached love from heterosexual marriage and later recoupled it to anchor and solidify difference, to position love as a scarce resource, partial to heterosexuality alone, so that it could satisfy the noble, natural end of marriage: the begetting of children. Here is the cataclysmic rendering of the move:

> The question of what is suitable for a marriage is quite separate from the matter of love, though of course it cannot be detached from love. The love of marriage is directed to a different end, or is woven into a different meaning, rooted in the character and ends of marriage. And to discover the "ends of marriage," we need only reflect upon this central, unimpeachable lesson of human nature: We are each of us, born a man

or a woman. The committee needs no testimony from an expert witness to decode this point: our engendered existence as men and women offers the most unmistakable, natural signs of the meaning and purpose of sexuality. And this is the function and purpose of begetting. At its core, it is hard to detach marriage from what may be called the "natural teleology of the body": namely, the inescapable fact that only two people, not three, only a man and woman, can beget a child.

Only conjugal heterosexual love has been granted the sanction of human nature, the proof of which resides in the large ontological task it had been handed in exchange, the begetting of children and "the propagation of the human race." Absent such a mandate, love could not signify by that name, it could not enter as kin to the love in heterosexual marriage, as kin to procreative love. These were the boundaries that had to be policed to disallow same-sex loving, which had to be dispensed with so that lesbian and gay folk could be entirely sexualized. To the extent that hegemonic heterosexuality is consonant with masculinity, the cosmic injury that disturbed the congressional deliberations pertained more particularly to an injured masculinity. Yet, in the context of the practice of power, that injury is more kin to violence than it is to loss.

For its part, "tradition" inhered in the "fact" that heterosexuality was the "most universal social institution." It was "ancient," "the keystone in the arch of civilization"; it constituted "sensible judgment," carrying the possibility "of begetting children," ultimately providing a "framework for lawfulness" with parents who were committed to nurturing themselves and their children. In the end, the committee reduced its interests to the simplest, most unequivocal terms: "Simply put, government has an interest in marriage because it has an interest in children." Without children, that crucial nexus between civilization and tradition would be a frayed enterprise, rendering futile heterosexual marriage itself.

Yet, the power of tradition did not derive solely from its ancient, transhistorical, commonsense, procreative and, therefore, ostensibly superior status. It carried moral authority and it drew its legitimacy from a "national consensus" among "many Americans." Here is how the committee was forced to marry its own aims to the predilections of civil society, this collectivized moral animus:

Civil laws that permit only heterosexual marriage reflect and honor a collective moral judgment about human sexuality. This judgment entails both moral disapproval of homosexuality, and a moral conviction that heterosexuality better comports with traditional (especially Judeo-Christian) morality. . . .

Same-sex marriage, if sanctified by law, if approved by law, legitimates a public union, a legal status that most people feel . . . ought to be illegitimate . . . And in so doing it trivializes the legitimate status of marriage and demeans it by putting a stamp of approval . . . on a union that many people . . . think is immoral.

This imputed capacity of same-sex marriage to do moral injury—to "demean" and "trivialize" that which has been legitimized as morally superior, that is, the heterosexual—does not in actual terms remove any of the murkiness that clothes the elements of this moral domain. What it does do is to use the moral as foil for the heterosexual, and that ideological foil is crucial since in order to prevent same-sex relations from being the same as (or, more important, from being *treated* the same as) heterosexual marriage those moral boundaries must be drawn and policed. Since this moral universe is also made to contain what is lawful, it also structures what is legal and illegal, which also means that it functions simultaneously as a mechanism to establish inequity—justifiable, righteous inequity—since this exalted moral domain simply cannot be contravened. But inequity could not be made to go by that name, so in a rhetorical sleight of hand it was transformed into "preferential status." Here is how the committee rendered this utilitarian transformation: "There are significant practical reasons why government affords preferential status to the institution of heterosexual marriage. These reasons of procreation and child rearing are in accord with nature and hence have a moral component."

Ultimately, the morality of childbearing, childrearing heterosexuality justified inequity. Put differently, heterosexism was being mobilized to justify itself as well as to protect democracy's potential demise. Also protected is the justification for instituting a measure that would prevent same-sex couples from being "eligible for a whole range of confirmed federal benefits." In order for the state to "[preserve] scarce government resources," noncitizen, nonlegitimized same-sex partners could not make claims on the state for the same benefits as legitimized heterosexual citizen unions. When the balance sheet was finally tallied heterosexism tipped the scales, offering up HR 3396 at "no cost" to the government. As the Congressional Budget Office reported, "HR 3396 would not affect direct spending or receipts; [it] will have no significant inflationary impact on prices and costs in the national economy."[63] Clearly, the costliness of installing heterosexual dominance cannot be rendered in monetary terms, by which I mean the social and political costs of partial citizenship and the psychic and bodily costs of violence, which the habits of heterosexual privilege foreclose. Lesbian, gay, bisexual, transgender, and two spirit peoples who survive hate violence perpetrated against them, or those who are forced to pay the price of violence in the currency of their very bodies and with their very lives, do not figure in this "no cost" inventory of privilege's zero-sum game. It is crucial that we apprehend this gesture in terms that delineate just how democracy operates through inequity (guarding heterosexuality's preferential status is guarding inequity) and, further, that we know that state managers are cognizant of this inequality, for it is this knowledge that will help to displace those liberal interpretations that divest state managers of the will to power and intentionality. We can simultaneously gain insight into the meaning of the force with which the self-representational impulse regarding free-market democracy is diffused in this moment of militarization and war. Such an impulse assumes this level of force in relation to the intentionality involved in creating and maintaining inequity.

It is not only a frayed democracy that is at further risk of being made transparent here. If we revisit the earlier formulation of the operation of an advanced capitalist colonial state that implicates the state within capital's simultaneous projects of neoliberalism, racialization and colonization, the mobilization against Hawai'i, whose promise (or threat, from the state's vantage point) of a queer nation instigated the Defense of Marriage Act against any "Indian tribe" and "U.S. possessions and territory" belongs in the pages of a colonial master narrative. Ambivalence regarding the ideologically coded terms "commonwealth status," in relation to Puerto Rico, or "tribal government," in the case of first nations, all disappear in favor of explicit colonial tropes of possession, thereby re-

establishing territorial propriety over Hawai'i, Puerto Rico, Indian nations, and, by extension, Guam, the U.S. Virgin Islands, and other American colonies. Ultimately the terms convey, first and foremost, the reminder that sovereignty is a conditional thing, indeed a fragile thing,[64]
and that the mission of rescue, to contain the dastardly spread of same-
sex coupling from infiltrating the conjugal bedrooms of the civilized
mainland, rested with the big state.[65] Indeed, Hawai'i had its own system
of referendum, which the congressional committee rhetorically recognized, but that fragile fact is displaced with a not-so-latent paternalism.
Indeed, heterosexuality continues to require colonization to extend its
civilizing mission. And, consonant with the habits of master narratives, it
remains incapable of delineating its own historical complicity in the
diffusion of heterosexuality in Hawai'i and among indigenous populations.[66] The irony here is that two of the same populations threatened
with state-engineered genocide at one historical moment become the
bodies on which another kind of state-legitimated violence is exercised at
another moment. Balboa thus reemerges, but with a different kind of
vengeance and in a much subtler guise.

None of these massive reconsolidations could have been undertaken,
however, outside of the context of violence. The legal violence of heterosexuality, the various ways in which it expands the cultural lexicon, enabling and supporting violence, tend to be positioned within the linear
telos as belonging to the neocolonial. But as I have shown (and will
demonstrate further), violence is intimately connected with the project
of modernity, no matter where it exists. It begs the question about
whether we are to apprehend violence as an indispensable dimension of
democracy or dispense with the category of democracy altogether.

Of course tradition, like any other socially constituted category, is not
simply immobile and fixed; rather, it is mobilized and utilized to ensure
its own longevity, and this is possible because there are avid interests that
attach themselves to it so that it might be deployed.[67] The congressional
Committee on the Judiciary traveled deep within the U.S. culture wars;
poured over the pages of the sexual revolution; ferreted out arguments
about the social acceptance of homosexuality among teenagers who had
experienced "sexual identity confusion" because they "believe[d] that
society was indifferent to their sexual orientation; surveilled the political

strategies of the Lambda Legal Defense and Educational Fund and the ACLU's Lesbian and Gay Rights Project; drove a wedge within the LGBTT community; footnoted authoritative texts; assembled legal precedents; and produced expert witnesses all of whom testified on tradition's behalf and on their intent to retain it at all costs so as to ensure that it be constitutionally sanctioned.[68] All of these differing class interests were folded into the interests of the state. Ultimately, they conferred on the state the power to legalize terror, in the form of homophobic violence, in such a way so as to displace criminality onto the hated and terrorized, a gesture that ultimately protected public patriarchy from ever having to confront its complicity in producing an archeology of terror and a political anatomy of hate. These effects are more easily cathected into "non-democratic," "traditional," and even uncivilized regimes, or apprehended in the nomenclature "hate crimes," which are committed by ordinary people on the street who are not affiliated with the state but who do state work.[69] All of these differing interests deployed homophobic violence to protect morality and tradition, to protect the Constitution, to protect terror, and ostensibly to protect themselves, all at the same time.

Tradition, when paired with civilization, can be invoked within the modern in ways that enable modernity to continue to signal the modern, not the traditional, as understood within the logic of the modernization narrative. But when tradition is paired with barbarism it is doomed to remain tradition, caught in a perennial struggle to beat back the modern in its unbounded desire for fixity and stasis. In the grand struggle between civilization and barbarism it is heterosexuality that emerges to occupy this nexus where the "natural teleology of the body" and the "propagation of the human race" conjoin. To push this further, we might see in this tradition elements of a fundamentalist belief structure in which heterosexuality emerges to uphold natural teleologies and trans-historical propagation narratives that rescue the human race from extinction. Of course, fundamentalism can be both of a religious and a secular nature. As I demonstrate below, a fundamentalist secularism can be based in a "free market" capitalism that requires neoliberal privatization to discipline a recalcitrant heterosexuality that refuses conjugal privatization, as in the case of women on welfare, or to promote structural adjustment of the economy in which privatization works to shift the fiscal responsibility from the public patriarch to the private patriarch, except that in the absence of the latter, provoked in no small degree by those very structural adjustments, it is women who assume the disproportionate fiscal burden. At a time of empire, heterosexuality emerges at the nexus of Judeo-Christian fundamentalism and militarization to uphold ostensibly natural teleologies of propagation and of market capitalism simultaneously, both of which require privatized heterosexuality and, increasingly, privatized homosexuality as well.

Financial Time: Neoliberal Capitalism, Privatization, and Poverty Curing Poverty: The Abolition of Welfare and the Promotion of "Healthy Marriage"

Heterosexual anxiety has a long, varied, and torturous history. DOMA's positioning of homosexuality as a threat to the "holy" union between "man" and "wife" indicates that state managers have authored and coauthored again heterosexuality's proclivities. This normalized imperative of heteromasculinity to be conjugally coupled with a domesticated femininity has a pedigree reaching far back to the nineteenth-century construction of the cult of white true womanhood;[70] to the construction of Chinese women as yellow peril and of loose and immoral character;[71] and in the early-twentieth-century debates that sexualized morality and translated it into the necessity of socializing impoverished women into the "benefits" of heterosexuality, illustrated, for instance, in the 1909 presidential report on dependent children.[72] Its terms parallel a similar gesture by black middle-class nationalist women who mandated mass marriages for Jamaican working-class women, a gesture that was promptly refused;[73] and in the more contemporary U.S. state deployment of the "welfare queen" who has been positioned to bear the scourge of unfit motherhood. By the time the Personal Responsibility Act of 1995, "To restore the American family, reduce illegitimacy, control welfare spending and reduce welfare dependence," morphed into the Personal Responsibility and Work Opportunity Reconciliation Act of 1996 (PRWORA), state managers had a vast repertoire of symbols from the interior of heteromasculine dominance from which to draw—symbols that had customarily latched themselves onto the large innards of racism and class hierarchy, gender, and nationality in order to perpetuate themselves.

The signatories of PRWORA, its companion Temporary Assistance to the Needy (which displaced Aid to Families with Dependent Children, AFDC), and DOMA are the same, but DOMA's fundamental claim that the state's interest in marriage emanates from its interest in children—a claim that positions children to anchor the meeting place of large processes of civilization, tradition, and heterosexuality—unravels in the face of the effects of the dissolution of AFDC. In its evaluation of the effect of PRWORA, the Children's Defense Fund has found, for instance, that "among children in single-mother families—the group most affected by welfare law—the number of children living below the poverty line rose by 26 percent from 1996 to 1997. In 1997, the percent of children in mother-only families with incomes at, or less than half of, the federal poverty line [which the Defense Fund has termed "extreme poverty"] was especially high for Latinos/as (12 percent), blacks (10.7 percent) and whites (9.5 percent)."[74] State interest may not, therefore, be as altruistically neutral as might first appear to be the case. Children are made to occupy an ideological conjuncture, in an apparent cosmic sense, but when those children wear the face of race-specific and class-specific homes in which their mothers refuse privatized heteromasculine dominance, neither these children nor the mothers who beget them (the most important marker that the state uses in DOMA to distinguish moral heterosexuality from immoral homosexuality) are deserving of state interest. Thus, we may understand state "interests" to mean an ideological investment in positioning children so as to facilitate the racialized and class-specific task of socially regulating them and their mothers who live outside of "lawful" conjugal heterosexual marriage. It is difficult not to conclude that the state constitutes itself through these very interests.

Historically this field called "welfare" has been crowded, contradictory, and, indeed, replete with the raucous memory of constitutionally legitimated yet culturally contested personhood; with the contradictory and shifting imperatives of the denial of motherhood to black women on the one hand, and the enforcement of compulsory motherhood on the other; with the ideological formulations of the black matriarch as the instigator of pathology and a "culture of poverty" in urban black communities—the discursive elements of which provide ample meeting ground for disciplining discourses within sociology, anthropology, and the state; with the legalization of sterilization that disallowed abortion for impoverished women under the Hyde Amendment; with the state-sanctioned population control practices done in the case of the sterilization of women in Puerto Rico, and of Indian, black, and white working-class women on the U.S. mainland, thereby anchoring the state's variant of cultural relativism that women's unruly sexuality posed a threat to the otherwise smooth evolutionary flow from tradition to modernity; and with the history of "regulating the poor" as a way of containing discontent prior to the fiscal crisis of the racial state and the "triumph" of neoliberalism. Race, class, and gender have historically operated as powerful markers to distinguish between the undeserving poor and the deserving elderly, but in the contemporary debates about "ending welfare as we know it," poverty had to be colored black (even though the majority of AFDC recipients were white) as a way to animate state policy and mobilize a manufactured popular memory that made (black) poverty the causal derivative of welfare.[75]

This blackening of welfare, in the production of what I demonstrated in chapter 3 as the production of the "welfare queen" (and what Kenneth Neubeck and Noel Cazenave call "Welfare Racism"),[76] provided the ideological anchor to install some of the most severe retrenchments of the last century. It parallels the "darkening" of the numbers of immigrants permitted entry into the United States after 1996,[77] the confluence of which provided potent ground for nativism and heterosexism to compete for a strategy that involved an unsettling ideological division of labor.

As dominant white heteromasculinity propelled these various discursive turns, it placed culpability on a pathologized black heteromasculinity while simultaneously rendering it absent and present. It was an irresponsibly absent black masculinity that made the potential conjugal couple incomplete and shifted the fiduciary obligations of the private patriarch onto the public patriarch, thereby forcing an uncomfortable and unwanted paternity onto the white public patriarch. In the context of white backlash, white state managers could not be seen as the proxies of irresponsible black paternity. Put differently, they could not be seen as white fathers to blackness. Of course, black womanhood is also implicated in this matrix, for it is her unbridled sexuality and irresponsible womanhood that begets children (not the children who provoked unequivocal state interest given that lesbian and gay marriage is essentially/naturally incapable of producing them) for whom the white public patriarch must assume proximate fiscal paternity. In the same way in which tradition is always already made to contain morality, so too womanhood is always already made to contain motherhood, but not under terms that entirely refuse wife and conjugal heterosexuality, and only during certain historical moments—under slavery black motherhood was essentially never permissible. We can only speculate on the longevity of the deep cultural memory of secret yet licit white paternity under slavery and its possible vengeful reemergence at a different historical moment to install a different structure of punishments that would make manly men out of black absent fathers by funneling them into the machineries of war or the machineries of prison, and consequently turning black women into domesticated wives or, otherwise, feeding them to work in the underside of capital's imperatives for cheap labor, and streamline both into marriage promotion projects underwritten by both the federal and local state.[78]

The ideological blackening of welfare ought not to imply that different racisms were not at work in the passage of PRWORA and in the strategies through which it took effect. According to Neubeck and Cazenave, "between 1996 and 1999 there was a 58 percent decline in the average monthly number of families enrolled in AFDC or its successor TANF. Whites left welfare more rapidly than persons of color. In 1999, two-thirds of TANF participants were people of color. The largest category of recipients was black, 38 percent, followed by white recipients who were 31 percent. Twenty-five percent were Latino/a, 3 percent were Asian and Pacific Islanders, and 1.5 percent were classified as American Indian or Alaskan Native."[79] Over half a million legal immigrants remain ineligible for food stamps under PRWORA.[80] These national figures do not convey, however, the extent of regional structural impediments experienced by particular racialized groups, such as the Vietnamese, Hmong, and other refugees dislocated from an earlier U.S. imperial war against Vietnam, and by American Indians historically dislocated as a consequence of the ongoing internal war. According to Linda Burnham, data from the federal government indicate that between 1994 and 1998 the number of Native Americans receiving public assistance climbed from 27 percent to 45 percent, with similar meteoric increases in Alaska, Arizona, New Mexico, Oklahoma, and Wyoming, thereby leading researchers to conclude that Native Americans have been "more severely affected" by welfare reform "than any other racial or ethnic group in the U.S."[81]

Nor do welfare policies subsist alone or in isolation. The ideological proximity between PRWORA, the Work Opportunity Reconciliation Act of 1996, and the Illegal Immigration Reform and Immigrant Responsibility Act also of 1996 works to make welfare, labor, and immigration deeply intertwined. In fact, processes of internal colonization and external colonization that have engendered the massive dislocation of huge segments of labor from Central and South America, from the Caribbean, and from Asia came to reside in PRWORA in some deeply problematic ways. Payal Banerjee's work is most instructive here, for it demonstrates the extent of the ideological traffic between and among these apparently unrelated state gestures. Banerjee argues that the state derived support for PRWORA from the widely held belief that "illegal" and "legal" immigrants relied on state public support and that prohibiting immigrants from receiving public assistance would act as a powerful deterrence to immigration. As a result, both "legal" immigrants (noncitizens) and "illegal" immigrants became ineligible for certain provisions under PRWORA. The Immigration Act of 1996 also sought to curtail "illegal" immigration by adopting more stringent law enforcement methods that tightened border policing, thereby strengthening its public image of being "tough on immigration." Yet, it was only a particular kind of immigrant that was positioned as undesirable, for this same state authorized the American Competitiveness and Workforce Improvement Act of 1998 and the American Competitiveness in the Twenty-first Century Act of 2002, the latter of which increased the quota for high-tech immigrant workers. In pointing to the ways in which "labor, immigration and welfare are organically tied," Banerjee notes, "the state worked in intimate collaboration with the Information Technology industry and increased the H1-B visa cap so that corporations had easier access to foreign labor. This happened amidst general anti-immigration sentiment and only a couple of years after the major cutbacks in welfare and tighter immigration regulations. Interestingly, even though H1-B workers are considered temporary (as they can work for a minimum of 6 years on this visa), the tax generated from these workers' incomes is seen as the solution to the imminent social security crisis."[82] At times nativism can act as a powerful social regulator—more powerful than heterosexuality—depending on the strength of those interests in whose name it is mobilized. More often both are needed, for in an undertaking as large as the rewriting of "civilization," "tradition," "heterosexuality," and "citizenship," there is ample room for nativism and heterosexuality to operate through a formidable division of ideological labor.

The Personal Responsibility, Work and Family Promotion Act of 2003 (HR4), like its predecessors, codifies a massive redrafting of the state's historic role in the provision of the social wage. The tropes of "personal responsibility," "work," and "family promotion" function as powerful shibboleths, the distinctive passwords for citizenship in an era in which poverty is the putative result of a dependency on welfare, a refusal to work, a lack of proper work habits, and a lack of "family values." Within the act, any promotion of marriage is legitimized as the provision of "welfare." The act lays out a detailed curriculum and the mechanisms of a whole tutelary complex in which the "promotion of family formation and healthy marriage" becomes the primary motor for transferring state accountability onto the individual and for targeting means-tested aid programs that are positioned as hostile to heterosexual marriage.[83] In it, states, territories, and tribal organizations are made to compete for grants "to develop and implement innovative programs to promote and support healthy, married, 2-parent families," to "advertise," "educate," "train," "enhance," and "mentor" "needy" families; in other words, to gaze at and surveil heterosexual habits so as to inculcate "healthy" norms of family.[84] According to the act, here is how the complex of heterosexualization through healthy marriage promotion is to be undertaken:

i. public advertising campaigns on the value of marriage and the skills needed to increase marital stability and health

ii. education in high schools on the value of marriage, relationship skills, and budgeting

iii. marriage education, marriage skills and relationship skills programs, that may include parenting skills, financial management, conflict resolution, and job and career advancement, for non-married pregnant women and non-married expectant fathers

iv. pre-marital education and marriage skills training for engaged couples and for couples or individuals interested in marriage

v. marriage enhancement and marriage skills training programs for married couples

vi. divorce reduction programs that teach relationship skills

vii. marriage mentoring programs which use married couples as role models and mentors in at-risk communities

viii. programs to reduce the disincentives to marriage in means-tested aid programs, if offered in conjunction with any of those described above.[85]

The ideological dominance of heterosexuality signals that it is under threat, as illustrated in the move in DOMA to "protect" it and in HR4 to introduce it within "at-risk communities," that is, communities that have refused middle-class heterosexual marriage norms as the locus in which to express intimacy.[86] At the moment of the passage of DOMA in 1996, state managers positioned same-sex love and marriage as threat to conjugal heterosexuality; in this instance, and with the knowledge that one out of two marriages end up in divorce, it is the population that has received "means-tested aid programs" defined as "needy" that is positioned as threat. It is this population that must be tutored within heterosexualizing projects as a condition of eligibility for state support. In the test between heterosexuality and means, heterosexuality wins out, but it is a "failed heterosexuality" that displaces the lack of means (i.e., poverty) now understood as a problem of individual morality—at once a problem of too much sex and insufficient investment in consumption—not one of structural inequity.[87] Participants in these marriage promotion programs recognize that institutionalized heterosexuality has failed, and what is "at risk" is not their refusal of marriage but marriage itself.[88]

If we hold on to the notion that ideologies do not die even when legislative maneuvers do, state managers are consistent in their allegiance to heterosexuality even as they mobilize different populations in its interests, including same-sex loving people, whether in the military, in the bedroom, or in the culture at large; and impoverished heterosexual men and women who are forced to rely upon the state, albeit less and less so, for financial support.

Failed heterosexuality, indeed, threatens a great deal. It threatens the privatized sphere of the household, for a "wanton" sexuality refuses to be contained. And it also severs the ideological reliance of the public patriarch on the private patriarch, in the sense that the former can no longer implicitly claim to be more progressive than the latter, against whom he has implemented sanctions against domestic violence, for instance. It threatens the neoliberal market's reliance on conjugal taxpaying, consuming coupling as a site of accumulation, hence the mandate to institutionalize work without any attention to the structures of racism and sexism in employment and to the cultural antipathy against hiring the immigrant or impoverished people on public assistance. These are the very households that have assumed the disproportionate task of care in the face of massive social divestment over the last two decades, the costs of social reproduction that Grace Chang maintains is more appropriately a state function.[89] It is for these reasons that "failed heterosexuality" cannot simply be allowed to exist; why the imperatives to pathologize and racialize morality within the project of heterosexualization are so strong, and why powerful faith-based interests are avidly aligned in these punitive projects to promote state imperatives. I say "punitive" here, for withholding loyalty to privatized patriarchy comes with a price: the travails of this peculiar institution is public knowledge, the notion of the widespread promotion of marriage mentoring through role models approaches the theater of farce.

The Structural Adjustment of Violence: Where "Private" and "Public" Heteropatriarchy Meet

The U.S. struggle for the Panama Canal in 1911 instigated two related developments: first, the massive restructuring of imperial interests away from Britain and Spain to America, particularly in the Caribbean and Latin America—including the Panama Canal, the same geography colonized by Balboa; and second, the global diffusion of neoliberal capital's market ideologies, the shape of which I outlined in chapter 3 under the contours of the new world order. This major shift enabled the U.S. national security state to claim in 2003 that "the United States [is] the top source of private capital to developing countries, averaging $36 billion annually between 1997 and 2000."[90] While it is difficult to ascertain the source of this figure, what the national security strategy fails to address is the disproportionate ways in which Third World countries subsidize the West, amounting to $120 billion in capital outflow (the euphemism for profits) in the same period.[91] In addition, the analysts of transnationalism who have examined the economic significance of diaspora to the Caribbean region in particular have found that financial remittances have become *the* largest, most stable source of external capital—larger than foreign investments and international aid combined. For example, per annum remittances to Haiti has escalated to as much as $900 million.[92] Thus, the fact of U.S. hegemony and its accompanying ideological pronouncements should not at all be taken to mean that U.S. capital is the primary motor of economic development in the region.

My focus at this point is the ideological production of privatization. I will plot specific routes of traffic by examining two apparently different sets of state discourses and practices: first, the Sexual Offences and Domestic Violence Act of the Bahamas,[93] which provides additional evidence that the category of the sexual carries weight in excess of the sexual; and second, the ideological parameters of privatization through Structural Adjustment Programs (SAP), which comport with the heterosexualization of welfare in the United States.

The impetus for the state legislation of domestic violence came, in the first instance, from a feminist campaign in the Bahamas, as well as from an organized regional movement. For my purposes here, what is significant is not so much the passage of the legislation, but the form it took and the fact that it was brought to life among a set of legal prescriptions that are apparently unrelated to it. The absence of a clear definition of domestic violence, its displacement with the terms of property and a textual fragmentation between bodily harm and psychic harm—the very practices that the feminist movement had brought together—provided an early indication that state interests had superseded those of organized feminism. Indeed, "protecting women against domestic violence" became displaced onto a set of terms to ensure that the disruption of heterosexual marriage would not result in the transfer of fiscal responsibility from the private patriarch to the state public patriarch. Put differently, the state needed to ensure that the asymmetries of gendered power, and the violences that derived from such power, remained in the household (i.e. the private sphere) within a larger practice that had already authorized massive retrenchments in the social wage. In the end, "domestic violence" became a state narrative about solidifying primogeniture.

Reconfiguring primarily middle-class households according to the terms of primogeniture was not the only site in which privatization was occurring. In line with my methodological strategy of placing discourses and practices into ideological proximity with one another, I will place this legal codification of privacy in the "domestic sphere" into proximity with SAP which anchors privatization in the economic sphere, thereby enacting a specific form of class violence on the part of ruling-class financial interests. The traffic between these two practices is quite substantial, as we shall see. Structural adjustment in the neocolonial context is the face that welfare wears within the neo-imperial.

The contemporary version of SAP finds expression in a powerful yet unequal alliance among financial interests that include the International Monetary Fund, the World Bank, and USAID (which might possibly be overtaken by the Department of Homeland Security in this new phase of empire). Its effects have been both long-standing and multiply pervasive: "Currency devaluations that increase the prices of food, housing, transportation, clothing, books, etc.; wage freezes which make it impossible to cope with the rapidly increasing cost of living; the massive breakdown of social services such as health and education; the absence of any consultation with the ordinary people who have been displaced from their lands to make way for huge dams to service the enterprises of multinational corporations while they themselves have no access to clean drinking water."[94] These developments have been most visually articulated in a film on Jamaica called *Life and Debt* that illustrates how the specific mandates of SAP destroyed the local milk and livestock industries, aligned the country's economy to serve, yet again, the interests of metropolitan capital through Export Processing Zones, and in general created conditions of economic hardship whose effects are disproportionately gendered.[95] Here is how the Caribbean Association for Feminist Research and Action (CAFRA) characterized the effects of SAP:

> Faced with the deepening economic crisis, women must work longer and longer hours of overtime to make ends meet, and also do more work at home so as not to spend cash, or to make up for declining social services. With less leisure time for themselves, their children, their families, and their social relationships, the quality of life declines. Despite women's efforts, thousands of children have had their life chances damaged by these policies, and the effect will be felt for generations to come.[96]

In the same way in which the consolidation of NAFTA produced significant economic displacements in Mexico, provoking rural-to-urban migration followed by off-shore migration to the United States, so too did the consolidation of SAP produce significant migrations, primarily of women, to the United States. These women have been hired as domestics and service workers, swelling the ranks of the noncitizen nonpatriot that is generally imagined outside of the new terms of the citizen patriot legislated under the ideological terms of empire.

Privatization and neoliberal globalization work hand in hand, and they are not merely economic processes because they reconfigure particular definitions of masculinity and femininity, both internal and external. The most significant retrenchments with the adoption of SAP have taken place in those sectors that have been historically coded as women's work: health, clinic and hospital service, caring for the sick and elderly, social services, and education. As women continue their work in the home and in the private or public service sector, they also work to care for the sick and elderly and continue, without state subsidies, the education of their children. The state relies on and operates within these dominant constructions of a servile femininity that is perennially willing and able to serve, a femininity that can automatically fill the gaps it has created. In contradistinction to the non-productive femininity drawn in the legislation, these are women doing work, and ironically, doing the work of the state.

Ideological registers are significant in another important regard, which has to do with the presumed disjuncture between the "public" and the "private" spheres. In one sense, one of the effects of a privatized state is that it becomes somewhat insulated from public demands; what was public responsibility is now shifted elsewhere, in this case to women who compensate for retrenchment in both spheres. But there is also a para-doxical collapse of this dichotomy, for the state is now relying on the private—private capital and private households—to consolidate its own quest for public economic and political power. We know that the house-hold has been an important ideological instrument for the state. It has been indispensable in the creation of the public against which it can be positioned. Because it has been an important space where a particular kind of hierarchical, patriarchal power has resided, the state must move to rehabilitate this sphere by specifically recoding women's experience of domestic violence and rape within it and, in general, by disallowing any household space for lesbians. Yet state economic practices are contribut-ing to the demise of the "male breadwinner" especially in working-class and working-poor households, which are the ones hit the hardest by SAP. In a racialized context, state practices are actually intervening to fix racial polarities as well.

This household, as I demonstrated in the context of chapter 1, is to be a heterosexual household according to the state. Nothing is to infiltrate this space. Yet state requirements for heterosexuality differ from those within the political economy. In the case of the former, there were vig-orous requirements for the kind of reproductive monogamous hetero-sexuality that consolidated respectable middle-class interests within nu-clear family, whereas within the sexual economy of tourism it was the mobile bodies of primarily black women sex workers, criminalized by the state as prostitutes, that fueled an underground nexus of forbidden desire on which imperial tourism rested.[97]

Privatization as a globalized practice straddles different geographic boundaries, as well as boundaries demarcated as "public" and "private." As a public discourse and practice, it makes the private public while conveying an ideological attachment to a private-only space, another of those spaces where hidden hegemonies reside. Within the United States, the retrenchments in welfare not only bolster market principles that require a nuclear accumulating household, they also help to demystify other important public formations such as those of militarization. The military has been positioned as the new citizenship school for women and men removed from public assistance, thereby making the downsizing of the social wage the corollary to the increases in the military budget whose expenditures finance both the war abroad and strategies against "domestic terrorism" at home.[98] This budget also finances the new kind of "order maintenance" policing that is authorized in central cities, which utilizes "warrior cops" trained in the military curriculum to police working-class communities that include immigrants. In addition, the police presence at toll booths, train stations, airports, bridges, and tunnels; the detention of large numbers of immigrants; the surveillance of foreign students; the wide diffusion of war propaganda on the Internet, on telephone, gas, and electricity bills, and public transportation media— all emendations of the private and the public—speak both to an escalation in the militarization of daily life, which the state positions as a necessary arm of the public war against domestic terrorism, and the safeguarding of the quasi-private/public space of the homeland as the basis of security. This public war is financed by the private tax-paying consumer, citizen and noncitizen alike, while private corporations intimately linked to public state managers, indeed state power, derive disproportionate profit.[99] Just how these ideological turns are pivoted is the topic I consider in the following section.

Not Just (Any) Body Can Be a Patriot: On Times of Empire both Here and There

At this point I will shift the site of analysis to the neo-imperial. I use the term neo-imperial in at least two senses: first, as the descriptive term for a form of globalization whose internal character reproduces a set of colonial relations with regard to indigenous peoples, immigrant people, people of color, and working-class white communities within the geographic borders of the United States as well as a set of related external colonial arrangements with, among others, Puerto Rico, Hawai'i, the U.S. Virgin Islands, and Guam; and second, as a way to denote the state's investments in a form of hyperconcentrated capital that is diffused in local/globalized economies with unequal gendered and class consequences. These contradictions form the basis for an understanding of the U.S. state that is not automatically, self-referentially democratic, although democracy characterizes its self-representational impulse.

"Neo-imperial" also refers to the constitution of a new empire, accelerated militarization, and war on the part of the United States. Its most recent discursive incarnation has been codified in three formative documents—the Patriot Act of 2001, its sequel of 2002, and the National Security Act of 20 September 2002—which explicitly and simultaneously link the imperial project to militarization and to nation building. However, nation building can be more accurately understood as a form of hypernationalism with a number of constituent parts: the manufacture of an outside enemy to rationalize military intervention and secure the annexation of land; the production of an internal enemy to rationalize criminalization and incarceration; the internal production of a new citizen patriot; the creation and maintenance of a permanent war economy, whose internal elements devolve on the militarization of the police and the resultant criminalization of immigrants, people of color, and working-class communities through the massive expansion of a punishment economy at whose center is the prison industrial complex. Neo-imperialism is constituted as well through those state practices I discussed earlier that are aimed at constituting a nation that is based in an originary nuclear family in ways that couple the nuclear with the heterosexual.

The confluence of this new moment of empire in which the invasion of Iraq is strategically central, the production of the national security strategy and the two emendations of the Patriot Act, signals a major reconstruction within, and a major reconsolidation of, the American state apparatus. I demonstrated earlier in the context of the 1991 Gulf War the ways in which the hypermasculine soldier was diffused as a symbol of U.S. might. Manufacturing the consent of "the American people" was carefully organized around this figure—more usually racialized externally as white so as to be juxtaposed against the dark enemy; and sometimes racialized as black internally to signal a dutiful return to family—the white soldier woman, and the "traditional oriental" woman who needed to be rescued from the enemy. At this moment, however, the state seems so assured of its legitimacy that it feels less compelled to invoke "the American people" as ideological foil. It is not so much that the hyper-masculine soldier has disappeared. Witness the feminized role of supporting the troops that has been assigned to the nation after the manly job of state decision making has occurred and the necessarily highly visible, "dangerous" rescue mission of Jessica Lynch, who had to be both white and a woman so that white masculine rescue could work.[100] It is, rather, that following the attacks on the heart of America's financial capital on September 11, 2001, state action has become more emboldened to promulgate the war against particular definitions of terror as the major vehicle around which to scaffold the national security state and secure its own class interests. Embedded in that militarized vehicle is the patriot who, like the soldier, is not only hypermasculine but heteromasculine, and there is an absolute requirement that emerges from the new legal mandate in which he has been produced: this patriot must be silent and must, as well, be the originary citizen who was "here" at the very beginning of the carving of the homeland, and therefore entrusted with its guardianship, which he presumably promised never to betray.[101] This (white) originary citizen is in sharp contradistinction to the (dark) naturalized citizen, the dark immigrant or even the dark citizen born of the dark immigrant whose (latent) "loyalty" is perennially suspect and, therefore, ultimately threatening.[102] It is this dark inside threat that must be cordoned off, imprisoned, expulsed and matched simultaneously with the extinction of the dark, external threat in order that the borders of the fictive, originary nation might be properly secured. There is no task that can legitimately rival this in terms of enormity; no ideological boundary that will not be contravened in its service, as illustrated by the words of President George W. Bush, "We will smoke those barbarians out of their caves." Within this matrix lies a collocation that is fundamental to the contemporary political constellation: empire building is national security. Since the latter is an indisputable task in the business of defense against the enemy, then empire building becomes a similarly indispensable undertaking. And since race and sex have historically been made to reside inside of empire, we will come to see how the making of the white heteromasculine patriot and the demasculinization of the dark enemy are twin processes that are themselves racialized and sexualized. Indeed, if empire-building did not require sexuality's garb, it would be altogether unnecessary to demasculinize the enemy. I now turn to examine more carefully the ideological traffic between these companion processes.

At first glance it might appear that the sheer scope of empire-building would necessitate the avid collaboration of all of "the American people." But on closer examination of the patriot acts and their attendant federal executive orders, we see that what is at stake is the production of a citizen patriot of a very specific sort. As a moment of nation building/hyperna-tionalism instigated by the state—although multinational corporations, independent contractors, and media are powerful allies in this consortium—they delineate just who this new citizen patriot is supposed to be: what he must look like, how he ought to behave, the terms of his silent support for a national security state, the criminalization of speech, all of these prerequisites where loyalty to the nation is conflated with loyalty to the state and where loyalty to the state can only be maximally fulfilled through defense of the nation. Just who becomes this citizen patriot whom the state feels compelled to legalize so that unpatriotic noncitizens can thus be criminalized? What social fragilities needed repair so that this figure is summoned in its service? How is patriotism secured and what are the specific tasks that ostensibly solidify it?

There are two crucial elements in these taxonomies on which my analysis will turn.[103] The first is an expansion of the conduct subject to state investigation under a crime called "domestic terrorism," which is defined as "acts dangerous to human life that are a violation of the criminal laws of the United States or of any State."[104] But it is not simply any act that is "dangerous to human life" that constitutes a crime, because if it were we could expect acts such as the bombing of abortion clinics, hate crimes, racist homophobic violence and domestic violence, re-trenchments of the social wage, and the destruction of the environment to count as violations.[105] It is, rather, specifically those acts that are directed against the state; those that "appear to be intended . . . to influence the policy of a government by intimidation or coercion." We can surmise at this point that anybody with such intent, who committed such acts, would be apprehended as a domestic terrorist.[106] And if we were to align this with my earlier discussion of the conduct and status categorizations of homosexuality on which the Military Working Group depended, we could further conclude that conduct alone—that is, "acts"—would mark the crucial distinction between the terrorist and the nonterrorist.

The second element in the taxonomy would undermine such a conclusion, however, for this is where an important conflation occurs and where the definitions of terrorist and nonterrorist shift. Provision 412 of the first Patriot Act calls for the "mandatory detention of suspected terrorists," suggesting that not acts alone but someone else's suspicion is the pivot on which the definition rests. But suspicion of whom? And by whom? It is here that the subject shifts suddenly from "domestic terrorist" to "immigrant," for it is in this provision that the attorney general is given broad powers to certify immigrants as risks. In this move from "act" to "risk," the distinction between terrorist and nonterrorist turns and the demarcation between citizen and immigrant is made. This provision is bolstered by the president's military order, which establishes trials by military tribunal, at the president's discretion, for noncitizens. And while the president can order both citizens and noncitizens to be made into "enemy combatants," the denotation of immigrant risk not only fuels detention but directs disproportionate suspicion onto the immigrant. In addition to the attorney general, up to two million Americans can secretly provide information to the government about any person whom they consider suspicious, on whom the state would subsequently establish a file. And in a massive reorganization of the agencies of the state, there are many more who have been authorized to pursue patriotism and suspect the suspicious: the secretary of state, the secretary of defense, the Department of Justice, the president, surveillance agencies such as the FBI and CIA (otherwise known as intelligence), the Bureau of Prisons, law enforcement agencies and the foreign intelligence apparatus including the Foreign Intelligence Surveillance Court), and even bookstore and library personnel. In the end, it is hardly conduct or "acts" but a status—that of immigrant—that shades "domestic terrorism" and that begins to hint, as well, at just whom this legalized patriot is supposed to be. Immigrant as perennial suspect, risky by virtue of status and bearing the disproportionate brunt of enemy is further criminalized in this act of patriotism and made to function as nonpatriot in this matrix where status and implied propensity meet, a propensity that is similar to, yet different from, "homosexual propensity" as established under the terms of the Military Working Group of 1993.

But the patriot is also designated by what he is not—that is, not immigrant; by what he has been authorized to do—that is, to comply with a legal mandate by actively participating in the task of surveillance: to secretly provide information to the state about suspects, and to disclose to the state information about the reading habits of those whom he has surveilled; and additionally by what he is being implicitly asked to do: to forfeit consent and to substitute participation in civil society with silence and loyalty to the state as a consummate patriot.[107] Legalized within the ambit of a militarized state apparatus at a moment of empire-building, this patriot is one of the major internal anchors at the nexus of empire-building and national security. This patriot citizen, like the soldier citizen, is a patriot for the consolidation of empire. But this is not the only nexus that the reconfigured map of empire draws.

There is a tacit, or not so tacit, ideological division of labor among the different kinds of patriots: state patriots securing their class interests through the annexation of land and territory, arguing the grand narratives of an ancient titanic call to freedom, civilization and Christian modernity through war, positioning free enterprise—which we shall understand as imperialism—as the tradition that requires protection; the citizen soldier patriot who comprises the imperial fighting force, the class and racial composition of which exposes the contradictions implicit in the racialization of empire (a point to which I return later); and the citizen patriot who, like the state patriot, stays home, but who exercises patriotism through another of the technologies of globalization—the Internet. This is one of the spaces where the companion nexus of empire building, enemy production, and failed heterosexualization are secured; in short, the place where the terrorist, the enemy, and the sexual pervert meet, the place where the sexual anxieties of domination and conquest thrive, enacting a form of violent spectacle similar in function to the postcard texts through which nineteenth-century European orientalism was produced[108] and the more grotesque photographic representations of lynching that pervaded the American South at the turn of the twentieth century.[109] It is not that state patriots have relinquished the heterosexualizing imperatives of nation-building. No lesbian, gay, bisexual, or transgendered family was made to signal national grief in the post– September 11 trauma. While DOMA risks the challenge from the recent antisodomy legislation in Texas, as well as other same-sex marriage initiatives in California and Massachusetts, the coalition of traditional interests will not die easily as illustrated in the call for the constitutional ban against gay marriage in terms that bear a sinister resemblance to those on which DOMA was argued.[110] Indeed, President George W. Bush called for this amendment prior to the 2004 elections as a mechanism to reinforce DOMA. The reevaluation of the "Don't Ask, Don't Tell" policy as a way to possibly enlist queer soldiering stands as a staunch reminder that there is a long arc between expediency and justice.

The meeting place that collapses the enemy, the terrorist, and the sexual pervert is the very one that secures the loyal heterosexual citizen patriot. Indeed, it is under his vigilant—one might even say vengeful— directives that the ostensible boundaries between the enemy and the patriot, the terrorist and the citizen, and the pervert and the morally abiding collide. These very boundaries dovetail simultaneously with policing the oppositional boundaries of Islamic tradition and Christian modernity. The enemy terrorist offered up by the state patriot to the citizen patriot appears in a garb that is far too incomplete, however, to accomplish fully the task of securing empire, which, as I established earlier, has historically relied on strategies of racialization and sexualization. As Jasbir Puar and Amit Rai have argued, "The construction of the [enemy] terrorist relies upon sexual perversity" and upon "deeply racist, sexist and homophobic suggestions" that become, at this historical conjuncture, the transformed technologies through which "heteronormative patriotism" is established.[111] At this point I wish to examine how these technologies accompany one another and how they work as a composite ideological field that is interdependent and that can demasculinize, feminize, sodomize, and racialize as a way of producing a grotesque enemy.

Puar and Rai, along with Robin Riley, have analyzed the representational impulses at work in different forms of media, including the Internet and email, following the destruction of the Twin Towers on September 11, 2001, that speak to this composite ideological field. Riley has found on a Web site (Osamayomama.com) thirty-six photographs in which

Osama bin Laden's head has been superimposed on the bodies of figures that include a hermaphrodite, a cross-dresser, a gay man, a heterosexual dominated by women, and a heterosexual having sex with animals. On other sites, the figure is routinely depicted as having sex with animals, and, in one case, of hiding in the rectum of a camel, thus reconciling the sexual pervert with the coward. One part of the representational perversity is cathected onto bin Laden, but its other face is rendered through specific gestures of "sodomizing" him. Puar and Rai analyze this imagery in the poster that was rapidly dispersed in New York City after the attack, which displayed a turbaned caricature of bin Laden being anally attacked by the Empire State building. The poster's caption—" 'The Empire Strikes Back,' or 'Do You Like Skyscrapers, Bitch?' "—is a combination of misogyny and heterosexism.

Another Web site invites its audience to assist in the torture of bin Laden with various weapons, including sexual torture through sodomy. And yet another Web site carries alternating portraits of bin Laden and O. J. Simpson, thereby placing, as Riley suggests, "a new face on an old body, the body of the man of color who has long posed threats," so that we identify and recognize "strangers . . . the stranger we know—O. J. and the 'Other' stranger. We can recognize bin Laden because we have seen him before."[112] No war can be waged without the production of an enemy, but the processes of militarization are never entirely externalized. Processes do not arbitrarily halt at geographical borders, and in this instance the production of an internal enemy carries the same type of sexual prerequisites as those of the external enemy. Indeed, "sexual perversity" is one of the ideological characteristics shared by the enemy at home and the enemy abroad. The enemy construction of blackness and the stranger shown on the Internet is palpably reminiscent of the crowds who assisted the celebratory rituals of lynching of an apparently earlier era, but it draws simultaneously from a larger state construction of sexual humiliation and torture illustrated in the sexual torture of Abner Louima by New York City police in 1997 and in the similar treatments meted out to the prisoners at Abu Ghraib, evocative of the pornographic.[113]

These varied heterosexual anxiety narratives—of violence, of injury and shame, and of punishment and retaliation—simultaneously produce the enemy and issue an invitation to the citizen patriot to attend to the propaganda mechanics of war. But there is an unspoken disciplining device at work here as well: "If you're not for the war you're a fag," a threat with disproportionate consequences for immigrants and queer people, particularly immigrants or immigrant-looking brown-skinned men.[114] Those immigrants not treated to the violence of the state patriot through detention meet with the violence of the citizen patriot on the streets; while LGBTT people of color in New York City, for instance, are met with the same. Once this sexualized heterosexual anxiety is unleashed, however, the enemy target can multiply. As we saw in the context of the 1991 Gulf War, violence against the "enemy" in the desert traveled into the U.S. soldier camps where a number of soldier women had been "forcibly sodomized."[115] Soldier citizens, "model soldiers" who served in the war against Afghanistan, brought the violence and war home during summer 2002 and unleashed it onto their wives in Fort Bragg, North Carolina, "the home of the Airborne and Special Operations Forces." They turned the gruesome techniques of the "activate to kill mode" of the war "out there" onto their military wives, battering, raping, and killing them, and in some instances also killing themselves.[116] And all this happened while their civilian citizen patriots, in the wake of September 11, instigated domestic violence in the privatized space of home.[117] The practices of violence on this continuum of violence render borders entirely inconsequential.

We should not assume that the militarization apparatus is mobilized only at the moment of war. Indeed, its swift mobilization elsewhere is indicative of a prior "local" existence, if you will, a prior episteme that bears close ideological resemblance to the war weaponry "over there," while at the same time assembling an entirely new vocabulary that intercepts yet intersects with the citizen patriot, the noncitizen nonpatriot or the disloyal suspect immigrant at home. This more local apparatus, assembled over the last two decades at the level of both the macrostate and mircostate, has been directed toward displacing the "war" on poverty with the "war" on crime, thus making imprisonment, as Angela Davis has argued, the "response of first resort to . . . the social problems that burden people who are ensconced in poverty."[118] In this war, the police are the transplanted soldiers drawing from the training curriculum of the police academy, which has targeted particular neighborhoods that are disproportionately inhabited by people of color and by immigrants. The curriculum has perfected a microscopic level of policing that is able to intervene more systematically in the daily lives of people through both increased surveillance and increased force attendant with its own system of categorizations: the "disorderly," and "symbolic assailants," those who look like people with the propensity to assail. Of course, these categorizations ultimately reinforce their own rationale for the existence of increased policing—what Jael Silliman and Anannya Bhattacharjee have called "policing the national body."[119] But it is policing of a very particular sort.

Urban policing has taken on an altogether different character in the past decade, spurred by what Diane Weber has called "the ominous growth of paramilitarism."[120] The elements of this culture of paramilitarization are constituted through the adoption of a military curriculum as the police curriculum, an increased role for the Pentagon in daily policing, and the use of the technologies of war on urban streets, including SWAT teams and special weapons and tactics units. As Weber reports, nearly 90 percent of the police departments surveyed in cities with populations over 50,000 had paramilitary units, as did 70 percent of the departments surveyed in communities with populations under 50,000.[121] This paramilitarism has been accompanied by another, related, technology of disciplining called "order maintenance policing," which is euphemistically called "community policing." At its center resides the broken windows theory, the notion that if left unattended misdemeanors such as aggressive panhandling and turnstyle-jumping will promulgate serious crime. The popular national diffusion of a methodology, which has been largely uncontested but whose findings are highly contestable, has produced some alarming but not surprising results: for instance, the majority of the over 140,000 women in the penitentiary system are black, Latina, and poor women incarcerated for petty crimes, and there has been a 50 percent increase in misdemeanor arrests in New York City in the mid-1990s.[122] On a nationwide basis, African Americans—who comprise a disproportionately low percentage of the population but a disproportionately high percentage of the imperial fighting force—constitute 46 percent of those arrested for vagrancy and 58.7 percent of those arrested for suspicion as "symbolic assailants."[123] Again, here there are powerful ideological symbols at play, as indicated in the apt assessment by Bernard

Harcourt: "The techniques of punishment create the disorderly person with a full biography of habits, inclinations and desires . . . as an object of suspicion, surveillance, control, relocation, micromanagement and arrest . . . while carefully managing its boundaries."[124] The technologies function in a way so as to maintain the boundaries they create.

Much like the categories, discussed above, of "homosexual propensity" and "immigrant propensity," the categories of the "disorderly" and the "symbolic assailant" create their own propensity apparatus, which propels conduct to devolve on status. The racialized citizen patriot, the noncitizen nonpatriot, the disloyal suspect immigrant, and the suspect citizen are all made to occupy this underworld as the urban internal enemy—the violence against whom underwrites the forms of massacre directed against the external enemy.

The link between militarization at home and militarization abroad also finds expression in the export and marketing of punishment technologies. The former commissioner of the New York City Police Department, Bernard Kerik, served in 2003 as Iraq's interim Minister of the Interior and subsequently became one of the top nominees to head the Department of Homeland Security; and the senior policy advisor to the U.S. presidential envoy, Paul Bremer, was entrusted with "the development and reconstruction of Iraq's police force." According to Kerik, within a five-month period thirty-five police stations were established "out of nothing"; and the police officers were to be trained according to "the principles of policing in a new society, a free and democratic society." It is significant that apart from the focus on the weaponry to be introduced—"handguns, rifles, long guns"—the training curriculum that would anchor freedom and policing remains largely unspecified.[125]

From the vantage point of the state patriot, now injured by a relation of the "sodomite/cross-dressers" with whom Balboa had presumably dispensed, punishment and retaliation must be even more severe. The enemy has to be made feminine enough to be subordinated, aberrant enough to be grotesque, barbaric enough to require civilization, Islamic enough to require Christianity, and yet potent and destructive enough to legitimize war: hence the invention of weapons of mass destruction. As ideological productions, these weapons of mass destruction need never be found, since the purpose of their production has already been served:

to reside in the imagination of the citizen patriot (indeed of the world) as the thing that had to be destroyed to bring about security, which only the national security state could provide: that is, the United States at the helm of the new world order. The weapons of mass destruction were publicly invented and fully integrated into the national security strategy first diffused on 17 September 2002. And even two years later with the 9/11 commission's findings that such weapons never existed, the weapons continue to live their intent: to serve as a major piece of ideological weaponry in the arsenal of militarized intervention.[126]

In a fundamental sense, the national security strategy laid out the template on which both Patriot Acts, full-scale war, the defense of imperialism, and the defense of America would rest. At the outset, however, this far-reaching project of empire was not rendered by that name, but was based instead in America's cosmic mandate to mind, in the wording of the text of the strategy itself, the "great struggles of the twentieth century between liberty and totalitarianism [that] ended with a decisive victory for the forces of freedom—and a single sustainable model for national success: freedom, democracy and free enterprise."[127] Further, "the duty of protecting these values against their enemies," the strategy reasoned, was "the common calling of freedom-loving people across the globe and across all ages." These terms by themselves do not necessarily carve out a special place for America, particularly in light of a common calling that has such a vast and long genealogy. How does freedom move from a common mandate to being a uniquely American mandate? And if it is a common mandate, how, or rather why, is it to be entrusted and managed by a singular entity—the United States of North America? The answers to these questions come through the positioning of what the president termed "a distinctly American internationalism" that emanated from its "unparalleled military strength and its great political and economic influence . . . its fundamental commitment to defend the nation against its enemies," and—here comes the twist—to seize this "moment of opportunity to extend the benefits of freedom, democracy, development of free markets and free trade." The special role of the United States is to build on common interests to promote global security. In a word, this unique American mandate is a capitalist mandate that has been thrust on itself by itself and in the face of the popular global opposition to the war and the opposition of a majority of nation-states—which at the very least suggests that the interests were not that common after all. The self-designated mandate to promote global security becomes all the more transparent in light of current disclosures of fabricated intelligence on the part of the state (which ironically play on the same oxymoronic impulse at work in the conflation of freedom, democracy, free market, and free trade) and a series of imperial tactics through which the provision of "development" is administered. Thus the link between national security and empire building is presumably secure. According to the president in the text of the strategy: "To defeat this threat, we must make use of every tool in our arsenal—military power, homeland defenses, law enforcement, intelligence, and vigorous efforts to cut off terrorist financing. The war against terrorists is of global reach, a global enterprise of uncertain duration. America will help nations that need our assistance in combating terror. And America will hold to account nations that are compromised by terror, including those who harbor terrorists—because the allies of terror are the enemies of civilization." The bombing of Falluja two days after the reinstallation of militarized masculinity in the face of the presidential elections of 2004 is a further attempt to consolidate this link between national security and empire building.

To be an enemy of civilization—which in essence suggests a propensity for barbarism—with the power, as the strategy outlines, "to turn the power of modern technologies" against a country that "enjoys a position of unparalleled military strength and great economic and political influence," invites conquest and a mode of perennial retaliation that is contradictory enough to undermine the very tradition of freedom that is presumably a cosmic responsibility to uphold. Some traditions are, however, more worthy of being upheld than others. For instance, the tradition of capitalism upheld by a modern militarized masculinity that is far superior to an outmoded barbaric masculinity, a caricature of modernity and heterosexual masculinity simultaneously—since its only power derives from the power of modern technologies itself. The paradox here is that both masculinities have been built on military might and on different forms of terror, but the struggle for empire can never be positioned as a struggle between equals.[128]

A Map Outside the Mandate for Conquest[129]

On this reconfigured map of palimpsestic time, the various parchments are not positioned by opposing a distant "then and there" to a proximate "here and now." Rather, I have sought to make them intelligible by bringing the "here" and "there" into ideological proximity within a single social formation as well as among and between social formations that have been positioned as opposites in the linear narration of time. Throughout, colonialism has been made to travel, functioning as an important metaphorical, discursive, and ideological fault line that refuses transhistoricity but has the capacity, nonetheless, to disrupt an altogether too easy alignment between modernity and neo-imperialism. Discourses are neither segregated from one another nor positioned as isolationist, cordoned off from crosscutting interests or geographies.

Bringing neocolonialism into ideological proximity with neo-imperialism has made visible the different ways in which ideologies and practices traffic within the two spheres, making visible, as well, the different investments in the simultaneous mobilization of tradition and modernity, not as fixed constructs but as profitable political currency. Neocolonialism chooses selectively from "modernity"; indeed, anticolonial nationalism was predicated on modernist claims about statehood and nation-building, and while neocolonial formations function within a subordinated relationship to neo-imperialism, it is these very imperial social relations that accord with one method of time keeping: that is, Christian neoliberal corporate financial time, which in its allegiance to the IMF and other strategies of privatization, compels it to assist in the production of subjectivities that would favor the social relations of global tourism above those of sovereignty. At a time of empire-building, heterosexuality emerges at the nexus of fundamentalism and militarization to uphold ostensibly natural teleologies of propagation and of market capitalism simultaneously, both of which require privatized heterosexuality and, increasingly, privatized homosexuality as well.

To the extent that heterosexualization is one of the processes through which globalization is aligned, neocolonial state managers avidly reinvigorate its elements as a way of signaling their allegiance to Western norms and their allegiance to the modern, since their repudiation of it would confirm racist challenges to their capacity to govern. Neo-imperial state managers, on the other hand, laud its tradition as the bedrock of the civilization from which they sprung. While the neo-imperial capitalist class does not bear the onus of the infantilizing, anxiety-ridden ideologies that accompanied colonization, its investment in an originary claim to the West has enabled it to be positioned, where visible, as the bearer of good tradition, the harbinger of modernity, and the guardian of democracy in spite of some of the most egregious infractions in its name.

On this map, heterosexuality's imperatives are quite large and necessarily differentiated. Among them are the acquisition of land and property—the territorial appropriation of land that is sealed through the territorial marking of whiteness; the consolidation of regimes of citizenship around various statuses that range from heteromasculine soldiering to the nuclear unit of the heterosexual family; the underwriting of the project of nation building in ways that paradoxically render the boundaries of the nation-state as fixed by designating loyal heterosexual citizenship along normative hierarchies of race, gender, and class in ways that guard the boundaries of the nation-state from sexual perversity and from certain classes of immigrants who ostensibly undo the nation's interests by relying on public assistance and whose movement across the borders of the nation must therefore be curtailed; and the rendering of those same boundaries as highly permeable for a hypermobile capitalist/corporate managerial class that does not require the nation-state to consolidate a set of global interests, including global citizenship.

And yet there are a number of practices that hypernationalism and anticolonial nationalism share as they go about the business of settling the question of just how the nation is to be peopled. Among them are the defense of originary nuclear family; the coupling of (hetero)sexualization and citizenship; the allegiance to the privatization of households and of economies both psychic and material, manifesting as structural adjustment in the Caribbean and retrenchments in the social wage in the United States; the allegiance to securing the longevity of their own class interests; and an injured masculinity (although the sources of infliction differ). For neocolonial state managers, injury devolves on the struggle for respectability and the colonized desire to be recognized as "civilized," while masculinity's neo-imperial injury emanates from a psychic memory of the Crusades, of being now outmaneuvered by the savage whom Christian Spanish civilization was supposed to have annihilated centuries ago but who reappears on a different continent, at a different historical moment, and in a different guise.[130] Hypernationalism and anticolonial nationalism share, as well, in the massive scope of violence that inheres in the simultaneous production of spectacularization. Both the violence of spectacularization and the violence of forced heterosexualization can be seen as operating hand in hand and as indispensable, therefore, to how these states conduct themselves. As I argued earlier, given what we have learned from the Combahee River Collective's analysis of the simultaneity of oppression, it would be difficult to establish a hierarchy of violence as a way to distinguish between democratic violence and savage violence, and it would indeed be difficult to sustain an argument in which the experience of democratic violence is somehow more desirable than that of savage violence.

In bringing discourses and practices into proximity with one another, we see how different populations are summoned to live on heterosexuality's behalf. The propensity apparatus that the Military Working Group developed to discipline lesbian, gay, and bisexual soldiers derives from a long and varied pedigree, echoed by neocolonial state managers in their reflection about whether it was the Soul or the mere body of the homosexual that was homosexual. Part of this belief was that these propensities could function as truth about character. In this sense, the manufacture of different propensities reinvokes the ideological taxonomies that were affixed to various African ethnic groups during the process of enslavement as a means of producing and solidifying divisions and of assuring the dominance of the planter class: the Ashanti and Fanti were positioned as intelligent, vengeful, and prone to kill their masters during insurrections; the Mandingoes gentle; the Kongos and Ibos suicide prone; the Angolans lazy. It reinvokes, as well, the taxonomies that underwrote the racialized and gendered U.S. Exclusion Acts that constructed Chinese as a "yellow peril."[131] These propensities also were intended to function as truth about character. But these are not the only propensities at work by playing on that odd slippage between conduct and status. The judgment of a reasonable heterosexual unit commander can identify the propensity of the lesbian soldier; legalized citizen patriots, "Americans," the attorney general, and the president can all make judgments about immigrant propensity for terrorism; and reasonable, tax-paying, consuming citizens can make judgments about the propensity for laziness of recipients of public assistance. Without being either reductionist or relativist, this analysis has shown that propensities work to marginalize, that is, they exact different forms of terror and violence on the bodies of different groups of people. What this also means, however, is that there is an opening on how to build strategic solidarities among these very marginalized constituencies once we refuse to mimic the practices of the state. Indeed, the question of just how not to do state work at a moment of empire is one of the most crucial questions we must confront in living a transformative politic.

The neo-imperial state's cordoning off of the originary citizen from the immigrant in order to delineate the legal loyal heterosexual patriot has implications for radical political projects, including political organizing. Histories of xenophobia and the various state mechanisms that keep "immigrants out" find ready settler places at moments of crisis. Because of the collusion between the media and the state, and because the task of figuring out a multivalenced political struggle is such a steep challenge (one can oppose the war yet continue to be an avid consumer that the war defends), only an eagle-eye vigilance can prevent state constructs from seeping into peace and justice movements. If the very terms on which we organize are constituted through the ideology of the secure citizen—the very construct that the state deploys to position the loyal patriot—then we will continue to make invisible the widespread detention of immigrants and their criminalization, and we will mystify the ways in which these detention practices work to secure the secure citizen. As Carole Boyce Davies has argued, citizenship is simply far too fragile, indeed, it is far too fraught and far too subject to state manipulation and co-optation for it to become the primary basis on which radical political mobilization is carried on.[132]

This analysis has not pivoted state power on contestation, on class struggle (although one might posit the predominantly working-class character of the imperial fighting force as a strategy of ruling-class warfare), or on other forms of political mobilization and social movements from below, or even on the category of resistance. Their apparent absence might suggest that the very mechanisms through which the state-nation nexus is mediated have been truncated. But there are two important caveats to be made in this regard. The first pertains to the categories that are dislodged at moments of crisis, and here I will pose the question in a way that parallels an articulation in the Bahamian context, that is, what are the productive breaks in the "heteropatriarchal symbolic order" that prompt the state to reclothe itself in heterosexuality's garb? The answer here bears on the second caveat, which is that the productive breaks in this symbolic order are provoked, and it is these provocations that are generated by political mobilizations of different kinds. To understand this in another way, while there is a level of violence that inheres in the very logic of state practices, the situational violences that are produced through law, for instance, such as the Defense of Marriage Act, the Sexual Offences and Domestic Violence Act, and the Personal Responsibility and Work Opportunity Reconciliation Act, are installed as the direct result of the provocation of "failed" heterosexuality—whether in the form of same-sex marriage contextualized through LGBTT political mobilization, feminist anti-imperialist movements read as lesbianism, or the heterosexual refusal of marriage as the domestic expression of love—contextualized through poor people's movements. These provocations are profound in contexts in which, for very different historical reasons, heterosexual marriage is not the primary locus of intimacy. But the fact that oppositional movements instigate state judicial violence suggests that we should move away from theorizations of resistance as reactive strategy to theorizing power as interwoven with, and living alongside, marginalization. It may not be a power that reverses state action—as these massive global antiwar mobilizations have demonstrated—but the very point of power and marginalization is evidenced in U.S. state attempts to position these global mobilizations as narrowly sectarian and self-interested. The threat of a rival global power that imagines a map outside of a mandate for conquest is quite profound. Conceiving of this power hinges on whether we think about moral agency and freedom as ontological categories with clear political expression but not necessarily derived, in the first instance, from the political, that is, from the outside, something that an outside entity more powerful than ourselves can confer.

If this analysis has convinced us about the value of palimpsestic time, then it must also mean that we are similarly convinced that the practices of imperialism cannot be hidden in an analytic closet. If from a privileged location in the United States of North America, some of us have been seduced into believing that imperialism was "then and there," this new round of empire consolidation and state restructuring must have brought a violent end to that seduction, for imperialism is simultaneously "then and there," "here and now," and "here and there." We must confront again the questions that Winona LaDuke, among others, posed about the importance of internal colonization and land struggles to the feminist project;[133] the claims that Puerto Rican feminists made more than three decades ago about U.S. imperial investments in the sterilization of Puerto Rican women; the arguments that Hawaiian feminists have made about American imperialism via tourism; the mobilization of Pacific women against U.S. military maneuvers that result in violence to the environment and to their bodies in the birth of abnormal fetuses;[134] Masai women from Kenya who have brought charges of rape against British militiamen stationed in their country;[135] the East Asia–U.S.–Puerto Rico Women's Network against Militarism, whose contemporary mobilizations have yielded new insights about the meaning of human security that are based in "a sustainable environment, the fulfillment of people's basic needs, respect for people's fundamental human dignity and cultural identities and protection of people and the natural environment from avoidable harm";[136] the various ways in which imperialism traffics in the war at "home"; the fact that every decade after the Second World War has been marked by U.S. intervention in other countries;[137] and the long-standing Israeli occupation of Palestine that is consistently being rewritten, even more so with the death of Yassir Arafat. The continued absence of empire in the study of American culture is complicitous with cultures of imperialism.[138] Charlotte Bunch's observation that U.S. feminist mobilizations have provoked transformations in the social relations of gender at the national cultural level but have been less successful in transforming state imperial policy is a strong reminder of the task ahead,[139] and it dovetails with Ella Shohat's assessment that the opposition to racism, sexism, and homophobia in the United States has never guaranteed the opposition to U.S. global hegemony.[140] The group Feminist Majority betrays the gains of solidary transnational praxis in its allegiance to this hegemony.[141] To ignore the centrality of imperialism is to continue to live a dangerous privilege that only the analytic habit of conflating capitalism and democracy can mistakenly confer.

At this moment of empire consolidation, the academy continues to figure prominently in what Jonathan Feldman identified more than a decade ago as the state's web of militarism and intervention.[142] The dominant iterations of our various disciplines continue a collusion with state practices that we can no longer ignore by virtue of a different institutional location in women's studies, queer studies, or postcolonial studies, particularly in light of our dual, sometimes triple, residence in these analytic homes. Sociology's implication in the punishment industry in ways that provide the rationale for "order maintenance policing" and the increased criminalization of daily life has almost wrenched it away from any plausible social justice claims. Normative political science has strong investments in a neutral, benign, and disinterested state, even as the state continues to preside over a racial, gendered, heterosexual order, and continues to position both this discipline and international relations schools as feeders for the managers of the militarized state. Normative economics remains wedded to explaining immigration according to push-pull factors, never paying attention to how assimilation functions as a form of violence, or how its own formulations prop up the nexus of capitalism's racialized, gendered inequities. In addition, the deployment of the academy within the policing functions of the state has been actualized most visibly in the regulations of the Patriot Act of 2001 in which international students, scholars, and their dependents on F and J visas are required to be registered on SEVIS—a student exchange visitor information system of Web-based data collection and monitoring designed to link institutions of higher education, the Bureau of Citizenship and Immigration Services (which replaces the INS) and other U.S. state agencies, consulates and embassies abroad, and ports of entry.

Not paradoxically, the academy has not escaped state surveillance. In the same way in which multicultural studies was positioned as scapegoat for the frayed economy of the 1980s, postcolonial studies is now being aligned with terrorist efforts that "undermine American foreign policy."[143] How will queer studies, ethnic studies, and women's studies engage the recent state attacks against postcolonial studies, particularly since radical transnational feminism has also been brought into the state's orbit?[144] There is a great deal of urgency for us to map—that is, to reimagine, practice, *and* live—some crucial analytic shifts that will prompt postcolonial studies to engage more strategically with the "here and there," to position immigration, for instance, as an important site for the local reconfiguration of subalternity and the local reconfiguration of race, and to develop a less-fraught relationship with a radically formulated ethnic studies by practicing what Donaldson, Donadey, and Silliman call "subversive couplings."[145] As certain strands of queer studies move to take up more centrally questions of political economy and racial formation, and of transnational feminism and immigrant labor, the analytic vise in the discipline will be sharpened between those who hold on to a representational democratic focus within U.S. borders and those who espouse an antipathy toward the links between political economy and sexuality. Addressing these questions can challenge a similar nationalist representational intellectual impulse insinuated within women's studies that renders the transnational and related critical approaches as consumptive or as an epistemic option.

What does a path outside of disciplinary intransigence or disciplinary segregation mean, bearing in mind that part of what is at stake in a radical project is the rewriting and living of a history that is fundamentally at odds with the intentions of the national security state; refusing the prescriptions of the permanent war economy that requires permanent enemies (both epistemic and political) as fuel. Some of its terms have already been suggested in the pages of this book. If there were ever a moment when interdisciplinarity is most needed it is now, but we need a kind of interdisciplinarity that fashions simultaneous articulations with radical political movements in ways that bring the necessary complexity to the multiple narratives about how history is made. We cannot escape the fierce contradictions that are posed for queer soldiering, for people of color soldiering, and for working-class soldiering on behalf of empire.

As we recognize that the nation-state matters more to some than to others, we also need to recognize that the borders of the nation-state cannot be positioned as hermetically sealed or epistemically partial. Our knowledge-making projects must therefore move across state-constructed borders to develop frameworks that are simultaneously intersubjective, comparative, and relational, yet historically specific and grounded. And because fragmentation is both material and metaphysical, and both epistemic and ontological, these frameworks would need to be attentive to the underbelly of superiority and the psychic economies of its entrails as part of an explicitly political project. The fiction of disappearing threat as a way to eliminate opposition has left a sort of residual psychic memory, the belief that physical removal ensures that that which has been expunged will never again reappear. And it leaves this memory precisely because it confuses the metaphysical with the material, believing that material removal is, simultaneously, a metaphysical removal. The metaphysical domain, however, cannot simply, easily, or arbitrarily be reduced to the material. So what appeared earlier in my discussion as purely materialized timekeeping is in reality metaphysical. Time as metaphysical is not disciplined by neat compartmentalizations of finance, the clock, the "here and now" and the "then and there," nor is it even governed by the "here and there" of our model of palimpsesis. Time transforms and, much like the serpent, that ancient figure of metamorphosis, returns to provoke the encounter with the lost double that memory makes impossible to forget.[146] These metaphysical questions, then, are the focus of the closing chapters of this volume.

III

DANGEROUS MEMORY

Secular Acts, Sacred Possession

6

Remembering *This Bridge Called My Back*, Remembering Ourselves

In March 2000, the Department of Gender and Women's Studies at Connecticut College organized an event to honor a multiracial group of women poets of distinction and to mark the twentieth anniversary of the publication of *This Bridge Called My Back*. "Poets on Location" was a way to bring back to memory an earlier historical moment in which the vision of a pancultural radical feminist politics seemed more vigorous and more visible in the United States. All six of the honorees had combined the search for beauty with the struggle for social justice in their life's work. As we wrote in the program notes: "These women poets have scrutinized their lives, wrestled with their different inheritances of geography, of place; with race, class, sexuality, body, nationality and belonging, and molded it all into sources of insight and wisdom. Among them, they have lived three hundred and sixty-three years, spanning continents, threading dreams, holding visions." Honored were Chrystos, Dionne Brand, Cherríe Moraga, Sonia Sanchez, Adrienne Rich, and Mitsuye Yamada, three of whom were original contributors to *Bridge*. Audre Lorde, Toni Cade Bambara, and Pat Parker joined us in spirit. Donna Kate Rushin read "The Bridge Poem" and, on the night of that honoring —nestled in between the overgrown stems of the most radiant sunflowers —she and Papusa Molina recalled the names of all thirty-two women who, as Lorde would have said it, put their pens in the full service of what they believed. The moment was electric: songs on drums; no land to light on; the heat of fire changing the shape of things; reminiscences of the desert and of the promise of oasis; listening for something; dreaming of a common language; moving radiance to trace the truth of history. On that evening in March, a "terrible beauty" had soaked the cadence of a playful flute and solemn drums and a not-so-silent hunger of a crowd, determined to smell the taste of a past now brought present. Yearning, memory, and desire. A powerful combination.

This past commemoration is not my only memory of *This Bridge Called My Back*. My earliest recollections were planted fifteen years ago as I was giving birth to myself in summer 1986. I navigated the passage in the waters of *Bridge, Homegirls, Cancer Journals,* and *Sister Outsider,* yearning, without knowing, for the company of lesbian women to help me swim in those gray Maine waters on Greenings Island, which appear to be strangers to their turquoise blue-green sisters thousands of miles away. Unrelated on the surface only, for down in that abyss their currents reach for each other and fold, without the slightest tinge of resentment, into the same Atlantic, the rebellious waters of which provided the path for a more violent passage, many, many centuries but not so many centuries ago. Secrets lie in the silted bottom of these waters. In that summer of a reluctant sun, incessant waves, and what seems now like an interminably full moon, I remember how much I have forgotten of that daily awakening. Stark outlines remain, to be sure, but the more tactile reminders have receded. There are no notes in the margins of my dissertation to indicate that, as I wrote those slow pages—heavy with the weight of the costs of medicine and the disproportionate brunt that workers bore at the hands of corporate and state managers—my heart was moving to a different rhythm. But I remember how my passion and love for a woman, a distant memory of a deep and necessary transgression, folded into a joy I felt on meeting the women in *Bridge* for the first time—women like me, bound in a collective desire to change the world. The experience of freedom in boundary crossing. I later went in search of *Zami,* but when these women "who work together as friends and lovers" announced a new spelling of their name under the section "Women of Color" at New Words Bookstore in Cambridge, my fingers became tentative with a memory of the harsh sound of the word *Zami* in Trinidad, and the whispers about two women whom my furtive friends and I had climbed over a fence to see, on the way home, from the convent high school I attended.

I couldn't live Caribbean feminism on American soil, and Caribbean soil had grown infertile to the manufacture of the needs of those to its north. Caribbean people had docked one ship too many; waved one goodbye too many to women recruited for the war in Britain or for work as domestics in Canada or the United States. They had grown one banana too many, thin and small—not Chiquita, not Dole—that would turn to manure before being eaten; heard one demand too many to smile for tourists because they presumably provided one's bread and butter. I was not in Jamaica with Sistren as they documented the rage of women who worked in the sugarcane fields (Sweet Sugar Rage), using theater to score the unequal vicissitudes of their lives; I would read only much later CAFRA's inaugural discussions.[1] Nor had I joined the droves of women who left the Caribbean and the metropolis with equal discontent to build the revolution in Grenada. I was not in Boston in 1979, as the bodies of black women fell, one after the other, twelve in all, at least that time—the same year the People's Revolutionary Movement came to power in Grenada—blood that defied the insistent rains and vowed to leave its mark on the harsh concrete, on the cluttered, winding corners of dark alleys. I was not in Pine Ridge, South Dakota, as the "red blood full of those arrested, in flight" flowed, as Sioux and Lakota alike occupied Wounded Knee.[2] Nor was I part of the "primary emergencies" confronting different women of color living on the other side of structural inequities; of violence within the false safety of home; of the unnatural disaster of imposed invisibility; of passing across the lines of color, different shades of light and brown, wearing "exhausting camouflages"; negotiating the pathologies of racism.[3] I had missed Nairobi completely, hidden in-between the stacks in the basement of Widener Library, forced instead to go in search of my blood sisters at one of the many post-Nairobi reports back to the community, which the Boston Women's Health Book Collective had sponsored. It was there that I met Angela Bowen for the first time, a sister traveler come to sojourn only four blocks away from where I lived in Cambridgeport. We have walked these dusty tracks before.

By the middle of the 1980s, then, when at least twenty thousand people had read *Bridge* and shared it with at least another twenty thousand of their friends, I had only begun the journey, and then only in text. For me, *Bridge* was both anchor and promise in that I could begin to frame a lesbian feminist woman of color consciousness and, at the same time, move my living in a way that would provide the moorings for that consciousness. Neither anchor nor promise could have been imaginable without the women in *Bridge*, who gave themselves permission to write, to speak in tongues.[4]

I was not a part of the sweat and fire that birthed a woman of color politics in this country in the 1970s and 1980s. This is why I want to remember that I have been shaped by it. It is why I am indebted to the women who literally entered the fire for me, on my behalf. What I found compelling was the plain courage and determination of a bunch of different women all tied to some kind of cultural inheritance, sometimes at a cost, sometimes isolated from it, at times yearning for it. The women were my age, many younger than I, saying so much about so many different things, gesturing to me about a forgetting so deep that I had even forgotten what I had forgotten.[5] I had not known that a love letter could still be a love letter, to one's mother no less, and deal with betrayal and wounds. I read Merle Woo's "Letter to Ma," my mouth open and aghast—and covered, of course. After all, I could not be caught staring at something, or someone, so impolitely, with my mouth open. I couldn't imagine speaking in this way within my family, a family in which speech was such a scarce commodity, the trade in silence the value. A system of silence, my uncle calls it. *How* do I come out to family? To all of my five brothers? No sister to tell. She closed her eyes for good only nine days after she had opened them, when I was just four and barely able to see the eyelet bonnet that caressed her soft face in the coffin. To my mother? For years I would think that as a lesbian I had a cosmic duty to perfect my relationship with my mother. My father, by then, had died alone without even a word to me. Months afterward, in one of those early hours before dawn, he visited me as a wraith, propped up on a walking stick. He saw my partner and me lying in bed, but said nothing. At least he knew. Later, I would see that my own hesitation about "coming out" in Trinidad was laced with the fears of a dutiful daughter's jeopardizing middle-class respectability. Anticolonial nationalism had taught us well about heterosexual loyalty, a need so great that it reneged on its promise of self-determination, delivering criminality instead of citizenship.[6] And yet my father's death released a different desire: a different form of loving and a new kind of politic that I found first in *Bridge*.

In Barbara Cameron's "Gee You Don't Seem Like an Indian from the Reservation," I saw reflected much of my first-year undergraduate experience in the United States where, for the first time in my life, the majority of people around me were white. Accented, foreign, and seen as friendly in this predominantly white environment, I had not yet known that I was being compared to black students (African American was not used then) and positioned in relation to the "unjustifiably angry" black American. I had not known until the slave auction, when white male students thought they could have fun by "hiring" white women as slaves for a day. And the campus exploded. In the midst of sit-ins and teach-ins, I was forced to confront the utter silence of white students who were my friends in the sudden shift to being a stranger. It was my most tactile experience of things of which I had only read or witnessed on television. It began to instill a daily awareness in me of seeing myself as black—and equally important—to begin thinking about what white people were seeing/ thinking as they saw me. I had not had to negotiate the daily assignment of racial superiority and inferiority, or its most egregious costs, as I grew up in Trinidad in the midst of an apparent black majority.[7] It would take me six more years, and a walk down the streets of Williamsburg, Virginia, with my friend Beverly Mason, to really understand how racism distorts and narrows the field and scope of vision. "Do you see how they look at us, Jacqui?" "No, no," I replied. "You don't see how they look at us!" "NO," I insisted, not knowing even intuitively what I was supposed to have seen. At that time I had not felt double-consciousness. I had known of its existence from Fanon's *Black Skins, White Masks*, but I had not known its taste.[8]

Nor had I known that the texture of identities could be made into a theory of the flesh, as Cherríe Moraga outlined. This idea echoed consistently throughout the collection and in the Combahee River Collective statement: "The most general statement of our politics at the present time would be that we are actively committed to struggling against racial, sexual, heterosexual, and class oppression, and see as our particular task the development of integrated analysis and practice based on the fact that the major systems of oppression are interlocking. The synthesis of these oppressions creates the conditions of our lives."[9] I had to work to understand this question of the conditions of our lives, how they are shaped daily through structures, and even how to use flesh-and-blood experiences to concretize a vision. I did not know how precisely the personal was political, since I had not yet begun to fully scrutinize much of what was personal.

The mobilization of Black Power in the mid 1970s in the Anglophone Caribbean spoke to the region's subordinate economic position in the world economy. Foreign ownership of banks, for instance, had guaranteed jobs for whites, but much of the contextual history of slavery and colonization—how we came to be there and got to be who we were—was largely missing from an educational system (nationalism notwithstanding) that asked smart students to learn the history of imperial might—British history, U.S. history and geography—and nothing of Caribbean history. All of Dickens, Shakespeare, Chaucer. None of Jean Rhys, George Lamming, Louise Bennett, Ismith Khan. It gave no clues about the connections between the operation of systems and the behaviors of people, no clues about our social sexual selves, or about how we could be agents in those selves.

The processes of colonization in *Bridge* wore a face different from the ones to which I had been accustomed. Articulated by Chicanas, Puertorriqueñas, and Native women, it spoke to the internal colonies of the reservations; the barrios; the labor regimes of the cotton fields of Texas; the contentious inheritance of Malintzín, and the confusion between devotion and obedience, usually cathected onto women in the secular sphere, or otherwise collapsed into the religious figure of the Virgin Mary, who had actually accompanied me throughout my thirteen years of Catholic school. I had longed to become a nun. Chrystos had learned to walk in the history of her people; she had come to know there were "women locked in [her] joints."[10] Who were my people? How does one know the stories and histories of one's people? Where does one learn them? Who were we as Trinidadians? We did not all come on the same ship, as the national(ist) myth held. Some of us, Indian, were captured/brought under indenture to work on plantations that had been evacuated after the "end" of slavery. We held in callused hands the broken promise of return to Calcutta, Bombay, Madras—a colonial betrayal consistently pushed under the surface in order to test Indian loyalty to Trinidad, the home of forced adoption. Some of us, Chinese, were smuggled/brought in as contract laborers, also to work on sugar plantations.[11] Some of us, black, were captured/sold from a geography so vast, the details would daunt memory to produce a forgetting so deep, we had forgotten that we had forgotten. Missing memory. Who are *my* people? How will I come to know the stories and histories of *my* people? With Chicanas and Puertorriqueñas, I shared a nonbelonging to the United States. Mirtha Quintanales was Cuban lesbian, a Caribbean lesbian. Like her, I did not belong in the United States, and while I was not Cuban, there was a family connection in my uncle's search for Oriente, Cuba, that place where the roots of trees travel without the need of a compass to the deep forests of Mayombe, Kongo, to Dahomey, Da-ha-homey, and to New York. Trees remember and will whisper remembrances in your ear, if you stay still and listen.

Charting the Journey

It was this sensibility of a politicized nonbelonging, with a capacity to fuel an imperative about self-determination, that persisted in the sister companion to *Bridge*, titled *Charting the Journey*—a journey that black women in Britain had undertaken by navigating a different set of waters. Immigrant waters. Colonial waters. The material substance of the "idea" of blackness, and the creation of a life in Britain, "of three to four million people and their descendants from former British colonies," worked as both scaffold and foundation to understand British imperialism, both outside and within, as it created "strangers at home" in an "Alien Nation."[12] The borders of that nation had been made porous long ago, so that when black women organized one of the campaigns, "we are here because you were there," they stood at the confluence of a set of historical forces that tied together a politics of dislocation and migration (which made ample room for solidarity with politics "at home" in Ireland, Palestine, Eritrea, Chile, Namibia, and El Salvador) with a consistent critique of state practices and of Zionism, and systematically folded it into the praxis of being black women in Britain.

In one sense, the weaving of a transnational intention into *Charting the Journey* is but implicit in *Bridge*. *Charting the Journey* made room for a dialectic of intersecting forces, splintered, as they constituted both the local (several localities simultaneously), and the global, across inherited maps but also within them. The bridge, in its first incarnation, is an internal one, crossing into different experiences of colonization, to be sure, but it largely assumes that the very borders of the American nation are intact, an assumption that is later dislodged and reimagined as a desire to be more explicitly international. As Moraga stated in the preface to the second edition, "The impetus to forge links with women of color from every region grows more and more urgent as the numbers of recently-immigrated people of color in the U.S. grows in enormous proportions."[13] These metaphors of links, charts, journeys, bridges, and borders are neither idle nor incidental, however, as we come to terms with the different cartographies of feminist struggle in different parts of the world; our different histories; where they change course and how they diverge.[14] It seems crucial that we come to terms with, and engage, that confluence of the local and the global in order not to view the transnational as merely a theoretical option. The fact that our standard of living here, indeed our very survival, is based on the raw exploitation of working-class women, white, black, and Third World in all parts of the world. Our hands are not clean.[15] We must also come to terms with that still largely unexamined faith in the *idea* of America, that no matter how unbearable it is here, it is better than being anywhere, elsewhere; that slippage between Third World and third rate. We eat bananas. Buy flowers. Use salt to flavor our food. Drink sweetened coffee. Use tires for the cars we drive. Depend on state-of-the-art electronics. Wear clothes, becoming of a kind of style that has called a premature end to modernity, to colonization. We travel. We consume and rely on multiple choice to reify consumption. All of those things that give material weight to the *idea* of America, and which conflate capitalism and democracy and demarcate "us" from "them." All of those things that give ideological weight to the *idea* of America, producing a constitutional fear, a fear of the disappearance of the very (American) self, of the erasure of the American nation, even as the borders of America become more permeable.

What might it mean to see ourselves as "refugees of a world on fire"?

"What if we declared ourselves *perpetual* refugees in solidarity with all refugees"?[16] Not citizen. Not naturalized citizen. Not immigrant. Not undocumented. Not illegal alien. Not permanent resident. Not resident alien. But refugees fleeing some terrible atrocity far too threatening to engage, ejected out of the familiar into some unknown, still-to-be-revealed place. Refugees forced to create out of the raw smithy of fire a shape different from our inheritance, with no blueprints, no guarantees. Some might die in flight: Palestine. Afghanistan. Rwanda. Kôngo. Bosnia. Haiti. Sierra Leone. Some live a different death: Marilyn Buck. Silvia Baraldini. Debbie Sims Africa. Leonard Peltier. Mumia Abu Jamal. Political prisoners.[17] And women and people of color shackled, in disproportionate numbers, at the height of their creativity in a privatized system of imprisonment.[18] Many undergo daily trials by fire: Women in Vieques, Puerto Rico, who since 1941 have lived with aerial bombardment and military maneuvers by the U.S. Navy, now suffer the effects of carcinogens in growing numbers. Some die a different death: 40,410 of us, every single year, of breast cancer in the United States.[19] Or the continuing deaths of African Americans from HIV/AIDS, in the face of reduced rates of infection in every other racial group; and the stunning increase in HIV/AIDS-infected babies to whom immigrant women give birth. A preventable phenomenon![20] And a general globalized violence producing rapid dispersals of people, some one hundred million, mostly women and children seeking asylum. What are the different intolerables from which we desire to flee? And how do we distinguish between those sites to which we must return and those from which we must flee entirely? What becomes of those who cannot flee, no matter how intolerable the conditions? In order to wrestle with these questions we would need to adopt, as daily practice, ways of being and of relating, modes of analyzing, and strategies of organizing in which we constantly mobilize identification and solidarity, across all borders, as key elements in the repertoire of risks we need to take to see ourselves as part of one another, even in the context of difference.[21] We would need to disappear the idiocy of "us" and "them" and its cultural relativist underpinnings, the belief that "it could never happen to *us,*" so that our very consciousness would be shaped by multiple histories and events, multiple geographies, multiple identifications.

And yet, we must remember the character of fire, its paradoxical dimension: it provides sustenance and warmth, but it can destroy, it can kill. But the difference between those of us who fear fire and "the welder" is her knowledge that she has to become intimate with this danger zone in order to re-create, to create anew; to enter the fire not figuratively, or metaphorically, but actually, that is, in flesh and blood.[22] The difference between the welder and those of us who fear fire is the consciousness and attentiveness she brings to the process of entering fire, and it is this consciousness that cultivates the intelligence to discern, embrace, and live that important, yet malleable, relationship between destruction and sustenance. Fire can kill, but without it we *will* die. Can we see that a lotus can bloom in the furnace without losing its freshness?[23] We would need to learn to make peace with contradiction and paradox, to see its operation in the uneven structures of our own lives, to learn to sense, taste, and understand paradox as the motor of things, which is what Marxian philosophy *and* the metaphysics of spiritual thought systems have in common: dialectics of struggle. Paradoxes of the Divine. Still, we know that living contradiction is not easy in a culture that ideologically purveys a distaste for it, preferring instead an apparent attachment to consensus.[24] But we know, as well, that living contradiction is necessary if we are to create the asylums of identification and solidarity with and for one another, without which our lives will surely wither.[25]

We Have Recognized Each Other Before

Who are we as women of color at this moment in history? Where is the political movement that calls itself a woman of color movement? Who mobilizes within it? On what terms? At the original writing of *Bridge,* women puzzled over these questions, even as they linked themselves to the emerging politic. Mirtha Quintanales got to the heart of the paradox of naming:

> Not all Third World women are "women of color"—if by this concept we mean exclusively "non-white" . . . And not all women of color are really Third World—if this term is only used in reference to underdeveloped . . . societies (especially those not allied with any superpower). Clearly then it would be difficult to justify referring to Japa-

nese women, who are women of color, as Third World women. Yet if we extend the concept of Third World to include internally "colonized," racial and ethnic minority groups in this country, the crucial issue of social and institutional racism and its historic tie to slavery in the U.S. could get diluted, lost in the shuffle. The same thing would likely happen if we extended the meaning of "women of color" to include . . . women . . . who are victims of prejudice . . . but who nevertheless hold racial privileges and may even be racists . . . Many of us who identify as "Third World" or "Women of Color," have grown up as, or are fast becoming "middle-class" and highly educated, and therefore more privileged than many of our white, poor and working-class sisters.[26]

Fractures of class and skin color, the different economic and cultural positions to which our countries of origin adhere in the capitalist hierarchy, all of these objective and lived conditions add considerable contention to this category of woman of color. At this historical juncture, it is structurally larger and more internally differentiated than at the moment of its inception more than two decades ago. The ongoing fact of "immigration" and its transformation of the complexion of racial politics, often jeopardizing relationships between indigenous and "immigrant" women, underscores the weight that the category woman of color is being called on to bear. And there are different violences: of continued forced removal; of (border) policing; of imprisonment and state sexual abuse.[27] In the mobilization of a hypernationalism following September 11, 2001, it is immigrant women in sweatshops who sew their alienation into the seams of a frayed democracy in the mass production of the U.S. flag. Yet, these are the very nonidentical conditions, the objective conditions—what Avtar Brah calls the "entanglements of the genealogies of dispersal and those of staying put"—that daily shape our consciousnesses *as* women of color, even as we negotiate the very different elements that constitute that consciousness.[28] As in all matters of racialization, both our identity (our social, cultural, and historical location) and our consciousness (the experiences, interpretations, and knowledge we use to explain that location) are constantly being thrown into contestation.[29]

The challenge of whom this category of woman of color can contain at this contemporary moment comes not only from the massive dislocations in women's labor that have by now become a permanent feature of imperialism but also in the destabilizing effects of the underside of capitalism, which communities of color and white working-class communities disproportionately suffer. This is partly what makes it politically, emotionally, and spiritually necessary for women of color to return to their geographies of origin. In addition, the movement that gave rise to *Bridge,* as well as *Bridge* itself, may well have helped to build a passing to the specificities of women's particular histories.[30] It would seem that at this moment many women of color have returned home, not necessarily to the homes they once vacated but to a new temporality, a new urgency, to the cultures we had not fully known. This is partially reflected in the growth of many culturally specific grassroots organizations, in aesthetic expression, as well as in more recent anthologies.[31]

Clearly a new moment has emerged that has produced the need for a different kind of remembering—the making of different selves. I shall not call it nationalism here, although I felt it as such as a Caribbean woman at the Black Women in the Academy conference in 1994, when a small group of African American women asserted that they needed to sort out their own identity, on their own, before considering solidarity politics. I had made home within the African American community, among and with African American women. Where was my place in this new map of identity? Who were its cartographers? To whom do I flee and where? I have grown sensitive to the taste of exclusion, which as a girl I sucked from birth. You see in my face neither sister, ally, nor friend. Only stranger. Not even in my eyes can you read your yearning, or mine. A loss so great, there is no safety in home. To whom do I flee and where? To whom do you flee? Had I not already earned the right to belong? These are some of the urgent questions I believe we must confront as women of color: How do we continue to be rooted in the particularities of our cultural homes without allegiance to the boundaries of nation-state, yet remain simultaneously committed to a collectivized politic of identification and solidarity? How do we remain committed to its different historical complexions?

There is a difference, for instance, between black consciousness (and its differentiations) and a woman of color consciousness. At the very least the latter requires collective fluency in our particular histories, an understanding of how different, gendered racisms operate, their old institutionalized link to the histories of slavery in the United States as well as their newer manifestations that partly rely on the "foreignness" of immigrants who have not been socialized into the racial/racist geographies of the United States.[32] If we were to bring a woman of color consciousness to the period designated as Reconstruction, for instance, at the very least it would cease to be qualified as black since the racial reconfiguration of the entire West and Southwest was at stake.[33] Some of the most severe restrictions of Native autonomy were undertaken during this time, including the 1867 Treaty of Medicine Lodge that compelled more than one hundred thousand Apache, Arapaho, Bannock, Cheyenne, Kiowa, Navajo, Shoshone, and Sioux to the militarized zones of the reservation.[34] Where is home? How do we cultivate new medicine on the forced soil of displacement to make the taste of despair unfamiliar, and therefore unwanted? Where is home? Who is family when labor means men only? In 1870, Mongolian, Chinese, and Japanese women were legislated against as prostitutes, women without "correct habits and good character," undeserving of forming family with their male spouses who were considered good enough to lay the base of the economy.[35] How do we frame our analyses, our politics, our sensibilities, and our being through the chasms of those different, overlapping temporalities? What are the different consequences of Republican-led militarized Reconstruction? Then and now? We are not born women of color. We *become* women of color.[36] In order to *become* women of color, we would need to become fluent in each others' histories, to resist and unlearn an impulse to claim first oppression, most-devastating oppression, one-of-a-kind oppression, defying-comparison oppression. We would have to unlearn an impulse that allows mythologies about each other to replace *knowing* about one another. We would need to cultivate a way of knowing in which we direct our social, cultural, psychic, and spiritually marked attention on each other.[37] We cannot afford to cease yearning for each others' company.

The expression in 1994 at the Black Women in the Academy conference was but a small episode in an ongoing choreography between African Americans and Caribbean people, oftentimes captured in fiction, all the time lived in the raucous seams of a predictable meeting, the

ground for which was set at the time of that earlier Crossing. It is predictable and more pronounced at this moment, four decades after the British, for instance, "announced" independence for certain parts of the
Anglophone Caribbean region. They buried their antipathy for the
United States without a single gunshot, a gentleman's agreement, the
perfect foil; they conceded their imperial role to America, setting the
stage for global capital to operate more fully and without regard for
nations, their sovereignty, or their boundaries. In keeping with its logic,
capital expelled large numbers of Caribbean women and men in successive waves, the majority of whom joined the ranks of an already dis-
gruntled proletarian class on American soil, with its own peculiar brand
of racial antipathies.[38]

Inscribed within these social relations is a set of tendentious claims
that need to be named. Caribbean people have charged African Americans with a lack of political savvy—had African Americans been vigilant
enough during slavery, they would not have fallen prey to its psychic
traumas; they would not have believed themselves inferior. African
Americans are charged, further, with mistakenly applying American
plantation slavery and institutionalized racism to all forms of black experiences. The very use of the term African American, Caribbean people
believe, contains and narrows the totality of black culture. Although
African Americans have been rejected by white Americans, they continue
to have a deep desire to be recognized by them, seeking validation from
the very group that has engineered their dismissal. The experience of
racism notwithstanding, African Americans believe in America, so Caribbean people say, and in America's superiority to any other black Third
World country. And the unkindest cut of all: African Americans have
squandered their economic chances and refused jobs that Caribbean
people are more willing to take.

African Americans have charged Caribbean people with diluting the
claims they have made about racism, by willingly participating in institutions that they have systematically critiqued. While feeling themselves
superior to African Americans, they allow themselves to be used in a set
of wedge politics between white Americans and African Americans,
aligning themselves with white structures of power (with white women in
the academy, for instance) wresting economic gains and a level of legit-

imacy that African Americans rarely enjoy.[39] Caribbean people refuse to understand that racism against African Americans has been formative of the entire structure of racism in the United States, or that they, and other black people, are better served by moving toward that analysis and its attendant politics.

Not far beneath the surface of these expressions lies a mirror refracting the twin companions of colonialism and slavery, their psychic and material legacies, their very historical antecedents, which have made this contemporary meeting possible. Neither one nor the other, but rather both, mutually aiding and abetting each other. The memory of slavery has receded in the lived experience of Caribbean people; colonization has greater force. The memory of colonization has receded in the lived experience of African American people; it is slavery that has carried historical weight. There is a cost to this polarized forgetting in the kinds of psychic distortions that both thought systems have produced: the hierarchies of inferiority and superiority and their internalizations; and the internecine struggles in a gendered, racialized political economy of global capital with its intrepid mobilization of race, gender, and nation as it manages crisis after crisis in this late stage of its evolution.

Racial polarization and contradiction is the face that decolonization wears in the United States at this moment.[40] As black people and people of color in this country, we are *all* living witnesses to the largely un-finished project of decolonization, some say a failed project, in the United States, Britain, the Caribbean, Asia, and Africa.

The racialized squabbles between African American and Caribbean communities are also mirrored within the academy in the struggles between postcolonial and African American studies, sometimes ethnic studies more broadly, playing out the same dominant iterations of the first arrived and the newcomer, the stepchild and the favored one, inten-tionally forgetting that dual operation of colonialism and imperialism against what Anne duCille calls "the academic merchandising of different difference."[41] Since the academy operates through its own brand of colo-nialism and imperialism, this unfinished project of decolonization is as urgent within these intellectual projects as within the relationships among intellectuals who continue to make theory out of studied myopia.

Of course, the failure of decolonization springs from different sources.

First, the avid embrace of new structures of imperialism, such as structural adjustment, that in essence adjust economic and political violence makes it almost impossible for the bulk of the population in "former" colonies, and for working-class communities and those of color in metropolitan countries, to live with dignity. Second, there is a fierce denial on the part of the state and other institutions, including the academy, that their own contemporary practices of racialization have been shaped by their refusal to admit and confront their historical complicity in racism against indigenous people of color on these shores. Third, the fierce revival of ethnonationalisms of different kinds has frustrated solidarity projects. Part of our own unfinished work, therefore, is to remember the objective fact of these systems of power and their ability to graft themselves onto the very minute interstices of our daily lives. It means that we are all defined in some relationship to them, in some relationship to hierarchy. Neither complicity (usually cathected onto someone else) nor vigilance (usually reserved for ourselves) is given to any of us *before* the fact of our living. Both complicity and vigilance are learned in this complicated process of figuring out who we are and who we wish to become. The far more difficult question we must collectively engage has to do with the political positions (in the widest sense) that we come to *practice,* not merely espouse; the mutual frameworks we adopt, as we live (both consciously and unconsciously) our daily lives.[42] No matter our countries of origin, decolonization is a project for *all.*

It is no longer tenable for Caribbean people to continue to seek immunity from racialized internalizations. It is no mere accident that it was Frantz Fanon of the Francophone Caribbean who formulated *Black Skin, White Masks.* Caribbean people of African descent may well have claimed a premature victory, and comfort in a black majority, without having sufficiently wrestled with the racial inequalities in our own countries of origin—the positions of Indians, for example, in Trinidad, which I came to understand as one of second-class citizenship only after experiencing racism in the United States. This is perhaps why sometimes we continue to reenact within Caribbean organizations in the metropolis the same dominant repetitions that position us as most targeted vis-à-vis Indians and Chinese, who are now defined as Asian, not Caribbean, whom we believe benefit more from the racial hierarchy in the United States than do we of African descent. Given the fact that this advanced capitalist colonial nation is constantly redrawing its own national borders, creating insiders and outsiders, African American claims for citizenship can no longer be undertaken as if these borders of the nation-state were fixed, or as if the borders of a mythic Africa are the only others that exist.[43]

Are there not fissures of class, skin color, shades of yellow and brown, within our respective nation/communities? Linguistic and regional differences that have created their own insiders and outsiders? At what historical moment does heterogeneity become homogeneity—that is, the moment to create an outside enemy? Neither of us as African American nor Caribbean people created those earlier conditions of colonialism and Atlantic slavery.[44] Yet we continue to live through them in a state of selective forgetting, setting up an artificial antipathy between them in their earlier incarnation, behaving now as if they have ceased to be first cousins.

We have recognized each other before. Blood flows, making a mockery of biology, of boundaries—within individuals, within families, within neighborhoods. One drop of blood is not sufficient to mark where one line begins and the other ends. Boundaries are never discrete. We have recognized each other before: in the streets of Harlem when we believed, along with six million black people worldwide, that Garvey's Black Star Line would sail clear to the continent above the objections of the black middle classes, who had distanced themselves from Africa and refused its proximity, believing they had arrived. Or in the heyday of Pan-Africanism when, as Baldwin elegantly framed it, "we were concerned with the immensity and variety of the experience called [black]," both by virtue of the fact of slavery *and* colonization, but not only because of it.[45] Neither of these movements were entirely free from exclusions, from sexism, from the contradictions and intrigue of class and color, from xenophobia. But they kept alive an idea that, for all of its fractiousness, lent public visibility and legitimacy to our humanity. We have stood in the same lines, under the El in New York, year after year, in the period after the Second World War, some reports say, to be chosen for work as maids in white wealthy households by the "Madames Jew and Gentile" alike.[46] We have recognized each other before. We agreed with Audre Lorde when she said that we are part of an international group of black women "taking care of business all over the world."[47] We have been neighbors, living in the raucous seams of deprivation. We have healed each other's sick; buried each other's dead. We have become familiar with the swollen face of grief that grows large in that stubborn space between love and loss.[48]

To be African American and exiled on the spot where one is born.[49] To be Caribbean and exiled on foreign soil producing a longing so deep that the site of neglect is reminiscent of beauty. We have grown up metabolizing exile, feeding on its main by-products—alienation and separation.[50] We walk these foreign caves crouched in stealth, searching for the bitter formations of betrayal and mistrust, seeking answers to who has betrayed whom. Crumpling expectations and desire into half-written notes of paper, barely legible, now lying in overstuffed baskets, never delivered. Hieroglyphic markings to an estranged lover.

Caribbean women ought to have come forward when African American women mobilized in their own defense in the midst of the attack on Anita Hill when she brought charges of sexual misconduct against Clarence Thomas. I signed the petition along with thousands of other women, knowing I was not born on U.S. soil. But it was not the time to raise objections about geographic and cultural accuracy. Our identity as Caribbean women was not the historical point to be made at that time. That ought to have been made later when Orlando Patterson claimed that had Thomas "harassed" Hill in Jamaica, it would not have been called sexual harassment. Caribbean women in the United States ought to have entered the debate then to say that Caribbean women in Jamaica and elsewhere in the Caribbean, both within and outside the context of feminist movement, had, in fact, culled a politics and language about sexual harassment and sexual violence in the region to counteract the very behaviors in which Thomas had engaged. Instead, silence worked on us like a vise, as we bought into the figment of ourselves that Patterson had constructed, and thus indirectly supported his and Thomas's (mis)representations of Hill, in a larger context in which, as Kimberlé Crenshaw has shown, the scales against Hill had been tipped from the very start.[51]

What kinds of conversations do we, as black women of the diaspora, need to have that will end these "wasteful errors of recognition"? Do we know the terms of our different migrations? Each others' work histories? Our different yearnings? What is to be the relationship with Africa in the term African American? What is to be our different relationships with Africa? On this soil? New Orleans? New York? Or reincarnated in Cuba? Brazil? Haiti? Shall we continue to read Edwidge Danticat while Haiti remains, like the Pacific, on the rim of consciousness, or enters our consciousness only in relation to continued U.S. dominance.[52] To which genealogy of Pan-African feminism do we lay claim? Which legacy of Pan-African lesbian feminism? These conversations may well have begun. If so, we need to continue them and meet each other eye to eye, black women born in this country, black women from different parts of the continent and from different linguistic and cultural inheritances of the Caribbean, Latin America, Asia, and the Pacific who experience and define themselves as black, for there is nothing that can replace the un-borrowed truths that lie at the junction of the particularity of our experiences and our confrontation with history.[53]

"Are You Sure, Sweetheart, That You Want to Be Well"?[54]

Women of color. Who are we now, twenty years later? Have we lived differently? Loved differently? What has become of the thinking that linked the internal colonization of women of color born here with women of color who had experienced colonization elsewhere? What has become of the women who have stayed in their countries of origin? Where are the refugees? Where does one come to consciousness as a woman of color and live it, at this moment? Have we developed a new metaphysics of political struggle? Did *Bridge* get us there, as Toni Cade Bambara believed? Did it coax us into the habit of listening to each other and learning each other's ways of seeing and being?[55] Have we made the crossing? In what shape have we reached shore? In whose company? With what in hand? Do we remember why we made the Crossing back then? Other crossings before, or since? Or had a desire to do so? Who are we now, twenty years later? Why do we need to remember?

Remembering is different from looking back. We can look back sideways and not bring things into full view.[56] We can look back to some past perceived to be wholly retrievable in the present, or some mirage of it, a gesture of nostalgia that can give rise to fascisms of different kinds. We live in a country that seems bent on inculcating a national will to amnesia, to excise certain pasts, particularly when a great wrong has been done. The calls for this American nation to move ahead in the wake of the presidential election of 2000 rest on forgetting. Forget intimidation at the polls and move on. Forget that citizenship is particular and does not guarantee a vote for everyone. Forget that we face the state reconsolidation of conservatism as the fragile seams of democracy come apart. Forget that law and order can be invoked so that a court can act with supreme expediency and not supreme ethics. Forget that as the media make the presidential election in the United States the only news, Palestinians continue to struggle for a homeland and Haitians continue to struggle for a democracy. Forget that in the midst of a "booming" economy, more people are hungry in New York now than they were ten years ago. Forget that capitalism does not bring democracy. "Once a great wrong has been done, it never dies. People speak the words of peace, but their hearts do not forgive. Generations perform ceremonies of reconciliation, but there is no end."[57] This is partly why the desire to forget does not rest only in one place.

At times, forgetting stands in for never having known or never having learned something, the difference between staying in tune with the source of our own wisdom and relying on borrowed substitutes, fleetingly fulfilling. As Audre Lorde says in the poem "Solstice": "We forgot to water the plantain shoots / when our homes were full of borrowed meat / and our stomachs filled with the gifts of strangers / who laugh now as they pass us / because our land is barren."[58] But, plantain shoots are tricky because the young can choke out the mother, or the mother can choke out the young, as *my* mother has instructed me. How do we learn the antidote to barrenness? And it may be not so much that we had never known about keeping things fertile and watered, the ancient sources of wisdom, but that at times the forgetting is so deep that forgetting is itself part of what we have forgotten. What is so unbearable that we even forget that we have forgotten?

"The scent of memory (our own and that of strangers)" can become faint, as faint as the scent of dried roses, when things become unspeakable and unbearable, when the terms of belonging get reshuffled.[59] This was the case in the white working-class community of Southall in London, where waves of South Asian immigration upset "origin stories." The memory of the turbulent Crossing, some of which still lies in the silted bottom of the deep, is a site of trauma and forgetting; a site of traumatized memory, as Elizabeth Alexander has called it. Such a memory of violence and violation begets a will to forget, to forget the innards of that violation. I remember Morrison's *Beloved,* whose character went to the depths of that silt. Her mother, Sethe, did not dare remember why she sent her there; she could remember only when it was safe to do so, when Paul D. returned: "The last color she remembered was the pink chips in the headstone of her baby girl."[60] To trust and remember. Love inspires remembering. It caused "floods and floods of blocked memories" to break when Barbara Cameron returned to the reservation after an eight-year absence and rediscovered herself, "walking on the Lakota earth," looking at the "cragged faces of her grandparents."[61]

So much of how we remember is embodied: the scent of home; of fresh-baked bread; of newly grated coconut stewed with spice (we never called it cinnamon), nutmeg, and bay leaf from the tree (not from the bottle). Violence can also become embodied, that violation of sex and spirit. Assimilation is another kind of violation that can be embodied, assimilating alienation, one's own as well as others.[62] We have to be sure we want to be well. "Are you sure, sweetheart, that you want to be well?" Minnie Ranson tests Velma Henry in the opening scene of *The Salt Eaters,* a necessary question, "just to caution folks," "and not waste . . . time."[63] A question that makes conscious the yearning to be healed. Conscious and practiced. Conscious and embodied. "A revolution capable of healing our wounds."[64] Healing wounds by touch, where touching is part of the work of decolonization. It explains why Baby Suggs, holy, took her heart—she had nothing left to make her living with, but her heart—to the Clearing, "in the heat of every Saturday," to deliver the weekly sermon:

> Here . . . in this here place, we flesh; flesh that weeps, / laughs;
> flesh that dances on bare feet in grass. Love it. Love it hard. . .
> O my people, / they do not love your hands. Those they only use,
> tie, bind, chop off / and leave empty. Love your hands! Love them.
> Raise them up and kiss / them. Touch others with them, pat them
> together, stroke them on / your face 'cause they don't love that either.
> *You* got to love it . . . Out yonder, hear me, they do not love your

neck unnoosed / and straight. So love your neck; put a hand on it, grace it, stroke it and / hold it up.[65]

Practicing again and again the ways in which we want to be well.

Women don't want to forget in the pages of *Bridge*. Barbara Cameron "will not forget Buffalo Manhattan Hat and Mani."[66] "When some lonesome half-remembered place" is reawakened in a sweat, Valerio remembers a past, a time before, before colonization."[67] What brings us back to remembrance is both individual and collective; both intentional and an act of surrender; both remembering desire and remembering *how* it works.[68] Daring to recognize each other again and again in a context that seems bent on making strangers of us all. Can we *intentionally* remember, all the time, as a way of never forgetting, all of us, building an archeology of living memory, which has less to do with living in the past, invoking a past, or excising it, and more to do with our relationship to Time and its purpose? There is a difference between remembering *when*—the nostalgic yearning for some return—and a living memory that enables us to remember what was contained in *Bridge* and what could not be contained within it or by it. What did it make possible? What else did we need? All are part of this living memory, of moments, of imaginings, which have never ended. And they will never end so long as we continue to dare yearning for each other. There is a writing exercise that Natalie Goldberg, author of *Thunder and Lightning,* has popularized. For ten minutes, or some other designated time, the exercise participant is asked to write uninterruptedly, beginning with "I remember," so as to bring to the present all things remembered. The exercise is then reversed with its supposed opposite: "I don't remember." As one participant negotiated the underbelly of her recollections, she observed, "It scares me that I remember what I don't remember."[69]

For me, remembering *Bridge* is a way of remembering myself, for even as I write I am aware that memory is not a pure act of access. I had not imagined, when I began *Remembering This Bridge* and named it after writing only three sentences, that it would require such excavation, such a rememory of deep forgettings, of feeding hungry ghosts.[70] As I bemoaned the travails of this writing, my friend Chandan posed his version of the question with which Minnie Ranson confronted Vilma Henry:

"What archaelogies have you undertaken, Jacqui?" "And I had promised myself," I continued by evading his question, "that I would begin to write in a different voice. But it is excruciating to keep that promise in the midst of impending deadlines." "You know, Jacqui," Chandan offered, "sometimes we can only authenticate our voice when we are up against a wall; if not, we are only an impostor in a new language, speaking in the name of populism." Authenticating a voice comes through the rediscovery of the underbelly, literally unearthing and piecing together the fragmented members of existence.

Remembering the unrelenting vision of *Bridge* in the multiple ways that remembering occurs is crucial in these times. It is a generous vision that was gifted two decades ago. And I want to insist on its generosity, for in the midst of uncovering the painful fault lines of homophobia, culture, and class within different communities of belonging, and advancing critiques of racism within the women's movement, it did not relinquish a vision of interdependence, of interbeing, if you will. It was not a transcendent vision, but one that was rooted in transforming the mundaneness of lived experience, the very ground on which violence finds fodder. Vision can only be as effective and as sturdy as our determination to *practice*. Novelist Toni Cade Bambara and interviewer Kalamu Ya Salaam were discussing a call Bambara made in *The Salt Eaters* through the Seven Sisters, a multicultural, multimedia arts troupe, a call to unite our wrath, our vision, our powers.

> KALAMU: "Do you think that fiction is the most effective way to do this?"
> TONI: "No. The most effective way to do it, *is to do it!*"[71]

It is the daily practice that will bring about the necessary shifts in perception that make change possible. Vision helps us to remember *why* we do the work. Practice is the *how;* it makes the change and grounds the work. A reversal of the inherited relationship between theory and practice, between how we think and what we do, the heart of engaged action. It is this that engages us at the deepest, most spiritual level of meaning in our lives. It is how we constitute our humanity.

El Mundo Zurdo and the Ample Space of the Erotic

If the gun and the cross have been used as instruments of oppression, we must learn to use them as instruments of liberation.
—CHERRÍE MORAGA, *Loving in the War Years*

And yet to act is not enough. Many of us are learning to sit per-
fectly still, to sense the presence of the Soul and commune with
Her. We are beginning to realize that we are not wholly at the mercy
of circumstance . . . We have come to realize we are not alone in our
struggles, nor separate, nor autonomous, but that we . . . are connected and interdependent.—GLORIA ANZALDÚA, "Refugees of a
World on Fire"

The dichotomy between the spiritual and the political is false resulting from an incomplete attention to our erotic knowledge, for
the bridge which connects them is formed by the erotic, the sen-
sual, those physical, emotional and psychic expressions of what is
deepest and strongest and richest within each of us being shared:
the passion of love in its deepest meaning.—AUDRE LORDE,
"The Uses of the Erotic"

Between 1997 and 2000 I participated in a series of meetings and discussions among a group of women and men—lesbian, gay, bisexual, transgendered, and heterosexual, of different nationalities and ages and with
different cultural and spiritual affinities—to learn what sex and spirit
(what sexuality and spirituality taken together) might tell us about who
we are. As a group, early in this work we found that many "secular"
activists were reluctant to come out spiritually. Some of that reluctance
came from the historical ways in which the Judeo-Christian church operated as an instrument of colonization: enforcing heterosexuality and the
nuclear family as the moral norm; attempting to erase the connection
between sexuality and land (in Hawai'i, for instance); splitting apart
mind, body, and spirit into the particularities of (white) manliness, colonized "other," and (Christian) religion, respectively. A more contemporary religious Right had mobilized globally to advance an antihuman
agenda, mistakenly attributing its authority to God. But this dominant

mythologized collapse of spirituality into religion was also operating among us, another indication of the subtle internalization of dominance. We found that we had a great deal of practice coming out politically, but many of us were timid about coming out spiritually as radical political people. It seemed that in combining the two we were on the brink of committing heresy of a different kind.

There was another kind of shared internalization that we identified as we moved to unite these powerful forces of sex and the spirit that belong together. As we grappled with the inherited division, we understood that it is sustained in part by an ideology that has steeped sex and sexuality in sin, shame and a general disavowal of the sacred. At the same time, this very ideology has attempted to contain all of what is of spirit and spiritual within the structure of religion, all with predictably devastating consequences. To this process of fragmentation we gave the name colonization, usually understood as a set of exploitative practices in political, ideological and aesthetic terms, but also linked in minute ways to dualistic and hierarchical thinking: divisions among mind, body, spirit; between sacred and secular, male and female, heterosexual and homosexual; in class divisions; and in divisions between the erotic and the Divine. We saw its operation, as well, in creating singular thinking: the mistaken notion that only one kind of justice work could lead to freedom. Presumably, organizing for a decent and fair living wage is not connected to antiracism work and to antihomophobia work. Such thinking always premised in negation, often translated into singular explanations for oppression. Breaking down these divisions and hierarchies, indeed making ourselves whole again, became the work that occupied us throughout our entire journey.

Since colonization has produced fragmentation and dismemberment at both the material and psychic levels, the work of decolonization has to make room for the deep yearning for wholeness, often expressed as a yearning to belong, a yearning that is both material and existential, both psychic and physical, and which, when satisfied, can subvert and ultimately displace the pain of dismemberment. Anticolonial and Left liberation movements have not understood this sufficiently in their psychology of liberation and, as a result, we have not made ample political room for it. This yearning to belong is not to be confined only to membership or citizenship in community, political movement, nation, group, or belonging to a family, however constituted, although important. Indeed, we would not have come to the various political movements in which we have been engaged, with the intense passion we have, had it not been for this yearning. With the help of Bernice Johnson Reagon, we recognized this yearning as a desire to reproduce home in "coalitions." As a consequence, our political movements were being made to bear too much—too much of a longing for sameness as home, the limits of nationalism.[73] But we needed to wrestle with that desire for home a bit longer, so as to examine a bit more closely the source of that yearning that we wanted to embed in the very metaphysics of political struggle, the very metaphysics of life. The source of that yearning is the deep knowing that we are in fact interdependent—neither separate nor autonomous. As human beings, we have a sacred connection to one another, and this is why enforced separations wreak havoc on our Souls. There is great danger, then, in living lives of segregation. Racial segregation. Segregation in politics. Segregated frameworks. Segregated and compartmentalized selves. What we have devised as an oppositional politic has been necessary, but it will never sustain us, for while it may give us some temporary gains (which become more ephemeral the greater the threat, which is not a reason not to fight), it can never ultimately feed that deep place within us: that space of the erotic, that space of the Soul, that space of the Divine.

"To sense the presence of the Soul and commune with her" is the job that excavation requires. It is a job of changing the self. And it is a job. It requires work. It requires practice. It cannot be someone else's excavation that we easily appropriate as our own and use as our own. It cannot be done as spectator or ventriloquist. It requires the work of each and every one of us, to unearth this desire to belong to the self in community, as part of a radical project that is not to be confused with a preoccupation with the self. The one has to do with a radical self-possession, the other with self-preoccupation on which individualism thrives. Self-determination is both an individual and collective project.

There is an inevitability (which is not the same as passivity) in this movement toward wholeness, this work of the spirit and the journey of the Soul in its vocation to reunite us with the erotic and the Divine. Whether we want it or not, it will occur. The question is whether we dare intentionally to undertake this task of recognition as self-reflexive human beings, open at the very core to a foundational truth: we are connected to the Divine through our connections with each other. Yet, no one comes to consciousness alone, in isolation, only for herself, or passively. It is here we need a verb, the verb *conscientize*, which Paulo Freire used to underscore the fact that shifts in consciousness happen through active processes of practice and reflection. Of necessity, they occur in community. We must constantly envision this as we devise ways to practice the building of communities (not sameness) over and over again. We can continue to hold onto a consciousness of our different locations, our understanding of the simultaneous ways in which dominance shapes our lives and, at the same time, nurture the erotic as that place of our Divine connection, which can in turn transform the ways we relate to one another.

When we have failed at solidarity work we often retreat, struggling to convince ourselves that this is indeed the work we have been called on to do. The fact of the matter is that there is no other work but the work of creating and re-creating ourselves within the context of community. Simply put, there is no other work. It took five hundred years, at least in this hemisphere, to solidify the division of things that belong together. But it need not take us another five hundred years to move ourselves out of this existential impasse. Spirit work does not conform to the dictates of human time, but it needs our courage, revolutionary patience, and intentional shifts in consciousness so that we can anchor the struggle for social justice within the ample space of the erotic.[74]

One of the earliest lessons we have all learned from feminism is that the personal is political: the insight that some of the most infinitesimal details of our lives are shaped by ideological and political forces much larger than our individual selves. In the midst of the pitched battle in New York to transform the curriculum at the New School University, I came to appreciate another shade of this insight as the School's administration sought to make me the entire political struggle. It was with a great deal of help and a deep level of self-scrutiny that I came to understand how a single individual could ignite a political struggle but ultimately had to be subsumed under it, simply be within it, if that struggle were to be successful. This interior work is indispensable in this journey to wholeness. In this conscious attention to the weaving of sex and Spirit that we undertook in the taskforce, and the spiritual political work I have undertaken in my life, I have come to see that an inside change in the personal is not entirely complete if it remains at the level of a shift in ideas, or even in practice, although both are necessary. Desire is expressed most fundamentally where change takes place, at the root of our very Souls, the base of the internal source of our power, the internal source of our yearning—the yearning and power we have been taught so much to fear. So when Gloria Anzaldúa asks us to commune with the Soul, or Audre Lorde urges us to find something that our Soul craves and do it, our first task is to become attentive to the desire of the Soul and to place ourselves in its service. It is a necessary and delicate undertaking in Spirit-based politics, this joining of the sacred and secular—to have, as Sharon Day states, "the ethics of spirituality inform daily life." It requires intention, a revolutionary patience,[75] courage, and above all humility. Once this work begins, the temptation to cross narrow boundaries becomes irresistible; connections, once invisible, come into full view. And I am assured that when the practice begins to bear fruit, the yearning itself is transformed.

There is an old man who has etched himself into an ancient slab of rock deposited in a park at the end of my street in Harlem. His face comes into view only from afar, with distance, with perspective. Close up, he simply folds himself back into the stone, disappearing or perhaps pretending not to be there. When I do not see him, does it mean he does not exist? Unlike the figures of Davis, Lee, and Jackson that are patiently chiseled into a mountain of stone in Georgia and pasted onto the tourist bus stationed opposite the park—figures that announce themselves from far and near—this old man works in stealth, through years of weather, bringing himself into my field of vision only by the angle of my gaze and the distance from which I stand. Although I lived for seven years on this same street that presumably goes in one direction, a one-way street leading directly to this slab of stone, I had never seen him before. Yet, he is there. The challenge for me is to see him in the present and to continue to know that he is there even when I cannot see him. Rocks hold memory.

Land holds memory. This is why the land and live oak trees rooted in the Georgia Sea Islands of the southern United States whisper in your ear when you allow yourselves to listen. The Georgia Sea Islands. The Ibo of Nigeria were captured and brought to these Islands. When they arrived and saw the conditions of their capture and homelessness, they turned around and walked to "wherever they was going that day."[76] The place, bearing the name Ibo Landing, holds the memory of that moment, which still lives in the heart of every Gullah child, and in the solid trunks of the live oaks. The live oaks will tell us these stories when we listen. And the mountains of Hawai'i will echo the ancient Kanaka Maoli belief that they are stewards of the land, eyes of the land, children of the land. Deep within their undulating folds, which drape themselves with the ease of velvet around the opulent embrace of mist and cloud, we will feel the ancient power of land to heal. Ocean will reveal the secrets that lie at the bottom of its silted deep. She requires no name before her. Not Pacific, not Atlantic, not Arctic, not Southern, not Indian. She is simply her watery translucent self, reaching without need of compass for her sisters whomever and wherever they are. She will call you by your ancient name, and you will answer because you will not have forgotten. Water always remembers.

Coda: Tribute to Gloria Anzaldúa . . .
Because Death Ups the Stakes

How many more must die before we internalize the existential message of our fundamental interdependence—any disease of one is a disease of the collectivity; any alienation from self is alienation from the collectivity? Your death was tragic, Gloria, not only because you died alone, but we relied on you as artist to provide our sanity, and we kept asking for more while you wrestled with terror day and night—the reality, as you said, of having a disease that could cost you your feet, your eyes, your creativity, the life of the writer you worked so hard to build . . . life itself.[77] Indeed, we demanded more. It's quite a pact to make, to demand without accountability. Yet we demanded more not knowing that giving and receiving are part of the same pendulum, that having received increases our responsibility to return the gift. You had no health insurance. You who wrote the borderlands that we appropriate to signal how "queer" we were. There is no romance or seduction to living on the borders. You taught us about the need to shift consciousness, to build common ground, to move from the militarized zone to the roundtable, to view the artist as healer, without separation. You taught us that our politics would not be effective without a spiritualized consciousness. *Conocimiento*. You taught us about Divine intelligence. But we consumed without digesting. You taught us; the question remains, What did we learn?

I did not *know* you, Gloria, although we worked together. I have only now learned to sense you through the grief of my beloved for whom you provided anchor. What might black women say to Chicana women to help ease the pain of this loss? We want to mourn with you the passing of your sister warrior. Your loss of her gentle footprints is also ours. We feel your loss. We hold your pain. We did not accompany you to those fields in Texas as you faced the noonday brunt of the sun. I myself never paid attention to your diabetes. I never looked at the statistics before now: diabetes is the fifth-deadliest disease in the United States. Over nine million women live with this disease, and Latina, African American, Native American, Asian, and Pacific Islander women are two to four times more likely to have this disease than white women.[78]

What might black women say to Chicana women? We grieve with you and we want ceremonies of reconciliation that link our goddesses and gods to each other, patterning new codices of forgiveness and triumph, sisters of the cornsilk and sisters of yam as your *comadre* Cherríe Moraga put it.[79] We petition the basket weavers to dream a new pattern of our knowing and loving that binds the permanent impermanence of our footprints in the sand.

7

Pedagogies of the Sacred:
Making the Invisible Tangible

One: The Memory of Mojuba:
A Spiritual Invocation to Remember

For more than six of my preteen years, I crossed the intersections of Mojuba in St. James during clandestine visits to friends or the more legitimate attendance at the Catholic Church, St. Mary's, not knowing that from Trinidad, Mojuba reached back to a lineage for which there were no signs, no visible ones at least. "Meet me at Mojuba Crossroads." No one could plead ignorance as the excuse for arriving late since everyone knew where it was—Mojuba, not far from Bengal Street. There was no apparent need to demarcate itself from the other streets from which the crossroad drew its name. Mojuba simply claimed the entire space of the intersection, and we crossed it over and over again without even a hint of knowing its secret or needing to know from whence it came. It took thirty years and another set of crossroads to point me to a path straight to a basement in the Bronx, New York, where, at a home that assumed the bearings of a spiritual workplace, I learned the lineage of Mojuba in a community of practitioners—Puertorriqueño/as, Cubano/as, Trinidadian, African American, Salvadorean, Brazilian—living an ancient memory in a city overcrowded with errant spirits, teeming with yearning not easily satisfied in towering buildings or in slabs of concrete.

A Spiritual Invocation to Remember

Omi Tutu / Cool Water / Freshen the Road / Freshen this House / Death is no more / Sickness is no more / Loss is no more / Obstacle is no more / To be overwhelmed is no more / The immortality of our ancestors / I Salute God / I salute all Orisa / I Salute all the mothers of Orisa, fathers of Orisa who are citizens of Heaven / Homage to the Sun, the Moon, the Earth / I salute all ancestors who sit at the feet of Olodumare who have no desire to return to Earth / I salute all my ancestors whose blood run in my veins. Mojuba. I greet you.

Mojuba: an expansive memory refusing to be housed in any single place, bound by the limits of time, enclosed within the outlines of a map, encased in the physicality of body, or imprisoned as exhibit in a museum. A refusal that takes its inheritance from the Crossing, which earlier prophets had been forced to undertake from the overcrowded passageways in a place called Gorée, the door of no return, still packed centuries later with the scent of jostled grief so thick that no passage of human time could absorb it. It hangs there, this grief, until today, an indelible imprint of the Crossing, fastened by a pool of tears below, constantly replenished by the tremors of human living.

Two: The Crossing

We lay in a dungeon. Many more of us lying in death, 21 times 21 times 21 and more. Crossing water on backs with sores and bellies empty except for those filled with air or swollen with child. Lying in rot and moon blood with skinless ankles and wrists, black skins turned yellow from chains acting like saws on our fearful flesh. Rocking. Wracked bodies numbed from pain. Rocking the dark noise, the loud silence of trembling hands and feet and whole bodies turned cold and numb from shock and heat and longing for the rhythm of daily living. Rocking. Crossing that line where humans force the sea and sky to meet so that their vastness would seem more bearable. Back then we crossed the horizon over and over again. Crossing the vortex of thick watery salt greenish gray bluish green turquoise spew of foam, only that time there were more of us on water. Some refused the Crossing, deciding instead to use their arms as wings, thousands of winged creatures flying free. Others simply kept each others company at the bottom of the Sea, becoming messengers from the spirits of the deep whose Souls had plunged there from the voyage before and the one before that and the one before that. O Yemaya, Achaba Peligrosísima / Haunting Sweet Verbena / Wise one / Hiding your age deep within the soft fold of waves, translucent / Amongst your treasures rest the captives shuffled through the door of no return / No longer imprisoned / You have restored their wings. No one knows the mysteries at the bottom of the Ocean. Crossing the line, the Kalunga line.

Once they crossed, they graced all things with the wisdom of Ashé. Wind. Sky. Earth. Fire. Thunder. They deposited it in *otanes,* stones, in the mossy underground of treacherous caves; in the caress of elegant waterfalls; in forests imposing enough to assume the name Mountain; in water salt and sweet to taste the opposite in things. In all winged creatures including the butterfly. All four-legged. And two-legged. And those who slithered on land, the color of coral, while their sympathies lived in Sky. And with those yet to be born. For once they intuited that the human will was long intent on capture, they all conspired to rest their Truth everywhere. And in the simplest of things. Like a raindrop. And therefore the most beautiful of things, so that Truth and Beauty would not be strangers to one another, but would rely one on the other to guide the footprints of the displaced, and those who chose to remain put; of those only once removed and those who had journeyed far in the mistaken belief that books were the dwelling place of wisdom; those who thought that the lure of concrete would replace or satisfy the call of the forest; those who believed that grace was a preoccupation of the innocent and the desire to belong a craving of the weak. Being everywhere was the only way, they reasoned, to evade capture and to ensure the permanence of change—one of the Truths of the Ocean.

Not only humans made the Crossing, traveling only in one direction through Ocean given the name Atlantic. Grief traveled as well.

The dead do not like to be forgotten, especially those whose lives had come to a violent end and had been stacked sometimes ten high in a set of mass graves, the head of one thrown in with the body of another, male becoming female, female becoming male, their payment for building the best stone fortress that hugged a steep hill, reputed to be the most well-secured in the Caribbean. Secure for the British, that is, who buried their antipathy for the French for one brief moment and killed off three hundred Indians in one day in the hope of proving ownership of the country. For months after the massacre, Indian blood usurped the place of mud and ran into the narrow channel that led to the Caribbean Sea, but not before depositing layers of bloody silt thick with suffering at the bottom of the river's floor. The bloody river took the story to the Sea, the Wide Sargasso Sea, which absorbed the grief, folding it into its turquoise jade until it assumed the color of angered sorrow. It spun into a vortex, a current in the Caribbean. The Trade Winds. North, pushing clear to Guineau, close to the shores of the Old Kôngo, Kingdom of the Bantu. Cabinda. Down, down Benguela. Angola. Forced upward again. Dahomey. Trade Winds South. Brazil. Nago. Candomblé. Jéjé. Swept into the Cape Horn up to Peru, Colombia, Ufaina. Spitting. Descending in the drift of the West Winding, climbing just underneath the dividing line that rests in the imagination. Equator. Kalunga. It joined the grief of those who had died emaciated, gasping for air in the two-storied house locked shut for months by the man who believed he could own flesh. Pain transforming their fingers into twisted scalpels that carved hieroglyphs on the walls. Reuniting with the current in Australia. Pacific. New Zealand. The Bone People. Washing over the Marrawuti. Sea Eagle. Dreamtime. Choosing a different route: Shanti, Bahini to India. Kala Pani. East? West? Monsoon. Mozambique. The bloodied vortex of angered sorrow plotting its way. Kuro Shio. The Pacific. Hawai'i Ascending. Arctic. Norwegian Current. Labrador. All the time announcing, spitting, grieving, as it washed itself up on different shores. The dead do not like to be forgotten.

Sentience soaks all things. Caresses all things. Enlivens all things. Water overflows with memory. Emotional Memory. Bodily Memory. Sacred Memory.

Crossings are never undertaken all at once, and never once and for all.

Three: Cosmologies

African-based cosmological systems are complex manifestations of the geographies of crossing and dislocation. They are at the same time manifestations of locatedness, rootedness, and belonging that map individual and collective relationships to the Divine. The complexity derives in part from the fact that the Sacred energies that accompanied the millions who had been captured and sold for more than four centuries had indeed inhabited a vast geography. But they had also traveled internally as a result of wars of conquest, in the name of religion, and for the sake of capturing people and owning territory. Even before the depletion of Yorubaland in its bound "cargo" headed to Cuba, Haiti, Brazil, Trinidad, and points in between, art historian Robert Farris Thompson tells us, "the deities of the Yoruba had already made their presence felt in Dahomey over hundreds of years. Yoruba deities were served under different manifestations in Allada before 1659 . . . transforming them into Ewe and Fon local spirits."[1] The pantheon of inheritance in what would come to be called the African diaspora collected itself on new soil through a combination of conditions: the terrain from which the trade drew its ambit; the specific and already transformed spiritual sensibility—the African provenance of belief structures and practices; the local pantheons that were encountered and transformed with successive waves of people; the degree of spatial autonomy that enslaved populations fought for and retained; and *Osanyin*, the ecology, a flora and fauna already inhabited by the Sacred.[2] By the time these energies began to plant themselves on the soil of the Americas, bringing different consciousnesses of culture, language, and region, they had long undergone various journeys and transformations.

In general terms, the cosmological systems of Kôngo Angola deposited themselves in the *minkisi*, medicines, of Kôngo Angola systems in Brazil; in the Petro Lemba of Haiti; the Palo Mayombe of Cuba; the Spiritual Baptist of Trinidad, St. Vincent, and Grenada, while they fused into the Winti system in Suriname. Those of the territories of West Africa, Dahomey, Yorubaland, Ghana, and Benin brought a varied and related spiritual lineage observed through *Lwa* Guinée, Spirits of Haiti, Lucumí of Cuba (more widely known as Santería), Shango of Trinidad, the Orixás, *minkisi* (medicines), and Vodun of Candomblé in Brazil, the Winti system of Suriname, and Vodou of New Orleans and the southern United States. Four centuries later, destined for the teeming metropoles of North America—New York, Boston, Chicago—these systems effected another migration, another cosmic meeting, this time forced underground to inhabit the most curious of dwelling places: the basement of immigrant homes. But the naming of place is somewhat misleading in light of the omnipresence of the Sacred, since naming implies that the Sacred has been cordoned off, managed, and made partial to a chosen geography, much like the invocation to God to bless America, while presumably leaving the rest of the world unblessed.

Migrations are one indication that these cosmological systems are marked by anything but stasis. Some energies have been fused; others apparently atrophy in certain places while becoming dominant in others. Yemayá, the goddess of the Ocean seems to have "disappeared" in Haiti, yet homage to Agwe the sea god and Mambo La Siren, the mermaid sister of the two Ezilis, Freda Dahomey and Dantò, attest to the sustained metaphysical significance of water in both systems. Yemayá reigns in Candomblé and Lucumí, assuming the position that had been accorded her River sister Oshún in Yorubaland, the recognition that it would have been impossible to have survived the Crossing without her. Often there are multiple avatars of the same Sacred force, while collectivities develop different relationships to the same multilayered entity as Sacred energies engage the different inventions of the social. Not paradoxically within Vodou, Lucumí, and Candomblé is retained the manifest energies of Eshu/Papa Legba/Elegba/Elegbara, guardian of Divine energy and communication, guardian of the crossroads, the force that makes things happen, the codification of potentiality and its indispensable tool, choice, which is multiplied at the crossroads—the place where judicious vigilance needs always to be exercised. Still, who is remembered—and how—is continually being transformed through a web of interpretive systems that ground meaning and imagination in principles that are ancient with an apparent placement in a different time. Yet, both the boundaries of those principles as well as what lies within are constantly being transformed in the process of work in the present; collapsing, ultimately, the rigid demarcation of the prescriptive past, present, and future of linear time. Both change and changelessness, then, are constant.

Housed in the memory of those enslaved, yet not circumscribed by it, these Sacred energies made the Crossing. But they did not require the Crossing in order to express beingness. They required embodied beings and all things to come into sentience, but they did not require the Crossing. There was a prior knowing, a different placement in the human idiom of constricted time. Still, the capacity to operate outside of human time does not mean that Divine energy has no facility within it. In this sense, there is no absolute transcendence—no transcendence, in fact—for if there were, there would be no intervention in, and no relationship with, the material, the quotidian, the very bodies through which divinity breathes life. Indeed, the Divine knits together the quotidian in a way that compels attunement to its vagaries, making this the very process through which we come to know its existence. It is, therefore, the same process through which we come to know ourselves, as in the words of María, an espiritista: "Yo soy mis santos; mis santos soy yo" (I am my saints; my saints are me).[3] How does one come to know oneself through and as Saints or Spirits? How does one not know oneself without them? What kind of labor makes this intelligibility possible?

The force of these questions at first came only imperceptibly to me, and in quite another guise. In 1989, I had embarked on a project on the ways in which African cosmologies and modes of healing became the locus of an epistemic struggle in nineteenth-century Trinidad, the period marking the establishment of the slave plantation economy and the con-solidation of the colonial state. My intent was to use an array of docu-ments surrounding the trial, torture, and execution of Thisbe, one of those captured and forced into the Crossing, who was accused of "sorc-ery, divination and holding frequent converse with the devil." I wanted to show the ways in which the body had become central in the contest between European and African systems: positioned as moveable property —chattel—and as repository of sin, or understood as the direct instru-ment of the Divine, mediator between the world of the living and the world of the dead. I used this approach in order to move beyond the more dominant understanding of African spiritual practice as cultural retention and survival, to get inside of the meaning of the spiritual as epistemological, that is, to pry open the terms, symbols, and organiza-tional codes that the Bântu-Kôngo people used to make sense of the world. I had surmised that cosmological systems housed memory, and that such memory was necessary to distill the psychic traumas produced under the grotesque conditions of slavery. How, why, and under what conditions do a people remember? Do spiritual practices atrophy? Or do they move underground, assuming a different form? What is the threat that certain memory poses?

What once seemed a legitimate set of questions to understand the plantation figure Thisbe were entirely inadequate to the task of knowing Kitsimba, who was waiting to be discovered. I first had to confront the limits of the methodology I had devised to know her. While legal and missionary documents gave me proximate access to daily life, they were unable to convey the interior of lived experience, the very category I needed to inhabit in order to understand how cosmological systems are grounded and expressed. Reading against the grain to fill in the spaces of an absent biography was simply not sufficient. I couldn't rely on the knowledge derived from books, not even on the analytic compass that I myself had drawn. Moreover, I had to scrutinize my own motivations for embarking on the project, as well as to figure out why I had been dele-gated to go in search of Thisbe's life. In short, I had to begin to inhabit that unstable space of not knowing, of admitting that I did not even know how to begin to know. Divested of the usual way of posing questions, I became vulnerable and experienced the kind of crisis that is named "writer's block." It was this that led me to examine the recalcitrance that masked an unacknowledged yearning for Spirit. Propelled to seek a dif-ferent source, I began to undertake linguistic spiritual work with a Bakôngo teacher so that I could follow Thisbe from a plantation located about seven miles from the Mojuba crossroads of my childhood back to the Mayombe region of Central Africa to discover Kitsimba, who refused to be cluttered beneath an array of documents of any kind, whether generated by the state, by plantation owners, or by me. It was in that basement in the Bronx, New York, that she manifested her true name, Kitsimba—not the plantation name Thisbe—and placed it back into the lineage that she remembered and to which she belonged. From then I began the tentative writing of a history that was different from the one I had inherited, knowing that I could no longer continue to conduct my-self as if Kitsimba's life were not bound inextricably with my own.

The idea, then, of knowing self through Spirit, to become open to the movement of Spirit in order to wrestle with the movement of history (as occurred in the process of how I came to know Kitsimba), are instances of bringing the self into intimate proximity with the domain of Spirit. It would make the process of that intelligibility into a spiritual undertaking. The manner in which Kitsimba emerged to render her own account of her life, including the narrative of the Crossing with which I began this chapter, was diametrically opposed to my research plan of using her body as the ground for an epistemic struggle. Kitsimba's plan required my engagement with the texture of her living. If texture of living were to be felt and analyzed as not only memory but, importantly, voice and identity, all seeming secular categories in which subjectivity is housed had to be understood as moored to the Sacred since they anchored a consciousness that drew its sustenance from elsewhere: a set of codes derived from the disembodied consciousness of the Divine. With what keys are these codes activated? Of what is its labor constituted? What is the purpose of such labor? Does rememory sharpen itself in the context of work, and is this project of rememory aligned with the Sacred? What is the self that is made in performing labor with disembodied energies that are themselves poised to work? These are the questions that Kitsimba provoked, and they are the very questions I use here to pivot our thinking through the constitutive elements of living a life that is propelled by the Sacred.

Work—spiritual work—is the major preoccupation of this final chapter. Drawing on ethnographic work and my own involvement in two African-based communities as a priest—one of Vodou and the other the Lucumí house that provoked my rememory of Mojuba—I wish to examine how spiritual practitioners employ metaphysical systems to provide the moorings for their meanings and understanding of self—in short, how they constitute or remember experience as Sacred and how that experience shapes their subjectivity. Experience is a category of great epistemic import to feminism. But we have understood it primarily as secularized, as if it were absent Spirit and thus antithetical, albeit indirectly, to the Sacred. In shifting the ground of experience from the secular to the Sacred, we can better position, as Lata Mani has proposed, the personal as spiritual.[4] But the designation of the personal as spiritual need not be taken to mean that the social has been evacuated for a domain that is ineluctably private. While different social forces may have indeed privatized the spiritual, it is very much lived in a domain that is social in the sense that it provides knowledge whose distillation is indispensable to daily living, its particular manifestations transforming and mirroring the social in ways that are both meaningful and tangible. Indeed, the spiritual is no less social than the political, which we no longer contest as mediating the traffic between the personal and the political.

Not only have we secularized experience but we have also secularized labor, both in our understanding of the work process and of its ideological construction, that is, the naturalization of women's labor. These formulations do not travel easily into the communities of the practitioners we meet here, communities that are marked by women's leadership as priests and practitioners who are themselves largely women, immigrant women. It is thus difficult to understand either what these women do or who they are when work is solely understood in relationship to the disciplining imperatives of global capital, in the terms that I crafted in chapter 3. Thus, part of the analytic challenge we face in considering the spiritual dimensions of work derives from the very nature of the epistemic frameworks we have deployed. Another part of that challenge derives from the hierarchies that are insinuated within our knowledge-making projects and in the geographies we have rendered inconsequential to them. As we saw in chapter 5, one of the consequences of the cultural relativist paradigm that undergirds the feminist-as-tourist model is the production of a distant alterity in which tradition is made subordinate to, and unintelligible within, that which is modern. Yet, it is not only that (post)modernity's secularism renders the Sacred as tradition, but it is also that tradition, understood as an extreme alterity, is always made to reside elsewhere and denied entry into the modern. In this context, African-based cosmological systems become subordinated to the European cosmos, not usually expected to accord any significance to modernity's itinerary, their provenance of little value in the constitution and formation of the very categories on which we have relied. It is not that (post)modernity's avowed secularism has no room for the Sacred (witness the Bush administration's avid mobilization of faith-based initiatives in the service of renewing American imperialism), it is rather that it profits from a hierarchy that conflates Christianity with good tradition while consigning "others" to the realm of bad tradition and thus to serve as evidence of the need for good Christian tradition. If Africa functions largely as an epistemic gap, as spectacularized homophobia dressed up in tradition—

its brand of feminism qualified, not for reasons of historical specificity but for cultural alterity, its religions designated as pejoratively animist—then its cosmological systems cannot be made to figure legitimately in (post)modernity's consciousness and, therefore, cannot be availed to assist in understanding the constitution and formation of self or the remapping of the major categories with which a transnational feminism has been engaged. And yet some of its most formative categories—migration, gender and sexuality, experience, home, history, and memory—can be made intelligible within these very systems.

Of what significance, then, is the body in the making of experience if it cannot merely be summoned instrumentally to serve or explain the axes of violence that stem from the crises of capitalism's various plantations or from its attendant modes of financial timekeeping? Clearly the focus on spiritual work necessitates a different existential positioning in which to know the body is to know it as medium for the Divine, living a purpose that exceeds the imperatives of these plantations. Put differently, it is to understand spiritual work as a type of body praxis, as a form of embodiment about which Nancy Scheper-Hughes offers an illuminating formulation: "Embodiment," she says, "concerns the ways people come to inhabit their bodies so that these become in every sense of the term 'habituated.' All the mundane activities of working, eating, sleeping, having sex, and getting sick and getting well are forms of body praxis and expressive of dynamic social, cultural and political relations."[5] Since the spiritual does not exist outside of these very social, cultural, and political relations, it too can be taken to constitute body praxis, and this, I believe, is what Karen McCarthy Brown means when she says that "religions such as Vodou inscribe [their traditions] in the bodies of the followers . . . the tradition, the memory of how to serve the spirits is held in the ritualized and ritualizing human body."[6] Far from being merely superficial, these markings on the flesh—these inscriptions—are processes, ceremonial rituals through which practitioners become habituated to the spiritual, and this habituation implies that requirements are transposed onto the body. One of these requirements is to remember their source and purpose. In this matrix the body thus becomes a site of memory, not a commodity for sale, even as it is simultaneously insinuated within a nexus of power. Body and memory are lived in the same body, if you will, and this mutual living, this entanglement, enables us to think and feel these inscriptions as process, a process of embodiment.

The purpose of the body is to act not simply, though importantly, as an encasement of the Soul, but also as a medium of Spirit, the repository of a consciousness that derives from a source residing elsewhere, another ceremonial ritual marking. To this end, embodiment functions as a pathway to knowledge, a talking book, whose intelligibility relies on the social —the spiritual expertise of a community to decode Sacred knowledge, since it is inconceivable to think about the Lwa or Orisha descending without a message to the collectivity gathered in their presence. Since body is not body alone but rather one element in the triad of mind, body and spirit, what we need to understand is how such embodiment provides the moorings for a subjectivity that knits together these very elements. How is a Sacred interior cultivated, and how does it assist practitioners in the task of making themselves intelligible to themselves? How does spiritual work produce the conditions that bring about the realignment of self with self, which is simultaneously a realignment of oneself with the Divine through a collectivity? These questions lead us to foreground practice (which is why I choose the term work) through which the Sacred becomes a way of embodying the remembering of self, if you will, a self that is neither habitually individuated nor unwittingly secularized.

Before proceeding further, I want to say a word about the coupling of Vodou and Santería. Historically, it has not been customary to speak Vodou and Santería in the same sentence, but the problem is neither of a linguistic nor grammatical sort. Within the community of practitioners in New York, for instance, suspicion and recriminations abound, laced with a peculiar strand of racialization and racism that paradoxically dislodges Santería from its African moorings and positions Vodou as bad witchcraft, thus mirroring popular cultural sentiments. Haiti still largely functions in the American imaginary as the accused for HIV infection, or otherwise as a projection for what Laënnec Hurbon has called a feeling of "disquieting strangeness," emerging primarily from phantasmagoric representations of Vodou, representations that have also been fanned by the American state.[7] And while Santería was thrust into public consciousness with the U.S. Supreme Court ruling that legitimized it, neither it nor

Vodou are widely understood to be religions.[8] To be sure, there are differences between the two systems. The elements of Vodou that are drawn from the Bântu Kôngo cultural zone and housed in its Petro pantheon of "hot" Spirits are not found in Lucumí, nor do Fon elements appear to be present. But these apparent differences are rather difficult to ascertain since Yoruba-based cosmologies morphed into the Fon and Ewe cultural zones. How can we be certain that the latter did not travel back into Santería once the Crossing was made? Yet similarities exist as well. Practitioners of both Santería and Vodou used Catholicism as the subterranean mask to sabotage colonial attempts to annihilate them. They walked the same celestial geography as they implored Catholic saints then, and they continue to do so now. Within Vodou's Rada rites and those of Lucumí are to be found the constitutive elements of both Yoruba and Dahomean ceremonial rituals. And it is this shared epistemological history that coheres around a similar set of foundational principles in which both systems are anchored—the most significant of which positions the energy force of the universe as a Sacred force emanating from God, Bondieu, Olodumare, the supreme quintessence of Ashé, the life force. Both attend to the idea of a multiply manifested or multidimensional god, avatars, that make the Sacred tangible, the most central of which are manifestations of Lwa and Orisha that inhabit physical elements as well as human beings. As healing systems anchored in the idea of the constant manifestations of spiritual power, they share the belief in the power of spoken medicine, the power of utterance, the literal understanding of Ashé, which means "so be it," as well as in the Sacred healing power of physical elements such as water, fire, and plants, *fèy*—Osanyin who functions both as forest-bearing medicinal plants and Orisha within Lucumí. Indeed, the fundamental metaphysical principles in which each is based collude in ways that nullify the very segregations that are produced and maintained. My intent here in bringing them together is not, however, to compare, conflate, or suggest that they are the same but to examine how they both illuminate the cosmological underpinnings of a world that uses Spirit knowledge/knowing as the medium through which a great number of women in the world make their lives intelligible. It is at these crossroads of subjectivity and collectivity, Sacred knowing and power, memory, and body, that we sojourn so as to examine their pedagogic content to see how they might instruct us in the complicated undertaking of Divine self-invention.

Four: Knowing Who Walks With You: The Making of Sacred Subjectivity

The Spirit is a wind. Everywhere I go they are going too . . . to protect me.—ALOURDES MARGAUX IN BROWN, *Mama Lola*

Winti (wind) come upon you in your dreams, they give you the strength and push you in a particular direction.—RENATE DRUI-VENTAK IN WEKKER, "One Finger Does Not Drink Okra Soup"

Yo soy mis santos, y mis santos soy yo (I am my saints, and my saints are me).—MARÍA, IN PROROK, "Boundaries Are Made for Crossing"

These statements, which reflect the spiritual sensibilities of practitioners immersed within the different practices of Vodou, Winti, Lucumí, and Espiritismo, encapsulate an understanding of self, knitted through a force—Spirit, Wind, Orisha—or through energies that are sacred. They are simultaneous expressions of mutual truths about both the self and that self's relationship to those Sacred forces. In being constituted as truths, we can imagine them as principles that one arrives at and literally wrestles with, and that then deepen over the course of time. Since this coming to know is both process and outcome, there is a strong suggestion that we need to become attentive to the inside in order to see the ways in which its elements are constructed. In the classes on Spirit propensity in which I participated at the outset of my own journey, my Madrina (god-mother) used the following phrase constantly: "You have to know who walks with you." These practitioners illustrate that they have come to know themselves as accompanied and as nonindividuated—that Winti walk with them, Spirit walks with them, and Orisha walk with them. They would not have been able to manifest these reflections as sensibilities, however, outside of a complicated, ongoing process of coming to consciousness, or what Donna Daniels calls "spiritual consciousness."[9] Thus, what appears at the outset as a first statement, "I am my saints," is actually the result of a series of moments of grounding one's consciousness in the idea and practice of Sacred accompaniment, Sacred guidance, and Sacred identity.

Taken together, the practitioners' statements speak to an intimacy of a lived experience in which the Sacred is embodied. They are woven through five interrelated elements: the idea that Sacred energies intervene in the daily lives of human beings; they surround, protect, push, strengthen, and bring a sense of purpose so that the individual is attuned to the Soul's purpose; they are present both everywhere, as in the Wind, and at specific moments, as in dreams; they mediate a process of interdependence, of mutual beingness, in which one becomes oneself in the process of becoming one with the Sacred; and they manifest their sacredness in nature as well as in their relationship with human beings, both of which take shape in a process of mutual embodiment. It would seem from these statements that Divine desire works to prod the self into believing that it does not exist of its own accord, free will notwithstanding. Such a formulation can be found in the cosmological anchor of the Bântu-Kôngo, as explained to me in the terms of Kia Bunseki Fu-kiau, my Bakôngo teacher:

> The same force that gave shape to the universe is the same force which resides within us. This force is Kalunga, a complete force by itself, the principle of God, the principle of change, vitality, motion, and trans- formation . . . There was nothingness, into which came this source of life, this energy, expressed as heat, cosmic fire after which there was a cooling that produced rivers, oceans, mountains. The world floated in Kalunga, endless water within subcosmic space, half emerging for terrestrial life, half submerging for marine life and the spiritual world. Kalunga is the ocean door between two worlds.[10]

In one sense the body's water composition seals our aquatic affinity with the Divine.

This idea of the intimacy between personhood and Sacred accompani- ment is also signified in the formative character of Winti in the lives of working-class Surinamese women. Gloria Wekker's ethnography, *The Politics of Passion: Women's Sexual Culture in the Afro-Surinamese Dias- pora,* hones in on this cosmological complex that, in her words, "shapes the ways working-class people think and talk about themselves and how they act from understandings of what a person is . . . It is the discursive context in which notions of working-class subjectivity and gender take shape . . . and also offers emic understandings of the bridges between subjecthood and sexuality."[11] When Renate Druiventak says that Winti come upon her in her dreams, she is drawing from a cosmology that frames a relationship with Winti, (which literally means Wind, and like Wind conveys the swiftness with which Spirits and ancestors can take possession of human beings and natural phenomena like trees and animals), and simultaneously her own understanding of who she is in the world. We will come later to see the purpose of this dream sequence, but for now it is enough to go deeper into this complex as a way of threading subjectivity with cosmology. To do so, I begin with Wekker's formulation:

> Within this cosmological system human beings are understood to be partly biological and partly spiritual beings. The biological side of humans, flesh and blood, is supplied by the earthly parents. The spiritual side is made up of three components, two of which are important here: all human beings have a *kra* or *yeye* (soul) and *dyodyo* (parents in the world of the gods). The *kra* and *dyodyo* together define a person's mind . . . [they] both consist of a male and female being and both of these parts are conceived of as human beings, with their own personality characteristics. The female and male part of the soul are determined by the day of the week on which the person is born. Thus, somebody born on Sunday is "carried" by Kwasi and Kwasiba, and is believed, therefore, to possess different characteristics that make her different from a person born on Wednesday who is "carried" by Kwaku and Akuba. Likewise a person like Renate, who has Aisa as a female godly parent, will, regardless of gender, display nurturing behavior, while somebody who has Leba (Elegba) will be very clean and orderly.[12]

The correlate of the *dyodyo* within Vodou and Lucumí is expressed in a parallel understanding of the Sacred energy that claims one's head, one's *mèt tète* or guardian angel, who is itself gendered. We can understand this claiming as the Sacred recognition of a likeness with someone whose primary "personal" sensibilities resemble the metaphysical principles that a particular Lwa or Orisha embodies. This likeness can be divined in a range of ways: sensed or seen by a seasoned practitioner, presented in dreams to the person herself, ascertained through a *lavé tèt,* washing of the head, in the case of Vodou, or through divination that relies on the Sacred corpus of the Ifa oracle, as is the case with Lucumí. The resemblance might be visible, but it might also be deeply hidden, or in need of reassembly, in which case the purpose of the *lavé tèt*, for instance, would be to activate latent or idle sensibilities so that they could steady the course of one's life. Still, the sensibilities are never singular but rather always pluralized, not only because we as human beings are made up of multiple energies, but also because those multiple energies exist within a single Orisha or Lwa as well. Knowing who walks with you, then, becomes a spiritual injunctive to activate a conscious relationship with the spiritual energies with whom one is accompanied, and who make it possible, in the words of Audre Lorde, "to do the work we came here to do."

But what are these energies or forces? What metaphysical principles do they codify? If we return to the Winti and to the figurative story of Kalunga, we see that these are forces of nature, the metaphysic of that which is elemental. Wind. Water. Fire. Thunder. Lightning. Volcano. The cosmic geography of Sky. Earth. Trees. Forest. Park. Mountain. River. Ocean. Rocks. Stones. They each have their own consciousness. They cluster at those places that the imagination fills with movement, upheaval, and contradiction: the crossroads, the railroad track, and the cemetery. Still, it is simply not possible to plumb their full depth, and we have come to know, through intuition and transmission, that there is a great deal of mystery constituting them, which explains why Vodou characterizes Lwa as *Les Mystères*. Finding the points of engagement is at once mystical, elusive, imaginative, and pragmatic, as Judith Gleason's artful rendition of Oya, Yansa, the Goddess of Wind and Fire conveys:

Oya at her most awesome, untrammeled Oya, is a weather goddess. This is how she appeared before the "world" as we know it and how she continues to manifest herself beyond the reach of meddlesome technological devices set up to simulate, alter, and pluck the heart out of the mystery of her storms. Caught in her updrafts, the religious imagination without apparatus seeks, though threatened with annihilation, to meet the weather goddess halfway, where sensuous experience remains possible. By reconnecting ourselves to the elements through which her urgent temperament expresses itself in patterns recognizable in our own swirls, inundations and disjunctive ardors, we come upon a language with which to invoke and reflect her power.[13]

It was on a stormy winter evening in New York City, the fifth in a series of unexpected blustering storms whose origin meteorologists designated as the North Pole, that I posed questions to Ekundayo and Sonia (both priest and devotee of Oya) aimed at understanding just how they connected themselves to Oya's convective currents—that is, what of her did they see in themselves. Although I had sat with Kitsimba's narration of the movement of the Trade Winds, I was slow to realize that they had come into being through the force of the energy of the dead—that is, in her telling, the grieving dead instigate their global movement. And it was that realization that pointed the direction to Oya. With Kitsimba and Gleason's updrafts buzzing in my mind, I posed those questions to both Ekundayo and Sonia. I explained Oya's updrafts as her capacity to move within multiple domains, possessing *ajè*—the power to do good and evil—yet refusing to admit it, the same way in which she refuses capture. As shape-shifter she is the River Niger, buffalo woman, dual symbol of the carrier of fire and mother of the cemetery, and mother of nine. "How do you find balance in turbulence?" I asked, "What does being one with the Wind of transformation mean?"

My questions came as an unexpected barrage, which Ekundayo generously greeted by asking me to repeat them. Here is the torrent that poured forth from her:

> It's being in the eye of the storm, which is the stillness. Oya takes me to different levels of consciousness . . . into a different plane, knowing that something is shifting in my mind. I am there (in the vortex) [though I am] not spinning. She allows me a different perspective on what's inside and outside of me and my role in it . . . Oya brings much peace, but will also move me when I am too still. You have to get up and do, hence the balance. She is also the gentle zephyr. [Here there was a long pause] Oya is also the first breath and the last breath . . . Oya moves people; moves the Ocean . . . moves me beyond fear, since movement is sometimes scary . . . moves us to grow as mother of transformation . . . She allows me to sit in the eye of the storm to grow.

As the world would have it, you can't sit in it for too long, but without wind there is stagnation, things will die . . .

Oya is very protective, she protects with a ferocity . . . what will a mother do to save her child? . . . There is no limit . . . I did not know how to do battle. There was always, well, too much emotion . . . I had to learn to sit with her and tell her what was going on . . . What seemed like such a problem with emotional strain, she would show me, look, move things here, go here, and when I follow, because I know it isn't me, when I follow I can take up my battle. She acts with a swiftness that is amazing. She does not like tears, so when I bring them the shift is even more immediate, more dramatic . . . She is equally as subtle; she can kiss you as a light breeze.

I really had a deeper sense of Oya going into Ifa. Everything was coming out right and then all of a sudden things started to go wrong, topsy turvy. I had to talk to Oya to say to her even though I was going into Ifa, I was still her daughter. And at the *bembé* for Oya this sister began doing this dance for her, swirling and swirling, and before I knew it I was brought into that swirl, saying "even though I am going to Ifa I am still your daughter . . ."

I had bronchial asthma that was killing me. Oya gave me life. She is the reason I am on this planet. She made it possible for me to breathe . . . Oya will call upon Yemayá to help her children . . . I know that some stories talk about the enmity between the two of them, but that is not what I experience . . . The dead are in the ocean, and the dead are also in the air . . . Oya teaches us to know the dance of life . . . We need to see the beauty of the dance . . . We can't be afraid to move . . . that is a rejection of life . . . One leg in life and one in death . . .

What is striking to me even as I now write Ekundayo's words is the degree to which they epitomize the sensuous intimacy, the ability to inhabit different planes of consciousness, that Gleason herself has conveyed. Clearly, she too has met the weather goddess halfway. But Ekundayo's rendering also reflects an agile movement between the metaphysic and the anthropomorphic, evincing again an embodiment of principles that are meaningful principally because she has threaded them through her daily life. The threat of death from asthma is no metaphor. The work of prayer, sitting with *ebbo,* offerings that Oya accepted, enables Ekundayo to say in just that matter-of-fact way, "[Oya] has made it possible for me to breathe," while her reflection on "one leg in life and one in death" pertains to a principle that has existential import. The challenge with which we are confronted here is how to move between death's clutches, and what Ekundayo suggests is that we do so by living in a particular way, by becoming still within Oya's multiple manifestations. It is no simple task.

And as shape-shifter, Oya could not be only one thing. Says Sonia, "She is an Orisha you have to deal with in the right way. I am still learning about her, still trying to understand her. I think I'm learning how to turn fear into power, like the power over darkness. I can sit and receive information . . . in the dark since darkness does not separate light for me."

There is a great deal to be understood about whether the character of the person and that of the Orisha or Lwa is indistinguishable; whether there is some degree of distance between that which demarcates person from Spirit; whether the process of being the ground in which the Sacred energies are planted fashions an entirely new self; and about the relative balance between the application of principles that are metaphysical or anthropomorphic in the living with these energies. These are indeed knotty issues that take the span of lifetimes to sort out. To be sure, the anthropomorphic mediates the distance between the physical and metaphysical as Ekundayo's reflection shows. But what is the context for learning? In places where Lwa, Orisha, and Winti are grounded in the soil, the multiple institutionalized instances of extended family yards that sometimes approximate small towns provide the sustained meeting place for the ceremonial rituals that school practitioners in the consciousness of the Spirit. But the fragmentation of urban living in places like New York City can sometimes make for what Gleason calls "a skittish pairing of the human and the divine."[14] There are principles to be adhered to, but there are no written maps that contour precisely how the pedagogic moments for Sacred learning are to be structured. And because in many instances there are ruptures in the lineage of practice—there was no homage to ancestors or to Orisha in my biological family, for instance—learning assumes a particular kind of deliberateness in communities that are multiply displaced. Donna Daniels was able to capture this slow process of deliberate embodiment that unfolded during her encounter with a West Coast community of Lucumí practitioners. She witnessed "a quality to spiritual learning [which women] described as a slow and deliberate coming to [spiritual] consciousness . . . predicated on vigilant observation of a sacred idea over time as it manifested itself in the devotee's life such that a personal understanding of its meaning was derived. Thus, spiritual knowledge . . . was acquired through a process of embodiment wherein understanding of a sacred idea was based on (in) the experience of living it or experiencing the idea in action, or 'seated' in one's life."[15]

In practice, the daily living of the Sacred idea in action occurs in the most simple of acts of recognition, such as pouring libations for and greeting the Lwa; attending to them on the days of the week that bear their signature; feeding ancestors first with the same meal we feed ourselves as a way of placing the purpose of our existence back with its source, as a gesture of mutual exchange and as a way of giving thanks and asking to be sustained; building an altar to mark Sacred ground and focus energies within the home, constructing a place to work, to touch down, discard, pull in, and practice reciprocity; and participating in collective ceremony. It is this dailiness that instigates the necessary shifts in consciousness, which are produced because each act, and each moment of reflection of that act, brings a new and deepened meaning of self in intimate concert with the Sacred. This idea to which Daniels refers of vigilant observation that rests at the heart of spiritual labor was also given form in these words of Kitsimba: "With careful attentive service and focused contemplation, the Divine is made manifest. It is why this work is never done." Thus, the cycle of action, reflection, and practice as Sacred praxis embodied marks an important reversal of the thinking as knowledge paradigm.

In the realm of the secular, the material is conceived of as tangible while the spiritual is either nonexistent or invisible. In the realm of the Sacred, however, the invisible constitutes its presence by a provocation of sorts, by provoking our attention. We see its effects, which enable us to know that it must be there. By perceiving what it does, we recognize its being and by what it does we learn what it is. We do not see Wind, but we can see the vortex it creates in a tornado. We see its capacity to uproot things that seem to be securely grounded, such as trees; its capacity to strip down, unclothe, remove that which draws the sap, such as leaves; its capacity to dislodge what is buried in the bowels of the earth. Wind brings sound, smells, messages that can at times be directionally deceptive so that we can be prompted to go in search of truth. Its behavior can be sudden, erratic; it can cleanse and disturb; provoke, destroy, caress and soothe. We learn about and come to know Wind by feeling, observing, perceiving, and recognizing its activity; in short, by remembering what it does as bodily experience. But it is bodily experience that demands a rewiring of the senses mirrored, for instance, in the aesthetic representations of figures whose ears, mouths, nostrils, and eyes assume a scale that is larger than life, so that they might convey a heightened grounding of the senses. Hearing is seeing and seeing is feeling.[16] An unbroken bottle with a thin elongated neck can contain a full-size wooden cross, challenging the naked eye. The feel of fire is strong, not hot.

That demand for the rewiring of the senses is even more provocative when the cycle of action, reflection, and practice cannot be automatically transposed to a curriculum whose learning requirements are sometimes neither straightforward nor self-evident. The very *how* of the manifestation of the Divine is a practice to which we have to become attuned and accustomed. This was brought home to me during one of the weekly sessions of the *mesa blanca*—spirit mediumship with the white table— when my Madrina was mounted by one of her main spirits, La Negra. La Negra is a firm, sympathetic spirit, one of whose embodied lives unfolded in Haiti. She spoke in the coded language of archaic Creole and Spanish combined, a border language, one might say, of another time. She often urged us: "Never be ashamed of your spiritual inheritance." And unity was a constant theme, a necessary one, in light of a good deal of racism, misogyny, and heterosexism that reigned in the temple. One day, however, she left us with a message in the form of an unexpected riddle: "The bourgeoisie sacrifice their children." I still remember the numinous silence enveloping the semidarkened room that encircled us. Those of us who were not mounted did not readily know to which time frame La Negra was referring, whether the bourgeoisie did so in the past, whether it was doing so then—that is now—or whether it intended to sacrifice its children in a time to come. Was/is sacrifice literal or metaphorical? "Bourgeoisie" in human idiom carries the understanding of a specific class extracting capital, not a term in popular currency at this moment. Its use was, therefore, unexpected in that space and at this time. To which particular bourgeoisie was La Negra referring? In which social formation? Haiti, the geography of another of her incarnations, one we do not know? Or the United States of North America? Or was she linking Haiti and the United States in a mutual complicity with bourgeois sacrifice? How did she come by that information? Did she experience it, that is, witness it, or was she told about it as a common practice? And why was it being revisited here and now? What modes of sacrifice was the bourgeoise exacting from members of their class, and could it be from members of a subordinated class? If sacrifice belonged in a "past," what key did it hold for decoding the "present"?

All of these questions press on our perceptions of, and relationship to, time with a capital T. In thinking about that moment of La Negra's pronouncement, as well as others, I am learning that the embodiment of the Sacred dislocates clock time, meaning linearity, which is different than living in the past or being bound by tradition. The feeling conveyed that afternoon of La Negra's announcement was one of being somewhat lost in time, of time standing still, the encounter with Time. Although the voice is present in the now, it collapses that tense we call present into a past and future combined. Notice that La Negra used the present tense. Spirit brings knowledge from past, present, and future to a particular moment called a now. Time becomes a moment, an instant, experienced in the now, but also a space crammed with moments of wisdom about an event or series of events already having inhabited different moments, or with the intention of inhabiting them, while all occurring simultaneously in this instant, in this space, as well as in other instants and spaces of which we are not immediately aware. Spirit energy both travels in Time and travels differently through linear time, so that there is no distance between space and time that it is unable to navigate. Thus, linear time does not exist because energy simply does not obey the human idiom. What in human idiom is understood as past, present, and future are calibrated into moments in which mind and Spirit encounter the energy of a dangerous memory, a second's glimpse of an entire life, of a dream or a sequence of dreams, of a shadow lying under a village, of the vibration of a feeling, of a letter to be delivered, a decision to be made, all penetrating the web of interactive energies made manifest. I can't say that I know in any definitive sense how the bourgeoisie sacrifice(d) their children, although the statement leaves me with a lot of possibilities to be decoded. Perhaps some historical record will, or perhaps already has, confirmed it. To be sure, confirmation in the historical record would be important only if we needed reassurance about Spirit truth-telling. Wrestling with the idea of Time, however, forces us to evacuate the desire for written confirmation, drawing us closer to observe and, therefore, to perceive how the mind of Spirit works. The demand is more exacting, for it would have us learn how to suspend inherited habits of knowing so as to better apprehend the very gestalt that is itself provoking the shifts in consciousness that scrambled time, turning its constructed fragments into one Time. Human beings are neither the guardians nor the owners of Time.

The work of rewiring the senses is neither a single nor individual event. Practitioners have to be present and participating in a community; they must show up, in other words, for this appointment, to the ceremonies that rehearse over and over again the meaning of Sacred accompaniment. To be sure, there is a compelling awe in the beauty of numinous ceremony, and there are no lengths to which practitioners will not go to bear its financial cost, but the bridge between that exterior and an interior, using what emerges from the contemplative and reflexive to shape exteriorized practice, whether in the form of ceremony in New York or in the form of hunting in Mali, has to be made. It is a crucial bridge, for without it we could indeed not address subjectivity of any kind.

The desire to cultivate this interior figured prominently among practitioners with whom Daniels worked. She found that "openness, poise, balance, alignment, clarity, humility, honesty and respectfulness [were] some of the spiritual principles and desirable inner states on which meaningfully living one's life and learning from life's lessons [were] predicated."[17] But working to achieve that alignment is pure challenge, not only because of the cultural dissonances in daily living that can undermine the evolution of character, but also because the spiritual is lived in the same locale in which hierarchies are socially invented and maintained. Within the Lucumí communities in New York, this social is invented through the very hierarchies that constitute the secular: heterosexism in the midst of the visible presence of lesbian, gay, bisexual, transgender, and two-spirit people; a peculiar brand of racism that positions Cuba as the seat of the religion, freed from its African moorings; a variant of indigenous black nationalism that interprets these moorings to mean the exclusion of lesbians and gay men and the paradoxical positioning of women's priestly function as marginalized mother in spite of women's numerical predominance; and a brisk trade and commodification of the Sacred that confuse the instrument with the source.

Yet dissonance results not only from the effects that these various exclusions produce but also because the old self, if you will, comes under siege once it begins the slow, indeterminate move toward its own dissolution. As my Madrina often asked rhetorically, as she linked the ego to a stone, "How would you know why the stone is there, whether you need to remove it, bury it, or ignore it?" The work, then, of traveling to the interior to unmoor, fracture, dislocate, and excavate those parts that are staunch in their defense of separation because they resist the idea of Divine guidance has to be intuited and projected as desire, injected into the very conviction of the choice of one's spiritual path. Knowing who walks with you and maintaining that company on the long journey is a dance of balance in which the fine lines between and among will and surrender; self-effacement and humility; doing and being; and listlessness and waiting for the Divine are being constantly drawn. This dance of balance is the work of healing, and it is to a discussion of the confluence between healing work and spiritual work that I now turn.

Five: Healing Work Is the Antidote to Oppression— Kitsimba

The idea that the fire that constitutes the center of human beings also constitutes the center of the universe anchors a Sacred connection between the two. It provides a theory of equilibrium, and, implicitly, of disequilibrium, since we can rightly assume that the result of moving away from that center is imbalance. The symbols and symbolism of centering—that is, of the concentration of Sacred energies—are numerous. Such centering, as opposed to scattering, coalesces in Vodou in the *djevo* (the altar room), the *poto mitan* (the central pole through which the Lwa descend), and the *vévé* (the Sacred ground etchings on which they come to ceremonial rest, which are not to be displaced once ceremony begins). But since no illness has a manifestation that is only of the individual, this theory of disequilibrium applies to the social, that is, to the collectivity as well. The two are, therefore, entangled.[18] And Kitsimba's particular formulation that healing work is the antidote to oppression not only implicates oppression in the production of disequilibrium but applies the solution—healing—at the point of the problem that everyone, it would seem, is called to address. She not only suggests that the work of healing is of various kinds, but also that it is at the very heart of spiritual labor, explaining why the healing instruments in Kikôngo are called *minkisi*, medicines, why *fèy*, leaves, in Vodou are also called *medicament*, medicine, and why in the Yoruba creation stories as told in the Ifá corpus medicines were allotted to Orisha as they were sent down to earth. To function as an antidote to oppression, healing work, that is, spiritual labor, assumes different forms, while anchored in reconstructing a terrain that is both exterior and interior.

For healing work to be undertaken there has to exist some understanding of cause, the precision of which is gained through a consultation of the Ifá oracle, or the Dillogun in the case of Santería, or the cards as in the case of Espiritísmo and Vodou. As Alourdes, a *mambo* (priest) of Vodou, explained:

> You do the cards for a person. In the cards you see the problem of the person. But when a person comes to see you he doesn't have anything to say. You have to read the cards. You going to spread out the cards to see what the person needs. You explain it. You tell the person . . . The cards tell you and then you speak with the person . . . And the person speaks to you and says, "What you say is true."
>
> If you see something in his face, you say, "Did this happen to you?" "Did you have an accident?" You search to see if the accident was natural or not . . . You have people who have things "thrown on them" (*voyé sou li*) but you have others who don't have that. It is a natural sickness they have, but people imagine that it is other people who have caused it. If someone has a *maladi* of the imagination, you can't do anything for them. You can survey someone's house . . . go there, read cards . . . you don't find a thing, because they have nothing. It is a

[medical] doctor's sickness they have. But they have an imagination and think that someone has done bad against them. There are people like that, but there are also people who really do bad. So you search to find where a malady comes from.[19]

No medicine or treatment comes without a theory of the cause of disequilibrium, *la causa*. What is the violation that displaces balance with disequilibria? Some crisis acts as the instigator for the healing work, but crisis is not the cause, yet it pushes the question of which set of explanations will one accept as the reason for the fractures that produced the crisis—the ones with which one has been living or the ones soon to be disclosed—and through which set of explanations will one begin to intuit the faint outlines of the self that succumbed to being constantly pushed aside, held at bay.[20] The crisis could be quite wrenching and deceptively self-evident, as in my earlier rendition of how I came to occupy that unstable space of not knowing in the pursuit of Kitsimba's life story. Might we think that writer's block could be the result of spiritual misalignment? Here is Kitsimba's version of my story:

> She lived a mere four miles from one of her two best friends, the one who lived right on top of the Yoruba cemetery, she, her clairvoyant aunt, Tantie, a hoard of boys and her parents, all of them laying their heads every blessed night, unknowingly, on the heads and bones of the dead; the friend who lived only two houses away from where they disturbed Sophie and unleashed the restless energy of other dead in order to build permanence in concrete houses in which they dreamed they could live in peace and luxury, but never really could . . . She and this friend would pass through the cemetery, always in a rush, taking a short cut. If they taking short cut why leave Diego Martin and go all the way to America and then to London to find out she wanted to study the plantation where I lived, right in Diego Martin, a stone's throw from where she grew up. She went to London to find out what the British put in their records about the plantation with someone called a research assistant. I was assisting her all this time, yet I never got any recognition. Well the British didn't put anything, and what they put was destroyed by fire. Fire destroyed records in St. Pierre too. What did the British have to do with snatching us from Kôngo. Absolutely nothing.

The second night, this reluctant, or rather hard-head, arrived in London. While taking a bath, she asked someone for assistance in completing all the work she had to do. And it was really a lot of work. But you know the distant way these nonbelievers do, needing assistance but self-conscious and skeptical about calling the higher power. I told her I would help her and in exchange she made a promise she vowed to keep. Yet, while in London, she still continued to introduce Allison as her research assistant. She never found anything about me in the archives, but she developed this fancy idea of which she became quite proud that I was somehow co-implicated in the psychic economy of slavery—such fancy words that meant nothing—and that there was some relationship between myself and Luisa Calderón. She fabricated that relationship only because the British were fond of collecting, and so they collected pages and pages about the trial and torture of Luisa Calderón. These were the pages she found, but there was nothing about me. Incidentally, there was a relationship, but it was not in the records. She had this fancy book all outlined, and I was the prop, for she had planned to rely on a skewed account of my life from one Pierre McCallum who was determined to seek revenge against the British by painting a picture of the horrors of slavery with us as the abject victims. Ask her to go back and find the chapter outlines, for she keeps meticulous records, never throwing away anything before time, and you can verify my story yourself. It was then I decided to create a block, to make it that she couldn't write what she had planned.

I told her she couldn't write about me unless she came to know and feel my daily life. She had to feel what it was like to get up before dawn and implore the protection of the fading dark to move in stealth to do what you had vowed to do in another place, another time, for another reason under different conditions. You could die in stealth and determination to pay the debt you were chosen to pay. She had to feel what it was like to survive above ground while really living underground by fire. She had to come as close to the ground as I did, learning to depend upon the damp rain smell of earth to clean her insides, jar her senses and to bring her to the heart of the oath I had sworn never to betray: all life is shared with those at the bottom of the Ocean, the bottom of the river, the bottom of water—the meeting point of the encircled cross. She had to feel the folds and dips against those places where earth becomes level again. I wanted her to come to feel how folds and dips provided security even more so than level ground, which could be deceptively friendly. Too level. Too even. Hostile to change.

And she was not one of those who learned by feeling. "Those who don't hear will feel," her mother was fond of saying, but no one learns to feel on demand, by dint of sheer threat. She had learned quite early, and in a way that did not serve her, that feelings had to be buried since they did not belong in the world of the living, except on auspicious occasions as when somebody died. So the ordinary feelings of daily life always eluded her; they came as a surprise to her. She found them excessive, almost always unexpected, out of the ordinary, for what was ordinary for her was to live devoid of feelings, having learned well to quietly predict the order of events, never their effects. I wanted her to feel the textured tapestry of my life in the soft markings of her flesh and through this feeling come to know it intimately, feel it as if she were the one who had lived it. She could no longer rely on what was written in books to convey or even arrive at Truth. What was written in those books was not even a faint shadow of me; it had nothing to do with me. They knew nothing about who I was. Relying on only one way of knowing to point a path to the wisdom of the Soul. This learning would take at least the span of one life, and only the Soul could decide what would be left over for a different time, a different place. It took her seven years of skeptical fits and starts to feel the power of that early revelation which was given in that place called London; and it would take her even longer to come to have faith in it, to know that her answers needed to come from a source different than the ones she had mastered in books; to begin to feel the difference between knowledge and wisdom—one could save you in the kingdom of the dead, the other gave you only temporary status in the kingdom of the living . . . To know that with careful focused attention and contemplative service, the Divine would be made manifest. The answer to many things lay in her hands, in her very own hands.

By the end of that day of being turned inside out, I had become convinced that Kitsimba's singular desire was not to have me author her life, but for her to author mine and make public my guarded secrets.

"How much more," I demanded, in a tearful fit of dampened rage, "are you going to divulge"? Now I struggle against the powerful urge to edit.

The *causa* can also manifest in attempts to beat back what was intentionally left behind, an intentional forgetting that is not the same as not knowing that one had something to remember. In a scene reminiscent of Julie Dash's "Daughters of the Dust" in which those bound for the city portend a misfit between the call of Spirit and the lure of concrete, Karen McCarthy Brown maps how Alourdes was jolted to remember the Lwa Kouzin Zaka, who was forced to leave his abode in the mountains of Haiti and appear on Forty-Second Street in New York City in the form of a relative's dream. "Tell Alourdes," he said, "if she dresses like me, everything going to be beautiful." It was the call to the portal of initiation, *kouché,* and a simultaneous call to remember her own family lineage of a mother and grandmother serving the Spirits.[21]

If healing work is a call to remember and remembering is embodied, then we would want to situate the body centrally in this healing complex. Brown rightly notes that "the healer's knowledge is carried in her body and it is addressed to the body of the client,"[22] and given that body praxis has been central in our mapping of subjectivity, it follows that it would be equally central in understanding the structure of healing as well. But we would also want to know how this healing work on the body travels, as well, to the inner self. Here is my reflection on a healing session in which I assisted Mama Lola, my spiritual mother in Vondou:

> Janice showed up to Mammie's basement in Brooklyn, a successful middle-class professional, wearing the strong scent of her grandmother, the scent of asafetida. From reading the cards Mammie saw that people were jealous of Janice's success and had consistently worked obeah on her, which resulted in her inability to keep money in her hands. Janice confirmed that she had a number of projects pending, but she had been in a spiral in which nothing came to fruition. "Other people go to church," she blurted with a twinge of lament and shame, "and they don't need any of this." Sensitive to the mixed scent of her grandmother's asafetida and Janice's own ambivalence, Mammie was quick on the uptake, "How do you know? You don't know that as an African woman your answers come from a different source!" The cards

indicated three cleansings, the first of which was to appease and activate Papa Legba, the guardian of doorways, the essence of choice. It began the very next day.

Standing on Legba's colors of black, red and white emblematic of the crossroads, with a lit white candle in her right hand, Janice prayed the prayer asking for protection against her enemies:

> . . . May the Peace of the Lord be with me! Divine Master, always accompany me, talk to me as you did to the disciples . . . walk in front of me and defend me against my enemies . . . May their eyes never see me, their hands never touch me, their ears never hear me, their wicked wishes never harm me and never overtake me on their way, neither on horse nor on foot, neither on earth, on the sea nor in the air. I beseech you, Lord, to spread your mighty arms to free me from unfair imprisonment . . .

"You finished?" With a limp nod from Janice, Mammie began the meticulous shredding of old clothes, snip, snip in a clockwise direction . . . snip, snip in a counterclockwise direction. The only sound was the snip snip of the new scissors and the sniffles from the steady stream of tears that mingled with the clothes discarded on the floor. Naked. Next came the food, cooked and uncooked grains, beans, ground provisions, cube sized, with two handfuls to be held for a different moment.

"I work on the outside, you work on the inside," the clear matter-of-fact announcement instruction to Janice. Again, the cleansing began with the head, this time with meat.

"If something is too heavy for your head, where will you put it?"

Not knowing whether or not it was a real question, Janice hesitated until the prompt, "On your shoulders," and so she repeated, hesitatingly, "On my shoulders."

"If it's too heavy for your shoulders where would you put it?" Still hesitating, and again the prompt, "In your hands."

"In my hands."

"If it's too heavy for your hands where would you put it?" This time with no need for a prompt.

"On the floor."

Each time the same set of questions pleading the same responses to the four directions, each time Janice's responses becoming more sure.

Next came the bad bath, strong smelling, again moving from top to bottom. "As soon as I put the bath on top of your head, drop what in your hand," one of the last vestiges of that which weighed down. With the last drop of water drained from the basin, Mammie cleaned Janice with black, red, and white cloth, each piece of fabric offered to the four directions, placed afterwards under Janice's feet. Standing on white cloth, Janice was sprayed with gin and agua florida, incensed, first the outstretched hands then the soles of the feet and head, the grounding to the earth and the seat of the Soul. She was then dressed with a new camisette of red and black with an emblazoned white cross. All clothes were incensed, including the shoes, to bring mindfulness to the road she walked.

At a different time a second steadying bath would follow, accompanied by a third white bath, the cooling signature of Papa Danbala, a good luck bath of milk, *malanguette,* a miniature family of bay leaves, cloves, cinnamon and star anise to be administered by Mammie when she traveled to complete the work at Janice's home and her place of work. It was not Papa Legba who made an appearance at Janice's workplace but Avandra, the animal spirit, come to disturb, dispel and outwit the obeah that was put there, and to teach the power of the difference between good strong medicine of the right hand and obeah of the left. The healing cycle had completed its trajectory from the bitter to the sweet. But healing takes time. Its mystery does not belong to us. It is now five years since that first moment in the basement. Janice continues to work with Mammie as she deepens her own internal sense of possibilities, still living in a place that continues to define the work *she* now does as obeah.

With the appropriate invocations and medicinal applications, the healer's work involves navigating an uninterrupted flow between the behavioral self, the inner self and the world of the disembodied.[23] To be successful, healing takes place at several levels, not the least of which is the symbolic—the peeling back of layers built up on the outside in order to get at that which resides on the inside, to which Janice had access. Temporarily, the body was unable to go the physical distance, but it could be prodded to go the metaphysical distance, within that space of the interior. Enemies lurked there, as well, not only on the outside. With the right prayer and concentration Janice could get to that inside while the body was being rid of burdens and blockages, its outer clothing, old, no longer required to adorn a body that needed to be rendered naked in order that it might be clothed differently—in the protective colors of Divine intermediary Papa Legba, guardian of the crossroads who opens the doorway to endless possibilities. The crisis had brought Janice to a crossroads, Legba's own domain, much the same way in which writer's block had catapulted me there. Invoking him was crucial to the success of this work. "I work on the outside; you work on the inside," demanded the participation of Janice, since no matter what shape one is in, one is never entitled to abdicate responsibility for one's healing or to assume the role of the passive bystander to obstruct it. "I work on the outside; you work on the inside," marked the necessary division of labor between Mammie and Janice that is required to knit the interior and exterior. And since the corporeal, physical body is not only body but of mind (inner self) and Spirit, the purpose of this body work is to bring them into synchronicity, into alignment.

Misalignment, then, is another way of thinking about alienation, that movement away from the center of fire. The pathway between the scent of asafetida and a middle-class professional does not necessarily point to alienation, but the loss of that scent may well be a powerful predictor of it. Janice did not spell out all of what she encountered on that pathway, but from Mammie's incisive uptake, "You don't know as an African woman your answers come from a different source," she did not need to. The sharp (astute) response articulated the perils associated with the journey: there is a cost associated with taking refuge in the borrowed gifts of alienation that cultivate the practice of forgetting, the refusal to pull on the ancestral cord, denying ourselves life source. But it also brings one face to face with genealogy, whether or not one is willing or ready to engage it. And those borrowed gifts of alienation are not simply passive, for ingesting the belief in obeah, another way of ingesting a deep mistrust of our senses, or the shame of our spiritual inheritance as La Negra put it, confronts the internalization of dominant religion's institutionalized disavowal of these practices, yet another form of oppression. The alignment of mind, body, and Spirit could be expected to assault the social practices of alienation wherever they may be practiced, whether within dominant religion, in the enclosure of the academy with its requirements of corporate time, or in day-to-day cultural prescriptions of disablement that call these Sacred practices into question and challenge their value. Ultimately, this alignment cannot but provoke a confrontation with history, both its Cartesian variant that produced the splits in the first place and the history that is being mobilized to displace it. This is what Kitsimba's rendition of my experience of writer's block so poignantly illustrates. Writer's block, like alienation—or rather, writer's block as an aspect of alienation—is a spiritual problem requiring a spiritual solution.

The knitting together of mind, body, and Spirit finds another pivotal anchor in the world of Spirit possession. Here, body becomes the means by which mind, which has fashioned itself as autonomous, is propelled outside of itself in order to invite the return of Spirit. Body, in this complex, becomes a means of communication, simply because Spirit requires it (although not only it) to mount its descent. There are many representations of possession that rely on exteriority to make the point about the visible transformation that takes place in outward appearance as a way of providing evidence for what practitioners take to be real. But that outside, visible dimension cannot be unmoored from an interior transformation that sets up the terms for the descent of Spirit. Crucial to those terms is surrender, a handing over of autonomy in the service of Spirit, without which that transformation, itself a struggle with sur-render, would never occur.

I say that the body is only one of the media for the housing of Spirit because there is no single place where this knowledge resides. Within the context of Orisha ceremony, for instance, the *Batá* themselves, the Sacred drums, are invested with the energies of the Orisha who reside there, Anya. They evoke and provoke those Sacred energies, but they also express through rhythm their own belief in their release. Doubling. At *bembés,* ceremonies that rely on the Batá, practitioners dance their belief in the rhythm of movement to guide them toward the energies of Yemayá who will manifest: *Hasta que muere,* "until I die," says Xiamara.

As she dances, soft waves begin to form a swaying circle, round and round, seduced by songs of praise and homage; skirts open, rise, and fall to a choreography aimed at the feet, tentative at first, mimicking the tidal way of the Ocean in search of a place to settle. Feet are the first to succumb to the shift in ground from concrete to water, throwing the dancer off balance until the body begins to rely on the weightlessness of water to sustain being upright. As the circle of movement widens, drums converse with the urgent plea of the bard. Waves become insistent, compelled by the roll of the drum call. Sharp. They crash as they reach shore. Sensitive to the spot where the water wants to settle, the bard moves closer, singing the resonance so that the eardrum would take the vibrations of its meanings to that meeting place: the vibrations of rhythm of drum beat released through Sacred energies; the vibration of song released through the rhythm of drum beat and movement.

As the rhythms complete the invitation by reminding the body of a prior promise of its ultimate surrender, darkness descends and a deep moan bursts through the artificial enclosure, rippling down the length and across the breadth of River, which, by this time, begins to remember. River assumes on its surface a delicate veil of moving tapestry, a rippled mirror flowing impatiently, yet revealing every manner of treasure: every tadpole ebony, shiny, slippery, every crayfish, each cowrie that had crawled into its protective spiral the color of ivory, each grain of silt hued to its finest having tumbled for eternity in this muddy vortex. The cry travels upward to Sky, downward again into the deep bowels of Earth until each molecule of air, each particle of soil, each sleeping star that planned to rise to brilliance later that night, each stone, each shard of leaf, each root of a tree that had crawled surreptitiously to lands grown distant from loss and from the fruits of its labor, the exploding scent of each flower, each expectant bud, each pig that had given life including those yet to be born, each fowl, each itinerant rooster, every drop of water including those hesitatingly formed, they all, each one of them began to feel the desire of the cry and agreed to conspire to make its power manifest.

The Divine call to the Divine, inside of a meeting of self with self, a practice of alignment with the Divine. Yemayá, that broad expanse of

Ocean, who lives both on sea and on land has pushed past modernity's mode of reason and taken up temporary sojourn on the insides of this artificial enclosure, come to accept, to cleanse, to bless, to remind us that in the same way the breaking of waves does not compromise the integrity of the Ocean, so too anything broken in our lives cannot compromise that cosmic flow to wholeness. The body cannot but surrender in order to make way for this tidal flow. And this, too, necessitates practice.

Six: Beginnings

While my focus here has been on African-based spiritual practices, it should not be taken to mean, as I indicated earlier, that the precinct of the Sacred is any way partial. Within the metaphysical systems of Native American, Hawaiian, the *I Ching,* ancient Hindu, and Jewish mysticism are to be found correlates of Vodou and Lucumí that can be interpreted through Fon, Ewe, Kikôngo, Yoruba, and Dahomean Sacred prisms. And since geography, culture, or religious systems cannot carry the capacity to annex the Sacred, we can safely assume that there must be multiple instances where its shades are inscribed. If it is to be found everywhere in the terrain of the everyday as part of the continuous existential fabric of being, then it lives simultaneously in the daily lives of everyone, in spiritual work that assumes a different form from those I have engaged here, but also in daily incidents, in those "things" we routinely attribute to coincidence, those moments of synchronicity, the apparently disparate that have cohesion but under another framework. It is to be found in direct revelation, in those domains that mystics routinely inhabit, but in work that in a purely secular realm would seem not to derive from Spirit. I am thinking here of Michael Cottman's project to uncover the sunken wreckage of the *Henrietta Marie*, a slave ship, off the coast of Florida and his explicitness about the spiritual character of the project: "We go to the sea to explore the depths of our Souls . . . the call that beckoned us under water came from the sea."[24] It is also to be found in the meeting ground of the erotic, the imaginative, and the creative, which Akasha Gloria Hull addressed in what she called the "union of politics, spiritual consciousness, and creativity that gave rise to a new spirituality among progressive African-American women at the turn of the 21st century."[25] This fusion helps to explain why black female theologians use Baby Suggs in Morrison's clearing as Sacred text. And it is not surprising that Donna Daniels found that many Santería practitioners in the Bay Area were artists, for in a larger sense there is no dimension of the Sacred that does not yearn for the making of beauty, an outer social aesthetic of expression whether in written or spoken word, the rhythm of drum, the fashioning of an altar, or any of the visual arts. The Sacred is inconceivable without an aesthetic. "We wanted to know God," Mbûta Kusikila explained in my trip to the Kôngo, "and that's why we carved all of these figures, not because we worshipped idols."[26] In an even larger sense, the sacred precinct is at once vast, proximate, and intimate. In Kitsimba's universe, the principle is quite simple: *You human beings have this fancy word—syncretism—for something quite simple: everything in the universe is interconnected!*

Interconnectedness, interdependence, and intersubjectivity as constructs or desire do not necessarily provoke resistance within the shared canon of materialist modernity. Indeed, we count on this for the making of successful political movements. It is not the fact of intersubjectivity, then, but the interjection of the Sacred in its matrix that renders it suspect. Let me examine the geographies of that suspicion. At times it is linked to the practitioner/believer, who ostensibly comes with a proclivity to disengage the world of politics. But that suspicion is simply not borne out in practice. There is a wide range of contexts that imbricate the Sacred with the political: the large-scale political movements that are based in liberation theology in Latin America; that phase of Indian anticolonial struggle inaugurated by Gandhi whose prayer life lay at the root of mass politics; and the political party in Suriname that was formed by Renate Druiventak, introduced earlier, based on the prompting of Winti in her dreams. Luisa Teish, who has been in a range of intersecting struggles, links the political to the spiritual in these terms: "We were political *because* we were spiritual,"[27] a formulation echoed in Marta Moreno Vega's apt sense of an intrinsic connection between the political and the spiritual: "The energy that naturally flows from initiation opens up inner channels, granting the initiate the ability to see, feel, smell, taste, and sense more acutely, and to be more present in the world. By combining my knowledge of the spiritual and the secular worlds, I have found a universe that unveils all of its wisdom and beauty before me. Like the great . . . goddess of the ocean,

Yemayá, who lives in the ocean and on the earth, we must avail ourselves of all the natural treasures of both worlds."[28] Indeed, the formulation of embodied praxis mounts a deep challenge to that suspicion of disengagement. Thus, to continue to argue from that suspicion not only denies the pedagogies derived from Sacred praxis but exposes an allegiance to that form of rationality that divests the secular of the Sacred in a way that both privileges and subordinates—privileging the former while subordinating the latter.

Or is the suspicion cathected onto women themselves whom feminism wants to cure of the desire to be consorts of manly male gods? To be sure, many of the immigrant women in Vodou and Lucumí practices do not claim the name feminist or woman of color. However, negotiating the social relations of gender and sexuality occurs within complicated inheritances of anthropomorphization. Within the Yoruba system Olodumare, god, is not gendered, and in the Kikôngo creation narrative what brings earth into existence is Kalunga, an energy force that is similarly nongendered. Thus moving from neutered conceptualization to the engendering of Sacred praxis maps a complex journey from energy to embodiment constitutive of a masculinization of the social organization of the Sacred, but it need not carry the immediate presumption of women's subordination. Lorand Matory's work is most instructive here, for in it he elaborates how cross-dressing and gender-bending in Oyo-Yoruba practices in Nigeria muddy the categories of male and female, husband and wife, in ways that carve a space for dominance by women.[29] The Vodou god Gede, a preeminently masculine god, dances the balance among sexuality, trickery, and death by mounting Mammie with consistency at every fete, replete with oversized penis, re-enacting the sensuous rhythms of sex on women—lesbian and heterosexual alike. There are then at least two kinds of mounting taking place, a process of doubling that makes the question of gendered memory of Spirit appropriate for both the mounted and mountee (the same person) and the woman who rides the sexual advance of Gede. Short of us all becoming practitioners, the urgent requirement here is not to presume a priori how gender and sexuality work but to lean on ethnographic work to create the proximate categories that convey a sense of the meanings of these gender transmutations.[30] The problematic here pertains to how we approach knowing when much of the service of that knowing emanates from being.

All of these questions heighten the importance of traveling within, of reaching on the inside of these cultural spiritual categories. In order to do so there are at least four areas we must examine. First, the critiques of patriarchal religions and fundamentalisms have, in some instances, kept us away from the search for Spirit. We have conceded, albeit indirectly so, far too much ground for fundamentalists to appropriate the terrain. And yet, the Sacred or the spiritual cannot be deployed as the ace in the political hole, that is, deployed only as a critique of fundamentalism.

Second, our legitimate repudiation of the category of naturalization as an instrument of domination ought not to be confused with the engagement of the forces, processes, and laws of nature, particularly because these forces of nature do not behave according to the terms prescribed by hegemonic thought systems. It is one reason that capitalist imperatives would have them "tamed" and "owned," or otherwise reconfigured as (Christian) paradise in order to be secularly consumed. The animus and activities of nature and the hegemonic processes of naturalization that would have social inequity originate in the natural are, simply put, not the same.

Third, critiques of the shifting faces of hegemony do not automatically provide the maps for an inner life, for redefining the grammar of the mind, for adjusting the climate of the Soul (in the words of Howard Thurman). Those maps have to be drawn, and drawing them is crucial since one of the effects of constructing a life based principally in opposition is that the ego learns to become righteous in its hatred of injustice. In that very process it learns simultaneously how to hate since it is incapable of distinguishing between good hate and bad hate, between righteous hate and irrational hate. My point here is not to reduce radical political movements to mass psychologies of hatred. Rather it is to suggest that the field of oscillation between the two might be quite small. The good righteous hatred of injustice solidifies in the same way in which, for instance, we learn how to class by living in a class system. We learn how to hate in our hatred of injustice, and it is these psychic residuals that travel, sometimes silently, sometimes vociferously, into social movements that run aground on the invisible premises of scarcity—alterity driven by separation, empowerment driven by external loss—and of having to prove perpetual injury as the quid pro quo to secure ephemeral rights.

Fourth, secular feminism has perhaps assisted, unwittingly, in the privatization of the spiritual—in the dichotomization of a "private" spiritual self from the corpus of work called feminism and from organized political mobilizations. There are personal, political, and epistemic ramifications here. Consider again Renate Druiventak. At the outset of her field project, Wekker was "wary of Winti, hoping that [she] might study the construction of gender and sexualities without having to get into it," to separate life from what she then thought of as the superstructure religion. As the evidence began to pile up, however, and "women frequently attended WintiPrey/ritual gatherings and consulted religious specialists in matters of love, sickness, health, and prosperity," Wekker admits that "it became inescapable."[31] If political work among Afro-Surinamese working-class women is taken merely to illustrate that "Third World women have agency too"—in short, if we theorize outside of that which gave impetus to the political work in the first place—we would have missed something quite crucial about how Winti knitted together the interstices of selfhood and the relationship between that self and community. We would not know Druiventak, although we would know *something* of what she did—that is, political work. Clearly the "success" of the political party in the secular world is not the only important "outcome" of the life she lives. Ultimately, excising the spiritual from the political builds the ground at the intersection of two kinds of alienation: the one an alienation from the self; the other, which is inevitable, alienation from each other.

What would taking the Sacred seriously mean for transnational feminism and related radical projects, beyond an institutionalized use value of theorizing marginalization? It would mean wrestling with the praxis of the Sacred. The central understanding within an epistemology of the Sacred is that of a core/Spirit that is immortal, at once linked to the pulse and energy of creation. It is that living matter that links us to each other, making that which is individual simultaneously collective. But as I outlined in the previous chapter, its presence does not mean it is passively given or maintained. Of course, the idea of core or essence signals essentialism, but the multiple praxis of embodiment I have explored here indicate requirements for a work life beyond the mere presence of a body. In this sense it marks a major departure from normative essentialism.[32] Yet core, like destiny, has been made to signal fixity and the unchanging, a move that opens the back door to conflate the Sacred with a primitive tradition that is resistant to change. Those who would characterize this world of the postmodern and the identities of its inhabitants as absent of this essence or core would seem to be at odds with the thought systems of a great number of people in the world who live the belief that their lives are intimately and tangibly paired to the world of the invisible. And this state of being at odds is to be expected since Enlightenment reason and its attendant psychologies have only a relatively short lifespan, coming into prominence as one mode of reasoning that achieved dominance, like any other hegemonic system, by beating out others. And although its diffusion as it accompanied imperialism in its quest to be imperial has, for the moment, promulgated some of its own essence on different shores, it need not follow that these are the only beings who can be produced, since each thought system has in fact its own attendant psychology, code of behaviors, and its own prerogatives to deal with impermanence that is not imagined as a recent by-product of modernity but as a permanent condition of the universe. Taking the Sacred seriously would mean coming to wrestle with the dialectic of permanent impermanence.

The constructs that constitute the praxis of the Sacred would thus have to be taken as real and the belief structure of its practitioners as having effects that are real. The constituents within its ambit, such as Truth, cannot be superficially positioned as multiple choice, contested situational claims, or lapses in communication, but as metaphysical principle. The knowledge derived from faith and belief systems is not uninformed epiphenomena, lapses outside the bounds of rationality to be properly corrected with rationality, but rather knowledge about Sacred accompaniment, knowledge that is applied and lived in as consistent and as committed a way as possible so as to feel and observe the meaning of mystery, not as secret, but as elusive—hence the constancy of work. Faith could not then live without spiritual literacy or competence, a shade of competence that does not rely on the tired exertion of an individuated will but on the knowledge of Divine accompaniment and guidance, itself the essence of Truth. And grace, the quality that, as Lata Mani says, picks us up and dusts us off over and over again, instills a sense, however faint, of its companion humility, since it comes through no merit of our own.[33] But for these anchors of Sacred praxis to shake the archives of secularism, they would have to be removed from the category of false consciousness so that they can be accorded the real meaning they make in the lives of practitioners.

Taking the Sacred seriously would propel us to take the lives of primarily working-class women and men seriously, and it would move us away from theorizing primarily from the point of marginalization. In chapter 3 I argued against the analytic tendency of turning women's indispensability in the labor market into narratives of victimhood, but that formulation remained narrowly materialist. Since in spiritual work inheres the lived capacity to initiate and sustain communication between spiritual forces and human consciousness, to align the inner self, the behavioral self and the invisible, we are confronting an engagement with the embodied power of the Sacred, collectivized self-possession, if you will. We can hardly think *empowerment,* then, premised as it is in the notions of need, lack and scarce resources that have to be shored up by an exterior source, since it would mean conferring on "theorists" the power to confer power, a power, quite simply, that we do not have. At the very least it should make us wary about theorizing from the point of marginalization, for even the most egregious signatures of new empire are not the sole organizing nexus of subjectivity, if we manage to stay alive, and even in death there are commitments and choices about the when, how, and the kind of provisions with which we return.

Since the praxis of the Sacred involves the rewiring of the senses, the praxis for secular feminism would involve a rewiring of its most inherited concepts of home and formulations of domesticity, for instance. Home is multiply valenced, a space and place in which Time centers the movement of Sacred energies; a place where those who walk with you—Orisha, Lwa, Spirit—live and manifest (drop in) apparently impromptu, or when called to work. They are fed, celebrated, and honored there because they reside there. It is one of the many places where they reside, whereas it may be the only place that we reside. Home is a set of practices, as John Berger notes, and at the heart of those practices are those that mark its conversion into a spiritual workplace.[34]

Of immediate importance to feminism is the meaning of embodiment and body praxis, and the positioning of the body as a source of knowledge within terms differently modulated than the materiality of the body and its entanglement in the struggle against commodification, as it continues to be summoned in the service of capital. But here again that materialism has absented Spirit, and so the contemporaneous task of a theory of the flesh, with which I think Cherríe Moraga would agree, is to transmute this body and the pain of its dismemberment to a remembering of the body to its existential purpose.[35] There are Sacred means through which we come to be at home in the body that supercede its positioning in materiality, in any of the violent discourses of appropriation, and in any of the formations within normative multiculturalism. That being at home in the body is one of the meanings of surrender, as in a handing over not a sacrificial giving up. Bodies continue to participate in the social but their raison d'être does not belong there, for ultimately we are not our bodies, and this contract cannot be settled cheaply. Sacred energies would want us to relinquish the very categories constitutive of the material world, not in the requisite of a retreat but as a way to become more attuned to their ephemeral vagaries and the real limits of temporality so as to return to them with a disciplined freedom capable of renovating the collective terms of our engagement.

Kit*simba* walks with me. She lives in springs, in water—that is, everywhere. She carves resistant rock. She lives in the roots of words: *Simba,* to bless, to grow into the gentle vibrations of our names. *Simbi,* the Soul of someone who holds the power of making community. *Simbi,* teacher, the Soul of someone who holds the power of touch. *Simbi,* healer, the Soul of someone who holds the power of words . . . *Simba Simbi,* hold onto what holds you up.

Yemayá holds the crown, having enabled the Crossing, Kitsimba's as well as my own. She has assumed the task of transforming what we most need to learn from the Crossing into what we most need to learn about ourselves. Pedagogies of the Sacred are pedagogies of Crossing.

Seven: Prayer Poem in Praise of Yemayá Achaba, Mediator of the Crossing

Without you I would not know life
I would   not be
Myself/Yourself
In me/In you
Sin tú no hay vida
Mother/Teacher
I learn how to caress from the cadence of waves
Supple
Gentle
Tumultuous Enveloping

In the vastness of Ocean surrounded by your treasures
Which passion alone could not coax you to reveal
Inle
Wash me . . . mother of life
of water
One in the beginning when there was no beginning
No time
Take me to that underground home on top of the sand
To your mirror turquoise jade inlay
Known in the land of gods to shatter
Illusion, Maya
Peligrosísima
Take me
Desnuda
Without pretense
Sin nada
Rebirthed in the cadence of waves

The end of your name is illusion
In another tongue
But there are no other tongues
For those who know your many names
Ancient names

You know you who love the ends of things
Who use them to sustain you
So that nothing may come to an end
Ashé

In the last cycle of Moon
We come paying homage
Gifts of Seven
No one mistakes your calm for weakness
When you tumble foam
Spew turquoise rage
No room for calm
In those times it is not weakness for which
We yearn but peace
That truth which passion alone
Could not entice you to divulge

O Achaba, Peligrosísima
Haunting Sweet Verbena
Wise one
Hiding your age deep within the soft fold of waves
translucent
amongst your treasures rest the captive
shuffled through the door of no return
no longer imprisoned
You have restored their wings
Bathe me
Goddess of Salt
Protector of the salt eaters
The salt pickers
Heal our wounds
You who rescued Lot's wife
Tongue-tied
From the scourge of generations
As I approach you in the early dawn
Wind whispers its welcome to the melody
Of the salmon violet horn

Moon rests from its full bloom
You in honor assume a stillness
Draped smooth in seamless silk
Awaiting a lover's return
In this early dawn
We coauthor
this day
                            of endless transformations
I rest my pen upon your altar
my Soul[36]

Introduction

1 See al-Radi, *Baghdad Diaries,* 125, for the environmental effects of the war.

2 Ibid., 21.

3 Wackernagel and Rees, *Our Ecological Footprint.*

4 I am referring here to the Reconstruction Act of March 2, 1867, in which the U.S. Congress stipulated that the former confederate states would be divided into five military districts, each headed by a general.

5 Stout, "Bush Pushes Faith-Based Agenda," www.nytimes.com/2003/02/10.

6 See Silliman and Bhattacharjee, *Policing the National Body;* Davis, *Are Prisons Obsolete?;* and Sudbury, ed., *Global Lockdown.*

7 Pitt, "Blood Money."

8 Lamming, *The Pleasures of Exile,* 158.

9 Ibid.

10 Lewis, correspondence with author, 2004.

11 Freire, *Pedagogies of the Oppressed.*

12 Mani, *Interleaves.*

13 Allen, *Off the Reservation.*

14 I am borrowing here from Thích Nhât H'ahn, *Our Appointment with Life.*

15 Moraga and Anzaldúa, eds., *This Bridge Called My Back;* Lorde, *Sister Outsider;* Smith, ed., *Home Girls.*

16 Alexander and Mohanty, eds., *Feminist Genealogies,* xiv.

17 Langton, "Speech Acts and Unspeakable Acts."

18 Frymer and Skrentny, "The Rise of Instrumental Affirmative Action"; and Mohanty, "Affirmative Action in the Service of Empire."

19 Paquet, Foreword, *Pleasures of Exile*, x.

20 Lorde, "Age, Race, Sex and Class," in *Sister Outsider*.

21 Gibran, *The Prophet*.

22 Rich, *An Atlas*.

23 Thurman, *A Strange Freedom*.

24 Baldwin, "The Creative Dilemma."

25 Neruda, "Notes on a Splendid City."

1. Erotic Autonomy

1   DAWN was formed in 1986, and from the outset it operated as an autonomous women's organization. Beginning with a multifaceted feminist ideology, one of its first tasks was to challenge the state and organized medicine in 1989 on the introduction of Norplant. It has simultaneously politicized questions of women's history, cultural and artistic production, domestic violence, and violence against women.

2   Bethel, "And the Trees Still Stand," 44.

3   Formed in the first decade of the twentieth century, these were international organizations with headquarters in London and chapters in the British Commonwealth countries. The following is a description of the aims of the Imperial Order of Daughters of Empire: "In May 1902, the first meeting in the Bahamas of the IODE was held. Its aims are loyalty to Queen and Country; service to others, (particularly to Commonwealth servicemen and their survivors); the promotion of education, with an emphasis on history; and the preservation of its records to assist in the relief of those in poverty or distress" (see Craton, *A History of the Bahamas*, 110).

4   Willis Carey, "Suffragettes Placed Goal above Threats to Jobs and Careers," *Nassau Guardian*, 25 January 1988; Edda Dumont, "Franchise Has Not Solved All Women's Problems," *Nassau Guardian*, 19 November 1987; Sharon Poites, "When Women Won the Vote, Men Began Taking Notice," *Nassau Guardian*, 5 November, 1987.

5   Hart, *Fatal Women*, 7.

6   See for instance, Parker, *Nationalism and Sexuality*; Williams, *The Alchemy of Race and Rights*; Sangari and Vaid, *Recasting Women*; Grewal et al., *Charting the Journey*; Enloe, *Bananas, Beaches, and Bases*; Truong, *Sex, Money and Morality*; Reddock, *Women, Labor and Politics in Trinidad and Tobago*; and French and Cave, "Sexual Choice as Human Rights." See also the special issue of *Feminist Review*, "The New Politics of Sex and the State" (no. 48, autumn 1994).

7   Connell, *Gender and Power*; Foucault, *Discipline and Punish*, 125.

8   Hart, *Fatal Women*, 8.

9   Alexander, "Not Just (Any) Body Can Be a Citizen."

10 Repression of other kinds also exists. For example, there is a section in the general

orders that curtails political activity by public servants. The injunction reads as follows: "A public officer must, in no circumstances, become publicly involved in any political controversy, unless he becomes so involved through no fault of his own, for example, in the proper performance of his official duties; and he must have it in mind that publication either orally, or in writing of any material, whether of direct political interest, or relating to the administration of the Government, or of a Department of Government, or any matter relating to his official duties or other matters do not affect the public service." Commonwealth of the Bahamas, general orders, "Utterance on Political and Administrative Matters, Statement 932," 1982, Nassau, Government Printing Office. See also Commonwealth of the Bahamas, Sexual Offences and Domestic Violence Act, "An Act To Amend the Law Relating to Sexual Offences and to Make Provisions in Respect of Related Circumstances Involving Parties to a Marriage" (date of assent 29 July 1991), Nassau, Government Printing Office.

11   Craton, *A History of the Bahamas*, 112.

12   Goldberg, "Sodomy in the New World," 3–18. The move here is an important foundational one. Goldberg draws from a sixteenth-century document regarding Balboa's entry into a Panamanian village, in which he ordered the killing of about six hundred "sodomitic" Indians and fed another forty to the dogs. Goldberg argues that the gesture served to establish a link between heterosexual imperial interests and heterosexual "native" interests, suggesting that "native" heterosexuals had more in common with imperial heterosexuals than with "native" homosexuals.

13   Warner, *Fear of a Queer Planet*, 15.

14   The recodification of primogeniture here is somewhat paradoxical since from 1982 women's groups have influenced the state to erase it.

15   Evans, *Sexual Citizenship*; Barry and Wood, *The Other Side of Paradise*, 259. This fact was also expressed to me in an interview with Michael Stevenson, College of the Bahamas, June 1993.

16   Hart, *Fatal Women*, 5.

17   This is one area that has been remarkably undertheorized in the understanding of the American state: the extent to which an advanced capitalist state can be simultaneously nationalist, or even hypernationalist, intervening abroad while vigorously engaged in the redrawing of its own borders at home. Unfortunately, nationalism has come to be more easily associated with the neocolonial than with the neo-imperial. The specific reference here is to the California mobilization in 1995, Proposition 187, against undocumented workers, whom the U.S. state defines as "illegal aliens." The effect of this right-wing mobilization would have been to deny schooling, health care, and a range of social services to undocumented workers and their children.

18   Robson, *Lesbian (Out)Law*, 58.

19 The most significant gesture here is the convergence of right-wing mobilization inside the American state regarding family values and the deployment of foreign aid in its service. The United States Foreign Relations Committee has, for instance, formulated a policy that links the terms of foreign aid to the outlawing of abortions, while increasing sterilization programs in Third World countries. In other words, population control is being institutionalized at the expense of birth control.

20 Grewal and Kaplan, *Scattered Hegemonies.*

21 Halley, "The Construction of Heterosexuality." See also Thomas, "*Bowers v. Hardwick.*"

22 Edda Dumont, "Franchise Has Not Solved All Women's Problems" (interview with Lady Bruder), *Nassau Guardian,* 19 November 1987.

23 There is a plethora of women's organizations that range from Girl Guides and trade unions to business and professional women's organizations and feminist groups. A listing compiled by the Women's Desk reveals that there are approximately sixty-seven women's organizations (Women's Affairs Unit, *Directory of Women's Groups,* Nassau, Government Printing Office, 1991).

24 The Women's Desk, established in 1981, was upgraded in 1987 to the Women's Affairs Unit, but it is still located within the Ministry of Youth, Sports, and Community Development. It has been consistently plagued by a lack of funds. Constraints faced in 1993 included the following: inadequate funds for execution of program activities; lack of trained staff; inability to meet the demands of the public; no approved national policy on women; and generally unclear status (Women's Desk, internal memorandum, 1989). See also Roberts, "The Changing Role of Women's Bureaux in the Process of Social Change in the Caribbean."

25 Sandra Dean Patterson, director of the Women's Crisis Center, interview by author, June 1993; Sharon Claire and Camille Barnett, College of the Bahamas, interview by author, June 1993. Interviews were conducted with Linda Carty.

26 Marion Bethel, Michael Stevenson, Sexual Offences Unit, Criminal Investigation Division, Bahamas, interviews by author, June 1993.

27 The following list of articles provides an indication of the kind of sensationalism generated in the media: "Sixteen-Year-Old School Girl Mother—Teenage Mothering Is No Fun," *Tribune,* 22 March 1986; "Thirteen-Year-Old Girls Sexually Molested by a Knife-Wielding Man," *Tribune,* 26 July 1986; "False Cry of Rape Puts Lady Accountant in Jail," *Tribune,* 18 September 1986; "Visitor Is Raped at Gunpoint at Paradise Beach," *Tribune,* 8 October 1986. Related information provided by Sears and Bethel, interview.

28 Sears and Bethel, interview. Almost all Commonwealth Carribean countries have passed some type of domestic violence or sexual offences legislation. The countries are as follows:

    Domestic Violence legislation: Domestic Violence (Summary Proceedings)

Act 1999 (Antigua and Barbuda); Sexual Offences and Domestic Violence Act 1991 (Bahamas); Domestic Violence (Protection Orders) Act, 1992, Cap 130A (Barbados); Domestic Violence Act 1992 (Belize); Domestic Violence Act 1997 (Bermuda); Domestic Violence (Summary Proceedings) Act 1992 (British Virgin Islands); Summary Jurisdiction (Domestic Violence) Law 1992 (Cayman Islands); Domestic Violence Act 2001 (Dominica); Domestic Violence Act 2001 (Grenada); Domestic Violence Act 1996 (Guyana); Domestic Violence Act 1995 (Jamaica); Domestic Violence Act 2000 (St. Kitts-Nevis); Domestic Violence (Summary Proceedings) Act 1995 (St. Lucia); Domestic Violence and Matrimonial (Proceedings) Act 1984, Domestic Violence (Summary Proceedings) Act 1995 (St. Vincent and the Grenadines); Domestic Violence Act 1999 (Trinidad and Tobago).

Sexual Offences Legislation: Sexual Offences Act 1995 (Antigua and Barbuda); Sexual Offences and Domestic Violence Act 1991 (Bahamas); Sexual Offences Act 1992, Cap 154 (Barbados); Criminal Code (Amendment) Act 1999 (Belize); Sexual Offences Act 1998 (Dominica); Sexual Offences and Domestic Violence Act 1991 (Bahamas); Sexual Offences Act 1998 (Dominica); Sexual Offences Act 1986, Amendment Act 2000 (Trinidad and Tobago). I thank Tracy Robinson for compiling this exhaustive listing.

29 See Commonwealth of the Bahamas, General Laws, "Personal Rights Arising from Marriage and Proprietary Rights During Marriage," part 3, subsection 2, relating to the rights of consortium and the duty of the wife to cohabit with her husband. It states: "It is the duty of the wife to reside and cohabit with her husband." There is no such requirement specified for a husband.

30 "DAWN Galvanizes Resources to Address Issues Arising from Sex Violence Bill," *Nassau Guardian,* 25 November 1989.

31 Therese Huggins, member of DAWN, interview by author, Bahamas, June 1993.

32 The link between domestic sexual violence and state economic violence has been made by CAFRA, the Caribbean Association for Feminist Research and Action, and by Sistren, a women's collaborative theater group. See, for example, the article "Women and Sexuality," in *CAFRA News* 8, nos. 1–2 (January–June 1994). See also Sistren, with Ford-Smith, *Lionheart Gal.*

33 Commonwealth of the Bahamas, Sexual Offences and Domestic Violence Act, 1991, emphasis added.

34 "Women's Crisis Week," *Nassau Guardian,* 29 September 1989; "MPs Passed the Sexual Offences Bill to Provide Greater Protection for Women on the Job," *Tribune,* 17 May 1991; Mondésire and Dunn, "Towards Equity in Development," 50.

35 Commonwealth of the Bahamas, Sexual Offences and Domestic Violence Act, 3.

36 Marion Bethel, attorney general's office, interview by author, Nassau, June 1993. For the question of rethinking issues of coverture in relation to domestic violence in the United States, see Marcus, "Thinking and Teaching about Terrorism in the Home."

37 Miller, *Family Property and Financial Provision,* 1–14.

38 Commonwealth of the Bahamas, Sexual Offences and Domestic Violence Act, 18–19.

39 Commonwealth of the Bahamas, "Family Law Provisions, Miscellaneous Amendments," no. 17, 1988, 851.

40 Miller, *Family Property and Financial Provision.*

41 Commonwealth of the Bahamas, Department of Statistics, "Labor Force and Household Income Report, 1989," Nassau, Government Printing Office, xii.

42 Ibid., x.

43 Bahamas Federation of Labor, "Salaries and Allowances for Cabinet Ministers," 1992, Nassau, Government Printing Office.

44 The point is excellently explicated by Williams, *The Alchemy of Race and Rights;* and Williams, "Attack of the 50-Foot First Lady."

45 Bahamas Department of Statistics, "Labor Force and Household Income Report, 1989," xvi.

46 Andrew Stuart, "Women Made up 60.5 Percent of Unemployed in 1989, Party Told," *Nassau Guardian,* 23 October 1989. See also Bahamas Department of Statistics, "Labor Force and Household Income Report," xiv–xv.

47 "Legislation for Women," *Nassau Guardian,* 20 November 1987.

48 Stevenson, interview. Haitians occupy a marginalized status in spite of their work and the fact that they have lived for several generations in the Bahamas. The conflation of the Haitian body with the AIDS-infected body has served to further make Haitians the object of state surveillance and repression and of misguided popular disaffection.

49 Claire and Barnett, interview.

50 Bahamas Department of Statistics, Vital Statistics Section, "Legitimate and Illegitimate Live Births, All Bahamas: 1970–2000."

51 This gesture of gender parity was first made explicit by women, endorsed by Myrtle Brandt, the principal drafter for the Sexual Offences and Domestic Violence Act, then enthusiastically endorsed by the state.

52 Mun Wong, City University of New York, conversation with author, May 1995.

53 The strictures of these surveillance mechanisms had already become clear to women and to women's groups and social service agencies almost immediately after the passage of the act. Ruth Bowe-Darville, Sandra Dean Patterson, and Zonta, interviews by author, June 1993.

54 Commonwealth of the Bahamas, Sexual Offences and Domestic Violence Act.

55 All of the quotes that follow are taken verbatim from tape recordings made during parliamentary hearings. At the time of my research in June 1993, four years after the debates, the testimonies, except for the then-opposition's statements, had not been transcribed. Thus we had access to information not yet known to many Bahamians.

56 Letter from Hunster to British Colonial Secretary, Trinidad and Tobago, 1804. British Museum Library, London.

57 Du Bois, *The Souls of Black Folk.*

58 Craton, *A History of the Bahamas*, 280–304; Saunders, *Slavery in the Bahamas*. See also Nandy, *The Intimate Enemy;* and Nandy, *Traditions, Tyranny and Utopias.*

59 All of these terms refer to women loving women, but there are nuances to which we need to pay attention that are illustrative of heterogeneity in the seemingly homogeneous category of lesbian. Mati is the Surinamese Creole word for friends of either gender. Mati work is an institution with its own rules and rituals in which Creole women openly engage in sexual relations with men and women simultaneously or consecutively. It is a behavior, not an identity and should not be configured as bisexuality. Wekker, "One finger does not drink Okra Soup," 336–338. Zami is the Carriacou name for women who are friends and lovers. The term kachapera is historically situated in Curaçao, while manroyals can be read as lesbian but carries a connotation of cross-gender mixture in Jamaica. Manroyal suggests a kind of third space, which might have a nuanced association with the designation butch. I thank Honor Ford Smith for this latter insight. See, for instance, Wekker, " 'I Am a Gold Coin (I Pass through All Hands, But I Do Not Lose My Value)' "; Clemencia, "Women Who Love Women"; Silvera, "Man Royals and Sodomites"; Lorde, *Zami*; and Brand, *Sans Souci.*

60 Hart, *Fatal Women*, 11.

61 The moment of transition from colonial rule to independence, symbolized by the new nation's flag, is being contested here. The point is that flag independence belies the significant ways in which foreign, imperial interests are still folded into those of the nation. While in the field, we first heard of the specter of a band of nationless men from some policemen after an interview at the Criminal Investigation Division. We found the image quite pervasive, and it was later corroborated by other interviewees.

62 Sears and Bethel, interview. See also Craton, *A History of the Bahamas*; Fawkes, *The Faith That Moved the Mountain*; and Johnson, *The Quiet Revolution in the Bahamas.*

63 Bethel, "Where Do We Go From Here?"; Saunders, "Women in the Bahamian Society and Economy in the Late Nineteenth and Early Twentieth Centuries."

64 Barthes, *Mythologies*, 109–58.

65 Evans, *Sexual Citizenship.*

66 The state, nonetheless, has to be careful of not entirely usurping the church's own divine mission of salvation. It must, therefore, legislate against these passions, these sins of the flesh, as a restorative gesture.

67 Evans, *Sexual Citizenship*, 111.

68 Pratt, *Imperial Eyes.*

69 The quotes here are pulled from the series of throne speeches printed in the

Nassau Guardian over the period from 1967 to 1992. These discussions are conducted in a way that suggests that Bahamians are not in need of an infrastructure.

70   "Rotarians Use Bumper Stickers to Highlight Tourism Campaign," *Nassau Guardian,* 20 August 1991.

71   *Bahamas Tourist Statistics,* 1990. Government of Bahamas Printing Office.

72   "Business Slump in Freeport Caused by Rudeness," *Guardian,* 6 October 1992.

73   Craton, *A History of the Bahamas,* 253.

74   Bahamas Ministry of Tourism, "The Bahamas: 1991 Guide to Cruising, Fishing, Marinas and Resorts," Nassau.

75   Hemingway, *Islands in the Stream;* Meyers, *Hemingway;* Baker, *Ernest Hemingway.*

76   Morrison, *Playing in the Dark,* 12.

77   Ibid., 10.

78   Barry and Wood, *The Other Side of Paradise,* 259; Deere, *In the Shadow of the Sun,* 125.

79   Barry and Wood, *The Other Side of Paradise,* 256.

80   Mercer, "Black Identity/Queer Identity."

81   Kincaid, *A Small Place.*

82   Evans, *Sexual Citizenship.*

83   There was apparently an opening for gay transvestite cultural expression in the mid to late 1970s that has since been foreclosed in this period of the commodification and fetishization of culture.

84   hooks, *Black Looks,* 21–27.

85   Bahamian law conforms to the Westminster model of British governance, with a balance among the legislative, judiciary, and executive branches and the charge to the legislature to "make laws for the peace, order and good government of the state." Moreover, British common law has been in full force since 1799, and laws relating to marriage are encoded in the Marriage Act of 1924. It still remains the case that changes made in metropolitan codes may not necessarily be enacted in former colonies. See Hall, "The Legal System of the Bahamas and the Role of the Attorney General"; see also Knowles, *Elements of Bahamian Law.*

2. Imperial Desire/Sexual Utopias

1   See, in particular, Alexander, "Not Just (Any) *Body* Can be a Citizen," 5–23. For a discussion of the operation of black capitalism, see Frazier, *Black Bourgeoisie.*

2   See Kempadoo, *Sun, Sex and Gold.*

3   Selvadurai, *Funny Boy,* 162–67.

4   See Morrison, *Playing in the Dark* (notably the chapter "Disturbing Nurses and the Kindness of Sharks") for an analysis of Hemingway's *To Have and Have Not* and *The Garden of Eden,* and for an incisive illustration of what she calls "American Africanism."

5   As demonstrated in the previous chapter, this incursion of the hegemonic into the oppositional can be found in neocolonial structures as well.

6   Gluckman and Reed offered one of the earliest analyses critical of the terms of this discursive formation. Their essay, "The Gay Marketing Moment," first appeared in *Dollars and Sense*, 16–19. See also Gluckman and Reed, eds., *Homo Economics*, xii.

7   Chasin, *Selling Out*. See also Urvashi Vaid, *Virtual Equality*.

8   Reed Abelson, "Welcome Mat Is Out for Gay Investors—They Have Cash, and Distinct Needs," *New York Times*, 1 September 1996, 1, 7.

9   As the irony of heterosexism would have it, the thoroughly heterosexualized masculine Marlboro man died of AIDS early in the life of the epidemic.

10 Karen Stabiner, "Tapping the Homosexual Market," *New York Times Magazine*, 2 May 1992, 34–35, 74.

11 This citation comes from a discussion about homoeconomics that appeared in Witt, Thomas, and Marcus, eds., *Out in All Directions*, 574–75. For an excellent discussion of the biased assumptions embedded in these data, see Badgett, "Beyond Biased Samples," 65–72.

12 Pritchard et al., "Reaching Out to the Gay Tourist," *Tourism Management*, 273–82. These statistics pertain specifically to travelers.

13 These data were prepared by Affluent Marketers Alert. There is, as well, a significant growth of these instruments of the information industry. They come from both gay and heterosexual marketers, including the Strub Media Group, Simmons Market Research Bureau, Overlooked Opinions, and others.

14 Pritchard, "Reaching Out to the Gay Tourist," 274.

15 Meyers, who manages the Meyers Sheppard Pride Fund, seeks companies whose portfolio of stocks return a good investment. She defines "gay friendly" as those corporations who are explicit in antidiscriminatory language against sexual orientation and those with health and other benefits for same-sex partners.

16 Lukenbill, *Untold Millions*; Reed Abelson, "Gay Friendly Fund Has Blue Chip Focus," *New York Times*, 1 September 1996, 7.

17 Kates, *Twenty-Million New Customers!*

18 Lukenbill, *Smart Spending*.

19 There are some in the lesbian and gay community who believe that heterosexism has necessitated these services and that viatics are in some instances underdeveloped. See Stone, "AIDS and the Moral Economy of Insurance."

20 *Windy City Times*, October 31, 1996, 61.

21 See Reed Abelson, "Gay Friendly Fund Has Blue Chip Focus," 7.

22 Davis, *Blues Legacies and Black Feminism*.

23 Baker, "A History in Ads," 112–24.

24 The Disney/Haiti Justice Campaign, "Fact Sheet Update," 12 November 1996. For a discussion of the challenges of the union-based gay rights movement, see Moir,

"Laboring for Gay Rights: An Interview with Susan Moir," 72–79. For an analysis of the role of the Disney Corporation in the sanitization of Times Square, see Delany, *Times Square Red.*

25 Gluckman and Reid, *Homo Economics,* xix.

26 See the excellent discussion in Clark, "Commodity Lesbianism," and also Jasbir Puar, "A Transnational Feminist Critique of Queer Tourism."

27 D'Emilio, "Capitalism and Gay Identity," 144.

28 I am leaning here on Morrison's notion of taint and stain; see the essay "Friday on the Potomac," in her *Race-ing Justice,* vii–xxx (especially xvi–xviii).

29 Clark, "Commodity Lesbianism," 199. See Puar for a discussion of lesbian tourism. Ibid., 937–39.

30 Witt, *Out in All Directions,* 45–46; 52–63. Marquis, "On Board w/ Outboard," *Vail Daily:* www.vaildaily.com. Accessed April 21, 2005.

31 At the time of this research, membership and financial information about IGTA was closed to members only. Lesbian became part of the title in 1997. The IGLTA's membership information is still restricted to members only.

32 For this research I first compared guides such as *Damron's Address Book* with the *Spartacus Guide,* before focusing on *The Spartacus International Gay Guides* from 1987 to 1996, and 1997 to 2004. See also, *Damron's Address Book: Canada.*

33 *The Spartacus International Gay Guide,* 1996–1997, 151.

34 Ibid., 141.

35 Ibid., 532.

36 I thank Silvia Panzironi for this point.

37 *The Spartacus International Gay Guide,* 1988, 129.

38 This construction of a pristine natural is not a neutral undertaking. According to Silvia Panzironi, "tour operators have to render their products attractive to Western consumers. Their marketing strategy emphasizes the quality and quantity of services, but especially in the case of tourist locations, which do not have much 'cultural' attractions (like ruins, temples, and the like) they must treat the location as a paradisiacal neutral/natural frame in which context the consumption of tourist services takes place. For example, sanitary information is rarely to be found in tour operators' brochures. It would be compromising to address the presence of parasites or simply insects to which urban people are presumably unaccustomed. Paradise must be paradoxically sold as quintessentially natural." Personal communication with author, August 2004. Thanks to Silvia Panzironi for these insights based on her former work as a tour operator in Italy and research she undertook to update this chapter.

39 *The Spartacus International Gay Guide,* 1988, 132.

40 I have been influenced here by three related analyses: Evans, *Sexual Citizenship,* 89–116; Bernard, "The 'Men of South Africa II' "; and hooks, "Eating the Other," *Black Looks,* 21–39.

41 *The Spartacus International Gay Guide*, 1996–1997, 98.

42 *The Spartacus International Gay Guide*, 1988, 129–30.

43 Ibid., 43. The significant difference between *Damron's* and *Spartacus* is that *Damron's* has (an admittedly extensive) listing of hotels, gyms, and the like, whereas *Spartacus* features extensive political commentary pertaining to the destinations of travel. The massacres in Rwanda occurred in 1994. The 2004 film *Hotel Rwanda* tells a wrenching story of that massacre.

44 Boone, *Vacation Cruises*, 100.

45 Boone, *Vacation Cruises*; see also Manderson and Jolly, *Sites of Desire*.

46 Shohat, *Talking Visions*, 52. There is an extensive literature on homosexual orientalism. Thailand stands out because of its role in the excessive ideological production of Asia and the fact that the cultural and sexual practices of men are highly regarded in the erotic geography of white gay tourism. See Truong, *Sex, Money and Morality*, for a careful argument on the institutionalization of exploitative sexual practices in Thailand and the ways in which the Thai state benefits disproportionately from the money made in prostitution.

47 Quoted in *J-Flag*, September 1999, 105.

48 Manalansan, *Global Divas*, 85.

49 Ibid., 86, 143.

50 Ibid., 19.

51 Shohat, *Talking Visions*.

52 According to its mission statement, "The Audre Lorde Project is a Lesbian, Gay, Bisexual, Two-Spirit, and Transgender People of Color center for community organizing, focusing on the New York City area. Through mobilization, education, and capacity-building," the project's work focuses on "community wellness and progressive social and economic justice. Committed to struggling across differences, [it] seeks to responsibly reflect, represent, and serve various communities." It is one of the few national organizations that has consistently made immigration and nationality a focus of LGBTT political organizing.

3. Whose New World Order?

1 Morrison, *Playing in the Dark*, 3.

2 Louie, "La Mujer Luchando," 63.

3 Quoted in Grossberg, "History, Politics and Postmodernism," 158. See also Grossberg's discussion of Hall's reformulation of Gramscian hegemony from Gramsci's *Selections from the Prison Notebooks*, 244–45.

4 "Destiny in Air, Leaders Arrive for Summit," *New York Times*, 1 December 1989, A1, 7–8.

5 Enloe, *The Morning After*, 195.

6   David Broder, "New World Order Galloping into Position," *Washington Post*, 20 December 1989, 1, 9.

7   Marshall Ingwerson, "Out of Troubled Times, A New World Order," *Christian Science Monitor*, 12 November 1990, A1, 5–6.

8   Enloe, *The Morning After*, 192; Said, *Orientalism*, 3; Lewis, *Gendering Orientalism*.

9   Hatem, "The Invisible Half: Arab American Hybridity and Feminist Discourses in the 1990s," 370–73.

10   Jakobsen, "Tolerating Hate? Or Hating Intolerance."

11   Hatem, "The Invisible Half," 373.

12   Enloe, *The Morning After*, 175–85.

13   Ibid., 202.

14   Ibid., 197. See also Okazawa-Rey, "Warring on Women."

15   Laclau, *Politics and Ideology in Marxist Theory*, 161.

16   Evans, *Sexual Citizenship*, 61.

17   Enloe, *The Morning After*.

18   Evans, *Sexual Citizenship*, 5.

19   See Ammott and Matthaei, *Race, Gender and Work*, 316–17; Mollenkopf and Castells, *Dual City*; Massey and Denton, *American Apartheid*; Sassen, *Globalization and Its Discontents*.

20   Nakano-Glenn, "From Servitude to Service Work"; Chang, *Disposable Domestics*. Both authors consider domestic work to be the work of social reproduction from which both the state and individual households (both wealthy and middle class) divest themselves. Nakano-Glenn argues that African American women, who worked in large numbers as domestics, enabled the privilege of well-to-do white women and men. In this current round of globalization, immigrant women have replaced African American women as domestics. There is also another element of privatization reflected in the demise of public health and the diffusion of a theory of disease etiology, which has privileged individual factors above environmental ones.

21   I am drawing on a range of research to make these arguments: see, notably, McAfee, *Storm Signals*, 36–40, which paved the way for a series of later research efforts on the shape and impact of structural adjustment policies in the Caribbean region. The work of Fernandez-Kelley and Nash was similarly influential, see their *Women, Men and the International Division of Labor*. Other work I drew on includes Mohanty, "Women Workers and Capitalist Scripts," and also the special issue of *Caribbean Perspectives* titled "NAFTA and the Caribbean."

22   See Chang, *Disposable Domestics*, 23–32; and Barndt, "Whose 'Choice'?" in her *Women Working the NAFTA Food Chain*. The term NAFTA refers to the North American Free Trade Agreement between the United States and Mexico that was instituted in 1994. Its policies of liberalizing trade and devaluing currency resem-

ble those enacted under structural adjustment programs elsewhere. Under NAFTA, the United States had a trade deficit with Mexico of over $15 billion in 1995, only one year after the start of the program. Testimony of Lori Wallach, May 1997, 1.

23   Rich, "Notes Toward a Politics of Location," 210–33.

24   National Labor Committee, *The U.S. in Haiti*; Kempadoo, "Women of Color and the Global Sex Trade"; Barndt, "Whose 'Choice'?" 70–75.

25   Sassen, *Globalization and Its Discontents*, 81–111.

26   Mohanty, "Women Workers and Capitalist Scripts," 3–29.

27   Sassen, *Globalization and Its Discontents*, 84; Barndt, "Whose 'Choice'?" 53–55.

28   Louie, *Sweatshop Warriors,* documents the existence of a large number of women's organizations, some that are union-based and others that are autonomous. Among the organizations are La Mujer Obrera (the Woman Worker) in El Paso, Texas; Fuerza Unida (United Force) in San Antonio, Texas; and the Thai and Latino Workers Organizing Committee of Los Angeles.

29   Rowbotham and Mitter, *Dignity and Daily Bread* (the title of which draws its name from women organizing in Gujarat, India); Louie, "La Mujer Luchando," 67.

30   Thompson and Tyagi, *Beyond a Dream Deferred,* xvi.

31   See Kelley, "The Proletariat Goes to College," 146; and the special issue of *Social Text* titled "Academic Labor."

32   Freire, *Pedagogy of the Oppressed,* 52–57.

33   Trumpbour, *How Harvard Rules,* 52; see also Shohat, *Talking Visions,* 34–46.

34   Mohanty, "Under Western Eyes"; Lazreg, "Feminism and Difference." Ella Shohat's "Area Studies, Transnationalism, and the Feminist Production of Knowledge" takes up these very questions.

35   Stuart Hall, "Cultural Studies."

36   Césaire, *Discourse on Colonialism,* 32.

37   Kincaid, *A Small Place,* 18–19.

38   Lazreg, "Feminism and Difference." See also Najmabadi's "(Un)Veiling Feminism," which makes a very interesting argument about the ways in which feminism does "veiling work" in that it acts as a boundary marker for secularism within Iranian modernity.

39   Parker, "Sunday," 56–57.

40   National Labor Committee, *Help End the Race to the Bottom*. The National Labor Committee is one of several community- and church-based groups that have aligned with students at more than a dozen campuses around the country to press for corporate accountability.

41   Evans, *Sexual Citizenship,* 5.

42   Morrison, *Lecture and Speech of Acceptance, upon the Award of the Nobel Prize for Literature.*

43 Foundation for Inner Peace, *A Course in Miracles*, 180.

44 Lorde, *The Marvelous Arithmetics of Distance*, back cover copy (written by Lorde).

4. Anatomy of a Mobilization

1 The Mobilization for Real Diversity, Democracy and Economic Justice, letter to President Jonathan Fanton, 2 February 1997. The vision of the Mobilization moved beyond definitions of redistributive justice. For the limits of the redistributive paradigm, see Young, *Justice and the Politics of Difference*, 15–38.

2 Wolfe-Rocca, Brignolo-Giménez, and Aucott, "The Politics of Education," 2–12. In this part of the essay, the authors engage the shifting meanings of "tradition" over time.

3 Krohn, *Intellectuals in Exile*, 5–16, 65–79.

4 See Said, *Culture and Imperialism*, 330, on the contradictions of providing educational leadership according to the terms of managing the nation-state.

5 New School for Social Research, "Status Report of the University Diversity Initiative," 1996, section 2, "Managing Diversity."

6 The entire summer 1997 issue of *Social Text* is devoted to academic labor (see, especially, Martin, "Academic Labor," 1–8. See also Nelson, ed., *Will Teach for Food*, which was prompted by the organizing efforts of teaching assistants at Yale University. Tuition increases and budgetary cutbacks at the School were the focus of many student newsletters. See, for instance, Lillian McMaster, "Where Has All the Money Gone?" *Newsletter of the Students of the Graduate Faculty*, April 1996, 11–13.

7 Gordon and Newfield, *Mapping Multiculturalism*; Bell, *Confronting Authority*; Lim Geok-Lin and Herrera-Sobek, *Power, Race and Gender in Academe*; Painter, "Black Studies, Black Professors, and the Struggle of Perception," *Chronicle of Higher Education*, 15 December 2000, B7–9.

8 Fish, *There's No Such Thing As Free Speech*, 113.

9 Morrison, *The Bluest Eye*, 206–9.

10 Carbado and Gulati, "Working Identity," 1279; Carbado and Gulati, "Conversations at Work," 103–46.

11 Walker, "Rights to Truth."

12 It is worth noting that militarization in the United States has never resulted in the formation of truth commissions. See Haynor, *Unspeakable Truths*.

13 Langton, "Speech Acts and Unspeakable Acts." See also MacKinnon, *Only Words*.

14 Langton, "Speech Acts and Unspeakable Acts," 299.

15 Ibid., 304, 299–305.

16 Morrison, "Unspeakable Things Unspoken"; Morrison, *Race-ing Justice*.

17 Habermas, *The Theory of Communicative Action*, 288–91.

18 In "Speech Acts and Unspeakable Acts" (315), Langton is theorizing in the spaces

Habermas left open. For applications of Habermas, see Panjabi, "Probing 'Morality' and State Justice"; and Jakobsen, "World Secularisms at the Millennium." See Young, *Justice and the Politics of Difference*, 30–38, for a discussion of both the limits and usefulness of Habermas.

19 Lorde, "The Transformation of Silence into Language and Action," *Sister Outsider*, 40.

20 *Newsletter of the Students of the Graduate Faculty*, November 1993, 3–4.

21 President Jonathan Fanton, memorandum to the New School community, 24 October 1996.

22 In both a metaphoric and practical sense, the Mobilization built on the earlier student movement of the 1960s and 1970s, members of which supported the 1996 struggle in several ways. At the launch of the New University in Exile, they brought the coffin they had built to signal the end of progressivism at the School in the 1970s.

23 Shohat, *Talking Visions*, 16.

24 West, "The New Cultural Politics of Difference," 33.

25 Dean Judith Friedlander, letter of welcome to students of the Graduate Faculty, 15 August 1995.

26 The New University in Exile, invoking the legacy of the GF's founding as the University in Exile, was a symbolic and actual project of the Mobilization aimed at connecting the historic and the contemporary legacies of exile. In taking over the lobby of the building that housed the GF, students created an alternative educational space, a liberated zone of sorts, where classes were held and guest speakers were invited, and which functioned as a meeting ground and central space for the Mobilization and its allies in spring 1997.

27 New School for Social Research, "University-wide Affirmative Action Data by Employee Type," fall 1996.

28 New School for Social Research, "A Handbook for Students of Color and Students Interested in Race, Ethnicity and Identity at the Graduate Faculty," 1996.

29 All references pertain to the "Affirmative Action Concept Paper," New School for Social Research, 1996.

30 Leslie Hill, letter to Dean Judith Friedlander, 27 March 1997; Hill, memorandum to members of the University Diversity Committee, 16 April 1997. Hill notes that she received two contradictory responses to her letter from Dean Friedlander: one handwritten, dated 28 March 1997, in which the dean thanked her for "such a thoughtful letter," the other typewritten, dated, 24 June 1997, in which the dean expressed her "quandary as to how to answer [Hill's] severe criticisms of the University's creation and management of the Diamond Post Doctoral Fellows program." Correspondence with author, 3 May 2005.

31 Stephanie Morgan, letter to President Jonathan Fanton, 16 December 1996.

32 Letter from bell hooks to END, 16 December 1996. This was among numerous

letters of support, both national and international, that addressed the national crisis and reinforced the links made by the Mobilization.

33 President Jonathan Fanton, "Memorandum to the University Community," 24 October 1996.

34 Fish, *There's No Such Thing As Free Speech*, 250.

35 "Court Finds New School Guilty of Gender Discrimination, Gender-Based Pay Gap at GF," *Newsletter of Students of the Graduate Faculty*, February 1996, 1, 9–10.

36 Eugene Lang College students, "Statement to the University Diversity Committee," read by Joe Townsend, 9 May 1996.

37 Statement by END at forum: "Faculty of Color Declare a State of Emergency," New School, 17 December 1996.

38 Young, *Justice and the Politics of Difference*, 35.

39 The Mobilization, "Know the Facts," 1 May 1997.

40 Steve Caton, Victoria Hattam, Rayna Rapp, M. Jacqui Alexander, Jerma Jackson, Gary Lemons, and Don Scott, "Rethinking Europe in a Global Context: A Proposal for Diversifying the Graduate Faculty within an Intellectual Program of Study," September 1997.

41 Richard Bernstein, memorandum to Rayna Rapp, 20 September 1996.

42 Student Mobilization Log, spring 1997; Schneider, "A Haven for Oppressed Scholars Finds Itself Accused of Oppression," *Chronicle of Higher Education*, 11 July 1997, A8–10.

43 First-year Graduate Faculty philosophy student, open letter, 4 April 1997.

44 Co-chair, Sub-committee on Curriculum, Gender Studies and Feminist Theory, letter to GSFT, 29 May 1998.

45 All quotes are from the Mobilization's letter to President Fanton, 2 February 1997.

46 President Jonathan Fanton, "Memorandum to the University Community," 3 February 1997.

47 The deflection strategy continued to exert a great deal of power, though not uncontested power, and gained a great deal of force in the forum of 6 May 1997, which I discuss later.

48 Schneider, "A Haven for Oppressed Scholars," *Chronicle of Higher Education* 43, no. 44 (1997): A8–11; *Lingua Franca*, August 1997, 34–43. There is a marked difference between these media and others, such as *In These Times*, which situated the hunger strike within similar student mobilizations at Columbia University and the University of California, Berkeley. See Chris Seymour, "Old Conflict, New School," *In These Times* 21, no. 3 (1997): 6–9.

49 New School for Social Research, "An Alternative," April 1997. There were eighty-six signatories to "An Alternative," including seventy-seven students and nine faculty members. The faculty signatures came from the chair of the Department of Philosophy, the chair of the Committee on Liberal Studies, the director of the

Center for Immigration Studies, members of the Department of Sociology and the Department of Political Science.

50   Ibid.

51   James Miller, "Remarks at the Open Forum on Diversity and Democracy," 6 May 1997.

52   Hall, "Cultural Studies and the Politics of Internationalization," 402–3.

53   Dean Judith Friedlander, letter to students, 21 January 1997.

54   "Advice to Graduates: Improve Society," *The New School Observer*, 1997, 1, 3.

55   Kimbwandende Kia Bunseki Fu-Kiau, "The Secret Power of *Mambu*, Words: The Essence of Kongo Ways of Life." Paper presented at the New York Open Center, New York, September 2003. The etymology of the term "mumbo jumbo" is quite torturous. According to Bunseki Fu-Kiau, it comes from *Diambu/Mambu*, a Kôngo word that means: word, issue, problem; action, reason, or topic. It also means to listen, to be able to listen, or to be listened to; a bundle (code) of what exits through the mouth, from within us, and re-renters us through the ears. Through enslavement of many Africans who were involuntarily lifted from the Kongo kingdom area, however, "this word Diambu/Mambu became diambo (djambo)/mambo and gave birth to '*Mambo djambo*,' an expression of total unintelligibility in the New World."

56   See challenges to Schneider's formulations: "Activist Protests at the New School," *Chronicle of Higher Education*, 12 September, 1997, B10. See also the response signed by a group of thirty-eight faculty and independent scholars from the United States and Canada who had to take "the unusual step of paying for space in the *Chronicle*," because of the paper's refusal to print their response. See "Advertisement," *Chronicle of Higher Education*, 31 October 1997, A31.

57   Rayna Rapp, meeting of the GSFT, March 1997.

58   Moya, "Postmodernism, 'Realism,' and the Politics of Identity," 140.

59   Cited in Chavez-Silverman, "Tropicalizing the Liberal Arts College Classroom," 132.

60   Moraga and Anzaldúa, *This Bridge Called My Back,* ix.

61   Ibid., 150.

62   Statement of Rayna Rapp, meeting of GSFT, April 1997. Emphasis added.

63   Statement of Rayna Rapp, meeting of GSFT, October 1994.

64   Kevin Plumberg, "The Gender Effect: Making a Little Noise at the GF," *Newsletter of Students of the Graduate Faculty,* winter 2001, 1, 2–3.

65   Said, *Culture and Imperialism,* 229–30.

66   Wolfe-Rocca, Brignolo-Giménez, and Aucott, "The Politics of Education," 15.

67   The quotes in this paragraph and in the one following are woven together from speeches given at various events of the Mobilization: "A Day of Struggle and Celebration," 17 December 1996; "Forum: The State of Emergency Continues," 18 February 1997; and "First Commencement Exercises of the New University in Exile," 12 May 1997. A number of poets, writers, activists, and scholars routinely

participated at the New University in Exile, including Derrick Bell, Chandra Talpade Mohanty, Brenda Joyner, Mab Segrest, Cheryl Boyce Taylor, Cherríe Moraga, and Leslie Feinberg.

68 TAP refers to the Tuition Assistance Program while PELL takes the name of Claiborne Pell, the senator who introduced financial allocations for student grants over thirty years ago. Attending the closing ceremonies were members of the Mobilization, including Leslie Hill, Diamond Fellow, and Colia Clarke, the chairwoman of Campus Action and the co-founder of the Student Non-violent Coordinating Committee (SNCC), whose talk was titled "Making Connections: A Moral and Ethical Agenda for the New Millennium."

69 This is the text of the degree granted by the New University in Exile.

70 Frymer and Skrentny, "The Rise of Instrumental Affirmative Action"; and Mohanty, "Affirmative Action In the Service of Empire."

5. Transnationalism, Sexuality, and the State

1 See also my essays "Redrafting Morality" and "Not Just (Any) Body Can Be a Citizen."

2 Note the shift of imperial interests from Spanish to American colonization in the case of Panama and from British to American colonization in the Anglophone Caribbean. In keeping with these shifts, Panama became the site of the U.S. construction of the Panama Canal, the site of U.S. invasion and home to one of the campuses of the School of the Americas. See Katz-Fishman and Scott, "Building the Peoples' Hemispheric Movement in the Midst of a Growing Police State," 13. For additional historical data, see http://www.ndfsk.to/081502.htm; and Tyler Jones, "The Panama Canal: A Brief History" at http://www.june29.com.

3 The G8 countries include: the United States, France, Canada, the United Kingdom, Italy, Japan, Russia, and Germany. The uneasy alliance has occurred in the face of French and Russian opposition to the U.S-led war against Iraq.

4 I do not mean to suggest that there has not been fruitful engagement between sexuality studies and transnational formulations. Here are some important interventions: Gopinath, *Impossible Desires*; "Queer Transexions of Race, Nation, and Gender," the special issue of *Social Text* (fall/winter 1997) that positions queer "to account for the social antagonisms of nationality, race, gender and class as well as sexuality"; the March 1995 conference Black Nations/Queer Nations? Lesbian and Gay Sexualities in the African Diaspora (sponsored by the Center for Lesbian and Gay Studies, and the Graduate Center of the City University of New York); Frilot, *Black Nations/Queer Nations*; Povinelli and Chauncey, "Thinking Sexuality Transnationally"; and Grewal and Kaplan, "Global Identities." I am especially indebted to the Thinking Sex in Transnational Times lecture series 2002, 2003 at the University of Washington, Seattle, as part of a collaborative research project.

5   See Mohanty, "Us and Them"; and Moody-Adams, *Fieldwork in Familiar Places*; see also Spiro, "Cultural Relativism and the Future of Anthropology." According to Spiro, there are three kinds of relativism: descriptive, normative, and epistemological, which are often conflated and muddled. I am referring here to Spiro's definition of "normative relativism" which, following his description, consists not of one but two judgments—one regarding culture itself and the other regarding its putative social and psychological products. Regarding culture, Spiro's claim is as follows: "Because all standards are culturally constituted, there are no available transcultural standards by which different cultures might be judged on a scale of merit or worth. Since all judgments regarding the relative merit or worth of different cultures are ethnocentric, the only valid normative judgment that can be made about them is that all are of equal worth. Normative cultural relativism in itself is comprised of two subtypes: cognitive (true/false) and moral (good/bad) relativism. Regarding the putative social and psychological products of culture, the claim of normative relativism is that since there are no universal acceptable valuable standards, any judgment regarding the behavioral patterns, cognitions, emotions, and the like of different social groups—judgments such as good or bad, right or wrong, normal or abnormal, and the like—must be relative to variable standards of the cultures that produce them; i.e., if the logical processes underlying Azande magic violate normal canons of logic, it is nevertheless impermissible to judge it as irrational because logical canons, like anything else, are culturally variable. In short, since all logic is *ethnologic* or sociologic, the judgment that Azande magic is irrational merely reflects an *ethnocentric* preference for the western logic" (125; emphasis added).

6   Narayan, *Dislocating Cultures*, 83–209.

7   For a well-argued formulation of the dialectics among capitalist, Christian, and Muslim fundamentalism, see Petchesky, "Phantom Towers," 15–29.

8   The Feminist Majority Foundation is active on a range of issues that derive from a liberal core, which is illustrated, for example, in its stance against trafficking in women, a long-standing point of mobilization on the liberal feminist political agenda. Here is its recommendation on the problem of trafficking in women in response to an invitation by the State Department to make suggestions for the U.S. delegation to the 1995 U.N. conference in Beijing: "Problem: Trafficking in women and girls is on the increase worldwide. It has been documented that U.S. military personnel stationed at overseas bases make use of local prostitutes. In addition, there are cases where retired U.S. military personnel return to cities adjacent to previous base assignments to profit from prostitution operations. Recommendation: Hold congressional hearings on the relationship between the U.S. military and the local prostitution trade at overseas U.S. bases. Through congressional action, reform the Uniformed Code of Military Justice to make the exploitation of prostitutes at or around military bases a punishable offense"

("Draft Commitments," Feminist Majority Foundation, Washington, D.C., August 1995, cited in Enloe, *Maneuvers*, 49–50).

9 Jakobsen and Pellegrini, in "World Secularisms at the Millennium," make this point in a thoroughly provocative and nuanced reading of the confrontation between the religious and the secular at the millennium.

10 RAWA, "An Open Letter to the Editors of *Ms Magazine*," in response to the magazine's article "A Coalition of Hope" in the spring 2002 issue. The critique by RAWA also rests on what it identifies as a collusion between Feminist Majority and the U.S. state in their support of the Northern Alliance. It must also be said that part of the animus of the "Open Letter" derives from RAWA's own erasure by Feminist Majority, yet RAWA's hypervisibility in terms to its speaking tour throughout the United States in 2001 was managed by the National Organization for Women, another liberal feminist organization. This hypervisibility, as Jasbir Puar and Amit Rai point out in their article "Monster, Terrorist, Fag: The War on Terrorism and the Production of Docile Patriots," bears its own contradictory costs: "The fetishizing of RAWA," they argue, "erases other women's groups in the region, ignores the relative privilege and access of resources that RAWA's members have in relation to the majority of women in Afghanistan, and obscures the network of regional and international political and economic interests that govern such organizations as NOW or even RAWA" (130). See also RAWA's Web site at www.rawa.org.

11 There is another interestingly paradoxical psychic somersault that I have witnessed in classrooms over the years, which involves a claim to superiority and privilege in relation to the Third World that masks a denial of agency in relation to the First World in students' claims that U.S. "society" is simply too dauntingly oppressive for them, as political actors, to bring about any meaningful social transformation. This position is maintained while at the same time cathecting an antipathy toward change on the part of the Third World. Teasing out how privilege continues to be exercised as it operates through a perceived powerlessness is one key in understanding the racial/cultural psychodynamics of the classroom as we move to pedagogic models of ethical interdependence.

12 Mohanty, *Feminism without Borders*, 239. Ella Shohat, in "Area Studies, Transnationalism, and the Feminist Production of Knowledge," explains the "sponge/additive approach" in these terms: "Paradigms that are generated from a U.S. perspective are extended onto 'others' whose lives and practices become absorbed into a homogenizing overarching feminist master narrative. This kind of facile additive operation merely piles up newly incorporated groups of women from various regions and ethnicities—all of whom are presumed to form a separate and coherent entity—easily demarcated as 'difference.' This form of multiculturalism and internationalism undergirds most global feminism" (1270).

13 Mohanty, *Feminism without Borders*, 239.

14　Narayan, *Dislocating Cultures*, 87. See also Moallem, "Am I a Muslim Woman?"

15　See, in general, Ahmed, *Strange Encounters*.

16　The phrase quoted here refers to Fabian, *Time and the Other*. See also Lévinas, "Time and the Other."

17　Shohat, *Talking Visions*, 20.

18　See Mohanty, "Us and Them."

19　Fabian, *Time and the Other*; see also Lévinas, "Time and the Other." Michel Trouillot, in "The Caribbean Region," has argued that the Caribbean is something of an "undisciplined region," in relation to anthropology, one in which "heterogeneity" and "historicity" have haunted the practitioners of the discipline, so much so that "as anthropology continues to nurture a legacy of tropes and concepts honed through the observation of societies once deemed simple (if not 'primitive'), outsiders continue to confront the fact that Caribbean societies have long been awkwardly, yet definitely, 'complex' (if not 'modern')" (20). In terms that are evocative of Barbara Christian's pathbreaking essay, "A Race for Theory," Toni Morrison (as cited in Gilroy, *Small Acts*) has offered another provocative challenge to the hegemonic tradition/modernity/postmodernity continuum in her formulation that black people were never not postmodern in that they are no strangers to the entanglements of loss and fragmentation.

20　Shohat, *Talking Visions*, 20.

21　Quoted in Grossberg, "History, Politics and Postmodernism," 159.

22　See Jakobsen and Pelligrini, "World Secularisms at the Millennium. Gita Patel, in "Ghostly Appearances," has advanced a most fascinating account of the ways in which multiple methods of timekeeping are simultaneously imbricated in the Hindu ordering of the Indian nation. See also Subramaniam, "Archaic Modernities."

23　Lisa Lowe and Judith Halberstam, "Perverse Modernities," book proposal to Duke University Press.

24　For important formulations of this dialectic between colony and metropolis, see Edmondson, " 'Race-ing' the Nation," 19–37. See also Colwill, "Sex, Savagery, and Slavery in the Shaping of the French Body Politic."

25　Many thanks to Gail Lewis and Avtah Brah for their provocative, ultimately indispensable, discussions about this framing of tradition and modernity during an earlier incarnation of my idea in which the comparative frame of reference was Zimbabwe, the Netherlands, and the United States.

26　See Guerrero, "Civil Rights versus Sovereignty." See also Cohen, *The Boundaries of Blackness*.

27　See, in general, Lewis, *"Race," Gender, Social Welfare*.

28　Jakobsen and Pelligrini, "World Secularisms at the Millennium."

29　Goldberg, "Sodomy in the New World," 4. According to Goldberg, his finding of the earliest account of the events of October 1513 is in Peter Martyr's *Decades*, first published in 1516. Goldberg cites from the 1555 English translation, *The Decades of the Newe Worlde or West India, March of America,* facsimile series, no. 4 (Ann Arbor, Mich.: University Microfilms, 1966). Goldberg purposely cites the English translation "as one way of immediately suggesting that these events cannot be thought of solely as episodes in Spanish-American history" (4). See Feinberg, *Transgender Warriors,* for a discussion of cultural understandings of two-spirit people. In this work, Feinberg refers readers to a number of writers who have addressed these questions. Regarding two-spirit people among Native Americans, for example, Feinberg writes: "Will Roscoe, who edited 'Living the Spirit,' explained that this more complex sex/gender system was found 'in every region of the continent, among every type of native culture, from the small bands of hunters to the populous, hierarchical city-states in Florida'" (24). Citing from Francisco Guerra's *The Pre-Columbian Mind,* Feinberg continues: "But the colonizer's reaction to two-spirit people can be summed up by the words of Antonio de la Calancha, a Spanish official in Lima. Calancha wrote that during Vasco Nuñez de Balboa's expedition across Panama, Balboa 'saw men dressed like women; Balboa learnt that they were sodomites and threw the king and forty others to be eaten by the dogs, a fine action of an honorable and Catholic Spaniard" (56). Feinberg also cites Cora Dubois as she further clarifies that "this was not an isolated attack. When the Spaniards invaded the Antilles and Louisiana, 'they found that men dressed as women were respected by their societies. Thinking they were hermaphrodites, or homosexuals, they slew them'" (23).

30 Goldberg, "Sodomy in the New World," 7. My point here does not pertain to the genealogy of the term or its subject formation.

31 A system of racial taxonomies was developed two centuries later, this time from Mexico, and submitted in 1774 as a colonial report to the king of Spain. (As Michelle Zamora, in "Malinally as Spiritual Epistemology," suggests, Spain struggled to manage the colonies through this hierarchical regime of racialized truth.) The author of *A Description of the Kingdom of New Spain, 1774,* Pedro Alonso O'Crouley, devised the following: Spaniard + Indian = mestizo; Spaniard + mestizo = castizo or albino; Spaniard + castizo = Spaniard; Spaniard + Negro = mulatto; Spaniard + mulatto = morisco; Spaniard + morisco = saltas atras; Spaniard + salta atras = tente en el aire. It takes three steps, as Zamora argues, "to reach the North, understood as Spanish blood." But in this racial map, "there is impending doom that rules the directions not to be followed. The 'salta atras' are 'steps backward,' 'tente en el aire' is worse, entirely up in the air, suspended and unknown" (19). See also McClintock, "The Lay of the Land," 21–74.

32 See Lewis, "From Sodomy to Superstition." In this analysis of colonial Mexico, Lewis draws an important parallel between the legal positioning of cross-dressing ("atypical sexual behaviors") and other kinds of social practices such as "witchcraft" in order to show how Indians embodied a paradox of the "pathic" woman,

who is condemned and pardoned (amenable to salvation), but who, in her words, "also returns 'from below' to contaminate the body politic" (3). The simultaneity of violence is clearly an old instrument of domination. In the context of Spain, the onset of the colonization of the Americas dovetails with the conflation of Jewishness and sodomy, the expulsion of the Jews from Spain and the marriage of Christianity and Catholicism (Dynes, *The Encyclopedia of Homosexuality*, entry on Spain). See also Greenberg, *The Construction of Homosexuality*; and Blackmore and Hutcheson, *Queer Iberia*.

33 *Bowers v. Hardwick*, 478 U.S. 186. This 1986 ruling has since been superceded by a 2003 Supreme Court ruling. In the 1986 decision the Supreme Court upheld the Georgia sodomy law (which had also applied to heterosexuals) pertaining to what it termed "homosexual sodomy." See Thomas, "Beyond the Privacy Principle."

34 Office of the Secretary of Defense, "Summary Report of the Military Working Group," Washington, D.C., 1 July 1993, 1.

35 Ibid.

36 Langton, "Speech Acts and Unspeakable Acts."

37 Halley, *Don't*, 7–8.

38 I am referring here specifically to the ideological work of enemy production during this ongoing war against Iraq. See Puar and Rai, "Monster, Terrorist, Fag."

39 *Windtalkers*, the 2001 film directed by John Woo and written by John Batteer and John Rice, brings this home. It documents the U.S. military use of the Navajo language as code during the Second World War. As the code and code talkers became public knowledge at the height of the cold war, the U.S. state justified its silence on the strategic role of Indians during the war as one of security. This major disjuncture between the role of Indians as strategic intelligence for the benefit of the state; the dire poverty of the material conditions that are faced on reservations; and the ongoing ideological war against Indian peoples is most stark.

40 "Enlistment of Men of Colored Race in Other than the Mesmen Branch," secret 1942 memorandum to the secretary of the Navy from its General Board, National Archives, G.B. No. 421/Serial No. 201. For mobilization of another kind, see Lane, "Black Bodies/Gay Bodies" for the conflation of queer struggles and civil rights struggles and the resultant conflicts.

41 The following quotations are from the Office of the Secretary of Defense, "Summary Report of the Military Working Group."

42 Halley, *Don't*, 8.

43 The following quotations are all from the "Summary Report of the Military Working Group," 2–5.

44 Halley, *Don't*, 126.

45 Ibid., 128.

46 Ibid., 7–8. See also Thomas, "Beyond the Privacy Principle."

47 I am addressing here the reversal of the Texas sodomy statute on 18 November 2003 by the U.S. Supreme Court. See also "Transcript of Bush Statement," 24 February 2004, at www.cnn.com.

48 Alturi, "When the Closet Is a Region," 1.

49 See my essay, "Redrafting Morality."

50 The Defense of Marriage Act: An Act to Defend and Protect the Institution of Marriage, 1993, PL 104–199.

51 Diamond, *Roads to Dominion*, 228.

52 Diamond, *Spiritual Warfare*, 35.

53 Hammonds, "Toward a Genealogy of Black Female Sexuality," 170–82.

54 Relevant here are two important essays by Tracy Robinson, "Fictions of Citizenship, Bodies Without Sex" and "Beyond the Bill of Rights," which explore the contradiction of producing and effacing gender while fetishizing sex. One of the earliest works to place the Caribbean sex trade within a global context while elaborating its implications for feminism is Kempadoo's *Sun, Sex and Gold* (see especially the introduction, "Five Centuries of Prostitution in the Caribbean," 3–36).

55 Tracy Robinson, in "Fictions of Citizenship," argues that the extent of legal activity belies the contradictory infantilization of women on the part of the state. Here is her analysis of that contradiction: "The result is that women, while not excluded from citizenship, are not conceived in law in the first instance as citizens, but as dependants of men, with de facto management of the family and responsibility for maintenance of family values . . . Second-class citizenship describes not only the hierarchy between men and women but also the hierarchy of roles for women: in one case, women are second to men as citizens, and in the other, citizenship is perceived as secondary for women" (19). For a similar argument in the case of Guyana, where the state positions women primarily as wives and mothers, see Peake, "The Development and Role of Women's Political Organizations in Guyana," 122.

56 This title is from my essay "Redrafting Morality." All references in this part of the text pertain to the Sexual Offences and Domestic Violence Act of Trinidad and Tobago.

57 Law Commission of Trinidad and Tobago, "Explanatory Note to the Sexual Offences Bill," internal document, 1985.

58 For a similar analysis of the inscription of erotic and legal discourses on the female body in Muslim societies, see Sabbah, *Woman in the Muslim Unconscious*. For a more recent formulation that twists the gaze to examine the veiling work in which feminism itself is engaged, see Najmabadi, "Unveiling Feminism."

59 See also Robinson, "Beyond the Bill of Rights," for a discussion of the subsequent watering down of Clause 4 and the increase in domestic violence in Trinidad and Tobago.

60 This formulation is taken directly from Warner's title *Fear of a Queer Planet*.

61 This turn of phrase bears a stark resemblance to the British formulation of "pretend families" in the United Kingdom, as illustrated in Section 28 of the Local Government Act of 1988: "A local government shall not intentionally promote homosexuality . . . as a pretended family relationship" (cited in Reinhold, "Through the Parliamentary Looking Glass: 'Real' and 'Pretend' Families in Contemporary British Politics," 61).

62 All quotations are taken from the text of the Defense of Marriage Act (DOMA).

63 Congressional Budget Office, "The Potential Budgetary Impact of Recognizing Same-Sex Marriages," U.S. Congress. Washington, D.C. 21 June 2004.

64 Carole Boyce Davies has made the point about the fragility of citizenship for black radical immigrants in her examination of the life and deportation of Claudia Jones.

65 The social forces that create the conditions that make sovereignty fragile are not simply passive. There is an indirect parallel that operates in the case of the Anglophone Caribbean.

66 See *Ke Kulana He Mahu—Remembering a Sense of Place: Colonization, Sexuality and Drag Queens in the Land of "Aloha,"* a film written and directed by Kathryn Xian and Brent Anbe, 2001.

67 The significance of a larger discourse on tradition and morality can be rendered in different terms. See my discussion in "Redrafting Morality."

68 There is a difference between questions of constitutionality and questions of justice; the procedural entanglements of the former do not necessarily enable the latter.

69 This immediate point is made by Thomas in his analysis of the relationship between state terror and street terror in "Beyond the Privacy Principle."

70 Giddings, *When and Where I Enter*.

71 Mohanty, "Cartographies of Struggle." See also Lowe, *Immigrant Acts*.

72 Proceedings of the Conference on the Care of Dependent Children, Washington, D.C., January 25, 26, 1909. Senate Document No. 721.

73 Clarke, *My Mother Who Fathered Me*, xxii–xxiii. The impact of that gesture on increasing women's desire for marriage was miniscule and in essence incapable of intruding on the cultural adaptive patterns established within working-class communities.

74 Cited in Neubeck and Cazenave, *Welfare Racism*, 218–19.

75 See Massey and Denton, *American Apartheid*, 6.

76 Neubeck and Cazenave, *Welfare Racism*, 153.

77 Ibid. See also Perea, *Immigrants Out!*

78 Heterosexual marriage is only one of the pivots that has been used by the state to promote sexual citizenship. But the danger for women on welfare—as many as 60 percent of whom are survivors of intimate partner violence—are quite severe if

this pressure to marry forces women to remain in already violent relationships. For an analysis of the risk of increase in domestic violence as a result of HR4, see "Bush's New Welfare Reform Promotes Marriage," *Manavi Newsletter* 13, nos. 1–2, (fall 2002): 1, 3–5. Another significant trope harkens back to elements in the Moynihan report, which positions militarism as the mechanism to transform black criminality into responsible law-abiding citizenship. See Rainwater and Yancey, *The Moynihan Report and the Politics of Controversy*, especially 44–46.

79   Neubeck and Cazenave, *Welfare Racism*, 217. See also Quadagno, *The Color of Welfare*.

80   Sen, "The First Time Was Tragedy."

81   Burnham, "Racism in US Welfare Policy." See also Neubeck and Cazenave, *Welfare Racism*, 202, as well as the analysis of the Feminism and Legal Theory Workshop at falcon.arts.cornell.edu/arms3/npmbasis.html.

82   Banerjee, "Integrated Circuits." Banerjee's empirical focus is on the immigration of Indian high-tech workers and the ways in which "the H1-B visa has been instrumental in the creation and consolidation of a subcontracting system of labor recruitment in the technology field" (3). In addition, her overall critique of a number of disassociations in the feminist literature between national and transnational processes, for instance, that mask the linkages that are drawn here are compellingly astute. See also Fragomen, "The Illegal Immigration Reform and Immigrant Responsibility Act of 1996"; and Leong, "How Public Policy Reforms, Shapes, and Reveals the Shape of Asian America." For a historicized analysis of the legal codification of immigration and its particular deployments in Asian America, see Lowe, *Immigrant Acts* (in particular the chapters "Immigration, Citizenship, Racialization: Asian American Critique" and "Work, Immigration, Gender: Asian 'American' Women").

83   Gail Lewis, in *"Race," Gender, Social Welfare*, has provided an indispensable analysis of the transformations in a racialized, gendered context of welfare in the British postcolonial state. In her analysis of the relations between state and family and the particular twists that the state takes as it sets up to discipline those on welfare, Lewis relies on the work of Donzelot, whose formulations resemble much of the analysis I offered in chapter 3. The term "tutelary complex" is Donzelot's, which he uses to examine the terms of unequal exchange between the state and the recipient of services. Here is his formulation of this complex: the state provides "the means to be self-sufficient by teaching you the virtues of saving in return for which the tutors of such virtues would have the right to gaze, to subject their tutees to a disapproving scrutiny of the demands for aid that you (the immiserised) might still pull forward, since they would constitute a flagrant indication of a breach of morality" (Donzelot, *The Policing of Families*, 55–56).

84   See the analysis by the Feminism and Legal Theory Workshop at www.falcon .arts.cornell.edu/arms3/npmbasis.html. Fifty percent of the monies budgeted

under HR4 are to be provided by the federal government, while the remaining 50 percent comes under the purview of the state.

85 We can be sure that a veritable industry will arise to market strategies for marriage promotion. One model, developed in Chattanooga, Tennessee, has caught the attention of the federal state. It uses local corporations, TV ads, and electronic newsletters as a way of "selling marriages to hard audiences" (Lerner, "Just Say 'I do,' " 23; see also Pollitt, "Shotgun Weddings"). In addition, two important essays scrutinize this area of "welfare reform": see Finn and Underwood, "The State, the Clock and the Struggle"; and Rabinowitz, "What Film Noir Can Teach Us about 'Welfare as We Know It.' " For an early analysis of how queer theory's category of the heteronormative needs to be extended beyond the boundaries of the queer community, see Cohen, "Punks, Bulldaggers, and Welfare Queens."

86 There is a resonance here in neocolonial social formations in the Caribbean where marriage functions primarily as a middle-class and upper-middle-class phenomenon.

87 This term is taken from Puar and Rai, "Monster, Terrorist, Fag."

88 Quote from participants.

89 See Chang's indispensable work *Disposable Domestics*, notably the introduction and the chapters "Immigrants and Workfare Workers: Employable but 'Not Employed,' " and "Global Exchange: The World Bank, 'Welfare Reform,' and the Trade in Migrant Women."

90 Discussed as part of the national security strategy, see "The Administration's Commitment to the Developing World" at www.whitehouse.gov/infocus/developing nations/developingworld.html. The United States is also the largest debtor nation, "living beyond its means and heavily dependent on foreign lenders," given that "the debt America owes abroad has now reached about $2 trillion" (Clyde V. Prestowitz, "The Unmighty Dollar," *Newsweek*, 24 March 2003, 32). Of course, the political manipulation of aid is a huge topic that is entirely related. One dimension of this has been reflected in what Caribbean state managers have called "arm twisting" in relation to the U.S. state's ultimatum to CARICOM countries to either support the U.S. position on the International Criminal Court or forfeit their aid. See Best, "Guess Who Is Coming to Breakfast in New York with President George Bush?"; and "Powell Snubs CARICOM Ministers." Another article by Best on Haiti, "U.S. Selling Torture Tools to Haiti but Blocking Development Aid," has revealed the operation of a politics of duplicity in which the U.S. Department of Commerce granted licenses to U.S. corporations to sell "torture tools" to Haiti while the Bush administration was involved in pressuring international financial institutions to withhold their development assistance.

91 Caribbean Association for Feminist Research and Action, "The Debt Crisis: Who Really Owes Whom?"

92 *Seeking the Soul of Freedom*, a film written and directed by Cynthia Carson and

Toni Brodber, 2004. A growing literature has developed in the field matching the meteoric increase in remittances and its effect on the GDP of different countries. See the following: Nurse, "Migration and Development in the Caribbean," 1; Cairncross, "The Longest Journey: A Survey of International Migration"; Peter Bate, "A River of Gold," at *www.iadb.org/idbamerica/English/OCT01E/oct01e3.html*; Orozco, "Globalization and Migration: The Impact of Family Remittances in Latin America"; *Tradewatch Newsletter*, "Remittances a Major Contribution to Regional Development," 6 June 2001. I thank Michele Reis for referring me to this body of literature.

93 This discussion will draw from the general terms I established in chapter 1.

94 Caribbean Association for Feminist Research and Action, "The Debt Crisis: Who Really Owes Whom?" 208.

95 *Life and Debt*, a film written and directed by Stephanie Black (A Tuff Going Pictures Production, 2001). See also New Internationalist, "Life or Debt?" 206–7; Harrison, "The Gendered Politics and Violence of Structural Adjustment in Jamaica"; Emeagwali, *Women Pay the Price*; and Persaud, *Counter-Hegemony and Foreign Policy*.

96 Caribbean Association for Feminist Research and Action, "The Debt Crisis: Who Really Owes Whom?" 208.

97 Since tourism is imagined to be one of the major conduits of economic viability, its placement within a sexualized economic practice makes it only partially intelligible. This apparently public-only discourse travels with different, oftentimes contradictory, requirements for the heterosexual middle-class bedroom, those of working-class, working-poor, or women-managed households and for sex-workers who are HIV-infected. See my discussion in chapter 1, which elaborates this point. See also Puar, "Transnational Circuits and Sexuality in Trinidad."

98 There has been an ongoing gendered and racialized discourse about whether women, single mothers in particular, enter the military for economic or patriotic reasons—a discourse partly instigated by the "rescue" of Jessica Lynch and the death of Lori Ann Piestewa, the first American servicewoman and the first Native American woman to be killed in Iraq. A good deal of the discussion has centered on Texas, the state that reportedly has the largest percentage of men joining the military. Ironically, Texas is also one of the poorest states and one that has experienced some of the most serious retrenchments in the social wage over the past two decades. See Jan Jarboe Russell, "Moms Shouldn't Sacrifice Their Lives for Their Kids' Survival," *San Antonio Express-News*, 13 April 2003, 7; and "Moms Seek a Better Life" (editorial), *San Antonio Express-News*, 20 April 2003, 4H.

99 See Pitt, "Blood Money," for an incisive report on the links between corporate and state power, the expansion of the military industrial complex, the formation of the Project for a New American Century, and the aspirations of the Bush administration. See also Roy, *Power Politics*, on who benefits from militarization.

100   An altogether different war story is told by Lynch herself. See Bragg, *I Am a Soldier Too: The Jessica Lynch Story*. See also "Debunking Early Rescue Myths, Lynch's Book Hits the Shelves," *USA Today*, 11 November 2003.

101   In his essay "Citizenship" Richard Delgado has examined the ways in which recent legislation evokes the premises of the Dred Scott decision of 1856, which held that black people could not be citizens since they were not "here" from the beginning.

102   Managing immigrant threat as a way to ensure homeland security has now been made official. As reported on the Web site of the U.S. Citizenship and Immigration Services, "On November 25, 2002, the President signed the Homeland Security Act of 2002 into law. This law transferred INS functions to the new Department of Homeland Security (DHS). Immigration enforcement functions were placed within the Directorate of Border and Transportation Security (BTS), either directly, or under Customs and Border Protection (CBP) (which includes the Border Patrol and INS Inspections) or Immigration and Customs Enforcement (ICE) (which includes the enforcement and investigation components of INS such as Investigations, Intelligence, Detention, and Removals).

"As of March 1, 2003, the former Immigration and Naturalization Service (INS) was abolished and its functions and units incorporated into the new Department. Below are links to Web information about the new locations, responsibilities, and contacts (HQs/field) of the former INS immigration services and immigration enforcement units." Web site of the U.S. Citizenship and Immigration Services: www.uscis.gov/graphics/othergov/roadmap.htm.

103   All subsequent quotes are taken from the USA Patriot Act 1.

104   ACLU, "How the USA Patriot Act Redefines 'Domestic Terrorism,'" at www.aclu .org/nationalsecurity/nationalsecurity.cfm?ID=11437&c=111. The power of discursive definition does not mean that the itinerary of the Patriot Act is not being contested. The Bill of Rights Defense Committee has been collecting data across the country on the grass-roots response to John Ashcroft's attempts to defend the Patriot Act. According to the committee, during the course of the attorney general's eight-month tour throughout the country, twenty-eight communities, representing 3.7 million pople passed resolutions opposing the Patriot Act. See the Bill of Rights Defense Committee Web site: www.bordc.org/ Ontheroad.html. Accessed 8 August 2004.

105   The ongoing bombing of abortion clinics and the state's refusal to intervene against this level of systematized misogynist violence has been carefully analyzed in Baird-Windle and Bader, *Targets of Hatred*.

106   ACLU also dicusses how Operation Rescue and mobilizations against the militarization of Vieques might well be put together under the heading "domestic terrorists" as abrogations of free speech. Free speech is not the category I am invoking here, even though it is important to recognize that constitutional rights are being fundamentally jeopardized and the category of citizen is being

consistently constrained. See "Interested Person's Memo: Section by Section analysis of Justice Department draft Domestic Security Enhancement Act of 2003," also known as "Patriot Act II" at www.aclu.org/safeandfree/safeandfree.cfm?ID=11835&c=206.

107 The Bill of Rights Defense Committee has conducted a very thorough analysis of the first Patriot Act, notably the ways in which it changes existing legislation and the various ways in which it can be misused. See their Web site at http://www.gjf/org/NBORDC.

108 See the classic by Malek, *The Colonial Harem*.

109 Allen et al., *Without Sanctuary*.

110 "Justices, 6–3, Legalize Gay Sexual Conduct in Sweeping Reversal of Court's '86 Ruling," *New York Times*, 27 June 2003.

111 See Puar and Rai, "Monster, Terrorist, Fag," especially the section, "Heteronormativity and Patriotism."

112 Robin Riley, " 'O(saddam)a': New Propaganda," 3. The Web sites that deal with the process of "enemyfication" are constantly in flux. Among the most recent are the ones that include Jessie Jackson and Bill Clinton in turbans (www.Politicalhumor.about.com/library/images/blosamabinlyin.htm) and a series of videos at www.newgrounds.com. For those asking the audience to participate in torture of bin Laden, there is a site called "Fists of Allah" that can be found at www.newgrounds.com/collections/osama/html. I thank Robin Riley for these specific references.

113 Seymour M. Hersh, "Torture at Abu Ghraib." *Annals of National Security*: www.newyorker.com/fact/content/?040510fa_fact. Posted 30 April 2004. A similar move has been made to make Abu Ghraib the work of a few rotten apples. A distinction needs to be made here between the ideological longevity of the representational impulses at work in the demonization of Simpson and the perpetration of domestic violence or murder. I am not arguing that Simpson did not engage in domestic violence.

114 Puar and Rai, "Monster, Terrorist, Fag."

115 Enloe, *The Morning After,* 197.

116 Orth, "Fort Bragg's Deadly Summer," *Vanity Fair*, December 2002, 222–40.

117 An entire issue of *Spare Change*, the newspaper of the Homeless Empowerment Project, was devoted to domestic violence just a month after 9/11. See *Spare Change,* special issue "Domestic Violence and the World Trade Center," October 2001, 18–31.

118 Davis, "Masked Racism: Reflections on the Prison Industrial Complex."

119 Silliman and Bhattacharjee, *Policing the National Body*.

120 Weber, "Warrior Cops: The Ominous Growth of Paramilitarism in American Police Departments."

121 Ibid., 1–2.

122   Silliman and Bhattacharjee, *Policing the National Body*, xv.

123   Bernard Harcourt, in "Reflecting on the Subject," presents a most compelling and extensive analysis of these technologies and their deployment in different parts of the country, underscoring the specious scientific evidence supporting them. There are, of course, implications for the organization of this symbolic archive that are manifested in the concrete committing of hate crimes. For the translation from symbol to hate, see Jakobsen, "Tolerating Hate? Or Hating Intolerance?" Here I am also drawing indirectly from my own research on the contradictory ways in which immigrant identities are mobilized not in the interest of assimilation, as melting-pot theories purport, but in the interest of violence. The empirical focus is the 1997 police torture of Abner Louima, whose bloodied body bore the mark of the reciprocal antagonisms between the war on crime and a global economy that relies on the very immigrants who have been criminalized. Louima's status as naturalized citizen had no bearing in media representations of him or in some of the violent anti-immigrant and homophobic sentiment that was unleashed. A 2003 report by the Justice Policy Institute (*State Spending on Prisons Grows at 6 Times the Rate of Higher Education; More African American Men Incarcerated Than Enrolled in College; African American Imprisonment Worsened During the "Good Times"*) has revealed that during the 1980s and 1990s state spending on prisons grew at six times the rate of higher education, and that by the close of the millennium there were nearly a third more African American men in prison and jail than in universities and colleges.

124   Harcourt, "Reflecting on the Subject," 293.

125   MSNBC News, *Hardball with Chris Matthews*, interview with Bernard Kerik, 3 October 2003, online at http://www.msnbc.com/news/976580.asp. Bernard Kerik's tenure as commissioner of the New York City Police Department coincided with the police torture of Abner Louima and a marked increase in civilian complaints filed against police brutality. In speaking about the "war at home," I am not referring to the normative stance in the *New York Times* that understands the war at home as the difficulties that the state confronts in marketing its economic agenda. A radical mobilization about the war at home is quite widespread. In addition to those movements already cited within *ColorLines* (in particular the spring 2002 special issue, "A New Era: Race After 9/11, 'The War at Home'") there are the following: *The Independent*, "From 9.11 to World War 3," Issue No. 21, September 2002; "Bush's Permanent War," *News and Letters*, March 2002, Editorial; *War Times*, "The First Casualty of War is Truth," September 2002, No. 5; Susan Webb, "Opposition Grows to War with Iraq," *People's Weekly World*, Saturday, August 31, 2002, Vol. 17, No. 14, 1–2; "Our Grief is not a Cry for War," http://www.notinourname.net; A.N.S.W.E.R. (Act Now to Stop War and End Racism) Coalition, "Against War, Colonial Occupation and Imperialism," May 3–4, 2002.

126 *The 9/11 Commission Report: Final Report of the National Commission on Terrorist Attacks Upon the United States.* Official Government Edition. Washington, D.C.: U.S. Government Printing Office, 2004.

127 A discussion of the national security strategy of the United States can be found at http://www.whitehouse.gov/nsc/nss.html. All subsequent quotes are taken verbatim from this text.

128 Petchesky, "Phantom Towers," 15–29.

129 These words are taken from Morrison, *Playing in the Dark*, 3.

130 Approximately four days after the attacks on the center of financial capital in the United States, the president remarked: "We will rid the world of evil doers . . . This crusade, this war on terrorism is going to take a while." The state alignment of the war on terrorism with the Crusades was stridently critiqued and resulted in the retraction of the statement. My interest, however, lies in its psychic production—its nostalgic anxiety for an earlier historical moment and the psychic residues it deposits. See "Bush Pledges Crusade against 'Evil Doers,' " at www.recordonline.com/archive/2001/09/17/rdp16.html.

131 See Mauge, *The Lost Orisha*, 118–19; and Mohanty, "Cartographies of Struggle," 25.

132 Davies, " 'Half the World': The Transnational Black Socialist Feminist Practice of Claudia Jones." See also Nobles, *Shades of Citizenship;* and Torpey, *The Invention of the Passport.*

133 LaDuke, "Radioactive Colonization." See also Trask, "Self-Determination for Pacific Island Women"; la Duke, "Nitassinan"; and Allen, *Off the Reservation.*

134 Women Working for a Nuclear Free and Independent Pacific, *Pacific Women Speak.*

135 "Kenyan women take rape case to the U.N." BBC News Online, 30 March 2005, newswww.bbc.net.uk/1/hi/4392147.stm. See also "Decades of Impunity: Serious Allegations of Rape of Kenyan Women by U.K. Army," Amnesty International Web site: web.amnesty.org/library/print/ENGEUR450142003. Accessed 27 April 2005. I thank Margo Okazawa-Rey for these references.

136 East Asia–U.S.–Puerto Rico Women's Network against Militarism, "Final Statement," Seoul, Korea, 15–19 August 2002. This network, initiated in 1997, links violence against women, children, and communities to the economic and military dominance of the United States around the world.

137 Roy, *Power Politics*, 128.

138 Kaplan and Pease, *Cultures of United States Imperialism,* 14.

139 Charlotte Bunch, "Talking and Doing Citizenship," Graduate Forum, Center for the Critical Analysis of Contemporary Culture, Rutgers University, 2 April 2004.

140 Shohat, *Talking Visions*, 38.

141 Cynthia Enloe, speaking at the conference of the National Women's Studies Association, Women in the Middle: Borders, Barriers, Intersections, gave a

strong reminder to participants that liberal feminists who placed these very questions on the political agenda are not the enemy. Milwaukee, June 2004.

142 Feldman, *Universities in the Business of Repression*.

143 The context here relies on a series of hearings in the U.S. House of Representatives, Committee on Education and the Workforce, pertaining to Title VI funding for "International Programs in Higher Education and Questions about Bias." The bias in question is postcolonial studies and "its efforts to potentially undermine American foreign policy." The companion legislation that has been introduced to curtail Title VI funding is HR 3077; see http://edworkforce.house .gov/hearings/108th/sed/titlevi61903/w161903.htm. These hearings can be considered part of what Kaplan and Grewal call "the backlash narrative" in their essay "Transnational Practices and Interdisciplinary Feminist Scholarship."

144 The consequences of this "backlash narrative" can be grave, particularly when immigrants are singled out for their "anti-American" politics. A statement by Stanley Kurtz, research fellow at the Hoover Institution, on 19 June 2003 cited the Hagop Kevorkian Center Web site at New York University: www.nyu.edu/ gsas/program/neareast, particularly the work of Ella Shohat. According to Kurtz, "Everyone that takes a stand sharply criticizes American policy." Note also that Shohat, in *Talking Visions*, criticizes America's "crimes" of "oil driven hegemony" and America's "murderous sanctions on Iraq."

145 Donaldson, Donadey, and Silliman, "Subversive Couplings"; Dirlik, *The Postcolonial Aura*. Postcolonial studies most often imagines the subaltern as residing elsewhere, rarely in conversation with local subalterns or with the political movements that provoked decolonization. See also Wing, "Educate to Liberate"; Grewal, "The Postcolonial, Ethnic Studies and the Diaspora"; and duCille, "Postcolonialism and Afrocentricity: Discourse and Dat Course."

146 Alarcón, *Snake Poems*.

6. Remembering *This Bridge Called My Back*

1 See the video documentary *Sweet Sugar Rage*, available from the Sistren Theatre Collective in Jamaica. See also the work by Sistren (with Ford Smith) titled *Lionheart Gal*. The term CAFRA stands for the Caribbean Association for Feminist Research and Action. Since its inception in 1986, the association has been explicit in its commitment to examine "the relations between men and women in capitalist and socialist societies; to use a framework inclusive of race, class and sex; to demonstrate the ways in which exploitative relations between men and women are facilitated, maintained and reproduced by exploitative capitalist relations, and to show, as well, how capitalism itself benefits in the process."

2 Chrystos, "I Walk in the Shadow of My People." The occupation in South Dakota by the people of Pine Ridge and members of the American Indian

Movement lasted for sixty-nine days in 1973. The conditions that led to the occupation still continue (conversation with Sharon Day, January 2001). See also Brown, *Bury My Heart at Wounded Knee*.

3   Quintanales, "I Paid Very Hard for My Immigrant Ignorance," 151; Yamada, "Invisibility Is an Unnatural Disaster," 35; Morales, "We're All in the Same Boat," 92; and Davenport, "The Pathology of Racism," 85.

4   Anzaldúa, "Speaking in Tongues," 173.

5   Walsh, *Communion with God*, 15.

6   See my argument in "Not Just (Any) Body Can Be a Citizen."

7   Nationalist regimes in the Caribbean have constantly mobilized race in the name of popular nationalism to generate the idea of a seamless nation. The national motto for Jamaica reads, "Out of many, one"; in the case of Trinidad and Tobago, it is: "Every creed and race has an equal place."

8   Du Bois's earlier analysis of double-consciousness is pertinent in this context. See Du Bois, *The Souls of Black Folk*. These formulations lie at the heart of the concept of internalized oppression used within feminism.

9   Combahee River Collective, "A Black Feminist Statement," 210.

10 Chrystos, "I Walk in the Shadow of My People," 57.

11 See Powell's *Pagoda* for a moving, complicated portrayal of Chinese migration to Jamaica and the different kinds of journeys it can represent.

12 Grewal et al., *Charting the Journey*, 1–6.

13 The politics of black women in Britain have always been infused with a more systematic critique of state practices than has been the case with women of color in the United States. The claim for black women's citizenship was anchored on a subjectivity as colonials, hence the notion that the borders of the British nation had never been fixed. Gail Lewis, one of the original editors of *Charting the Journey*, believes (at the time of this writing) that black women are posing questions of belonging in ways that are changing the very character of Britishness. There is a fruitful set of transatlantic conversations that black women in Britain and women of color in the United States still need to have.

14 Mohanty, "Cartographies of Struggle," 1–50; Moraga, "Refugees of a World on Fire," i–iv.

15 This is taken from the text of a song by Sweet Honey in the Rock, "Are My Hands Clean?" (reproduced in Enloe, *Bananas, Beaches and Bases*, 158).

16 Moraga, "Refugees of a World on Fire"; Jordan, *Affirmative Acts*, 94. There is an important distinction here between wealthy refugees who flee to protect privilege: for instance, the light-skinned/white Cuban refugees who fled to Miami with the triumph of communism in Cuba; the Asian Ugandans who were expelled by the 1972 edict of Idi Amin who had business interests in different parts of the world (see Brah, *Cartographies of Diaspora*, 35); and the *comprador* classes of many Third World countries who flee to metropolitan countries partly out of a

refusal to rebuild civil society in their own countries of origin (this latter insight came from a conversation with Chandan Reddy). See also Bhattacharjee, "The Public/Private Mirage."

17 The Prison Activist Resource Center has assembled a listing of political prisoners in the United States and the various mobilizations on their behalf (www .prisonactivist.org.pps+pows). See also the addendum in Davis, *Are Prisons Obsolete?* See also post–September 11 implications for political prisoners: Harvard Black Letter Law Journal C. 18 (2002): 129–37; Prison Activist Web site (www .prisonactivist.org/pps+pows/info?SERijah_reality_of_pps.pdf).

18 Sudbury, *Global Lockdown*; Davis, *Are Prisons Obsolete?*

19 Jordan, *Affirmative Acts*, 159. Web site of the Breast Health Resource: http:// imaginis.com/breasthealth/statistics.asp.

20 Cohen, *The Boundaries of Blackness: AIDS and the Breakdown of Black Politics*, 123. I learned about these disturbing data and their implications in conversation with Barbara Herbert. They refer primarily to African and Brazilian women in Massachusetts. African American women who have had this disease since it became visible in 1981 continue to suffer disproportionate morbidity and mortality rates, even with the advent of new medications. Clearly the question of the kinds of political interventions we adopt to make breast cancer, HIV/AIDS, and other diseases central parts of our organizing is an urgent one.

21 Freire, *Pedagogies of the Oppressed*, 31.

22 Moraga, "The Welder," 219; Clarke, "Althea and Flaxie," in *Living as a Lesbian*, 24.

23 These lines are taken from the haiku of Ngo An, an eleventh-century Vietnamese Zen monk: "The jade burned on the mountain retains its natural color, / The lotus, blooming in the furnace, does not lose its freshness." They also serve as the epigraph to Nhat Hanh's *Vietnam: Lotus in a Sea of Fire*. Nhat Hanh traces the history of Vietnamese Buddhism and its engagement in the conflagration called the Vietnam War. I thank Mab Segrest for this reference.

24 Levins Morales, " . . . And Even Fidel Can't Change That!" 53–56.

25 Jordan, *Affirmative Acts*, 95.

26 Quintanales, "I Paid Very Hard for My Immigrant Ignorance," 151.

27 The sexual abuse of women in prisons is part of the violent sexualization of prison life: see Davis, *Are Prisons Obsolete?* 62–83; and *ColorLines*, especially the winter 2001 issue titled "Conferences on the Color of Violence."

28 Brah, *Cartographies of Diaspora*, 242.

29 For an exceptional analysis of dominant postmodernism's premature theoretical abandonment of the category of social location and identity, see Moya, "Postmodernism, 'Realism' and the Politics of Identity."

30 Cherríe Moraga, "A Tuna Bleeding in the Heat: A Chicana Codex of Changing Consciousness." Moraga, the recipient of the CLAG's Kessler award, noted that her recent work has a stronger Chicano/a audience.

31 See, for instance, the Latina Feminist Collective, *Telling to Live*; Women of South
    Asian Descent Collective, *Our Feet Walk the Sky*; and Khadi, *Food for Our Grand-
    mothers*.

32 Brah, *Cartographies of Diaspora*, 154.

33 Du Bois, *Black Reconstruction*.

34 The official period of Reconstruction is 1865–1877. Certainly the ideology of race
    was taking dramatic turns during this period, but it sets the stage for an even
    more vigorous legislation of whiteness in the 1880s and 1890s. See also Haney-
    López, *White by Law*; Montejano, *Anglos and Mexicans in the Making of Texas*;
    Perdue, *Cherokee Women*; and Porter, *Black Seminoles*, 175. This was also the
    period of sustained guerrilla wars by the Lumbee in North Carolina, for instance,
    that heightened the threat of revolt and the Red River War (conversation be-
    tween David Sartorious and Theda Purdue, research notes of David Sartorious,
    2003).

35 Lowe, *Immigrant Acts*, 11; Mohanty, "Cartographies of Struggle," 25.

36 Alexander and Mohanty, *Feminist Genealogies*, xiii–xv.

37 Brah, "The Scent of Memory," 6.

38 There are, of course, different class migrations that are in turn linked to the
    categories and quotas deployed by the Immigration and Naturalization Service.
    For a comparison of South Asian migration to the United States, see Bhattachar-
    jee, "The Public/Private Mirage," 210.

39 Here I have benefited enormously from discussions with Andrée Nicola Mc-
    Laughlin, founder of the Black Women's Cross-Cultural Institute, Gloria I.
    Joseph, Chandan Reddy, Tamara Jones, Gayatri Gopinath, Judith Halberstam,
    and Liza Fiol-Matta.

40 I thank Chandan Reddy for this point. This polarization is also reflected in a
    theoretical schism between postcolonial studies and ethnic studies. A larger
    analysis is warranted here, which should also entail an analysis of hiring practices
    within the academy.

41 DuCille, "Postcolonialism and Afrocentricity: Discourse and Dat Course," 30. See
    also Grewal, "The Postcolonial, Ethnic Studies and the Diaspora." For a critique of
    the popularity of postcolonial studies in the academy, see hooks, *Yearning*, 93–94.

42 Brah, "The Scent of Memory," 13.

43 Our understanding of this American social formation would benefit enormously
    from analyses that do not automatically premise a democratic U.S. state. Such a
    refusal would help to reduce the anomaly of positioning the state as democratic at
    home and interventionist abroad. See Guerrero, "Civil Rights versus Sover-
    eignty," for an understanding of how the U.S. state negotiates a set of advanced
    capitalist *and* colonial relations, particularly in relation to Native peoples; and
    Cohen, *The Boundaries of Blackness*, for an astute reading of the "advanced
    marginalization" of African American communities. See also Lewis, "*Race*," *Gen-*

der, Social Welfare, for an exceptional formulation of Britain as a postcolonial social formation.

44 The fact of African complicity in the Atlantic slave trade is a different point from the one I am making here.

45 Baldwin, "Princes and Powers," in *The Price of the Ticket,* 56. Of course Baldwin's conflation of Pan-Africanism with royal manliness is not to be missed here.

46 Marshall, *The Fisher King,* 56. A closer analysis of the new racial composition of domestic labor needs to be undertaken.

47 Lorde, *Burst of Light,* 109.

48 I recall here the shared mobilizations in New York City around the death of Galvin Cato, the police torture of Abner Louima, and the police shooting of Amadou Diallo.

49 Baldwin, "The American Dream and the American Negro," in *The Price of the Ticket,* 404; Phillips, *The Atlantic Sound,* 252.

50 See Lorde's "Eye to Eye," an important essay on which I lean heavily (in *Sister Outsider,* 145–75).

51 Crenshaw, "Whose Story Is It Anyway?" 402.

52 David Rudder, a Calypsonian from Trinidad, has penned an exceptional Pan-African tribute to Haiti, titled, "Haiti I'm Sorry." The last stanza goes as follows:

> When there is anguish in Port-au-Prince
> is still Africa crying
> We're outing fires in far away places
> when our neighbors are just dying
> Dey say the middle passage is gone
> so how come overcrowded boats still haunt our lives
> I refuse to believe that we the people
> will forever turn our hearts and our eyes away
> *Chorus*: Haiti, I'm sorry, we misunderstood you
> one day we'll turn our heads and look inside you
> one day we'll turn our heads and restore your glory.

53 Nhât H'ahn, *Fragrant Palm Leaves,* 89.

54 Bambara, *The Salt Eaters,* 1.

55 Moraga, "Refugees of a World on Fire," vii.

56 Brand, *No Language Is Neutral,* 26. Brand is talking here about the sidelong glances that Caribbean people give to slavery.

57 Epigraph taken from the "Tiv of West Africa," in Marshall, *The Chosen Place, the Timeless People.*

58 Lorde, "Solstice," in *Black Unicorn,* 117.

59 Brah's excellent essay, "The Scent of Memory" plays on the title of an autobiographical account by a man named Lott of his mother's suicide in Southall. In

the work, Brah reconstructs Lott's family genealogy in this white working-class community in the context of interviews that Brah herself conducted earlier with Lott's contemporaries, and she analyses South Asian migration and the attendant violence against South Asians (which interrogate "origin stories" of belonging) in order to understand how Lott's mother was implicated in Brah's world, and Brah in the mother's world. The essay is an excellent methodological piece that demonstrates how to think about identification across difference.

60 Morrison, *Beloved,* 38. Carole Boyce Davies makes the point that there is a heterosexualizing move at work here in the fact that it is the manly presence of Paul D. that makes Sethe's womanly remembering possible. Davies argues that after all Sethe went through she was compelled to "leave her breasts" in Paul D.'s hands, to entrust her womanliness to heterosexual manhood. Davies, *Migration of the Subject,* 130–51.

61 Cameron, "Gee, You Don't Seem Like an Indian from the Reservation," 52.

62 Fonesca, *Bury Me Standing,* 281.

63 Bambara, *The Salt Eaters,* 3–4.

64 Morales, " 'And Even Fidel Can't Change That!' " 56.

65 Morrison, *Beloved,* 88.

66 Cameron, "Gee, You Don't Seem Like an Indian from the Reservation," 46–52.

67 Valerio, "It's in My Blood, My Face—My Mother's Voice, The Way I Sweat," 43.

68 Morrison, *Beloved,* 20.

69 Natalie Goldberg, "Writing the Landscape of Your Mind" (Austin, Writer's AudioShop, 1993, tape 1). Goldberg also discusses how the idea for this exercise of writing at the place of what is seen and not seen, and the space in between, comes out of her Zen practice.

70 Nhât H'ahn, *Touching Peace,* 53.

71 Bambara, "Foreword," viii.

72 El Mundo Zurdo is the left-handed world as envisioned by the editors of *Bridge.* See *Bridge,* 195–96.

73 Reagon, "Coalition Politics."

74 Lorde, "The Uses of the Erotic," in *Sister Outsider,* 58.

75 I borrow the term "revolutionary patience" from Gloria Joseph.

76 Marshall, *Praisesong for the Widow.*

77 Keating and Anzaldúa, *This Bridge We Call Home.*

78 American Diabetes Association, December 2004. These data have been taken from the Web site for the American Diabetes Association, National Diabetes Information Clearinghouse: www.diabetes.niddk.nih.gov/populations/index .htm.

79 Moraga, "From Inside the First World," xxvi (foreword to the twentieth anniversary edition of *This Bridge Called My Back*).

7. Pedagogies of the Sacred

1 Thompson, *Flash of the Spirit*, 166.

2 Murphy, *Working the Spirit*, 178, 179.

3 Prorok, "Boundaries are made for Crossing," 7.

4 Mani, *Interleaves*, 73.

5 Scheper-Hughes, *Death without Weeping*, 184–85.

6 Brown, "Serving the Spirits," 216.

7 Hurbon, "American Fantasy and Haitian Vodou," 250. See also Farmer, *AIDS as Accusation.*

8 In 1993 the U.S. Supreme Court ruled in the case of the *Church of Lukumi Babalu Aye, Inc. v. City of Hialeah* that Santería could legitimately be practiced.

9 Daniels, *When the Living Is the Prayer.*

10 Interview with author, 2000.

11 Wekker, *The Politics of Passion*, 54.

12 Wekker, "One Finger Does Not Drink Okra Soup," 335.

13 Gleason, *Oya*, 21.

14 Ibid., 289.

15 Daniels, *When the Living Is the Prayer*, 86.

16 Fu-kiau, *Tying the Spiritual Knot.*

17 Daniels, *When the Living Is the Prayer*, 95.

18 Fu-Kiau, *Tying the Spiritual Knot*, 73.

19 Brown, "Serving the Spirits," 236.

20 See the following for different renditions of this crisis that provides the starting point for healing: Anzaldúa, *Borderlands*, 46; Fernandes, *Transforming Feminist Praxis*, 43; and Hull, *Soul Talk*, 150.

21 Brown, "Serving the Spirits," 236.

22 Ibid., 260.

23 Gleason, *Oya*, 119.

24 Cottman, *Spirit Dive*, 155.

25 Hull, *Soul Talk*, 1–26.

26 Interview with author, 1999.

27 Teish, "Still Crazy After All These Years," 507.

28 Vega, *The Altar of My Soul*, 56.

29 Matory, *Sex and the Empire that Is No More.*

30 See Conner, with Hatfield Sparks, *Queering Creole Spiritual Traditions.*

31 Wekker, *I Am a Gold Coin*, 30.

32 See Fernandes, *Transforming Feminist Practice.*

33 Mani, *Interleaves.*

34 The term spiritual workplace is Daniel's. Berger cited in Brown, "Serving the Spirits," 261.

35 Moraga, "The Dying Road to a Nation."

36 Praisepoem composed at Punta Caracól, Puerto Morellos, México.

BIBLIOGRAPHY

Aarmo, Margaret. "How Homosexuality Became "un-African": the Case of Zimbabwe." In *Female Desires*, edited by Evelyn Blackwood and Saskia Wieringa, 255–
80. New York: Columbia University Press, 1999.

Abimbola, Wande. *Ifá Will Mend our Broken World: Thoughts on Yoruba Religion and
Culture in Africa and the Diaspora*. Roxbury: Aim Books, 1997.

Ahmed, Sara. *Strange Encounters: Embodied Others in Post-coloniality*. New York:
Routledge, 2000.

Alarcón, Francisco X. *Snake Poems: An Aztec Invocation*. San Francisco: Chronicle
Books, 1992.

Alexander, M. Jacqui. "Not Just (Any) Body Can Be a Citizen: The Politics of Law,
Sexuality and Postcoloniality in Trinidad and Tobago and the Bahamas." *Feminist
Review*, no. 48 (1994): 5–23.

——. "Redrafting Morality: The Postcolonial State and the Sexual Offences Bill of
Trinidad and Tobago." In *Third World Women and the Politics of Feminism*, edited
by Chandra Talpade Mohanty, Ann Russo, and Lourdes Torres. Bloomington:
Indiana University Press, 1991.

Alexander, M. Jacqui, and Chandra Talpade Mohanty, eds. *Feminist Genealogies,
Colonial Legacies, Democratic Futures*. New York: Routledge, 1997.

Allen, James, Hilton Als, John Lewis, and Leon F. Litwack, eds. *Without Sanctuary:
Lynching Photography in America*. Santa Fe, Calif.: Twin Palms Publishers, 2000.

Allen, Paula Gunn. *Off the Reservation: Reflections on Boundary-Busting, Border-
Crossing, Loose Canons*. Boston, Mass.: Beacon Press, 2000.

Al Radi, Nuha. *Baghdad Diaries, 1991–2002*. London: Saqi, 2003.

Alturi, Tana. "When the Closet Is a Region: Homophobia, Heterosexism and Nationalism in the Commonwealth Caribbean." Centre for Gender and Development Studies, Cave Hill, Barbados, West Indies, Working Paper no. 5 (March 2003).

Ammott, Teresa L., and Julie Matthaei, eds. *Race, Gender, and Work: A Multicultural Economic History of Women in the United States.* Boston: South End Press, 1991.

Anzaldúa, Gloria. "Speaking in Tongues: A Letter to 3rd World Women Writers." In *This Bridge Called My Back: Writings by Radical Women of Color,* edited by Cherríe Moraga and Gloria Anzaldúa, 165–75. New York: Kitchen Table: Women of Color Press, 1981.

Anzaldúa, Gloria and Analouise Keating. *This Bridge We Call Home: Radical Visions for Transformation.* New York: Routledge, 2002.

Badgett, M. V. Lee. "Beyond Biased Samples: Challenging the Myths on the Economic Status of Lesbians and Gay Men." In *Homo Economics: Capitalism, Community, and Lesbian and Gay Life,* edited by Amy Gluckman and Betsy Reed. New York: Routledge, 1997.

Baird-Windle, Patricia, and Eleanor J. Bader. *Targets of Hatred: Anti-Abortion Terrorism.* New York: Palgrave Macmillan, 2001.

Baker, Carlos. *Ernest Hemingway: A Life Story.* New York: Charles Scribner's Sons, 1969.

Baker, Dan. "A History in Ads: The Growth of the Gay and Lesbian Market." In *Homo Economics: Capitalism, Community, and Lesbian and Gay Life,* edited by Amy Gluckman and Betsy Reed. New York: Routledge, 1997.

Baldwin, James. "The Creative Dilemma." In *American Literature,* Ginn Literature, edited by Andrew J. Porter, Robert A. Bennett, and Henry L. Terrie. Lexington, Mass.: Ginn, 1981.

Bambara, Toni Cade. *The Salt Eaters.* New York: Vintage Books, 1992.

——. "Foreword." In *This Bridge Called My Back: Writings by Radical Women of Color,* edited by Cherríe Moraga and Gloria Anzaldúa, vi–viii. New York: Kitchen Table: Women of Color Press, 1981.

Banerjee, Payal. "Integrated Circuits: Capital, Race, Gender and Nation in the Making of Indian Immigrant Information Technology Workers in the United States." Ph.D. dissertation, Syracuse University, 2006.

Barndt, Deborah. "Whose 'Choice'? 'Flexible' Women Workers in the Tomato Food Chain." In *Sing, Whisper, Shout, Pray: Feminist Visions for a Just World* edited by M. Jacqui Alexander, Lisa Albrecht, Sharon Day, and Mab Segrest, 77–90. Berkeley: EdgeWork Books, 2003.

——. *Women Working the NAFTA Food Chain: Women, Food and Globalization.* Toronto: Second Story Press, 1999.

Barry, Tom, Beth Wood, and Deb Preusch. *The Other Side of Paradise: Foreign Control in the Caribbean,* New York: Grove Press, 1984.

Barthes, Roland. *Mythologies.* New York: Noonday Press, 1957.

Bell, Derrick. *Confronting Authority: Reflections of an Ardent Protester.* Boston: Beacon Press, 1994.

——. *An Atlas of the Difficult World: Poems, 1988–1991.* New York: W. W. Norton, 1991.

Bellegarde-Smith, Patrick. *Haiti: The Breached Citadel.* Toronto: Canadian Scholar's Press, 2004.

Bernard, Ian. " 'The Men of South Africa II': Constructing Gay Whiteness." Paper delivered at the Lesbian and Gay Studies Association conference, Iowa City, November 1994.

Best, Tony. "Guess Who Is Coming to Breakfast in New York with President George Bush? Some CARICOM Leaders have been Invited While Others Left Off the List." *CaribNews* 19, no. 1091 (24–30 September 2003): 5.

——. "U.S. Selling Torture Tools to Haiti but Blocking Development Aid." *CaribNews* 19, no. 1100 (26 November–2 December 2003): 3.

Bethel, Marion. *Guanahani, mi amor y otros poemas,* Cuba: Casa de las Americas, 1994.

——. "Where Do We Go From Here?" Keynote presentation, Second National Women's Conference, Nassau, 6 December 1986.

Bhattacharjee, Anannya. "The Public/Private Mirage: Mapping Homes and Undomesticating Violence Work in the South Asian Immigrant Community." In *Feminist Genealogies, Colonial Legacies, Democratic Futures,* edited by M. Jacqui Alexander and Chandra Talpade Mohanty, 308–329. New York: Routledge, 1997.

Blackmore, Josiah, and Gregory Hutcheson. *Queer Iberia: Sexualities, Cultures, and Crossings from the Middle Ages to the Renaissance.* Durham: Duke University Press, 1999.

Blackwood, Evelyn and Saskia Wieringa, eds. *Female Desires.* New York: Columbia University Press, 1999.

Boone, Joseph A. "Vacation Cruises; or the Homoerotics of Orientalism." *PMLA* 110, no. 1 (1995): 89–107.

Bragg, Rick. *I Am a Soldier Too: The Jessica Lynch Story.* New York: Knopf, 2003.

Brah, Avtar. *Cartographies of Diaspora: Contesting Identities.* New York: Routledge, 1997.

——. "The Scent of Memory: Strangers, Our Own, and Others," *Feminist Review,* no. 61 (spring 1999): 6.

Brand, Dionne. *No language is Neutral.* Toronto: Coach House Press, 1990.

——. *Sans Souci.* Toronto: Williams-Wallace, 1988.

Brandon, George. *Santería from Africa to the New World: The Dead Sell Memories.* Bloomington; Indianapolis: Indiana University Press, 1993.

Brown, Dee Alexander. *Bury My Heart at Wounded Knee.* New York: Washington Square Press, 1981.

Brown, Karen McCarthy. "Serving the Spirits: The Ritual Economy of Haitian

Vodou." In *Sacred Arts of Haitian Vodou,* edited by Donald J. Cosentino. Los Angeles: Fowler Museum of Cultural History, University of California, 1995.

Brown, Karen McCarthy, and Mama Lola. "The Altar Room: A Dialogue." In *Sacred Arts of Haitian Vodou,* edited by Donald J. Cosentino. Los Angeles: Fowler Museum of Cultural History, University of California, 1995.

Burnham, Linda. "Racism in US Welfare Policy: A Human Rights Issue." In *Sing, Whisper, Shout, Pray! Feminist Visions for a Just World,* edited by M. Jacqui Alexander, Lisa Albrecht, Sharon Day, and Mab Segrest. Berkeley: Edge Work Books, 2003.

Cabrera, Lydia. *Yemayá Y Ochún: Kariocha, Iyalorichas Y Olorichas.* New York: Lydia Cabrera, 1980.

Cairncross, Francis. "The Longest Journey: A Survey of International Migration." *Economist* 365, no. 8287 (2 November 2002): 3–16.

Cameron, Barbara, "Gee You Don't Seem Like an Indian From the Reservation." In *This Bridge Called My Back: Writings by Radical Women of Color,* edited by Cherríe Moraga and Gloria Anzaldúa, 46–52. New York: Kitchen Table: Women of Color Press, 1981.

Carbado, Devon W., and Mitu Gulati. "Conversations at Work." *Oregon Law Review* 79, no. 1 (spring 2000): 103–46.

——. "Working Identity." *Cornell Law Review* 85, no. 5 (July 2000): 1259–1308.

Caribbean Association for Feminist Research and Action. "The Debt Crisis: Who Really Owes Whom?" In *Women's Lives: Multicultural Perspectives,* edited by Gwyn Kirk and Margo Okazawa-Rey. London: Mayfield Publishing Company, 1998.

Caribbean Perspectives 1, no. 1 (1998). Special Issue: "NAFTA and the Caribbean."

Césaire, Aimé. *Discourse on Colonialism.* New York: Monthly Review Press, 1972.

Chang, Grace. *Disposable Domestics: Immigrant Women Workers in the Global Economy.* Cambridge, Mass.: South End Press, 2000.

Chasin, Alexandra. *Selling Out: The Gay and Lesbian Movement Goes to Market.* New York: St. Martin's Press, 2000.

Chavez-Silverman, Susana. "Tropicalizing the Liberal Arts College Classroom." In *Power, Race, and Gender in Academe: Strangers in the Tower,* edited by Shirley Geok-Lin Lim and María Herrera-Sobek. New York: Modern Language Association, 2000.

Christian, Barbara, "Race for Theory." In *Contemporary Literary Criticism: Literary and Cultural Studies,* edited by R. Davis and R. Schleifer. New York: Longman, 1994.

Churchill, Ward, and Winona LaDuke. "Native North America: The Political Economy of Radioactive Colonialism." In *The State of Native America: Genocide, Colonization, and Resistance,* edited by M. Annette Jaimes. Boston: South End Press, 1992.

Chrystos, "I Walk in the History of My People." In *This Bridge Called My Back: Writings by Radical Women of Color,* edited by Cherríe Moraga and Gloria Anzaldúa, 57. New York: Kitchen Table: Women of Color Press, 1981.

Clark, Danae. "Commodity Lesbianism." In *The Lesbian and Gay Studies Reader,* edited by Henry Abelove, Michèle Aina Barale, and David M. Halperin. New York: Routledge, 1993.

Clarke, Cheryl. *Living as a Lesbian.* New York: Firebrand Books, 1991.

Clarke, Edith. *My Mother Who Fathered Me.* London: George Allen and Unwin, 1966.

Clemencia, Joceline. "Women Who Love Women: A Whole Perspective from Kachapera to Open Throats." Paper presented at the Caribbean Studies Association conference, Curaçao, 23–26 May 1995.

Cohen, Cathy J. *The Boundaries of Blackness: AIDS and the Breakdown of Black Politics.* Chicago: University of Chicago Press, 1999.

——. "Punks, Bulldaggers, and Welfare Queens: The Real Radical Potential of Queer Politics?" *GLQ: A Journal of Lesbian and Gay Studies* 3 (1997): 437–65.

Colwill, Elizabeth. "Sex, Savagery, and Slavery in the Shaping of the French Body Politic." In *From the Royal to the Republican Body,* edited by Sara Norberg and Kathryn Mezler. Berkeley: University of California Press, 1998.

Combahee River Collective. "A Black Feminist Statement." In *This Bridge Called My Back: Writings by Radical Women of Color,* edited by Cherríe Moraga and Gloria Anzaldúa, 210–18. New York: Kitchen Table: Women of Color Press, 1981.

Connell, R. W. *Gender and Power.* Stanford: Stanford University Press, 1987.

Conner, Randy P., with David Hartfield Sparks. *Queering Creole Spiritual Traditions: Lesbian, Gay, Bisexual, and Transgender Participation in African-Inspired Traditions in the Americas.* New York: Harrington Park Press, 2004.

Cornell, Drucilla. *Defending Ideals: War, Democracy and Political Struggles.* New York: Routledge, 2004.

Cottman, Michael H. *Spirit Dive: An African American's Journey to Uncover a Sunken Slave Ship's Past.* New York: Three Rivers Press, 1999.

Craton, Michael. *A History of the Bahamas.* Waterloo, ON: San Salvador, 1986.

Crenshaw, Kimberlé. "Whose Story is it Anyway? Feminist and Antiracist Appropriations of Anita Hill." In *Race-ing Justice, En-gendering Power,* edited by Toni Morrison, 402–40. New York: Pantheon Books, 1992.

Dangarembga, Tsitsi. *Nervous Conditions.* New York: Seal Press, 2003.

Daniels, Donna D. "When the Living Is the Prayer: African-Based Religious Reverence in Everyday Life among Women of Color Devotees in the San Francisco Bay Area." Ph.D. dissertation, Stanford University, 1997.

Danielsen, Dan, and Karen Engle, eds. *After Identity: A Reader in Law and Culture.* New York: Routledge, 1995.

Danticat, Edwidge. *The Farming of Bones: A Novel.* New York: Soho Press, 1998.

Davenport, Doris. "The Pathology of Racism: A Conversation with Third World

Wimmin." In *This Bridge Called My Back: Writings by Radical Women of Color*, edited by Cherríe Moraga and Gloria Anzaldúa, 85–90. New York: Kitchen Table: Women of Color Press, 1981.

Davies, Carole Boyce. *Black Women, Writing and Identity: Migrations of the Subject*. New York: Routledge, 1994.

———. " 'Half the World': The Transnational Black Socialist Feminist Practice of Claudia Jones." Paper presented at the conference by African American Studies: Transnationalism, Gender, and the Changing Black World, Syracuse University, April 2002.

Davis, Angela. *Are Prisons Obsolete?* New York: Seven Stories Press, 2003.

———. *Blues Legacies and Black Feminism: Gertrude "MA" Rainey, Bessie Smith and Billie Holiday*. New York: Pantheon Books, 1998.

———. "Masked Racism: Reflections on the Prison Industrial Complex." In *Sing, Feminist Visions Whisper, for a Shout, Just World Pray!* Edited by M. Jacqui Alexander, Lisa Albrecht, Sharon Day, and Mab Segrest, 52–57. Berkeley: EdgeWork Books, 2003.

Deere, Carmen Diana. *In the Shadow of the Sun: Caribbean Development Alternatives and United States Policy*. Boulder: Westview Press, 1990.

Delany, Samuel R. *Times Square Red, Times Square Blue*. New York: New York University Press, 1999.

Delgado, Richard. "Citizenship." In *Immigrants Out! The New Nativism and the Anti-Immigrant Impulse in the United States*, edited by Juan Perea. New York: New York University Press, 1997.

D'Emilio, John. "Capitalism and Gay Identity." In *Powers of Desire: The Politics of Sexuality*, edited by Ann Snitow, Christine Stansell, and Sharon Thompson. New York: Monthly Review Press, 1983.

Deren, Maya. *Divine Horsemen: The Living Gods of Haiti*. Kingston, New York: McPherson & Company, 1991.

Diamond, Sara. *Roads to Dominion: Right-Wing Movements and Political Power in the United States*. New York: Guilford Press, 1995.

———. *Spiritual Warfare: The Politics of the Christian Right*. Boston: South End Press, 1989.

Dillard, Cynthia B, Daa'iyah Abdur-Rashid, and Cynthia A. Trons. "My Soul is a Witness: Affirming Pedagogies of the Spirit," *Qualitative Studies in Education* 13, no. 5 (2000): 447–62.

Dirlik, Arif. *The Postcolonial Aura: Third World Criticism in the Age of Global Capitalism*. Boulder: Westview Press, 1997.

Donaldson, Laura E., Anne Donadey, and Jael Silliman. "Subversive Couplings: On Antiracism and Postcolonialism in Graduate Women's Studies." In *Women's Studies on Its Own*, edited by Robyn Wiegman. Durham: Duke University Press, 2002.

Donzelot, J. *The Policing of Families: Welfare versus the State*. London: Hutchinson, 1979.

Dubois, J. Cl. "Transsexualism and Cultural Anthropology." *Gynecologié Practique* 20 (1969): 431–40.

Du Bois, W. E. B. *Black Reconstruction.* New York: Harcourt, 1935.

——. *The Souls of Black Folk.* New York: Penguin, 1969.

duCille, Ann. "Postcolonialism and Afrocentricity: Discourse and Dat Course." In *The Black Columbiad: Defining Moments in African American Literature and Culture,* edited by Werner Sollors and Maria Diedrich. Cambridge, Mass.: Harvard University Press, 1994.

Dynes, Wayne, ed. *The Encyclopedia of Homosexuality.* New York: Garland, 1990.

Edmondson, Belinda. " 'Race-ing' the Nation: Englishness, Blackness, and the Discourse of Victorian Manhood." In *Making Men: Gender, Literary Authority, and Women's Writing in Caribbean Narrative.* Durham: Duke University Press, 1999.

Eisenstein, Zillah. *Against Empire: Feminisms, Racism, and the West.* Melbourne: Spinifex Books, 2004.

Emeagwali, Gloria T. *Women Pay the Price: Structural Adjustment in Africa and the Caribbean.* Trenton, N.J.: Africa World Press, 1995.

Enloe, Cynthia. *Bananas, Beaches, and Bases: Making Feminist Sense of International Politics.* Berkeley: University of California Press, 1989.

——. *Maneuvers: The International Politics of Militarizing Women's Lives.* Berkeley: University of California Press, 2000.

——. *The Morning After: Sexual Politics at the End of the Cold War.* Berkeley: University of California Press, 1993.

Epega, Afolabi A. and Phillip John Neimark. *The Sacred Ifá Oracle.* San Francisco: Harper, 1995.

Evans, David T. *Sexual Citizenship: The Material Construction of Sexualities.* London: Routledge, 1993.

Fabian, Johannes. *Time and the Other: How Anthropology Makes Its Object.* New York: Columbia University Press, 2002.

Farmer, Paul. *AIDS as Accusation: Haiti and the Geography of Blame.* Berkeley: University of California Press, 1992.

Feinberg, Leslie. *Transgender Warriors: Making History from Joan of Arc to Dennis Rodman.* Boston: Beacon Press, 1996.

Feldman, Johnathan. *Universities in the Business of Repression: The Academic-Military-Industrial Complex in Central America.* Boston: South End Press, 1989.

Feminist Review, no. 48 (autumn) 1994. Special issue: "The New Politics of Sex and the State."

Fernandes, Leela. *Transforming Feminist Practice: Non-Violence, Social Justice, and the Possibilities of a Spiritualized Feminism.* San Francisco: Aunt Lute Books, 2003.

Fernandez-Kelley, Maria Patricia, and June Nash. *Women, Men, and the International Division of Labor.* Albany: State University of New York Press, 1983.

Finn, Janet L., and Lyne Underwood. "The State, the Clock, and the Struggle: An

Inquiry into the Discipline of Welfare Reform in Montana." *Social Text* 62 (spring 2000): 110–34.

Fish, Stanley. *There's No Such Thing as Free Speech . . . and It's a Good Thing Too.* New York: Oxford University Press, 1994.

Fonseca, Isabel. *Bury Me Standing: The Gypsies and their Journey.* New York: Alfred A. Knopf, 1996.

Foucault, Michel. *Discipline and Punish.* New York: Vintage, 1979.

Foundation for Inner Peace. *A Course in Miracles.* New York: Viking Press, 1996.

Fragomen, Austin T. "The Illegal Immigration Reform and Immigrant Responsibility Act of 1996: An Overview." *International Migration Review* 31, no. 2 (summer 1997): 438–60.

Frazier, E. Franklin. *Black Bourgeoisie.* Glencoe, Ill.: Free Press, 1957.

Freire, Paulo. *Pedagogies of the Oppressed.* Translated by Myna Bergman Ramos. New York: Continuum, 2000.

French, Joan, and Michelle Cave. "Sexual Choice as Human Rights: Women Loving Women." Paper presented at the Critical Perspectives in Human Rights in the Caribbean conference, Trinidad and Tobago, 26–28 January 1995.

Frilot, Shari. *Black Nations/Queer Nations.* New York: Videocassette, 1995.

Frymer, Paul, and John D. Skrentny. "The Rise of Instrumental Affirmative Action: Law and the New Significance of Race." *Connecticut Law Review* 36, no. 3 (2004): 665–76.

Fu-Kiau, Kimbwandende Kia Bunseki. *Tying the Spiritual Knot: African Cosmology of the Bântu-Kôngo, Principles of Living.* New York: Athelia Henrietta Press, 2000.

Gibran, Kahil. *The Prophet.* New York: Knopf, 1922.

Giddings, Paula. *When and Where I Enter: The Impact of Black Women on Race and Sex in America.* New York: Morrow, 1984.

Gilroy, Paul. *Small Acts: Thoughts on the Politics of Black Cultures.* London: Serpent's Tail, 1993.

Gleason, Judith. *Oya: In Praise of the Goddess.* Boston: Shambhala Publications, 1987.

Gluckman, Amy, and Betsy Reed. "The Gay Marketing Moment: Leaving Diversity in the Dust." *Dollars and Sense* 190 (1993): 16–19.

———, eds. *Homo Economics: Capitalism, Community, and Lesbian and Gay Life.* New York: Routledge, 1997.

Goldberg, Jonathan. "Sodomy in the New World: Anthropologies Old and New." In *Fear of a Queer Planet: Queer Politics and Social Theory,* edited by Michael Warner. Minneapolis: University of Minnesota Press, 1993.

Gopinath, Gayatri. *Impossible Desires: Queer Diasporas and South Asian Public Cultures.* Durham: Duke University Press, 2005.

Gordon, Avery F., and Christopher Newfield, eds. *Mapping Multiculturalism.* Minneapolis: University of Minnesota Press, 1996.

Gramsci, Antonio. *Selections from the Prison Notebooks*. London: Lawrence and Wishart, 1973.

Green, Richard. *Sexual Identity Conflict in Children and Adults*. New York: Basic Books, 1974.

Greenberg, David. *The Construction of Homosexuality*. Chicago: University of Chicago Press, 1988.

Grewal, Inderpal. "The Postcolonial, Ethnic Studies and the Diaspora: The Contexts of Ethnic Immigrant/Migrant Cultural Studies in the U.S." *Socialist Review* 24, no. 4 (1995): 45–74.

Grewal, Inderpal, and Caren Kaplan. "Global Identities: Theorizing Transnational Studies of Sexuality." *GLQ* 7, no. 4 (2001): 663–79.

——, eds. *Scattered Hegemonies: Postmodernity and Transnational Feminist Practices*. Minneapolis: University of Minnesota Press, 1994.

Grewal, Shabnam, et al., eds. *Charting the Journey: Writings by Black and Third World Women*. London: Sheba Feminist Publishers, 1988.

Grossberg, Lawrence. "History, Politics and Postmodernism: Stuart Hall and Cultural Studies." In *Stuart Hall: Critical Dialogues in Cultural Studies*, edited by David Morley and Kuan-Hsing Chen. New York: Routledge, 1996.

Guerrero, Marie Anna Jaimes. "Civil Rights versus Sovereignty: Native American Women in Life and Land Struggles." In *Feminist Genealogies, Colonial Legacies, Democratic Futures*, edited by M. Jacqui Alexander and Chandra Talpade Mohanty. New York: Routledge, 1997.

Habermas, Jürgen. *The Theory of Communicative Action*. Vol. 1: *Reason and the Rationalization of Society*. Boston: Beacon Press, 1984.

Hall, Burbin. "The Legal System of the Bahamas and the Role of the Attorney General." *Bahamian Journal* 1, no. 1 (1985): 10–13.

Hall, Catherine. "Competing Masculinities: Thomas Carlyle, John Stuart Mill and the Case of Governor Eyre." In *White, Male and Middle-Class: Explorations in Feminism and History*. Cambridge: Polity Press, 1992.

Hall, Stuart. "Cultural Studies and the Politics of Internationalization." In *Stuart Hall: Critical Dialogues in Cultural Studies*, edited by David Morley and Kuan-Hsing Chen. London: Routledge, 1996.

——. "Cultural Studies: Two Paradigms." *Media, Culture, and Society* 2, no. 1 (1980): 52–72.

Halley, Janet. "The Construction of Heterosexuality." In *Fear of a Queer Planet: Queer Politics and Social Theory*, edited by Michael Warner. Minneapolis: University of Minnesota Press, 1993.

——. *Don't: A Reader's Guide to the Military's Anti-Gay Policy*. Durham: Duke University Press, 1998.

Hammonds, Evelynn M. "Toward a Genealogy of Black Female Sexuality: The Problematic of Silence." In *Feminist Genealogies, Colonial Legacies, Democratic Futures*, edited by M. Jacqui Alexander and Chandra Talpade Mohanty. New York: Routledge, 1997.

Haney-López, Ian. *White by Law: The Legal Construction of Race.* New York: New York University Press, 1996.

Harcourt, Bernard E. "Reflecting on the Subject: A Critique of the Social Influence Conception of Deterrence, the Broken Windows Theory, and Order-Maintenance Policing New York Style." *Michigan Law Review* 97, no. 2 (November 1998): 291–389.

Harrison, Faye V. "The Gendered Politics and Violence of Structural Adjustment in Jamaica." In *Gender in a Transnational World: An Introduction to Women's Lives,* edited by Inderpal Grewal and Caren Kaplan. Boston: McGraw-Hill, 2001.

Hart, Lynda. *Fatal Women: Lesbian Sexuality and the Mark of Aggression.* Princeton: Princeton University Press, 1994.

Hatem, Mervat F. "The Invisible Half: Arab American Hybridity and Feminist Discourses in the 1990s." In *Talking Visions: Multicultural Feminism in a Transnational Age,* edited by Ella Shohat. Cambridge, Mass.: MIT Press, 1998.

Hawley, John C. *Postcolonial and Queer Theories: Intersections and Essays.* Westport, Conn: Greenwood Press, 2001.

Haynor, Priscilla B. *Unspeakable Truths: Confronting State Terror and Atrocity.* New York: Routledge, 2001.

Hemingway, Ernest. *Islands in the Stream.* New York: Charles Scribner's Sons, 1990.

hooks, bell. "Eating the Other." In *Black Looks: Race and Representation.* Boston: South End Press, 1992.

——. *Yearning: Race, Gender and Cultural Politics.* Boston: South End Press, 1990.

Hughes, Howard. "Holidays and Homosexual Identity." *Tourism Management* 18, no. 1 (1997): 3–9.

Hull, Akasha Gloria. *Soul Talk: The New Spirituality of African American Women.* Rochester, Vt.: Inner Traditions, 2001.

Hurbon, Laënnec. "American Fantasy and Haitian Vodou." In *Sacred Arts of Haitian Vodou,* edited by Donald J. Cosentino. Los Angeles: Fowler Museum of Cultural History, University of California, 1995.

Ingwerson, Marshall. "Out of Troubled Times, A New World Order." *Christian Science Monitor* (12 November 1990): A1, 5–6.

Jackson, Helen Hunt. *A Century of Dishonor: A Sketch of the United States Government's Dealings with Some of the Indian Tribes.* Minneapolis: Ross and Haines, 1964.

Jakobsen, Janet R. "Tolerating Hate? Or Hating Intolerance? Why Hate Crimes Legislation Won't Work." *Sojourner: The Women's Forum* (August 1999): 9–11.

Jakobsen, Janet, and Ann Pellegrini. "World Secularisms at the Millennium: Introduction." *Social Text* 64 (fall 2000): 1–27.

Johnson, Doris L. *The Quiet Revolution in the Bahamas.* Nassau: Family Islands Press, 1972.

Jordan, June. *Affirmative Acts.* New York: Anchor Books, 1998.

Kadi, Joanna. *Food for Our Grandmothers: Writings by Arab-American and Arab-Canadian Feminists.* Boston: South End Press, 1994.

Kaplan, Amy, and Donald E. Pease, eds. *Cultures of United States Imperialism.* Durham: Duke University Press, 1993.

Kaplan, Caren, and Inderpal Grewal. "Transnational Practices and Interdisciplinary Feminist Scholarship: Refiguring Women's and Gender Studies." In *Women's Studies on Its Own,* edited by Robyn Wiegman. Durham: Duke University Press, 2002.

Kates, Steven. *Twenty Million New Customers! Understanding Gay Men's Consumer Behavior.* Bingham: Haworth Press, 1998.

Katz-Fishman, Walda, and Jerome Scott. "Building the Peoples' Hemispheric Movement in the Midst of a Growing Police State." *From the Left* 24, no. 2 (2003): 7–8.

Kelley, Robin D. G. "The Proletariat Goes to College." In *Will Teach for Food: Academic Labor in Crisis,* edited by Cary Nelson. Minneapolis: University of Minnesota Press, 1997.

Kempadoo, Kamala. *Sexing the Caribbean: Gender, Race and Sexual Labor.* New York: Routledge, 2004.

——. *Sun, Sex and Gold: Tourism and Sex Work in the Caribbean.* Lanham, Md.: Rowman and Littlefield, 1999.

——. "Women of Color and the Global Sex Trade: Transnational Feminist Perspectives." *Meridians: Feminism, Race, Transnationalism* 1, no. 2 (spring 2001): 28–51.

Kincaid, Jamaica. *A Small Place.* New York: Farrar, Straus and Giroux, 1988.

Kingsolver, Barbara. *The Poisonwood Bible.* New York: Harper Perennial, 1998.

Knowles, Sir Leonard, *Elements of Bahamian Law.* Nassau: Business and Law, 1978.

Krohn, Claus-Dieter. *Intellectuals in Exile: Refugee Scholars and the New School for Social Research.* Amherst: University of Massachusetts Press, 1993.

Laclau, Ernesto. *Politics and Ideology in Marxist Theory.* London: New Left Books, 1977.

LaDuke, Winona. "Nitassinan: The Hunter and the Peasant." In *Sing, Whisper, Shout, Pray! Feminist Visions for a Just World,* edited by M. Jacqui Alexander, Lisa Albrecht, Sharon Day, and Mab Segrest. Berkeley: EdgeWork Books, 2003.

Lamming, George. *The Pleasures of Exile.* London: M. Joseph, 1960.

Lane, Alycee J. "Black Bodies/Gay Bodies: The Politics of Race in the Gay Military Battle." In *The Black Studies Reader,* edited by Jacqueline Bobo, Cynthia Hudley, and Claudine Michel, 1074–88. New York: Routledge, 2004.

Langton, Rae. "Speech Acts and Unspeakable Acts." *Philosophy and Public Affairs* 20, no. 2 (spring 1992): 293–30.

Latina Feminist Group, ed. *Telling to Live: Latina Feminist Testimonios.* Durham: Duke University Press, 2001.

Lazreg, Marnia. "Feminism and Difference: The Perils of Writing as a Woman on Women in Algeria." *Feminist Studies* 14 no. 1 (spring 1988): 81–107.

Leong, Andrew. "How Public Policy Reforms, Shapes, and Reveals the Shape of Asian America." In *Contemporary Asian American Communities: Intersections and Divergences,* edited by Linda Trinh Vo and Rick Bonus. Philadelphia: Temple University Press, 2002.

Lerner, Sharon. "Just Say 'I Do.'" *Nation* 275, no. 18 (25 November 2002): 22–23.

Lévinas, Emmanuel. "Time and the Other." In *The Levinas Reader,* edited by Sean Hand. Cambridge, Mass.: Blackwell Publishers, 1996.

Levins Morales, Aurora. "And Even Fidel Can't Change That!" In *This Bridge Called My Back: Writings by Radical Women of Color,* edited by Cherríe Moraga and Gloria Anzaldúa, 53–56. New York: Kitchen Table: Women of Color Press, 1981.

Lewis, Gail. *"Race," Gender, Social Welfare: Encounters in a Postcolonial Society.* Cambridge, U.K.: Polity Press, 2000.

Lewis, Laura. "From Sodomy to Superstition: The Active Pathic and Bodily Transgressions in Colonial Mexico." Paper prepared for the conference The Body and the Body Politic in Latin America, Center for Historical Studies, University of Maryland at College Park, April 2003.

Lewis, Reina. *Gendering Orientalism: Race, Femininity, and Representation.* London: Routledge, 1996.

Lim, Shirley Geok-Lin, and María Herrera-Sobek, eds. *Power, Race, and Gender in Academe: Strangers in the Tower.* New York: Modern Language Association, 2000.

Lorde, Audre. *A Burst of Light: Essays.* New York: Firebrand Books, 1988.

——. *The Marvelous Arithmetics of Distance.* New York: Norton, 1993.

——. *Sister Outsider.* Trumansburg, N.Y.: Crossing Press, 1982.

——. *Zami: A New Spelling of My Name.* Trumansburg, N.Y.: Crossing Press, 1982.

Louie, Miriam Ching Yoon. "La Mujer Luchando, El Mundo Transformando! Mexican Immigrant Women Workers." In *Sweatshop Warriors: Immigrant Women Workers Take on the Global Factory.* Cambridge, Mass.: South End Press, 2001.

Lowe, Lisa. *Immigrant Acts: On Asian American Cultural Politics.* Durham: Duke University Press, 1996.

Lukenbill, Grant. *Smart Spending: The Gay and Lesbian Guide to Socially Responsible Shopping and Investing.* Los Angeles: Alyson Books, 1999.

——. *Untold Millions: Positioning Your Business for the Gay and Lesbian Consumer Revolution.* New York: Harper Business, 1995.

MacKinnon, Catharine A. *Only Words.* Cambridge, Mass.: Harvard University Press, 1993.

Malek, Alloula. *The Colonial Harem.* Minneapolis: University of Minnesota Press, 2000.

Manalansan, Martin F., IV. *Global Divas: Filipino Gay Men in the Diaspora.* Durham: Duke University Press, 2003.

Manderson, Lenore, and Margaret Jolly, eds. *Sites of Desire, Economics of Pleasure: Sexualities in Asia and the Pacific.* Chicago: University of Chicago Press, 1997.

Mani, Lata. *Interleaves: Ruminations on Illness and Spiritual Life.* Northampton, Mass.: Interlink Publishing Group, 2001.

Marcus, Isabel. "Thinking and Teaching about Terrorism in the Home." Paper presented at the Feminism and Legal Theory workshop, Columbia University, June 1992.

Marshall, Paule. *The Chosen Place, the Timeless People.* New York: Harcourt, Brace & World, 1969.

———. *Praisesong for the Widow.* New York: Penguin, 1983.

———. *The Fisher King: A Novel.* New York: Scribner, 2000.

Mason, John. *Four New World Yorùbá Rituals.* New York: Yorùbá Theological Archministry, 1993.

Massey, Douglas S., and Nancy A. Denton. *American Apartheid: Segregation and the Making of the Underclass.* Cambridge, Mass.: Harvard University Press, 1993.

Matory, J. Lorand. *Sex and the Empire that Is No More: Gender and the Politics of Metaphor in Oyo Yoruba Religion.* Minneapolis: University of Minnesota Press, 1994.

Maugé, Conrad E. *The Lost Orisha.* Mount Vernon, N.Y.: House of Providence, 1996.

Mbiti, John S. *African Religions and Philosophy.* Portsmouth, NH: Heinemann International, 1969.

McAfee, Kathy. *Storm Signals: Structural Adjustment and Development Alternatives in the Caribbean.* Boston: South End Press, 1991.

McAlister, Elizabeth. *Rara! Vodou, Power, and Performance in Haiti and Its Diaspora.* Berkeley: University of California Press, 2002.

McClintock, Anne. "The Lay of the Land: Genealogies of Imperialism." In *Imperial Leather: Race, Gender, and Sexuality in the Colonial Context.* New York: Routledge, 1995.

Mercer, Kobena. "Black Identity/Queer Identity." Paper presented at the conference Black Nation/Queer Nation? Lesbian and Gay Sexualities in the African Diaspora, New York, April 1995.

Metraux, Alfred. *Voodoo in Haiti.* New York: Schocken Books, 1972.

Meyers, Jeffrey. *Hemingway: A Biography.* New York: Harper and Row, 1985.

Miller, J. G. *Family Property and Financial Provisions.* London: Sweet and Miller, 1983.

Moallem, Minoo. "Am I a Muslim Woman? Nationalist Reactions and Postcolonial Transactions: Colonizing and Decolonizing Practices in Academia." Paper presented at the conference Practicing Transgressions, University of California at Berkeley, February 2002.

Mohanty, Chandra Talpade. "Affirmative Action in the Service of the Empire?" Paper delivered at the annual meeting of the Modern Language Association, Syracuse, December 2003.

———. "Cartographies of Struggle." In *Third World Women and the Politics of Feminism,* edited by Chandra Talpade Mohanty, Ann Russo, and Lordes Torres. Bloomington: Indiana University Press, 1991.

——. *Feminism without Borders: Decolonizing Theory, Practicing Solidarity.* Durham: Duke University Press, 2003.

——. "Under Western Eyes: Feminist Scholarship and Colonial Discourses." In *Third World Women and the Politics of Feminism,* edited by Chandra Talpade Mohanty, Ann Russo, and Lourdes Torres. Bloomington: Indiana University Press, 1991.

——. "Women Workers and Capitalist Scripts: Ideologies, Domination, Common Interests, and the Politics of Solidarity." In *Feminist Genealogies, Colonial Legacies, Democratic Futures,* edited by M. Jacqui Alexander and Chandra Talpade Mohanty. New York: Routledge, 1997.

Mohanty, Satya P. "Us and Them: On the Philosophical Bases of Political Criticism." *Yale Journal of Criticism* 2, no. 2 (1989): 1–23.

Moir, Susan. "Laboring for Gay Rights: An Interview with Susan Moir." In *Homo Economics: Capitalism Community and Gay and Lesbian Life,* edited by Amy Gluckman and Betsy Reed, 229–240. New York: Routledge, 1997.

Mollenkopf, John H., and Manuel Castells, eds. *Dual City: Restructuring New York.* New York: Russell Sage Foundation, 1991.

Mondésire, Alicia, and Leith Dunn. "Towards Equity in Development: A Report on the Status of Women in 16 Commonwealth Caribbean Countries." Paper presented at the Fourth World Congress on Women, Georgetown, Guyana, May 1994.

Montejano, David. *Anglos and Mexicans in the Making of Texas, 1836–1986.* Austin: University of Texas Press, 1987.

Moody-Adams, Michele M. *Fieldwork in Familiar Places. Morality, Culture, and Philosophy.* Cambridge, Mass.: Harvard University Press, 1997.

Moraga, Cherríe. "The Dying Road to a Nation: A prayer para un Pueblo." In *Sing, Whisper, Shout, Pray: Feminist Visions for a Just World,* edited by M. Jacqui Alexander, Lisa Albrecht, Sharon Day and Mab Segrest, 687–703. Berkeley: Edge-Work Books, 2003.

——. "From Inside the First World." In *This Bridge Called My Back: Writings by Radical Women of Color 20th Anniversary Edition,* edited by Cherríe Moraga and Gloria Anzaldúa, xv–xxxiii. Berkeley: Third Woman Press, 2002.

——. *Loving in the War Years: lo que nunca pasó por sus labios.* Boston: South End Press, 1983.

——. "A Tuna Bleeding in the Heat: A Chicana Codex of Changing Consciousness." Lecture delivered at the Center for Lesbian and Gay Studies, City University of New York, December 2000.

Moraga, Cherríe, and Gloria Anzaldúa, eds. *This Bridge Called My Back: Writings by Radical Women of Color.* Berkeley: Third Woman Press, 2002 [1983].

Morales, Rosario. "We're All in the Same Boat." In *This Bridge Called My Back: Writings by Radical Women of Color,* edited by Cherríe Moraga and Gloria Anzaldúa 91–93. New York: Kitchen Table: Women of Color Press, 1981.

Morrison, Toni. *The Bluest Eye.* New York: Penguin Books, 1994.

——. "The Nobel Lecture in Literature 1993." In *Nobel Lectures, 1991–1995*, edited by Sture Allén. Singapore: World Scientific Publishing Company, 1997.

——. *Playing in the Dark: Whiteness and the Literary Imagination.* Cambridge, Mass.: Harvard University Press, 1992.

——. *Race-ing Justice, En-gendering Power: Essays on Anita Hill, Clarence Thomas, and the Construction of Social Reality.* New York: Pantheon, 1992.

——. "Unspeakable Things Unspoken: The Afro-American Presence in American Literature." *Michigan Quarterly Review* 28 (winter 1989): 1–34.

Moya, Paula M. L. "Postmodernism, 'Realism,' and the Politics of Identity." In *Feminist Genealogies, Colonial Legacies, Democratic Futures,* edited by M. Jacqui Alexander and Chandra T. Mohanty. New York: Routledge, 1997.

Murphy, Joseph M. *Working the Spirit: Ceremonies of the African Diaspora.* Boston: Beacon Press, 1994.

Murphy, Joseph M. and Mei-Mei Sanford, eds. *Ọṣun across the waters: A Yoruba Goddess in Africa and the Americas.* Bloomington: Indiana University Press, 2001.

Najmabadi, Afsaneh. "(Un)Veiling Feminism." *Social Text* 64 (fall 2000): 29–45.

Nakano-Glenn, Evelyn. "From Servitude to Service Work: Historical Continuities in the Racial Division of Paid Reproductive Labor." *Signs* 18, no. 1 (autumn 1992): 1–43.

Nandy, Ashis. *The Intimate Enemy.* Oxford: Oxford University Press, 1983.

——. *Traditions, Tyranny and Utopias: Essays on the Politics of Awareness.* Oxford: Oxford University Press, 1987.

Narayan, Uma. *Dislocating Cultures: Identities, Traditions, and Third World Feminism.* New York: Routledge, 1997.

National Labor Committee. *Help End the Race to the Bottom.* New York: National Labor Committee Education Fund, 1998.

——. *The U.S. in Haiti: How to Get Rich on 11 Cents an Hour.* New York: National Labor Committee Education Fund, 1996.

Nelson, Cary, ed. *Will Teach for Food: Academic Labor in Crisis.* Minneapolis: University of Minnesota Press, 1997.

Neruda, Pablo. "Notes on a Splendid City." In *Nobel Lectures: Literature, 1968–1980,* edited by Sture Allen. Singapore: World Scientific Publishing Co., 1993.

Neubeck, Kenneth J., and Noel A. Cazenave. *Welfare Racism: Playing the Race Card against America's Poor.* New York: Routledge, 2001.

Nhât H'ahn, Thích. *Fragrant Palm Leaves: Journals, 1962–1966;* translated by Mobi Warren. Berkeley: Parallax Press, 1998.

——. *Our Appointment with Life: The Buddha's Teaching on Living in the Present.* Berkeley: Parallax Press, 1990.

——. *Vietnam: Lotus in a Sea of Fire.* New York: Hill and Wang, 1967.

Nobles, Melissa. *Shades of Citizenship: Race and the Census in Modern Politics.* Stanford: Stanford University Press, 2000.

Nurse, Keith. "Migration and Development in the Caribbean." Presentation at the Workshop on Hemispheric Integration and Transnationalism, Institute of International Relations, February 2004.

O'Crouley, Pedro Alonso. *A Description of the Kingdom of New Spain, 1774.* Translated by Sean Galvin. San Francisco: John Howell Books, 1972.

Okazawa-Rey, Margo. "Warring on Women: Understanding Complex Inequalities of Gender, Race, Class and Nation." *AFFILIA* 17, no. 3 (2002): 371–83.

Ong, Aihwa. *Flexible Citizenship: The Cultural Logics of Transnationality.* Durham: Duke University Press, 1999.

Orozco, Manuel. "Globalization and Migration: The Impact of Family Remittances in Latin America." *Latin American Politics and Society* 44, no. 2 (summer 2002): 41–66.

Painter, Nell Irvin. "Black Studies, Black Professors, and the Struggle of Perception." *Chronicle of Higher Education* (15 December 2000): B7–9.

Panjabi, Kavita. "Probing 'Morality' and State Violence: Feminist Values and Communicative Interaction in Prison Testimonios in Argentina." In *Feminist Genealogies, Colonial Legacies, Democratic Futures,* edited by M. Jacqui Alexander and Chandra Talpade Mohanty. New York: Routledge, 1997.

Paquet, Sandra Puchet. *The Novels of George Lamming.* Kingston, Jamaica: Heinemann Educational Books, 1982.

Parker, Andrew. *Nationalism and Sexuality.* New York: Routledge, 1991.

Parker, Pat. "Sunday." In *Movement in Black: The Collected Poetry of Pat Parker, 1961–1978.* Trumansburg, N.Y.: Crossing Press, 1983.

Patel, Gita. "Ghostly Appearances: Time Tales Tallied Up." *Social Text* 64 (fall 2000): 47–66.

———. "Sleight(s) of Hand in Mirror Houses." Paper presented at the Queer Theory on Location conference, New York, April 1996.

Patullo, Polly. *Last Resorts: The Cost of Tourism in the Caribbean.* London: Cassell, 1996.

Peake, Linda. "The Development and Role of Women's Political Organizations in Guyana." In *Women and Change in the Caribbean,* edited by Janet Momsen. London: James Currey, 1993.

Perdue, Theda. *Cherokee Women: Gender and Culture Change, 1700–1835.* Lincoln: University of Nebraska Press, 1998.

Perea, Juan, ed. *Immigrants Out! The New Nativism and the Anti-Immigrant Impulse in the United States.* New York: New York University Press, 1997.

Persaud, Randolph B. *Counter-Hegemony and Foreign Policy: The Dialectics of Global Forces in Jamaica.* Albany: State University of New York Press, 2001.

Petchesky, Rosalind P. "Phantom Towers: Feminist Reflections on the Battle between Global Capitalism and Fundamentalist Terrorism." In *Sing, Whisper, Shout, Pray! Feminist Visions for a Just World,* edited by M. Jacqui Alexander, Lisa Albrecht, Sharon Day, and Mab Segrest. Fort Bragg, Calif.: EdgeWork Books, 2003.

Phillips, Caryl. *The Atlantic Sound*. London: Faber and Faber, 2000.

Pitt, William Rivers. "Blood Money." In *t r u t h o u t*. www.truthout.org/cgi-bin/ artman/exec/view/cgi?archive=1&num+53. 27 February 2003.

Pollitt, Katha. "Shotgun Weddings." *Nation* 274, no. 4 (4 February 2002).

Porter, Kenneth Wiggins. *The Black Seminoles: History of a Freedom-Seeking People*. Gainsville: University Press of Florida, 1996.

Povinelli, Elizabeth, and George Chauncey. "Thinking Sexuality Transnationally." *GLQ* 5, no. 4 (1999): 439–50.

Powell, Patricia. *The Pagoda: A Novel*. New York: Knopf, 1998.

Pratt, Mary Louise. *Imperial Eyes: Travel Writing and Transculturation*. London: Routledge, 1992.

Preston Blier, Suzanne. *African Vodun: Art, Psychology, and Power*. Chicago; London: University of Chicago Press, 1995.

Pritchard, Annette, Nigel Morgan and Diane Sedgely. "Reaching Out to the Gay Tourist: Opportunities and Threats in an Emerging Market Segment." *Tourism Management* 19, no. 3 (1998): 273–82.

Prorok, Carolyn, V. "Boundaries are Made for Crossing: The Feminized Spatiality of Puerto Rican Espiritismo in New York City." *Gender, Place and Culture* 7, no. 1 (2000): 57–79.

Puar, Jasbir. "Transnational Circuits and Sexuality in Trinidad." *Signs* 26, no. 4 (summer 2001): 1039–65.

——. "A Transnational Feminist Critique of Queer Tourism." *Antipode* 34, no. 5 (2002): 935–946.

Puar, Jasbir K., and Amit Rai. "Monster, Terrorist, Fag: The War on Terrorism and the Production of Docile Patriots." *Social Text* 72 (fall 2002): 117–48.

Quintanales, Mirtha. "I Paid Very Hard for my Immigrant Ignorance." In *This Bridge Called My Back: Writings by Radical Women of Color*, edited by Cherríe Moraga and Gloria Anzaldúa, 150–56. New York: Kitchen Table: Women of Color Press, 1981.

Rabinowitz, Paula. "What Film Noir Can Teach Us about 'Welfare as We Know It.' " *Social Text* 62 (spring 2000): 135–41.

Rainwater, Lee, and William L. Yancey. *The Moynihan Report and the Politics of Controversy: A Trans-action Social Science and Public Policy Report*. Cambridge, Mass.: MIT Press, 1967.

Reagon, Bernice Johnshon. "Coalition Politics: Turning the Century." In *Home Girls: A Black Feminist Anthology*, edited by Barbara Smith. New York: Kitchen Table: Women of Color Press, 1983.

Reddock, Rhoda. *Women, Labor and Politics in Trinidad and Tobago*. London: Zed, 1994.

Reinhold, Susan. "Through the Parliamentary Looking Glass: 'Real' and 'Pretend' Families in Contemporary British Politics." *Feminist Review*, no. 48 (autumn 1994): 61–79.

Rich, Adrienne. *An Atlas of the Difficult World: Poems 1988–1991*. New York: W. W. Norton, 1991.

———. "Notes Toward a Politics of Location." In *Blood, Bread, and Poetry*. New York: Norton, 1986.

Rigaud, Milo. *Secrets of Voodoo*. City Lights: San Francisco, 1985.

Riley, Robin. "O(saddam)a: New Propaganda, Masculinity and Enemification on the Information Highway." Paper presented at the International Studies Association Meeting. New Orleans, March 2000.

Roberts, Audrey. "The Changing Role of Women's Bureaux in the Process of Social Change in the Caribbean." Keynote presentation, tenth anniversary celebration of the Women's Affairs Unit, Nassau, Bahamas, 17 June 1991.

Robinson, Tracy. "Beyond the Bill of Rights: Sexing the Citizen." In *Confronting Power, Theorising Gender: Interdisciplinary Perspectives in the Caribbean*, edited by Eudine Barriteau. Kingston, Jamaica: University of the West Indies Press, 2003.

———. "Fictions of Citizenship, Bodies without Sex: The Production and Effacement of Gender in Law." *Small Axe* 7 (March 2000): 1–27.

Robson, Ruthann. *Lesbian (Out)law: Survival Under the Rule of Law*. Ithaca, NY: Firebrand Books, 1992.

Roscoe, Will. *The Zuni Man-Woman*. Albuquerque: University of New Mexico Press, 1988.

Rosenthal, Judy. *Possession, Ecstasy, & Law in Ewe Voodoo*. Charlottesville, Virginia: University of Virginia Press, 1998.

Rowbotham, Sheila, and Swasti Mitter, eds. *Dignity and Daily Bread: New Forms of Economic Organising among Poor Women in the Third World and the First*. New York: Routledge, 1994.

Roy, Arundhati. *Power Politics*. Cambridge, Mass: South End Press, 2000.

Rustin, Bayard. *Down the Line: The Collected Writings of Bayard Rustin*. Chicago: Quadrangle Books, 1971.

Sabbah, Fatna A. *Woman in the Muslim Unconscious*. New York: Pergamon Press, 1984.

Said, Edward W. *Culture and Imperialism,* New York: Knopf, 1993.

———.*Orientalism: Western Conceptions of the Orient*. New York: Vintage Books, 1979.

Sangari, Kumkum, and Sudesh Vaid. *Recasting Women: Essays in Indian Colonial History*. New Brunswick: Rutgers University Press, 1990.

Sassen, Saskia. *Globalization and Its Discontents*. New York: New Press, 1998.

Saunders, Gail. "Women in the Bahamian Society and Economy in the Late Nineteenth and Early Twentieth Centuries." Paper presented at the Twenty-Third Annual Conference of Caribbean Historians, Dominican Republic, March 1991.

Scheper-Hughes, Nancy. *Death without Weeping: The Violence of Everyday Life in Brazil*. Berkeley: University of California Press, 1992.

Schneider, Alison. "A Haven for Oppressed Scholars Finds Itself Accused of Oppression: A Bizarre Battle over Faculty Diversity Divides Students and Professors at the New School." *Chronicle of Higher Education* (11 July 1997): A8–10.

Selvadurai, Shyam. *Funny Boy.* New York: Harcourt Brace and Co., 1994.

Sen, Rinku. "The First Time Was Tragedy." *ColorLines* 3, no. 3 (fall 2000): 19–21.

Shahjahan, Siyad Ahmed. "Centering Spirituality in the Academy: Towards a Transformative Way of Teaching and Learning," *Journal of Transformative Education* 2,
no. 4 (2004): 294–312.

Shohat, Ella. "Area Studies, Transnationalism, and the Feminist Production of
Knowledge." *Signs* 26, no. 4 (summer 2001): 1269–73.

——, ed. *Talking Visions: Multicultural Feminism in a Transnational Age.* Cambridge,
Mass.: New Museum of Contemporary Art; MIT Press, 1998.

Silliman, Jael, and Anannya Bhattacharjee. *Policing the National Body: Race, Gender,
and Criminalization.* Cambridge, Mass.: South End Press, 2002.

Silvera, Makeda. "Man Royals and Sodomites: Some Thoughts on the Invisibility of
Afro-Caribbean Lesbians." *Feminist Studies* 18, no. 3 (1992): 521–32.

Sistren, with Honor Ford-Smith. *Lionheart Gal: Lifestories of Jamaican Women.* London: Women's Press, 1994.

Smith, Barbara, ed. *Homegirls: A Black Feminist Anthology.* New York: Kitchen Table:
Women of Color Press, 1983.

Social Text 51 (summer 1997). Special issue: "Academic Labor."

Social Text 52–53 (fall/winter 1997). Special issue: "Queer Transexions of Race,
Nation, and Gender."

Somé, Malidoma Patrice. *Of Water and the Spirit: Ritual, Magic, and Initiation in the
Life of an African Shaman.* New York: G. P. Putnam's Sons, 1994.

Spare Change (18–31 October 2001). Special issue: "Domestic Violence and the World
Trade Center."

Spartacus International Gay Guides. Leck, Germany: Clausen & Bosse. Editions from
1987–2004.

Spiro, Melford. "Cultural Relativism and the Future of Anthropology." In *Rereading
Cultural Anthropology,* edited by George E. Marcus. Durham: Duke University
Press, 1992.

Stone, Deborah. "AIDS and the Moral Economy of Insurance." In *Homo Economics:
Capitalism, Community, and Lesbian and Gay Life,* ed. Amy Gluckman and Betsy
Reed. New York: Routledge, 1997.

Subramaniam, Banu. "Archaic Modernities: Science, Secularism, and Religion in
Modern India." *Social Text* 64 (fall 2000): 67–85.

Sudbury, Julia, ed. *Global Lockdown: Race and Gender in the Prison Industrial Complex.* New York: Routledge, 2005.

Tambiah, Yasmin. *Defining the Female "Body Politic": Sexuality and the State.*
SEPHIS: The Netherlands, 2002.

Teish, Luisa. "Still Crazy after All These Years." In *This Bridge We Call Home: Radical
Visions for Transformations,* edited by Gloria Anzaldúa and Analouise Keating.
New York: Routledge, 2002.

Thomas, Kendall. "Beyond the Privacy Principle." *Columbia Law Review* 92, no. 6 (October 1992): 1431–516.

———. "*Bowers v. Hardwick*: Beyond the Pleasure Principle." In *After Identity: A Reader in Law and Culture,* edited by Dan Danielsen and Karen Engle. New York: Routledge, 1995.

Thompson, Becky, and Sangeeta Tyagi, eds. *Beyond a Dream Deferred.* Minneapolis: University of Minnesota Press, 1993.

Thompson, Robert F. *Flash of the Spirit: African and Afro-American Art and Philosophy.* New York: Vintage Books, 1984.

Thurman, Howard. *A Strange Freedom: The Best of Howard Thurman on Religious Experience and Public Life,* edited by Walter Fluker and Catherine Tumber. Boston: Beacon Press, 1998.

Torpey, John. *The Invention of the Passport: Surveillance, Citizenship and the State.* Cambridge: Cambridge University Press, 2000.

Trask, Haunani-Kay. "Self-Determination for Pacific Island Women: The Case of Hawai'i." In *Sing, Whisper, Shout, Pray! Feminist Visions for a Just World,* edited by M. Jacqui Alexander, Lisa Albrecht, Sharon Day, and Mab Segrest. Fort Bragg, Calif.: EdgeWork Books, 1998.

Trouillot, Michel-Rolph. "The Caribbean Region: An Open Frontier in Anthropological Theory." *Annual Review of Anthropology* 21 (1992): 19–42.

Trumpbour, John, ed. *How Harvard Rules: Reason in the Service of Empire.* Boston: South End Press, 1989.

Truong, Thanh-Dam. *Sex, Money and Morality.* London: Zed, 1990.

Vaid, Urvashi. *Virtual Equality: The Mainstreaming of Lesbian and Gay Liberation.* New York: Anchor Books, 1995.

Valerio, Anita. "It's in My Blood, My Face—My mother's Voice, The Way I Sweat." In *This Bridge Called My Back: Writings by Radical Women of Color,* edited by Cherríe Moraga and Gloria Anzaldúa, 41–45. New York: Kitchen Table: Women of Color Press, 1981.

Vega, Marta Moreno. *The Altar of My Soul: The Living Traditions of Santeria.* New York: One World, 2000.

Wackernagel, Mathis, and William Rees. *Our Ecological Footprint: Reproducing Human Impact on the Earth.* Gabriola Island, BC.: New Society Press, 1996.

Walker, Margaret Urban. "Rights to Truth." Paper presented at the Women's Rights as Human Rights conference, South-Eastern Women's Studies Association, Boca Raton, March 2001.

Wallach, Lori. "Public Citizen's Global Trade Watch Before the International Trade Commission, May 15, 1997: Impact of NAFTA on the U.S. Economy, NAFTA's Failure at 41 Months." http://www.islandhosting.com/~contempo/library/mai/wallach.html.

Walsch, Neale Donald. *Communion with God.* New York: G.P. Putnam's Sons, 2000.

Warner, Michael. *Fear of a Queer Planet: Queer Politics and Social Theory*. Minneapolis: University of Minnesota Press, 1993.

Weaver, Lloyd and Olukunmi Egbelade. *Maternal Divinity: Yemonja: Tranquil Sea Turbulent Tides: Eleven Tales from Africa*. Brooklyn: Athelia Henrietta Press, 1999.

Weber, Diane Cecilia. "Warrior Cops: The Ominous Growth of Paramilitarism in American Police Departments," Cato Institute Briefing Papers, 26 (August 1999).

Wekker, Gloria. *The Politics of Passion: Women's Sexual Culture in the Afro-Surinamese Diaspora*. New York: Columbia University Press, 2006.

——. "One Finger Does Not Drink Okra Soup: Afro-Surinamese Women and Critical Agency." In *Feminist Genealogies, Colonial Legacies, Democratic Futures*, edited by M. Jacqui Alexander and Chandra Talpade Mohanty. New York: Routledge, 1997.

West, Cornel. "The New Cultural Politics of Difference." In *Beyond a Dream Deferred, Multicultural Education and the Politics of Excellence*, edited by Becky Thompson and Sangeeta Tyagi. Minneapolis: University of Minnesota Press, 1993.

Wiegman, Robin. *Women's Studies on its Own*. Durham: Duke University Press, 2002.

Williams, Patricia. *The Alchemy of Race and Rights*. Cambridge, Mass.: Harvard University Press, 1991.

——. "Attack of the 50-Foot First Lady: The Demonization of Hillary Clinton." *Village Voice* 36 (1991): 35.

Wing, Bob. "Educate to Liberate!: Multiculturalism and the Struggle for Ethnic Studies." *ColorLines* 2, no. 2 (summer 1999): 1–7.

Witt, Lynn, Sherry Thomas, and Eric Marcus, eds. *Out in All Directions: The Almanac of Gay and Lesbian America*. New York: Warner Books, 1995.

Wolfe-Rocca, Ursula, Claudia Veronica Brignolo-Giménez, and Jasmine E. Aucott. "The Politics of Education." Archiving Project for the Mobilization, New School for Social Research, New York, 1996.

Women of South Asian Descent Collective, ed., *Our Feet Walk the Sky*. San Francisco: Aunt Lute Books, 1993.

Women Working for a Nuclear Free and Independent Pacific. *Pacific Women Speak, Why Haven't You Known?* Oxford: Green Line, 1987.

Yamada, Mitsuye. "Invisibility is an Unnatural Disaster: Reflections of an Asian American Woman." In *This Bridge Called My Back: Writings by Radical Women of Color*, edited by Cherríe Moraga and Gloria Anzaldúa, 35–40. New York: Kitchen Table: Women of Color Press, 1981.

Young, Iris Marion. *Justice and the Politics of Difference*. Princeton: Princeton University Press, 1990.

Zamora, Michelle. "Malinally as Spiritual Epistemology: Revisiting La Malinche through Náhuatl Cultural Forms." Masters thesis, Gender Studies and Feminist Theory, New School University, 1997. File with author.

American Competitiveness in the Twenty-first Century Act (2002), 225
American Express, 75
American Indian Movement, 365 n.2
And the Trees Still Stand (Bethel), 21
Anguilla, 104
anthropology, 189
anticolonialism, 182, 247–248, 260–261
Antigua, 104
Anya, 320
Anzaldúa, Gloria, 15, 283, 285–286
Apache, 269
apartheid, 123, 142
Arab Americans, 96–97
Arapaho, 269
Argentina, 122
artist, the, 18
Aruba, 82–83
Ashé, 289, 299
Asian Americans/Pacific Islanders, 133, 224, 251, 266, 269, 357 n.82
Aspen, Les, 199
Atlas of the Difficult World (Rich), 18
Audre Lorde Project, the, ix, 88, 343 n.52

backlash narratives, 364 nn.142, 143
Bahama Mama, 61
Bahamas, the: criminalization of sexuality in, 27–28, 52–53, 62–63; criminalization of women in, 24–25, 27–28, 62–63; domestic violence in, 11, 24–26, 29–34, 192–193; feminisms and, 21–22, 27, 29–34, 62–65; Haitians in, 338 n.48; heterosexualization within, 206; homosexuality within, 40–52; international women's organizations and, 334 n.3; marriage within, 340 n.85; national liberation movements and, 24–25, 49–50, 182–183; neocolonialism and, 182; recolonization within, 25, 26, 27, 182–183, 340 n.85; sexual and reproductive rights in, 32–34; tourism and, 26–27, 53–62, 67–68, 104; women's movements in, 21–22, 29–34, 50, 62–65, 334 n.3, 336 n.24. *See also* Caribbean, Anglophone

Balboa, Vasco Nuñez de, 191, 196–199, 335 n.12, 353 n.29
Baldwin, James, 18, 152–153, 273, 368 n.45
Bambara, Toni Cade, 257, 275, 279
Banerjee, Payal, 13, 190, 225, 357 n.82
Bannock, 269
Bântu-Kôngo, 290, 293–294, 299
Baraldini, Sylvia, 265
Barbados, 84, 104
Batá (Sacred drums), 320–321
belonging, 280–284
Beloved (Morrison), 277–278
Bennet, Louise, 262
Berger, John, 328
Bernard, Ian, 84
Bethel, Marion, 21, 22
Bhattacharjee, Anannya, 242
Bill of Rights Defense Committee, 361 nn.104, 107
bin Laden, Osama, 239–240
bisexuality, 84–85, 201, 310
blackness: African Americans and, 269–270; in Britain, 263; Caribbean people and, 269–270; citizenship and, 263; colonization and, 269–271; diasporic, 261–262, 272–275; exile and, 274; feminisms and, 268; heteromasculinity and, 223; heteropatriarchy and, 62–63; poverty and, 223–225; racialization and, 271–273; sexual commodification and, 60–61; whiteness and, 261; women and, 223–225, 263, 268, 274–275, 366 nn.13, 20; women of color politics and, 268. *See also* African Americans; black women; race; racialization
black women, 223–225, 263, 268, 366 nn.13, 20. *See also* women of color
Black Women in the Academy conference, 268, 269–270
body praxis, 291, 297–298, 318, 323–324, 326–327. *See also* embodiment
Bondieu, 299
Boone, Joseph, 85
borders/borderland, 17, 264
Bosnia, 265

Fish, Stanley, 121, 141

Fon, 291, 322

Ford-Smith, Honor, 259, 337 n.32

forgetting: *causa* and, 316; not forgetting and, 14, 284; remembering and, 14, 275–279; wisdom and, 276–279

fragmentation, 253–254, 280–284, 306–307, 352 n.19

France, 84

freedom, 11–12, 17, 18, 121, 142–143. *See also* pedagogies of crossing

Freire, Paulo, 6, 7, 107, 282

Fuerza Unida (Texas), 345 n.28

fundamentalisms, 193, 220–221

Funny Boy (Selvadurai), 67

Gaia's Guide, 82, 85

Garvey, Marcus, 273

gay consumers, 71, 72–78

gay men, 11, 40–46

gay travel guides, 71, 81–84

Gede, 324

G8 countries, 182, 350 n.3

gender: marriage and, 34–40; memory and, 324; militarization and, 97–100; modernity and, 96–97; poverty and, 36–37; power and, 4; property ownership and, 35–37; sexual commodification and, 27, 60–61; sexuality and, 324; spiritual practice and, 324; the state and, 23; studies of, 170–175, 185–188; transgender people and, 310; transmutations of, 324

gender studies, 170–175, 185–188

General Motors Corporation, 75

Georgia Sea Islands, 284

Gleason, Judith, 303–304, 306

globalization: class development and, 100–103; heterosexualization and, 246–247; tourism and, 86–87. *See also* corporatization

Gluckman, Amy, 69

God, 299

Goldberg, Jonathan, 196–197, 335 n.12, 353 n.29

Goldberg, Natalie, 278, 370 n.69

Gopinath, Gayatri, 368 n.39

Gorbachev, Mikhail, 94–95

Gramsci, Antonio, 93

Grenada, 49, 259

Grewal, Inderpal, 364 n.142

Guadeloupe, 82–83

Guam, 219, 233

Guerrero, Maria Anna Jaimes, 368 n.43

Gulf War (1991), 10, 107, 190, 199, 234, 241

Guyana, 356 n.55

Habermas, Jürgen, 125

Haiti, 103, 122, 265, 298, 338 n.48, 359 n.91, 369 n.52

"Haiti, I'm Sorry" (Rudder), 369 n.52

Haiti Justice Campaign, 76

Halberstam, Judith, 191, 368 n.39

Hall, Stuart, 2, 93, 190

Halley, Janet, 200, 205

hambre de justicia, 12–13, 103, 104, 105–106, 108

Harcourt, Bernard, 242, 362 n.123

Hart, Lynda, 23, 24

hate crimes, 213–222

Hatem, Mervat, 96–97

hatred, 213–222, 325

Hawai'i, 212, 213, 218–219, 233, 251, 280

healing, 293, 299, 311–323, 329, 371 n.20

"healthy" marriage, 226–228

hegemony, 4, 5–6, 325

Hemingway, Ernest, 57–58, 67–68

Herbert, Barbara, 366 n.20

heteromasculinity: blackness and, 223; patriotism and, 236–239; whiteness and, 236–239. *See also* heteropatriarchy; masculinities

heteropatriarchy, 23–24, 25, 28, 29–34, 62–65

heterosexualities, 4–5, 11, 227–228, 335 n.12

heterosexualization: the Caribbean and, 205–207; of citizenship, 25; class struggle and, 249–250; democracy and, 13–14; "Don't Ask, Don't Tell" policy and, 204–205; globalization and, 246–247; legal codes and, 207; linearity and, 13–14;

through marriage, 226–228; militarization and, 199–205; Military Working
Group and, 192–193; morality and, 205–
207; nationalism and, 11, 45–46; regionality and, 205–207; the state and, 23–24;
time/temporality and, 13–14, 183; of tradition, 2–3, 205–207; transnationalism,
181; violence and, 219; of welfare programs, 226–228. *See also*
heteropatriarchy

hierarchies, 5, 141–143, 189–190

Hill, Anita, 274

Hill, Leslie, 347 n.29, 349 n.65

HIV/AIDS, 24, 61, 265, 338 n.48, 341 n.9,
366 n.20

Hmong, 224

home, 281, 328

Homegirls (Smith), 9, 258

Homeland Security Act of 2002, 360 n.102.

homophobia, 75, 83

homosexuality: Bahamian, 40–52; category
of, 201; citizenship and, 46–53; colonization and, 48; criminalization of, 40–46;
marriage and, 213–221; militarism and,
199–205; the nation and, 46–53; orientalism and, 343 n.45; privacy and, 203–
204

Hong Kong, 104

hooks, bell, 15, 136–137

households, 231–232. *See also* private
sphere

Hull, Akasha Gloria, 322

hunger strikes, 159–163

Hurbon, Laënnec, 298

hypernationalism, 5, 247–248

hypervisibility, 351 n.10

Ibo Landing, 17, 284

identities: hegemonic, 4–5

identity: knowledge and, 151, 172–174, 177

Ifá, 302, 312

IGLTA (International Gay and Lesbian Travel
Association), 342 n.31

IGTA (International Gay Travel Association), 342 n.31

illegal aliens, 335 n.17. *See also*
immigrants/immigration

Illegal Immigration Reform and Immigrant
Responsibility Act of 1996, 225

illocutionary acts, 123–124, 159

IMF (International Monetary Fund), 195,
230, 245–246

immigrants/immigration: Asian Ameri-
cans/Pacific Islanders, 357 n.82; citizenship and, 28, 249; homeland security, 360
n.102; homeland security and, 360 n.102;
nationalism and, 335 n.17; refugee status
and, 366 n.16; violence and, 362 n.123;
welfare programs and, 224–225. *See also*
citizenship

Immigration and Naturalization Service,
368 n.38. *See also individual nations*

imperialism: feminist political organizations and, 184; homosexuality and, 49;
the neocolonial and, 182; recolonization
and, 182; the Sacred and, 327; tourism
and, 61–62; of the United States, 244–
245. *See also* empire; neocolonialism;
neo-imperialism

Imperial Order of Daughters of Empire,
334 n.3

imprisonment, 362 n.123

incarceration, 3, 242–243, 362 n.123, 367 n.27

incest, 30–32

India/Indians, 104, 262–263, 272

Indians (indigenous), 196–197, 204, 335
n.12. *See also individual nations*

individualism, 140–141, 175–176

Indonesia, 83

Ingwerson, Marshall, 94–95

intellectuals: progressive tradition, 176–178;
radical, 3

interconnectedness, 6, 323–324

interdisciplinarity, 253–254

International Gay and Lesbian Travel Association (IGLTA), 70, 80, 81, 86, 342 n.31

International Gay Travel Association
(IGTA), 342 n.31

International Monetary Fund (IMF), 195,
230, 245–246

intersubjectivity, 108–110, 109–112, 323–324
Iraq, 10, 185, 199, 243
Ireland, 104, 263
Islamic tradition, 239, 243
Israel, 251

Jakobsen, Janet, 196, 351 n.9
Jamaica, 49, 66–67, 86, 103, 259, 365 nn.1, 7, 366 n.11
Jewish peoples, 354 n.32
Jones, Claudia, 356 n.64
Jones, Tamara, 368 n.39
Jordan, 104
Joseph, Gloria I., ix, 368 n.39
journeys (of memory), 258–261
Judeo-Christian traditions, 196, 206, 221, 239, 243, 247–248, 262, 280, 339 n.66, 354 n.32
justice, 121–125, 346 n.1

kachapera, 49, 339 n.59
Kalunga, 303, 324
Kanaka Maoli, 284
Kaplan, Caren, 364 n.142
Kenya, 251, 259
Kerik, Bernard, 243, 363 n.125
Khan, Ismith, 262
Kikôngo, 312, 322, 324
Kimbwabdende Kia Bunseki Fu-kiau, 300, 301, 349 n.54
Kincaid, Jamaica, 59, 108–109
Kingsolver, Barbara, 186
Kiowa, 269
Kitsimba: antidotes to oppression and, 312; the Crossing and, 6–7, 293, 329; healing work and, 312–315, 320, 323, 329; inter-subjectivity and, 323; Mayombe (Kôngo), 293; methodologies of knowing and, 17, 294–295; the Middle Passage and, 6–7; at the Mojuba Crossroads, 293; not know-ing and, 294, 313–315; pedagogies of crossing and, 7, 17, 320, 329; power and, 7; the Sacred and, 323, 329; the Soul and, 329; spiritual work and, 7, 17, 294–295, 307, 313–315, 320, 323, 329; as Thisbe, 6–7,

293, 294; time/temporalities and, 7, 313–315; writer's block and, 320
knowledge: embodiment and, 297–298, 316–319; fragmentation of, 253–254; identity and, 151, 172–174, 177; Kitsimba and, 17, 294–295, 313–315; militarism and, 251–254; not knowing and, 17, 109–110, 294–295, 313–315; people of color and, 132; praxis and, 91; production of, 6, 13, 91, 132, 251–254; whiteness and, 13
Kôngo, 9, 186, 263, 265
Kôngo Angola (Brazil), 291
Korea, 104
Kouzin Zaka, 316
kra, 302
Kurtz, Stanley, 364 n.143
Kusikila, Mbûta, 323
Kuwait, 104
Kwaku, 302
Kwasi, 302
Kwasiba, 302

labor: academic, 113, 120, 142, 156, 346 n.6; exploitation of women's, 103–106; non-academic, within the academy, 142, 156–157; secular, 295–298; secularization of women's, 295–298; service economies, 59–60; spiritual, 7–8; sweatshop labor, 103–106, 345 n.28; tourism and, 59–60; women's, 59–60, 103–106, 259, 295–298; working class, 141–142
LaDuke, Winona, 251
Lakota, 259
Lamming, George, 2, 262
La Mujer Obrera, 345 n.28
La Negra, 308–309, 319
Langton, Rae, 123–125, 129, 141
Latino/Latinas, 133, 134, 136, 222, 224, 225, 262
lavé tèt (washing of the head), 302, 303
law of the father, 29, 34–40
Lazreg, Marnia, 107, 109
Leba, 302
legal codes: consent and, 207–213; domestic violence and, 32–40; heterosexualization

and, 207; marriage and, 205, 213–222, 227, 238–239, 250; production of hatred and, 213–222; sexual and reproductive rights and, 223

lesbians: Bahamian, 40–46; butch, 49; category of, 23, 49–51, 77, 339 n.59; citizenship and, 11; criminalization of, 25, 27–28, 62–63, 208–210; feminisms and, 275; pan-African, 275; privatization and, 231–232; as prostitutes, 23

"Letter to Ma" (Woo), 260

Levi Strauss and Company, 105

Lewis, Gail, 358 n.83, 366 n.13, 368 n.43

Lewis, Laura, 354 n.32

Life and Debt (Black), 230–231

linearity, 189–190, 309

Local Government Act of 1988, 356 n.61

Lorde, Audre, 16, 116, 125, 257, 273–274, 276, 303

Louie, Miriam Ching Loon, 345 n.28

Louima, Abner, 362 n.123, 363 n.125

love, 215–216

Lowe, Lisa, 191

low-wage work, 103–106

Lucumí (Cuba), 291, 292, 299, 302, 310, 322, 324

Lukenbill, Grant, 73–74

Lwa, 302, 303, 306, 311, 328

Lwa, Kouzin Zaka, 316

Lwa Guinée (Haiti), 291

Lynch, Jessica, 235, 360 n.98

Malintzín, 262

Malta Summit of 1989, 93–95

Mama Lola, 300, 316–319

Mambo La Siren, 292

Mammie, 316–319, 324

Manalansan, Martin, 87

Mani, Lati, 7, 15, 295, 327

manroyal, 49, 339 n.59

maquilas, 105

María (espiritista), 293, 300

marketing groups, gay, 71–72, 84, 341 n.13

marriage: in the Caribbean, 340 n.85, 358 n.86; citizenship and, 357 n.78; Defense

of Marriage Act of 1996 (DOMA), 205, 213–221, 222, 227, 238–239, 250; domestic violence and, 34–40, 219, 357 n.78; gender and, 34–40; "healthy," 226–228; heterosexualization through, 226–228; homosexuality and, 213–221; love and, 215–216; market strategies and, 358 n.85; morality and, 217–218; personal rights and, 337 n.29; property rights and, 35–37; same-sex, 213–221; sexual citizenship and, 357 n.78; tradition and, 215–217; violence and, 219; women and, 337 n.29, 357 n.73

Marriage Act of 1924, 340 n.85

Martinique, 82–83

Martyr, Peter, 353 n.29

Marvelous Arithmetics of Distance, The (Lorde), 116

Masai women (Kenya), 251

masculinities, 50–51, 238–241, 245

Mason, Beverly, 261

materialism, 6–7

materiality, 6–7

mati, 49, 339 n.59

Matory, Lorand, 324

Mayombe (Kôngo), 9, 263

McAfee, Kathy, 344 n.21

McLaughlin, Andrée Nicola, 368 n.39

memory: embodiment and, 297–298; gendered, 324; intersubjectivity and, 109–112; land/rock holding, 283–284; the Sacred and, 14–15; transformations and, 14, 253–254; transgenerational, 14

metaphysical, the, 15–16, 295–296, 302–303, 305–306, 318–319

methodologies: of anthropology, 189; of cultural relativism, 183; of knowing, 17, 294–295. *See also* pedagogies of crossing

Mexico, 103, 105, 344 n.22, 354 n.32

Meyers Sheppard Pride Fund, 341 n.15

Middle East, the, 107, 109

Middle Passage, the, 6–7, 288

militarism: the academy and, 251–252; citizenship and, 357 n.78; "Don't Ask, Don't Tell" policy and, 204–205; hetero-

militarism (*continued*)

sexualization and, 192–193, 197–199; homosexuality and, 199–205; incarceration and, 242–243; knowledge production and, 251–254; Military Working Group and, 192–193, 199, 200–203, 248–249; Native Americans and, 269; racialization and, 99–100; women and, 96–99, 360 n.98

militarization: the academy and, 92–93, 251–252; citizenship and, 100, 235–236; consent and, 97–98; domestic policing and, 241–242; gender and, 97–100; heterosexualization and, 199–205; military-industrial complex and, 362 n.123; neo-imperialism and, 234; paramiltarism and, 242–243; public sphere and, 232–233; race and, 200, 360 n.98; women and, 200, 351 n.8, 360 n.98

military-industrial complex, 362 n.123

Military Working Group, 192–193, 199, 200–203, 236, 248–249

minkisi (medicines), 291, 292, 312

misalignment, 319–320

Mobilization for Real Diversity, Democracy and Economic Justice: accountability of Faculty Initiative for Diversity, 145–148; Alexander hire and, 127–128, 145–147, 151, 153–154, 160–163, 168, 169, 175; "An Alternative," 164, 166–169, 348 n.48; coalition-building and, 129–130, 151–154; constituency-building and, 154–159; demands of, 157–158; demystification and, 130, 140–142, 156; economic justice issues and, 141–143; END (Education Not Domination), 144–148; faculty retention and, 144–148; financial aid concerns and, 142; hunger strike and, 159–163; non-academic labor and, 142, 156–157, 179; ongoing work and, 178–180; overview of, 118, 125–132, 143; praxis and, 129–130; "Rethinking Europe in a Global Context," 148–152; specificity of location and, 156; whiteness and, 140–142, 155–157

modernity: African cosmologies and, 296;

in the Caribbean, 352 n.19; colonialism and, 194–195; cultural relativism and, 13; gender and, 96–97; intersubjectivity and, 323–324; neocolonialism and, 194–195; neo-imperialism and, 194–195; patriarchy and, 188; pedagogies of crossing and, 7–8; perverse modernities and, 191; time/temporality and, 189–190, 192–193; tourism and, 26–27; tradition and, 191–193, 220–221, 296–297, 353 n.25; violence and, 219–220. *See also* postmodernity

Mohanty, Chandra Talpade, 9, 107, 187–188

Mojuba Crossroads, 287–288, 294, 295

Molina, Papusa, 257

Moraga, Cherríe, 174, 257, 261, 264

moral emergencies, 122

morality: consent and, 207–213; heterosexualization and, 3, 205–207; sexualization of, 221

Morgan, Stephanie, 135

Morrison, Toni, 91, 121, 124, 141, 277, 322, 352 n.19

Moya, Paula, 172, 174–175, 367 n.29

Moynihan Report, The (Rainwater and Yancey), 357 n.78

multiculturalism, 133–140. *See also* diversity, discourse of

multinational corporations, 26, 58–59, 103–106

mumbo-jumbo, 169, 349 n.54

Muslim tradition, 356 n.58

mysticism, 322–323

NAFTA (North American Free Trade Agreement), 231, 344 n.22

Najmabadi, Afsaneh, 345 n.38, 356 n.58

Nakano-Glenn, Evelyn, 344 n.20

Namibia, 263

Narayan, Uma, 184, 188

Nash, June, 344 n.21

nation, the: heterosexualization of, 11, 40–46; homosexuality and, 46–53; masculinity and, 50–51

nationalism, 45–46, 96–97, 181, 281, 310–311, 335 n.17, 365 n.7

National Labor Committee, 345 n.40
national liberation movements, 24–25
National Organization for Women, 351 n.10
National Security Act of 2002, 234
national security strategies, 182, 241–244
Native Americans, 133, 134, 219, 223, 224, 262, 263, 354 n.31
nativization, 70–71, 87
naturalization, 325; of violence, 10
Navajo, 269, 355 n.39
neocolonialism: in the Caribbean, 182–183; colonization and, 194–195; imperialism and, 182; modernity and, 194–195; neo-imperialism and, 245–246; racialization and, 194–195; state formations and, 4; structural adjustment policies and, 230–231; tourism and, 54–62
neo-imperialism: citizenship and, 248–250; modernity and, 194–195; national security strategies and, 182, 241–245; neocolonial and, 245–246; new world order and, 12; racialization and, 194–195; state formations and, 4; time/temporalities and, 245–246; welfare and, 230. See also empire; imperialism
neoliberal globalization, 229–232
Neruda, Pablo, 18
Neubeck, Kenneth, 223, 224
New School for Social Research. See New School University
New School University: affirmative action and, 127–129, 133–135, 137–139, 147; Alexander hire and, 127–128, 145–147, 151, 153–154, 160–163, 168, 169, 175; "An Alternative," 164, 166, 167–169, 348 n.48; Committee on Gender Studies and Feminist Theory, 126, 170–176; counter-mobilization of, 131–133, 163–170; cultures of silencing at, 141; curriculum development and, 126; discourse of diversity within, 10, 130, 133–144, 167–168; Faculty Initiative for Diversity (FIND), 126, 136–137, 138, 145; failure to transform, 170–178; financial aid, 142; Graduate Faculty, 126, 177–178; history and structure of, 119–120, 126; Mobilization for Real Diversity, Democracy and Economic Justice, 118, 126; nonacademic labor within, 142, 156–157, 179; overview of, 13; production of knowledge and, 166–167; "Rethinking Europe in a Global Context," 126, 132–133, 148–152; University Diversity Initiative, 126, 133, 135, 137–138; whiteness and, 138–140, 167–168
New University in Exile, the, 119, 133, 178, 347 n.25
new world order, 10, 12, 91, 92–95
Ngo An, 367 n.23
Nigeria, 104
nodes of instability, 4–5
noncitizens, 25, 28
normalization, 71, 190–196
North Africa, 109
North American Free Trade Agreement (NAFTA), 344 n.22

Ocean, 117, 284, 320–322
O'Crouley, Pedro Alonso, 354 n.31
Olodumare, 299, 324
oppositional consciousness, 2, 6
oppositional knowledge, 5
oppositional movements, 28
oppositional practice, 5–6
oppression, healing work and, 294, 311–312, 316–322
oracle, consulting the, 312–313
orientalism, 87–88, 107, 343 n.45
Orişa, 288
Orisha, 299, 300, 302, 303, 306, 312, 320, 328
Orixás (Brazil), 291
Orozco, José Clemente, 135
Osanyin, 291, 299
Overlooked Opinions, 72
Oya, 303–306
Oyo-Yoruba (Nigeria), 324

Pacific Islands, 82–88, 224
Palestine, 251, 263, 265, 276
palimpsestic time, 190, 194, 245–246
Panama, 196–199, 228–229, 335 n.12, 350 n.2

tion and, 196–199; militarism and, 99–
100; patriotism and, 236–239; of power,
4, 140–141; privatization and, 231–232;
racial taxonomies of, 354 n.31; sexual
consumption of, 82–88; of welfare, 221–
228; white women and, 140–141; women
of color and, 262–263, 267. *See also*
blackness; whiteness
racial taxonomies, 354 n.31
racisms, 113–115, 125, 261–262, 268–269,
270–271, 310–311
Rada rites, 299
radical projects, 253–254
Rai, Amit, 239–240, 351 n.10
RAWA (Revolutionary Association of the
Women of Afghanistan), 185–186, 351 n.10
Reagon, Bernice Johnson, 281
recolonization, 24–27, 182
Reconstruction Act (1867), 333 n.4
Reddy, Chandan, 278–279, 368 nn.39, 40
redistributive justice, 346 n.1
Reed, Betsy, 69
refugees, 264–265
regionality, 205–207
Reis, Michelle, 359 n.93
relativism, cultural, 13, 183–184, 189, 296,
350 n.5
religion, 207–208, 280. *See also* Judeo-
Christian traditions
remembering: *la causa* and, 316; forgetting
and, 275–279; not remembering and,
278; purposes of, 275–279; of the Sacred,
291–292; theory of the flesh and, 261–
262, 328–329; time/temporalities and,
268–269. *See also* forgetting; pedagogies
of crossing
rescue narratives, 196–199
Revolutionary Association of the Women of
Afghanistan (RAWA), 185–186, 351 n.10
Rhys, Jean, 262
Rich, Adrienne, 18, 257
Riley, Robin, 239–240
Robinson, Randall, 136, 140
Robinson, Tracy, 207, 211, 356 n.55
Rudder, David, 369 n.52

Rushin, Kate, 257
Rwanda, 85, 265

Sacred, the: body praxis and, 306–307; embodiment of, 300–311; experience and, 295;
feminism and, 295; imperialism and, 327;
intersubjectivity and, 323–324; Kitsimba
and, 323, 329; memory and, 14–15; pedagogies of praxis and, 322–324; the political and, 323–324; the secular and, 295, 307;
time/temporalities and, 308–310; transnational feminisms and, 326–329
Said, Edward W., 346 n.4
Salt Eaters, The (Bambara), 277, 279
same-sex marriage, 213–221
Sanchez, Sonia, 257
Santa Anita Packers, 105
Santería, 15, 298–299
SAP (Structural Adjustment Policies), 102,
229, 230–231
"Scent of Memory, The" (Brah), 369 n.59
Scheper-Hughes, Nancy, 297
secular, the: power of, 7; the Sacred and,
295, 307; women's labor and, 296–298
Seeking the Soul of Freedom (Carson and
Brodber), 359 n.93
segregation, 5, 183, 281–282
self-determination, colonialism and, 181
selfhood, 326, 329
self-possession, 16–18, 282, 328
Selvadurai, Shyam, 67, 186–187
Seminole, 367 n.34
Senegal, 104
September 11, 238–241, 243–244, 267, 366 n.17
SEVIS (Student and Exchange Visitor Information System), 252
sexual agency, women's, 22–23, 269
sexual and reproductive rights, 30–34, 223–
224, 269
sexual commodification, 27, 60–61
sexual consumption, 82–88
sexuality: criminalization of, 24; gender
and, 324; heterosexualization and, 196–
199; intelligibility of, 186; spirituality
and, 280–284, 324; studies, 183, 350 n.4

sexualization: of hegemony, 4; of power, 4;
of subjectivity, 11
Sexual Offences and Domestic Violence Act,
11, 24, 33, 61, 207–212, 250, 336 n.28, 338 n.51
sexual violence, 30–34, 39–40
sex workers, 104
Shangó (Trinidad), 291
Sheppard and Meyers (mutual fund), 73–74
Shohat, Ella, 189, 190, 251, 352 n.12, 364 n.143
Shoshone, 269
Sierra Leone, 265
Silliman, Jael, 242, 253
Sioux, 259, 269
Sister Outsider (Lorde), 258
Sistren, 259, 337 n.32, 365 n.1
slavery, 224, 262–263, 271, 273–274
Smith, Bessie, 75
social movements, 120, 207, 268, 325
sodomy, 51–52, 197–199, 215, 335 n.12, 354
nn.32, 33
Sonia, 306
Soul, the, 282, 325, 329
South Africa, 84
South Asians, 369 n.59
South Dakota Occupation, 365 n.2
Spartacus International Gay Guides, The, 70,
81–82, 85–86, 342 n.32, 343 n.43
spectacularization, 248
speech acts, 10, 120–121, 123–124, 153–154,
165–166
Spirit, 295, 300, 325, 328
Spirit-based politics, 283
Spirit knowledge/knowing, 15–16, 299–300,
306–307
Spirit possession, 320–322
Spiritual Baptist, 291
spirituality, 15–16, 280–284, 290–311, 324–326
spiritual practices, 322–324
spiritual work, 7, 14–15, 294–298, 307, 311–
322, 329
Spiro, Melford, 350 n.5
spoken medicine, 299
Sri Lanka, 67
state, the: citizenship and, 181; corporate
class and, 95–96; gender and, 23; hetero-

sexualization and, 23–24; race and, 23;
salvation and, 339 n.66; violence of, 249–
250; welfare programs and, 358 n.83. *See
also* legal codes; nation; national security
strategies
state formations: nation-building, 181; neocolonial, 4; neo-imperial, 4; neoliberal
feminism and, 185–186; sexuality and, 181
Structural Adjustment Policies (SAP), 102,
229, 230–231, 344 nn.21, 22
Subaru of America, Inc., 76
subjectivity: cosmologies and, 302; the
Sacred and, 300–311; sexualization of, 11
subordination, discourse of, 141–142
subversive couplings, 253
Sudbury, Julia, 265
"Sunday" (Parker), 110–111
Suriname, 49, 339 n.59
sweatshop labor, 103–106, 345 n.28. *See also*
export processing zones
Sweet Sugar Rage (Sistren Theatre Collective), 365 n.1

TANF (Temporary Aid to Needy Families),
222, 224
TAP (Tuition Assistance Program), 349 n.65
teaching for justice, 9, 12–13, 92–93, 107–
113, 114–116
Teish, Luisa, 323
Temporary Aid to Needy Families (TANF),
222, 224. *See also* Welfare
terrorism, 361 n.106, 363 n.130
Thai and Latinos Workers Organizing
Committee, 345 n.28
Thailand, 84, 343 n.45
theory of the flesh, 261–262, 329
Third World, the: First World and, 187–189,
228–229, 352 n. 11; tourism and, 82–88;
women of color and, 266–275; writers
and texts of, 186–187
Thisbe, 6–7, 293, 294. *See also* Kitsimba
This Bridge Called My Back, 14, 187, 257–
258, 260–263, 268, 275, 279
Thomas, Clarence, 274
Thomas, Kendall, 203

Thompson, Becky, 106

Thurman, Howard, 18, 143, 325

Time, 7, 309–310

time/temporalities: colonialisms and, 182; cosmologies and, 302; embodiment and, 308–310; financial, 195; healing and, 318–319; heterosexualization and, 13–14, 183; hierarchies of, 189–190; homogenization of, 192; Kitsimba and, 7, 294–295, 307, 313–315, 320, 329; modernity and, 189–190; narratives of, 190–196; neo-imperialism and, 245–246; normalization and, 190–196; remembering and, 268–269; Sacred praxis and, 328; Time and, 309–310; tradition/modernity and, 189–190, 192–193; transformations and, 253–254; transnational, 190; women of color politics and, 268–269

tour guides, gay, 343 n.43

tourism: in the Bahamas, 26–27, 53–62; bisexuality and, 84–85; the colonial and, 82–83; feminism as, 187–188; gay, 71, 78–88; homosexual orientalism and, 343 n.45; in Jamaica, 66–67; modernity and, 26–27; neocolonialism and, 11–12, 54–62; orientalism and, 87; service labor for, 103–104; sexual commodification and, 60–61; sexualized economic practices and, 360 n.97; in Thailand, 343 n.45; the Third World and, 82–88; the West and, 80–83, 85, 86; white gay, 79–88; women's labor within, 59–60

tradition: children and, 222; heterosexualization of, 2–3, 205–207; linearity and, 309; modernity and, 191–193, 220–221, 296–297, 353 n.25; patriarchy and, 188; religion and, 207–208; Sacred praxis and, 326–327; time/temporality and, 189–190; violence and, 185

transformations, 16–18, 253–254, 304–306

transgender people, 310

transnational feminism, 183, 350 n.4

transnationalism: feminism and, 183, 350 n.4; heterosexualization and, 181; local/global and, 264; sexuality studies and, 183, 350 n.4; women of color politics and, 263–265

travel guides, gay, 342 n.32

Treaty of Medicine Lodge (1867), 268

Trinidad and Tobago, 182–183, 206, 208–211, 258–260, 262–263, 272, 365 n.7, 369 n.52

Trouillot, Michel-Rolph, 352 n.19

Truong, Thanh-Dam, 343 n.45

truth, 10, 121–125

truth commissions, 122, 346 n.12

Tuition Assistance Program (TAP), 349 n.65

tutelary complex, 358 n.83

two-spirit people, 310, 353 n.29

Tyagi, Sangeeta, 106

Uganda, 366 n.16

United States: colonization and, 262–263; debts of, 359 n.91; imperialism of, 244–245; superiority of, 264

United States Foreign Relations Committee, 336 n.19

United States of North America: imperialism of, 250–251

University in Exile, the, 119, 133, 178, 347 n.25

unspeakability, 121, 123–124

Uraguay, 122

USAID, 230

U.S. Virgin Islands, 219, 233

Valéry, Paul, 174

Vega, Marta Morena, 323

vévé, 311

viatics, 74, 341 n.19

victimhood, narratives of, 109, 328

Vieques (Puerto Rico), 265, 361 n.106

Vietnamese, 224

violence: citizenship and, 362 n.123; civilization and, 3; democracy as, 4–5; domesticating, 29–34; heterosexualization and, 196–199, 219; hierarchies of, 248; immigrant identities and, 362 n.123; marriage and, 34–40, 219, 357 n.78; modernity and, 219; naturalization of, 10; paramiltarism and, 242–243; perpetual refugees and, 265; sexual, 24, 30–31, 39–40, 274; the state and,

violence (*continued*)
25–26, 249–250; tradition and, 185. *See also* domestic violence; militarism
visions, 279
Vodou, 15, 291, 297–299, 302, 311, 322, 324
Vodou (New Orleans), 291
Vodun of Candomblé, 291, 312
voice, 16–18, 278–279

Walker, Margaret Urban, 121–122
Walt Disney Corporation, 75, 76–77
war, 233, 363 nn.125, 130
water: crossings of the, 259; the Divine and, 301; goddesses of, 291; healing rhythms and, 320–321; holding memory, 284; spirituality work and, 322–323
Weber, Diane, 242
Wekker, Gloria, 301–302, 326
welfare, 99–100, 221–228, 230, 358 n.83
West, Cornel, 15, 129
whiteness, 71, 77, 124, 134, 139–141, 150–151, 174, 261, 367 n.34. *See also* racialization
wholeness, 280–284. *See also* fragmentation
Wind, 300, 302, 303, 307, 326
Windtakers (Woo), 355 n.39
Winti (Suriname), 291, 306, 326
Winti (Wind), 291, 300, 302, 303, 307, 326
women: autonomy of, 22–23; blackness and, 223–225; breast cancer and, 265; criminalization of, 24; diabetes and, 285, 370 n.79; exploitation of, 103–106; gender-bending, 324; genealogies of consciousness and, 103–106; heteropatriarchy and, 63–65; infantilization of, 356 n.55; labor and, 59–60, 103–106, 259, 295–298; loving, 339 n.59; low-wage work of, 103–106; Middle Eastern, 107, 109; militarism and, 96–99, 360 n.98; North African, 109; organizing/organizations, 29–30, 336 n.23, 345 n.28; in prisons, 367 n.27; secularization of, 295–298; sexual agency of, 22–23; sexual commodification of, 60–61; social movements, 21–22, 30, 31, 50, 62–65, 334 n.3, 336 n.24; spiritual practice

and, 296–297, 324; trafficking of, 351 n.8; whiteness and, 140–141. *See also* lesbians; women of color
women of color: becoming, 9; blackness and, 263–265, 268; category of, 260–263, 266–270, 274–275; feminism and, 251; hypervisibility and, 13; nationalism and, 262–263, 265–267; as perpetual refugees, 265; relationships between, 14, 285; the Third World and, 266–275; time/temporalities and, 268–269; transnationalism and, 263–265; women's studies and, 172
women of color politics, 260–261; blackness and, 268; British black women, 263–265; time/temporalities and, 268–269; transnationalism and, 263–265
Women's Affairs Unit, 336 n.24
Women's Crisis Center, 30, 31
Women's Desk, The, 30, 336 n.24
women's studies, 107, 170–175, 185–188, 252
Woo, Merle, 260
World Bank, the, 230
Wounded Knee, 259
writing: healing work and, 320; Kitsimba and, 320; memory and, 16–18; spiritual work and, 320

Xiamara, 320–321

Yamada, Mitsuye, 257
Yansa, 303
Yarbro-Bejarano, Yvonne, 148
Ya Salaam, Kalamu, 279
Yemayá, 289, 292, 320–323, 329–332
Yemayá Achaba, 329–332
yeye, 302
Yoruba, 291, 299, 312, 322
Young, Iris, 146

zami, 49, 339 n.59
Zami (Lorde), 258
Zamora, Michelle, 354 n.31
Zionism, 263
Zonta, 30

M. Jacqui Alexander is a professor of women's studies and gender studies at the University of Toronto. She is a coeditor of *Sing, Whisper, Shout, Pray! Feminist Visions for a Just World* and *Feminist Genealogies, Colonial Legacies, Democratic Futures.*

Library of Congress Cataloging-in-Publication Data
Alexander, M. Jacqui.
Pedagogies of crossing : Meditations on feminism, sexual politics, memory, and the sacred / M. Jacqui Alexander.
p. cm. — (Perverse modernities)
Includes bibliographical references and index.
ISBN 0-8223-3607-3 (cloth : alk. paper)
ISBN 0-8223-3645-6 (pbk. : alk. paper)
1. Equality. 2. Social justice. 3. Feminism—Cross-cultural studies. 4. Women—Social conditions—Cross-cultural studies. 5. Racism. 6. Postcolonialism. 7. Transnationalism. I. Title. II. Series.
HM821.A49 2005
323.1—dc22
2005016114